Public and Private Social Policy

Also by Daniel Béland

NATIONALISM AND SOCIAL POLICY: The Politics of Territorial Solidarity. Oxford: Oxford University Press, (*with André Lecours (2008)*).

SOCIAL SECURITY: A Documentary History. Washington, DC: Congressional Quarterly Press, (*with Larry DeWitt and Edward D. Berkowitz (2007)*).

STATES OF GLOBAL INSECURITY: Policy, Politics, and Society. New York: Worth Publishers ("Contemporary Social Issues Series"), (*Author (2007)*).

SOCIAL SECURITY: History and Politics From The New Deal To The Privatization Debate. Lawrence: University Press of Kansas ("Studies in Government and Public Policy" series), (*Author (2005)*).

Public and Private Social Policy

Health and Pension Policies in a New Era

Edited by

Daniel Béland
Professor of Public Policy
University of Saskatchewan, Canada

and

Brian Gran
Associate Professor, Department of Sociology and Law School
Case Western Reserve University, USA

First published 2008 by
PALGRAVE MACMILLAN

Palgrave Macmillan in the UK is an imprint of Macmillan Publishers Limited, registered in England, company number 785998, of Houndmills, Basingstoke, Hampshire RG21 6XS.

Palgrave Macmillan in the US is a division of St Martin's Press LLC, 175 Fifth Avenue, New York, NY 10010.

Palgrave Macmillan is the global academic imprint of the above companies and has companies and representatives throughout the world.

Palgrave® and Macmillan® are registered trademarks in the United States, the United Kingdom, Europe and other countries.

ISBN-13: 978–0–230–52733–1 hardback
ISBN-10: 0–230–52733–7 hardback

This book is printed on paper suitable for recycling and made from fully managed and sustained forest sources. Logging, pulping and manufacturing processes are expected to conform to the environmental regulations of the country of origin.

A catalogue record for this book is available from the British Library.

Library of Congress Cataloging-in-Publication Data

Public and private social policy : health and pension policies in a new era / edited by Daniel Béland, Brian Gran.
    p. cm.
Includes bibliographical references.
ISBN 978–0–230–52733–1
    1. Social policy. 2. Welfare state. 3. Public welfare. 4. Subsidies. I. Béland, Daniel. II. Gran, Brian, 1963–

HN18.3.P83 2008
362.1—dc22   2008020599

10 9 8 7 6 5 4 3 2 1
17 16 15 14 13 12 11 10 09 08

Printed and bound in Great Britain by
CPI Antony Rowe, Chippenham and Eastbourne

To Angela and Julie

Contents

Figures

Tables

Acknowledgments

This book is a true collective project, and we would like to start by thanking our excellent contributors for their hard work. Without their expertise and professionalism, this book would not have been possible. At Palgrave, we would like to thank commissioning editor Philippa Grand and her assistant Olivia Middleton for their support as well as the reviewers for their insightful comments. We are grateful to Michael Flatt and Robin Shura Patterson for their assistance. Thank you to Jacob Hacker, Jennifer Klein, John Myles, and Ann Orloff for their advice and support. This volume has its beginnings with a 2005 workshop, and we collectively thank its participants for their enthusiasm. Thanks to Fritz Von Nordheim Nielsen for prescient conversations on these issues years ago, and scholars whose work on which this book has its foundation. Finally, we must thank our respective wives, Angela and Julie, for their constant love and patience.

Daniel Béland
and
Brian Gran

Notes on Contributors

Karen M. Anderson is Associate Professor in the Political Science Department at the University of Nijmegen in the Netherlands. Her current research focuses on the political economy of welfare state reform in Europe as well as the role of the left in processes of welfare state restructuring. She has published several book chapters and articles on welfare state reform in Sweden, and her most recent work investigates the politics of pension reforms in Sweden, Germany, and the Netherlands. With Ellen Immergut and Isabella Schulze, she coedited *The Handbook of West European Pension Politics* (Oxford University Press, 2007).

Toni Ashton (PhD) is an Associate Professor in Health Economics in the School of Population Health. Her primary field of research and publication is in the analysis of the organization and funding of health systems from an economic perspective, with the ongoing restructuring that has taken place with the New Zealand health system since the early 1990s being her main focus in recent years. Her extensive range of publications have appeared in international medical journals, public health journals, economics journals, working papers, and health professional publications. Professor Ashton has also been a member of many Government working parties covering health policy, health structures, health funding, and health needs. She has also been a consultant to international agencies such as WHO and OECD and nationally for Government agencies, health professional bodies, and nongovernment organizations.

Keith G. Banting is Professor in the School of Policy Studies and the Department of Political Studies at Queen's University, and holder of the Queen's Research Chair in Public Policy. His research interests focus on public policy, especially social policy, in Canada and other Western nations. He is the author of *Poverty, Politics and Policy* (Macmillan 1979) and *The Welfare State and Canadian Federalism* (McGill-Queen's University Press, second edition 1987). In addition, he is an editor or coauthor of another 15 books, including *Federalism and Health Policy: A Comparative Perspective on Multi-Level Governance* (McGill-Queen's University Press 2001, coedited with Stab Corbett). Much of Professor Banting's current research focuses on ethnic diversity, multiculturalism, and the welfare state. In this field, he is coeditor (with Will Kymlicka) of *Multiculturalism and the Welfare State: Recognition and Redistribution in Contemporary Democracies* (Oxford University Press 2006).

Daniel Béland is Professor of Public Policy at the University of Saskatchewan (Canada). A political sociologist studying public policy from a comparative and historical perspective, he has published more than three-dozen articles in peer-reviewed journals. His recent books include *Social Security: History* *and Politics from the New Deal to the Privatization Debate* (2005), *States of Global Insecurity: Policy, Politics and Society* (2007), *Social Security: A Documentary History* [with Larry DeWitt and Edward D. Berkowitz] (2007), and *Nationalism and Social Policy: The Politics of Territorial Solidarity* [with André Lecours] (2008).

Edward D. Berkowitz is Professor of History and of Public Policy and Public Administration at George Washington University. He writes on the history of American social welfare policy, including eight books on aspects of Social Security, disability, and health care. His most recent book is *Something Happened: A Political and Cultural Overview of the Seventies* (Columbia University Press, 2006). His articles have appeared in journals such as the *Milbank Memorial Quarterly* and the *Social Service Review* and he has written opinion pieces for the *Washington Post* and the *Boston Globe*. His government service includes a stint as a senior staff member of the President's Council for a National Agenda for the Eighties.

Fabio Bertozzi is scientific collaborator at the social policy unity of the Swiss Graduate School of Public Administration (IDHEAP) associated with the University of Lausanne. He has taken part in several national and international research projects in the area of comparative welfare state analysis, with a special focus on pensions and labor market policies. Recent publications include "The Swiss Pension System and Social Inclusion" in T. Meyer, P. Bridgen, and B. Riedmüller (eds), *Private Pensions versus Social Inclusion?* Edward Elgar, 2007: 107–135 (with G. Bonoli) and "The Swiss Road to Activation: Legal Aspects, Implementation and Outcomes" in W. Eichhorst, O. Kaufmann, and R. Konle-Seidl (eds), *Bringing the Jobless Into Work? Experiences with Activation Schemes in Europe and the US*, Heidelberg: Springer (with G. Bonoli and F. Ross, 2008).

Paula Blomqvist is Associate Professor at the Department of Government, Uppsala University. She received her PhD in political science from Columbia University in 2002. Her research focuses on health care and welfare state policy in comparative perspective, particularly the introduction of privatization and market-oriented reforms. Paula's research has appeared in *Governance* and *Social Policy and Administration*, as well as in Swedish and Nordic journals. She is editor of four books, *Välfärdsstatens nya ansikte* ("The New Face of the Welfare State" with Bo Rothstein) and *Den gränslösa välfärdsstaten* ("The Borderless Welfare State"), *Vem styr vården?* ("Who Governs Swedish Health Care?") and *Mellan Folkhem och Europa. Svensk politik i brytningstid* ("Between Europe and the People's Home. Swedish Politics in Transition," with Li Bennich-Björkman).

Gerard W. Boychuk is the Director, Ph.D. in Global Governance, Balsillie School of International Affairs and Associate Professor in the Department of

Political Science, University of Waterloo (Ontario, Canada). His areas of interest include global social policy and comparative social and health policy. He is the author of numerous articles and book chapters as well as two books including *National Health Insurance in the United States and Canada: Race, Territory and the Roots of Difference* (Georgetown University Press, 2008) which examines the historical development of public health insurance in the United States and Canada. He is a coeditor of the Georgetown University Press series, *American Governance and Public Policy*.

Christina Ewig is Assistant Professor in the Departments of Gender & Women's Studies and Political Science at the University of Wisconsin-Madison. Her research focuses on gender and social policy reform in Latin America. She is the author of *Second Wave Neoliberalism: Gender, Race and Health Sector Reform in Peru* (under contract with Penn State Press). She has also carried out research on the politics of health reform in Chile, Colombia, and Mexico with the support of a Fulbright New Century Scholars fellowship. Her articles have appeared in *Social Politics, Latin American Research Review* and *Feminist Studies*.

Fabrizio Gilardi is an Associate Professor of Public Policy at the University of Zurich (Switzerland). His research interests include regulation, comparative political economy, welfare state policy and politics, political delegation, and policy diffusion processes. His work has been published in the *Annals of the American Academy of Political and Social Science, Comparative European Politics, Comparative Political Studies*, the *Journal of European Public Policy*, the *Journal of Theoretical Politics, Politica y Gobierno, Politische Vierteljahresschrift*, and the *Swiss Political Science Review*. He is also the author of a book on independent regulatory agencies in Europe (Edward Elgar, 2008), and the coeditor of a volume on delegation in contemporary democracies (Routledge, 2006).

Brian Gran is an Associate Professor in the Sociology Department, with a secondary appointment in the Law School, of Case Western Reserve University. His research focuses on comparative social policy as it is formed in the intersection of the public and private sectors, in particular, how laws are used to draw boundaries between public and private social policies. His most recent work appears in the *International Journal of the Sociology of Law, Sociological Focus, Buffalo Public Interest Law Journal*, and *International Journal of Health Services*.

Christopher Howard is the Pamela C. Harriman Professor of Government and Public Policy at the College of William and Mary. He is the author of *The Welfare State Nobody Knows: Debunking Myths about U.S. Social Policy* (Princeton University Press, 2007), *The Hidden Welfare State: Tax Expenditures and Social Policy in the United States* (Princeton University Press, 1997), as well as a number of scholarly articles and book chapters. Howard has won research fellowships from the American Council of Learned Societies and the National Endowment for the Humanities.

Ellen M. Immergut is Professor of Comparative Politics in the Department of Social Sciences at Humboldt University Berlin. She did her graduate work at Harvard University, was appointed as Assistant and Ford Career Development Associate Professor in the Department of Political Science at the Massachusetts Institute of Technology, Visiting Professor at the Instituto Juan March in Madrid, and Professor of Political Theory at the University of Konstanz. She is author of the book *Health Politics* (Cambridge University Press, 1992), coeditor of a special issue of *Governance* on crises of governance in coordinated market economies, as well as various articles on the new institutionalism, institutional design, and the politics of constitutional reform.

Sven Jochem is Lecturer in Political Science at the University of Luzern, Switzerland. His research interests include political theory as well as the comparative analysis of contemporary welfare state reforms. His publications include his Habilitation: *Reformpolitik im Wohlfahrtsstaat: Deutschland im internationalen Vergleich* [Reforming the Welfare State: Germany Compared] (2007) and *Das skandinavische Modell: Grundlagen, Vorzüge, Probleme* [The Scandinavian Model: Politics, History, Economy] (2008). He has additionally published several book chapters and journal articles on welfare state reforms in Germany, Sweden, and other European countries.

Stephen J. Kay is the coordinator of Latin American analysis in the Research Department of the Federal Reserve Bank of Atlanta and the coordinator of the Bank's Americas Center. His research focuses on public policy in Latin America. His articles on pension reform in Latin America have appeared in scholarly journals and he coedited *Lessons from Pension Reform in the Americas* (Oxford University Press, 2008). He has testified twice before committees of the United States Congress on pension reform in Latin America.

Patrik Marier is Canada Research Chair in Comparative Public Policy and Associate Professor of Political Science at Concordia University (Canada). His current research focuses on challenges to the welfare state and the impact of population aging on public policy. He has published articles on pension reforms in various journals such as *Governance, Social Politics, West European Politics, Journal of Social Policy, Mobilization,* and *Social Policy & Administration.* His book *Pension Politics: Consensus and Social Conflict in Ageing Societies* was recently published by "Routledge (2008)."

Lavinia Mitton is a lecturer in social policy at the University of Kent, UK. Her main area of research is financial exclusion, household income, and social security policies. Her recent publications have appeared in the journals

Policy & Politics, Culture, Health & Sexuality, Critical Social Policy, Journal of Further and Higher Education, Social Policy & Society and in the book *Europäische Wohlfahrtssysteme [European Welfare Systems]*, edited by Klaus Schubert, Simon Hegelich, and Ursula Bazant (eds.) (VS Verlag für Sozialwissenschaften: 2007).

Toshimitsu Shinkawa is Professor of Political Science at Kyoto University (Japan). His research interests are comparative social policy and labor market studies. His recent works include *Nihongata Fukushi Rejimu no Hatten to Henyo* [The Development and Transformation of the Japanese-Style Welfare Regime] (Kyoto: Minerva, 2005), *Ageing and Pension Reform around the World* (coedited with Giuliano Bonoli) (Edward Elgar, 2005), and "Democratization and Social Policy Development in Japan" in *Democratization and Social Policy Development*, edited by Yusuf Bangura and Carl-Johan Hedberg.

Suzanne Skinner Suzanne Skinner holds a Master in Public Policy and Public Administration from Concordia University, Montréal. She currently serves as policy advisor to the government of Ontario. Her research interests concern welfare state politics relating to gender and immigration. Prior to this Suzanne was program manager of a nongovernmental organization serving immigrant and refugee women.

Susan St John is a senior lecturer in Economics, and codirector of the Retirement Policy and Research Centre at the University of Auckland. Publications include (with Alison McClelland) "Social policy responses to globalisation in Australia and New Zealand," *Australian Journal of Political Science*, 41(2), 2006 and "Retirement Income in New Zealand," *The Economic and Labour Relations Review*, 15(2) 2005.

Debra Street is an Associate Professor of Sociology at the University at Buffalo, SUNY. She conducts comparative research on the life course implications of natiojn-specific health and income policies. Her current work focuses on health and long-term-care policies and the politics of income and health security. Author of numerous journal articles and book chapters, Street is coeditor of *Aging for the Twenty-First Century* [with Jill Quadagno] (St. Martin's, 1995) and *Women, Work and Pensions: International Prospects* [with Jay Ginn and Sara Arber] (Open University Press, 2001).

Peter Taylor-Gooby is Professor of Social Policy at the University of Kent and Director of the ESRC Social Contexts and Responses to Risk network and the EU Welfare Reform and the Management of Societal Change program. He is a founding academician at the Association of Learned Societies in the Social Sciences, a Fellow of the Royal Society for the encouragement of Arts, Manufactures and Commerce (RSA), and current President of the

Sociology and Social Policy section of the British Association for American Studies (BAAS). Recent publications include *Risk in Social Science* (Oxford University Press, 2006); *Ideas and the Welfare State* (Palgrave, 2005); *New Risks, New Welfare* (Oxford University Press, 2004); *Making a European Welfare State?* (Blackwell, 2004); and *Risk, Trust and Welfare* (Macmillan, 2000).

Introduction: Public *and* Private?

Daniel Béland and Brian Gran

Since the late 1970s, the rise of neoliberalism has intensified the traditional debate over the relationship between public and private social policy (Esping-Andersen 2002: 4).[1] Based on the idea that markets are more efficient than states at distributing resources and regulating the economy, neoliberalism promotes the application of market solutions to social policy issues (Campbell and Pedersen 2001; Harvey 2005). Although a number of neoliberal privatization efforts have failed due to intense political opposition (Pierson 1994), the idea of a growing reliance on private benefits has gained traction in this era of economic globalization and fiscal austerity (Gilbert 2002). Beyond national parties and politicians, think tanks and international organizations have actively promoted neoliberalism and, more specifically, social policy privatization. In 1994, for example, the World Bank issued a widely debated report on pension reform entitled *Averting the Old Age Crisis*. Through this report, the World Bank directed policymakers to reduce the state's role in order to make more room for private efforts (World Bank 1994). Beyond spectacular neoliberal statements such as this 1994 World Bank report, market liberalism is the dominant economic creed in most advanced industrial societies. Many states have promoted the development of private social policies to offset cutbacks in—or to prevent the expansion of—public provisions (Shalev 1996).

Concerns about demographic aging and economic competitiveness legitimized this quest for a greater reliance on private benefits. The World Bank (1994) report was framed as a response to growing concerns about unfavorable demographic pressures on long-term welfare state finances (O'Higgins 1986: 141–42; Ruggie 1996: 186). The World Bank and others claimed that dependency ratios, the ratio of recipients to payers, would weaken to the point that public pension programs would be unsustainable (on this debate see Béland 2007).

At the same time, other experts raised alarms that global economic competition would place severe pressures on national states (on this literature see Helliwell 2002). In particular, the ability of companies to move to more favorable business conditions, especially locations with low tax rates and business costs, would force states to lower their tax levels in a bid to retain both capital and jobs. One way to mitigate these pressures was to reduce commitments to public programs, including pensions and health insurance, perhaps reducing taxes by shifting responsibilities onto the private sector. Overall, the redefinition of the boundaries between public and private social policy has become a major economic and political issue in most advanced industrial societies (Rein and Schmähl 2004; Seeleib-Kaiser 2008; Shalev 1996; West Pedersen 2004).

Although scholars have paid close attention to these matters, more systematic comparative research may offer unique, crucial insights into understanding why and how boundaries change between the public and private spheres in the provision of social benefits. This awareness is especially crucial now, as the push for privatization and market-based social policy not only remains influential in most advanced industrial countries, but is expected to become stronger (Gilbert 2002). This push raises three main questions, which are related to policy design, politics, and social inequality, respectively. First, concerning policy design, what is the nature of the public-private dichotomy and what forms can and does it take? Second, what politics drive states to employ public-private collaborations? What are the impacts of private benefits on the politics of social policy? Third, does reliance on private benefits promote social inequality? What is the relationship between gender and class inequality, on the one hand, and the public-private dichotomy, on the other hand? Is the growing reliance on private benefits necessarily at odds with economic redistribution and the struggle against social inequality? As suggested below, the existing literature on social policy raises these questions without fully answering them. An overarching objective of this volume is to further address these important questions.

A look at the literature

Three bodies of literature shed light on the above questions: the international scholarship on welfare regimes; the relatively recent and growing US literature on the history and politics of private social policy; and finally, the reemerging comparative scholarship on the public-private dichotomy for social policy. As evidenced below, more comparative work is needed to answer the questions mentioned above.

The scholarship on welfare regimes

The work of British scholar Richard Titmuss is the starting point of the modern literature on welfare regimes. Like Gøsta Esping-Andersen years later, Titmuss (1974) classifies countries based on the nature of the social policy arrangements that characterize them. Following this logic, he identifies three main welfare models: the residual, the industrial achievement-performance, and the institutional redistributive models. For Titmuss, the residual model "is based on the premise that there are two 'natural' (or socially given) channels through which an individual's needs are properly met; the private market and the family. Only when these break down should social welfare institutions come into play and then only temporarily" (Titmuss 1974: 30–1). As for the industrial achievement-performance model, it is characterized by a close relationship between work performance, occupational solidarity, and social policy (Titmuss 1974: 32). Finally, the institutional redistributive model "sees social welfare as a major integrated institution in society, providing universalist services outside the market on the principle of need" (Titmuss 1974: 32). These three models are defined in relationship to the role of market forces within them, among other things (Titmuss 1974: 30–2). Beyond this well-known but conceptually underdeveloped typology, Titmuss paid significant attention to what he described as the regressive nature of private social policy schemes. For example, he notes that "Private enterprise social service institutions have to operate on the principle of excluding the 'bad risks' and the social casualties of change" (Titmuss 1974: 42). Furthermore, Titmuss stressed the tension between the multiplication of occupational benefits and the expansion of the state-centered welfare state: "as they grow and multiply... [occupational schemes] come into conflict with the aims and unity of social policy; for in effect (whatever their aims may be) their whole tendency at present is to divide loyalties, to nourish privilege, and to narrow the social conscience as they have already done in the United States, in France and in Western Germany" (Titmuss 1963: 52).[2]

Although what Titmuss defines as occupational welfare is not always *private* in the strict sense of the term, the reference to the United States points to the potentially negative impact of private social benefits on welfare state development, which is a significant aspect of the recent US literature on public-private social policy discussed below (Béland and Hacker 2004; Hacker 2002; Klein 2003). Consequently, the work of Titmuss explicitly deals with policy design as well as impacts of private social policy on politics and on social inequality.

Another major British author who directly contributed to the early debate on the relationship between inequality and social policy is sociologist T. H. Marshall (1964). For Marshall, citizenship consists of three rights that were developed in the following sequence for England: civil, political, and social rights. Developed in the eighteenth century, civil rights are legal rights, such as the freedom of speech and right to form a contract, and are usually employed in legal systems. Coming about in the nineteenth century, according to Marshall, political rights include rights to vote and run for elected office, and thus are employed in political systems. In the last century, social rights were established and include rights to education, health care, and an income that provides at least a modicum of well-being. According to Marshall, without protections afforded by social rights, many citizens would face difficulties in deploying their civil and political rights.

In his book *The Three Worlds of Welfare Capitalism*, Gøsta Esping-Andersen (1990) takes Marshall's notion of citizenship and, in particular, social rights to examine how different types of national social policy systems promote decommodification. For Esping-Andersen, decommodification is the process through which *state*-granted social rights free workers and citizens from market dependency (Esping-Andersen 1990: 37). "Decommodification occurs when a service is rendered as a matter of right, and when a person can maintain a livelihood without reliance on the market" (Esping-Andersen 1990: 21–2). For example, when studying decommodification in pension policy, the overarching question is whether a public pension benefit permits an individual to avoid market dependency during older age. Furthermore, nonincome benefits, such as rights to health care, can weaken dependence on the paid labor market, and therefore can be understood as decommodifying.

Esping-Andersen's understanding that social rights are key to decommodification leads to his discussion of the role of private benefits, for instance, private pensions and health insurance. Because private benefits typically arise from an employee-employer relationship, or are purchased from an individual's or family's income earned in the paid labor market, private benefits usually do not enhance decommodification.[3] Instead, private benefits often reinforce inequalities arising from market opportunities and other sources of disparites between workers.

Esping-Andersen employs the concept of decommodification to characterize welfare regimes according to three types: social-democratic, conservative, and liberal. Social rights are strong in the social-democratic regime. The social-democratic regime tends to rely on state programs, which are extensive in coverage and generous in benefits, while offering high levels of decommodification. Social rights are moderately strong in the conservative regime. This regime also tends to rely on state programs, but these programs often reinforce occupational inequalities and, as a result, offer moderate levels of decommodification. Social rights are weak in the liberal welfare regime because it takes a safety-net approach; benefits are provided to individuals who cannot obtain them in the market. According to Esping-Andersen (1990, 1999), private benefits are especially prominent in this regime, found in the United States and other Anglo-American countries. In addition to their greater reliance on means-tested public benefits, liberal countries stimulate the development of a large private yet frequently subsidized welfare system (Esping-Andersen 1999: 73). For Esping-Andersen, liberal welfare regimes only weakly decommodify.

In his influential research, Esping-Andersen suggests that the reliance on private benefits (liberal welfare regime) or on occupationally fragmented social insurance schemes (conservative welfare regime) exacerbates social inequality instead of mitigating it. For this author, the social-democratic welfare regime is more efficient at fighting market dependency and social inequality than its liberal and conservative counterparts (Esping-Andersen 1990, 1999).

From debates over Esping-Andersen's three-worlds typology, which have been strenuous and wide ranging, has emerged a substantial and important comparative literature on welfare regimes. Criticisms of this typology range from a general discussion about social—especially gender—inequality (for example Lewis 1992; Orloff 1993; O'Connor et al. 1999) to concerns about the problematic status of particular countries within the typology (for example Castles and Mitchell 1993; Ferrera 1996). From the perspective of the present volume, Esping-Andersen's typology of welfare regimes offers an invaluable starting point for the selection of the cases, which is discussed in the last section of this Introduction. Although his work rightly stresses the broad impact of the public-private dichotomy on social inequality, however, Esping-Andersen has done little to explore the multiple facets of this dichotomy, both in terms of policy designs and political impacts. While taking into account Esping-Andersen's typology, this volume offers a more detailed analysis of the public-private dichotomy and its implications for policy design, political development, and social inequality.

The US literature

The United States is considered a major social policy laboratory when it comes to the politics of public and private social policies (Hacker 2002). In the United States, a number of prominent scholars have systematically examined the development and the political effects of private social benefits. Following pioneers such as Edward D. Berkowitz and Kim McQuaid (1980), Jill Quadagno (1988), Beth Stevens (1988), Martin Rein (1989), and Neil and Barbara Gilbert (1989), scholars like Jacob Hacker (Hacker 2002; 2004; Béland and Hacker 2004), Marie Gottschalk (2000), Christopher Howard (1997; 2006), and Jennifer Klein (2003) offer detailed analyses of the history and politics of public and private social policy in the United States. In *The Hidden Welfare State*, for example, Howard (1997) explores the central yet low profile role of tax benefits and regulations in US social policy. In his recent *The Welfare State Nobody Knows*, Howard (2006), following Hacker (2002) and Klein (2003), also underlines the fact that the United States' strong reliance on private social benefits exacerbates social inequality. Overall, this growing literature clearly demonstrates that, in the United States, the development of *private* social programs is closely related to *public* tax and regulatory policies that favor the expansion of private benefits at the expense of public benefits.

Theoretically, Hacker probably goes the farthest in exploring the political and institutional consequences of the public-private dichotomy. According to Hacker (2002; Béland and Hacker 2004), private benefits create the same type of "policy feedback" as public social programs. This means that, although rarely spectacular and explicitly political in nature, the development of private benefits can strongly impact welfare state politics. According to Hacker, public and private institutions are closely related, and private benefits have the power to constrain the development of *public* social programs through the creation of enduring vested interests among employers, professionals (for example doctors), insurance companies, and workers. In the field of health care, for example, Hacker (Hacker 2002; Béland and Hacker 2004) argues that the early expansion of private health insurance created strong vested interests that proved instrumental in preventing the enactment of national health insurance during and after the Truman presidency (1945–53).

An interesting concept Hacker has introduced to the social policy literature is the one of "policy drift" (Hacker 2004). According to Hacker, without significant reforms, new social and economic trends as well as the reconfiguration of private benefits can eventually render existing policy arrangements incapable of adapting to changing social circumstances. In the United States, the current growth in personal retirement savings accounts and the decline of employment-based, defined-benefit pensions illustrate how the interaction between changing circumstances and relative political inaction can gradually transform the social policy arrangements that impact the lives of many workers and citizens. For example, the transition from defined-benefit to defined-contribution pensions is shifting financial risks from the employer to workers (Hacker 2004; Klein 2003).

The recent US literature on private social policy excels in its exploration of institutional diversity of private social benefits as well as their possible impacts on welfare state politics and social inequality. Yet, this literature rarely offers comparative insights due to its generally exclusive focus on US social policies. The above-mentioned authors refer to other countries in their works, but seem to take for granted the fragmented nature of US political institutions and welfare state without considering application of their concepts to other countries' experiences. One of the objectives of the present volume is to explore the impact of national institutions—especially political institutions—on the changing relationship between public and private social benefits. This book will assess, for instance, whether Hacker's claim of a strong political impact of private benefits on the development of public social programs such as national health insurance applies—beyond the US case—to other countries' experiences.

Comparative research on the public-private dichotomy for social policy

An overarching objective of this volume is to examine the utility of the public-private dichotomy for studying social policies. Although the comparative literature on the public-private dichotomy for social policy remains limited, important research was undertaken nearly 20 years ago, and more recently several publications have improved our understanding of this dichotomy. Reviewing this literature will help clarify some of the objectives of the present volume.

Take Michael Shalev's *The Privatization of Social Policy?* (1996), for example. As opposed to the present volume, Shalev's edited collection focuses almost exclusively on occupational pensions and, despite the inclusion of Canada and Japan, is essentially framed as a comparison between the United States and Scandinavia. Despite these geographic limitations, Shalev's volume is important because it looks at private benefits from the perspective of social policy rather than business, economic, and financial analysis. We take the same approach in this volume, which is devoted to the *social policy* role of private benefits (that is, the ways they protect workers and citizens against economic deprivation and insecurity) rather than their impacts on the economy and the development of financial capitalism, for example. Although pension funds and other types of private social schemes play a major role in advanced industrial economies, their social policy aspect is essential and worthy of scholarly attention.

Beyond such a broad social policy perspective on private benefits, this volume stresses the potentially ambiguous and fuzzy nature of the public-private dichotomy, which raises issues for policy design. In the introduction to their volume on pension reform, Martin Rein and Winfried Schmähl (2004) argue that the boundaries between "public" and "private" are fuzzy and that the public-private dichotomy is ambiguous. This conclusion is true because, as mentioned above, the state is involved in the regulation of private benefits, and often is a financial contributor through tax expenditure support. This research is based on Rein's long-term studies of the public-private dichotomy for social benefits social policy.

In their groundbreaking volume, *Public/Private Interplay in Social Protection*, Martin Rein and Lee Rainwater (1986: vii, 203) set the goal of clarifying the "murky terrain" of distinguishing between public and private social policy efforts. Rein and Rainwater introduce their book by stating the task is difficult (Rein and Rainwater 1986: vii): "The boundary question turned out to be as fascinating as it was illusive. The state penetrates private activities and blurs the distinction between them. We believe this blurring of sectoral boundaries is an essential feature of the modern welfare state." In the same volume, Ellen Immergut (1986: 89) states "that the stark contrast often made between the public and the private sectors is overdrawn." Rein and Rainwater's volume was followed by other important studies, some of which reemphasized blurred boundaries between public and private (von Nordheim Nielsen 1991; Ruggie 1996: 186, 127–74).

One major contribution made by this public-private research was to reconceptualize what is public and private by identifying multiple providers (Starr 1989). Rather than a dichotomy, a trichotomy was presented, often market, state, and nonprofits (Rein and Rainwater 1986: 39) or household, market, and state (Rose 1989: 79). Esping-Andersen (1999: 85) seems to adopt the latter trichotomy by incorporating the market, state, and family in his analyses of welfare regimes. Seeking to bring the nonprofit sector in, Jane Jenson (2004: 2) proposes a "welfare diamond," a four-sided typology of welfare providers comprised of the state, the market, the family, and the community. The importance of each side of the diamond varies across countries and policy areas. Jenson's (2004) work considers what may happen when contributions made by one side of the diamond weaken but another side does not necessarily shore up the difference. Jenson (2004: 5) recommends a balance of the four sides of the diamond to achieve welfare. A second important contribution made by this line of research is its observation that rather than a line separating public and private efforts, a continuum better describes efforts to provide social benefits. As opposed to a dichotomy, Rein and Rainwater (1986: 17) conceptualize the state's role in the provision of socioeconomic benefits as along a *continuum*. Other research (Gran 2003) proposes an analytical framework of collaborations among different sectors, emphasizing that the state often works with market, social, and individual actors to provide social benefits.

This volume starts from the perspective that the public-private dichotomy is often fuzzy, and that public and private policies can form a complex network where the boundaries between the state and the private sector are blurred at best. Yet, because this volume recognizes the diversity in policy design that characterizes the public-private dichotomy, it is not grounded in the assumption that the line between the public and the private sector is *always* fuzzy. Under some institutional arrangements, for example, the division of labor between the state and the private sector is relatively unproblematic. Offering a number of historically minded case studies will reveal key variations in the institutional fuzziness of the public-private dichotomy.

Lastly, as far as policy design is concerned, the existing literature on private social policy does not provide a compelling answer to the question of whether public and private benefits complement or substitute one another (West Pedersen 2004). Economists such as Martin Feldstein (1974) have argued that there is a mechanical relationship between public and private benefits: the expansion of private benefits necessarily leads to the decline of public ones, and vice versa (Hagestad and Herlofson 2007). Alternatively, scholars such as Frank Dobbin and Terry Boychuck (1996) stress the complementary relationship between public and private benefits. According to Dobbin and Boychuk, the expansion of public benefits can trigger the development of private schemes, as public benefits can increase social and economic expectations about economic security, which can in turn stimulate the development of private schemes.[4] From this perspective, social benefits are a social construction and the level of protection that workers expect from the state and employers vary according to the economic, social, and political context (West Pedersen 2004: 8). The present volume will contribute to this debate about the nature of the relationship between public and private social schemes.

Although this literature demonstrates that the line separating public and private provision is often difficult to draw, it is not clear whether impure provision promotes inequality. Immergut (1986: 89) questions whether employer-provided benefits work against public benefits' objectives of security and equity, although Rein and Rainwater suspect it is difficult to identify these impacts given blurred boundaries between public and private benefits (1986: 203). Questions remain whether reliance on public-private collaborations for social policy increases socioeconomic inequalities.

This volume

Focusing on health care and pensions, this volume provides some answers to our three questions about the nature, the politics, and the impacts on social inequality of the public-private dichotomy for social policy. First, regarding the nature of this dichotomy, the volume challenges the utility of a clear-cut vision of the dichotomy as both straightforward and identical, no matter the country or policy area. Beyond the claim that public-private boundaries are often fuzzy, the volume shows that the public-private dichotomy takes different meanings depending on the national and institutional contexts. From this perspective, the public-private dichotomy may take a different meaning from one country to another, as well as from one policy area to another within the same country.

Second, regarding the politics of public and private benefits, this volume suggests that although existing public and private institutions may act as strong constraints to change, path-departing reforms can reshape well-established public and private social programs. This means that taking into account the structuring role of existing political institutions and policy legacies should not hide the fact that political mobilization and other powerful forces can deeply reshape these legacies.

Finally, previous research provides some evidence that a strong reliance on private benefits can increase social inequalities. Because the state frequently plays a major role in regulating private benefits, however, public regulations can mitigate the potentially negative impact of a strong reliance on such private benefits.

Eleven substantive chapters comprise this volume. The first two chapters explore broad trends about health and pension policies across time and countries. In her first chapter, Debra Street uses quantitative approaches to study cross-national patterns in health policies, whereas, in the second chapter, Patrik Marier and Suzanne Skinner take a similar approach to study cross-national developments in pension policies. These chapters examine transformations in public-private, social-policy expenditures and their impacts on social inequality, among other major issues.

The subsequent chapters offer detailed, qualitative analyses of prevailing institutional and political circumstances in nine different countries. These chapters are written by known specialists of each country: the United States (Christopher Howard and Edward Berkowitz), Canada (Gerard Boychuk and Keith Banting), the United Kingdom (Peter Taylor-Gooby and Lavinia Mitton), New Zealand (Toni Ashton and Susan St John), Japan (Toshimitsu Shinkawa), Switzerland (Fabio Bertozzi and Fabrizio Gilardi), Germany (Sven Jochem), Sweden (Karen Anderson, Paula Blomqvist, and Ellen Immergut), and Chile (Christina Ewig and Stephen Kay).

Public and private benefits are believed to play major and distinct roles in Canada, New Zealand, the United Kingdom, and the United States. Although the United States is more liberal than the three other cases, these four liberal countries share a common reliance on private benefits in at least one of the two policy areas under study here. This volume not only stresses crucial differences among and within these four liberal democracies, it will demonstrate that national states often have surprisingly important roles in providing health care and pensions. In contrast to the US experience, national states in Britain, Canada, and New Zealand play a more direct role in their health care systems. Private pension plans are key components of the British and Canadian retirement-income systems, but the state influences private provision through tax benefits and regulations. Major differences in political institutions characterize these liberal countries. This factor helps explain differences between countries in the development of public-private social policies.

Public-private collaborations in social-policy provision can become quite complex. Meriting attention are the cases of Japan and Switzerland, where health care and pension provision are made through public-private collaborations. Complexity in Japan arises from state-private relationships, whereas in Switzerland it largely results from the country's federal structure, which gives cantons authority to regulate social policy, producing different forms of public-private health care and pensions. Once again, political institutions seem to play a major role in shaping the public-private dichotomy.

Often overlooked in debates about the future of the public-private dichotomy for social policy are Germany and Sweden. The state is believed to dominate health and pension policies in both countries, but in Germany and Sweden these policies take important, distinct approaches. On the one hand, Germany belongs to the conservative welfare regime where occupationally fragmented social insurance schemes traditionally provide the bulk of the protection. On the other hand, Sweden is one of the best examples of the social-democratic welfare regime, which is grounded in universal coverage and a central role of the state in the allocation of welfare (Esping-Andersen 1990). Private benefits are believed to be less prominent in these two countries, yet in the last ten years, private plans have played an increasing role in both countries, with varying success. Germany and Sweden represent cases in which introductions of private alternatives have encountered barriers arising from strong public provision. Consideration of the German and Swedish approaches offers invaluable insights to debates on the fate of public-private social policies in advanced industrial societies.

Finally, the book covers a fascinating and highly debated policy innovator: Chile. Now the most prosperous country in Latin America, Chile has long been considered a "model" for neoliberal privatization, both in developing and in advanced industrial countries. Yet, reform efforts are underway for the Chilean model. In 2000, for example, Chile initiated health care reforms focused on greater state regulation of private health insurers, whereas pension reforms proposed in 2006 included the introduction of universal needs-based pensions. Because of intense discussions about the so-called "Chilean model"—especially its form of privatization and as a striking example of policy creating vested interests among private actors—inclusion of this country further enriches our analysis.

Each of the case study chapters follows the same basic template: an introduction; thoughtful analysis of the public-private qualities of dominant health care policies and pension policies; and a concluding discussion on the future of public and private components of the health care systems and pension systems. More specifically, each chapter discusses the history and the current transformation of the public-private dichotomy for social policy for the particular country. Beyond dealing with mere technical details, the country chapters offer the "big picture," allowing readers to understand why each country took the public-private path it has followed for health care and pension policies.

The volume's conclusion synthesizes ideas and evidence from the substantive chapters, presenting insights into this volume's main contributions regarding policy design, politics, and social inequality. This final chapter integrates findings on health and pension policies with a discussion of ramifications of the changing nature of the public-private dichotomy for the three main issues raised in this volume: policy design, politics, and social inequality. Finally, the chapter sketches a comprehensive research agenda for the comparative exploration of the public-private dichotomy for social policies in advanced industrial countries and beyond.

As argued in the final chapter, the boundaries separating public from private social provisions are seldom clear cut. This is why we must reject the idea of a strict separation between public and private social policies. Moreover, considering the enduring nature of profound institutional and political variations, the public-private dichotomy can take a very different meaning from one society to another or, within the same society, from one policy area to another. Overall, drawing on the rich empirical material discussed throughout the volume, the final chapter illustrates these claims, which all point to the complexity of the public-private dichotomy for health and pension policies.

Notes

1. Throughout this volume, *public* social policy refers to 'the policy of governments with regard to action having a direct impact on the welfare of the citizens by providing them with services and income.' (Marshall 1965: 1) The emphasis here is on the direct role of the state, which is a key characteristic of public social policy. Conversely, *private* social policy refers to forms of protection often regulated by the state but operated mainly by private actors, both in the nonprofit and the for-profit sectors, as well as other social and individual efforts.
2. For an historical discussion about the sources of social-policy fragmentation in Western European countries see Baldwin, 1990.
3. Esping-Andersen's work on decommodification is extended to defamilialization, which asks whether a welfare state offers benefits that enable an individual to enjoy a socially acceptable standard of living independent of his or her family. Decommodification primarily concerns itself with relationship between state and market, while defamilialization is concerned with state and family.
4. For Bruno Palier and Giuliano Bonoli (2000), the opposite can also be true, as cutbacks in mature public programs can leave more room for—and facilitate—the development of private benefits.

References

Baldwin, Peter. 1990. *The Politics of Social Solidarity: Class Bases of the European Welfare State, 1875–1975*. New York: Cambridge University Press.

Béland, Daniel. 2007. *Social Security: History and Politics from the New Deal to the Privatization Debate* [paperback edition with new afterword]. Lawrence, KS: University Press of Kansas.

Béland, Daniel and Jacob S. Hacker. 2004. "Ideas, Private Institutions, and American Welfare State 'Exceptionalism': The Case of Health and Old-Age Insurance in the United States, 1915–1965." *International Journal of Social Welfare* 13(1): 42–54.

Berkowitz, Edward D. and Kim McQuaid. 1980. *Creating the Welfare State: The Political Economy of Twentieth-Century Reform*. Westport, CT: Praeger.

Campbell, John and Ove Kaj Pedersen. (eds). 2001. *The Rise of Neoliberalism and Institutional Analysis*. Princeton, NJ: Princeton University Press.

Castles, Francis G. and Deborah Mitchell. 1993. "Worlds of Welfare and Families of Nations." In Francis G. Castles (ed.), *Families of Nations*. Aldershot: Darmouth: 93–128.

Dobbin, Frank and Terry Boychuk. 1996. "Public Policy and the Rise of Private Pensions: The US Experience since 1930." In Michael Shalev (ed.), *The Privatization of Social Policy? Occupational Welfare and the Welfare State in America, Scandinavia and Japan*: 104–35. Houndmills: Macmillan.

Esping-Andersen, Gøsta. 1990. *The Three Worlds of Welfare Capitalism*. Cambridge: Polity.

Esping-Andersen, Gøsta. 1999. *Social Foundations of Postindustrial Economies*. Oxford: Oxford University Press.

Esping-Andersen, Gøsta. 2002. "Towards the Good Society, Once Again?" In Gøsta Esping-Andersen et al. (eds), *Why We Need a New Welfare State*. Oxford: Oxford. University Press: 1–25.

Feldstein, Martin. 1974. "Social Security, Induced Retirement, and Aggregate Capital Accumulation." *Journal of Political Economy* 82(5): 905–26.

Ferrera, Maurizio. 1996. "Southern Model of Welfare in Social Europe." *Journal of European Social Policy* 6(1): 17–37.

Gilbert, Neil. 2002. *Transformation of the Welfare State: The Silent Surrender of Public Responsibility*. Oxford: Oxford University Press.

Gilbert, Neil and Barbara Gilbert. 1989. *The Enabling State: Modem Welfare Capitalism in America*. New York: Oxford University Press.

Gottschalk, Marie. 2000. *The Shadow Welfare State: Labor, Business, and the Politics of Health Care in the United States*. Ithaca, NY: Cornell University Press.

Gran, Brian. 2003. "A Second Opinion: Rethinking the Public-Private Dichotomy for Health Insurance." *International Journal of Health Services* 33(2): 283–313.

Hacker, Jacob S. 2002. *The Divided Welfare State: The Battle over Public and Private Social Benefits in the United States*. Cambridge: Cambridge University Press.

Hacker, Jacob S. 2004. "Privatizing Risk without Privatizing the Welfare State: The Hidden Politics of Social Policy Retrenchment in the United States." *American Political Science Review* 98(2): 243–60.

Hagestad, Gunhild O. and Katharina Herlofson. 2007. "Micro and macro perspectives on intergenerational relations and transfers in Europe." In *Report from United Nations Expert Group Meeting on Social and Economic Implications of changing Population Age Structures*. New York: United Nations (Department of Economic and Social Affairs): 339–57.

Harvey, David. 2005. *A Brief History of Neoliberalism*. Oxford: Oxford University Press.

Helliwell, John F. 2002. *Globalization and Well-Being*. Vancouver: University of British Columbia Press.

Howard, Christopher. 1997. *The Hidden Welfare State: Tax Expenditures and Social Policy in the United States*. Princeton, NJ: Princeton University Press.

Howard, Christopher. 2006. *The Welfare State Nobody Knows: Debunking Myths about U.S. Social Policy*. Princeton, NJ: Princeton University Press.

Immergut, Ellen. 1986. "Between State and Market: Sickness Benefits and Social Control." In Martin Rein and Lee Rainwater (eds), *Public/Private Interplay in Social Protection*: 57–98. Armonk, NY: M.E. Sharpe, Inc.

Jenson, Jane. 2004. *Canada's New Social Risks: Directions for a New Social Architecture* Ottawa: Canadian Policy Research Networks.

Klein, Jennifer. 2003. *For All These Rights: Business, Labor, and the Shaping of America's Public-Private Welfare State*. Princeton, NJ: Princeton University Press.

Lewis, Jane. 1992. "Gender and the Development of Welfare State Regimes." *Journal of European Social Policy* 2: 159–73.

Marshall, T. H. 1964. *Class, Citizenship and Development*. Garden City, N.Y: Doubleday.

Marshall, T. H. 1965. *Social Policy*. London: Hutchinson.

O'Connor, Julia S., Ann Shola Orloff, and Sheila Shaver. 1999. *States, Markets, Families: Gender, Liberalism and Social Policy in Australia, Canada, Great Britain and the United States*. Cambridge: Cambridge University Press.

O'Higgins, Michael. 1986. "Public/Private Interaction and Pension Provision." In Martin Rein and Lee Rainwater (eds), *Public/Private Interplay in Social Protection*: 99–148. Armonk, NY: M.E. Sharpe, Inc.

Orloff, Ann Shola. 1993. "Gender and the Social Rights of Citizenship: The Comparative Analysis of Gender Relations and Welfare States." *American Sociological Review* 58: 303–28.

Palier, Bruno and Giuliano Bonoli. 2000. "La montée en puissance des fonds de pension." *L'Année de la régulation* 4: 71–112.

Pierson, Paul. 1994. *Dismantling the Welfare State? Reagan, Thatcher, and the Politics of Retrenchment*. New York: Cambridge University Press.

Quadagno, Jill. 1988. *The Transformation of Old Age Security: Class and Politics in the American Welfare State*. Chicago, IL: University of Chicago Press.

Rein, Martin. 1989. "The Social Structure of Institutions: Neither Public Nor Private." In Sheila B. Kamerman and Alfred J. Kahn (eds), *Privatization and the Welfare State*: 49–71. Princeton, NJ: Princeton University Press.

Rein, Martin and Lee Rainwater. 1986. "The Future of the Public/Private Mix." In Martin Rein and Lee Rainwater (eds), *Public/Private Interplay in Social Protection*: 202–14. Armonk, NY: M.E. Sharpe, Inc.

Rein, Martin and Lee Rainwater. 1986. "The Institutions of Social Protection." In Martin Rein and Lee Rainwater (eds), *Public/Private Interplay in Social Protection*: 25–56. Armonk, NY: M.E. Sharpe, Inc.

Rein, Martin and Lee Rainwater. 1986. "Introduction." In Martin Rein and Lee Rainwater (eds), *Public/Private Interplay in Social Protection*: vii–viii. Armonk, NY: M.E. Sharpe, Inc.

Rein, Martin and Winfried Schmähl. (eds). 2004. *Rethinking the Welfare State: The Political Economy of Pension Reform*. London: Edward Elgar.

Rose, Richard. 1989. "Welfare: The Public/Private Mix." In Sheila B. Kamerman and Alfred J. Kahn (eds), *Privatization and the Welfare State*: 73–95. Princeton, NJ: Princeton University Press.

Ruggie, Mary. 1996. *Realignments in the Welfare State*. New York: Columbia University Press.

Seeleib-Kaiser, Martin (ed.) 2008. *Welfare State Transformations: Comparative Perspectives*. Basingstoke: Palgrave.

Shalev, Michael. 1996. *The Privatization of Social Policy? Occupational Welfare and the Welfare State in America, Scandinavia and Japan*. London: Macmillan.

Starr, Paul. 1989. "The Meaning of Privatization." In Sheila B. Kamerman and Alfred J. Kahn (eds), *Privatization and the Welfare State*: 15–48. Princeton, NJ: Princeton University Press.

Titmuss, Richard M. 1974. *Social Policy: An Introduction*. London: George Allen and Unwin.

Titmuss, Richard. 1963. *Essays on "The Welfare State."* (Second Edition). London: Unwin University Books.

von Nordheim Nielsen, Fritz. 1991. "The Politics of Aging in Scandinavian Countries." In John Myles and Jill Quadagno (eds), *States, Labor Markets, and the Future of Old-Age Policy*. Philadelphia, PA: Temple University Press: 127–74.

West Pedersen, Axel. 2004. "The Privatization of Retirement Income? Variation and Trends in the Income Packages of Old Age Pensioners." *Journal of European Social Policy* 14(1): 5–23.

World Bank. 1994. *Averting the Old Age Crisis: Policies to Protect the Old and Promote Growth*. Washington, DC: The World Bank.

1
Balancing Acts: Trends in the Public-Private Mix in Health Care

Debra Street

Introduction

Across the globe, health expenditures constitute a large and growing share of both public and private spending on social welfare. Levels of health spending vary widely between countries, reflecting pressures of different domestic economic circumstances, sociopolitical factors, demographic conditions, and the particular financing and organizational arrangements of national health care systems. Two major components of health expenditures are spending on personal health care (however its financing and delivery are arranged) and spending on population-level public health interventions. The need for these publicly financed, public health measures is presumed, even in the most market-oriented societies. Only governments can efficiently undertake collective measures on the scale needed to preserve population health for public health activities ranging from ensuring clean food and water supplies, to regulating the safety and efficacy of pharmaceutical products, to implementing population immunization programs and responding to epidemics, and the like (Gostin 2000; IOM 1988, 2003; WHO 2000).

Although the largest financial contribution that some governments make is to collective public health, citizens most directly experience their nation's health care spending in the ways they consume health care as individuals, not as beneficiaries of macro-level public health measures. Yet macro-level trends such as population aging have a number of implications for government and private spending on health care and pensions and, more generally, for economic growth and welfare (OECD Factbook 2007). Increasing costs associated with public social welfare spending are among the reasons that countries pursue reforms to rebalance public and private provision across social welfare domains, health care included.

More so than most other types of social welfare, citizens' entitlements to health care are widely accepted across both the developed and developing world. Market-based arguments used to promote private housing, education, and pension policies often fall flat when stakeholders discuss dismantling a fundamental right to basic health care. Still, national perspectives on what the "basic care" package should cover and how a right to basic care should be enacted implicate private and public provision differently. Adding to the challenge of clearly understanding the complexities of health care systems is a lack of national health expenditure data that are truly comparable. Some kinds of health services, such as dental care or long-term care, are not included in health expenditure policy data for some countries, but are in others.

Regardless of what countries now spend on health care, which services are mainly delivered through public programs or purchased privately, or which sector pays the bills, the sheer size of national health expenditures make health care a target for policy reform in an era of global competition and fiscal belt-tightening, much like its pension cousin. Additional impetus for reform comes from a variety of sources, for example: (1) a neoliberal political climate that denigrates public programs and promotes markets and individual responsibility; (2) attention to the role national health care arrangements play in positioning national economies for global competitiveness; (3) constant medical innovation accompanied by medical inflation that outstrips national economic growth in most Organisation for Economic Co-operation and Development[1] (OECD) countries; (4) the increasing role of pharmaceuticals in managing chronic diseases; and (5) predicted increases in levels of health system demands due to aging population. Advocates of collective responsibility for health care defend the status quo of dominantly public funding as the best tool to meet future health care demands. Proponents of market-style reforms argue that increased reliance on private provision could improve the responsiveness of national health care systems, heighten efficiency, and relieve some pressures on the public purse, topics on national agendas around the world (see Drache and Sullivan 1999; Figueras and Saltman 1997; Saltman et al. 1998).

National health care systems present an intriguing case of how public and private provision are elaborated and balanced in one social welfare domain. This chapter provides a comparative context for the country-specific discussions provided later in this volume, exploring the nature and extent of the public-private dichotomy by describing trends in national health care provision arrangements, focusing on evidence bearing on questions raised in the introductory chapter: Do trends indicate a steady retreat from publicly funded health care? Which health outcomes appear to be linked to the balance of public and private arrangements for health care? What are the implications of greater private responsibility for health care?

This chapter broadly outlines health care mechanisms within the context of national social expenditure patterns. It traces the empirical contours of trends related to current funding arrangements to consider adjustments in the historical balance of public-private provision for health care. Health-related outcomes may indicate, among other factors, the partial impact of the public-private balance of health care delivery on national health statistics. Finally, this comparative chapter sets the stage for the more nuanced and detailed country chapters that follow, highlighting several key questions about the complexities and the future of the public-private character of health care systems for countries across the world.

The public-private mix of health policies

Alongside public social spending on income support for working-age citizens, pensions, and other social services (such as family allowances and child care), health care is a major area of domestic social expenditure. The share of public spending devoted to particular social welfare areas varies from country to country and over time, in response to a myriad of distinctive national circumstances. Figures 1.1 and 1.2 show total health expenditure as a percentage of gross domestic product (GDP) for OECD countries (Figure 1.1), and the share of that spending that is public (Figure 1.2). The proportion of GDP devoted to total health spending varies widely across OECD countries (see Figure 1.1). Occasional exceptions notwithstanding, wealthier countries (see Figure 1.2) within particular welfare state types (for example, liberal

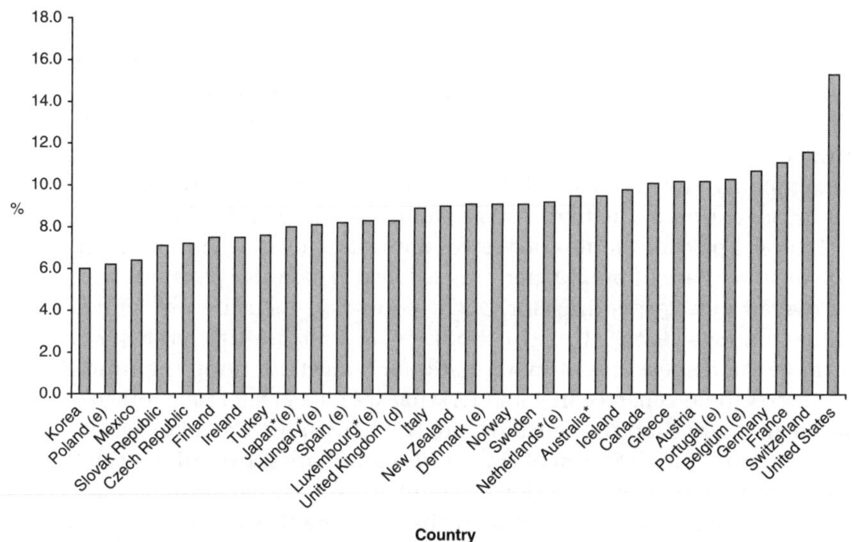

Figure 1.1   Total national health expenditures as a percentage of GDP, 2005
Note: * = 2004; (e) = estimate; (d) = different methodology.
Source: OECD (2007).

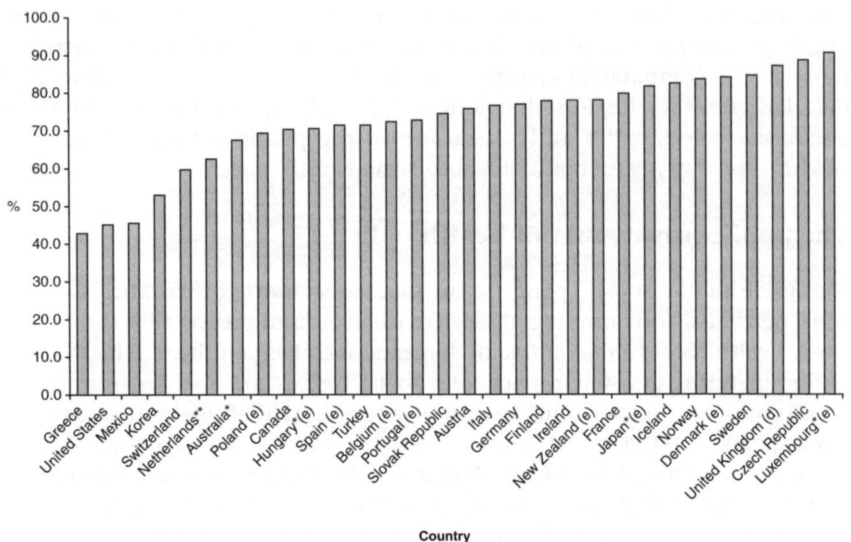

Figure 1.2   Percentage of total national health care expenditure from public sources, 2005

Note: * = 2004; ** = 2002; (e) = estimate; (d) = different methodology.

Source: OECD (2007).

[Anglo-American countries], social democratic [Scandinavian], and conservative/corporatist nations [continental European]) tend to have higher public spending per capita[2] than less wealthy nations (OECD 2007). Greece, the United States, and Mexico have the lowest levels of public spending, whereas Luxembourg, the Czech Republic, the United Kingdom, and the Scandinavian countries cluster at the high end of public spending on health care.

Table 1.1 provides some context for national social expenditures, showing the relative share of public spending for health care and pensions compared to overall public spending for OECD countries, focusing on eight[3] of the nine countries featured in this book. Note that health care expenditures rival pension spending in many national budgets. Among the nine OECD countries (bold typeface in Table 1.1) that spend a greater percentage of GDP on health care than on pensions, are five (Australia, Canada, Ireland, New Zealand, the United States) of the six *liberal* welfare states (all but the United Kingdom). With few exceptions, countries from other welfare state types generally spend more on pensions than on health care. There are several likely reasons for this pattern. First, with the exception of the United Kingdom, liberal countries have relatively young demographic age structures (due to relatively higher fertility and/or immigration rates), and hence proportionately fewer pensioners require income support. Second, in-kind

Table 1.1   Social spending as a percentage of GDP, 2001

	Public social spending		
	Total public social spending, percent of GDP	**Public spending for pensions, percent of GDP**	**Public spending for health, percent of GDP**
Australia	18.0	4.3	6.2
Austria	26.0	12.9	5.2
Belgium	27.2	11.2	6.4
Canada	17.8	5.3	6.7
Czech Republic	20.1	7.6	6.7
Denmark	29.2	6.5	7.1
Finland	24.8	8.0	5.3
France	28.5	11.9	7.2
Germany	27.4	11.2	8.0
Greece	24.3	13.4	5.2
Hungary	20.1	7.7	5.1
Iceland	19.8	4.7	7.5
Ireland	13.8	3.2	4.9
Italy	24.4	13.8	6.3
Japan	16.9	7.6	6.3
Korea	6.1	1.3	3.2
Luxembourg	20.8	8.0	4.8
Mexico	11.8	7.6	2.7
Netherlands	21.8	6.4	5.7
New Zealand	18.5	4.9	6.1
Norway	23.9	4.8	6.8
Poland	23.0	10.6	4.4
Portugal	21.1	9.1	6.3
Spain	19.6	8.7	5.4
Sweden	28.9	7.4	7.4
Switzerland	26.4	13.1	6.4
Turkey	13.2	6.3	3.9
United Kingdom	21.8	8.3	6.1
United States	**14.8**	**6.1**	**6.2**

Source: OECD (2004); Social Expenditure database (1980–2001) (www.oecd.org/els/social/expenditure).

transfer of health care goods and services is qualitatively different from redistributive cash transfers required to support pension income. Norms of reciprocity which influence the generosity, the types (cash or in-kind benefits), and the basis for claiming social welfare benefits comprise the moral economy foundation that shapes the character of different types of welfare states (Mau 2003; Minkler and Estes 1999). The moral economy of liberal welfare states is characterized by an individualistic ethos of self-sufficiency that stigmatizes recipiency of most cash benefits as undesirable welfare dependency. The bounded usefulness of publicly funded health care may satisfy social control components of grudging redistribution to market "failures" in liberal welfare states, in that resources provided only for consumption of health care services cannot be reallocated to other, more discretionary consumption. The data in Table 1.1 reflect only public social spending, not total social spending which would also include resources from the private sector for health care or pensions.

How do privatizing trends in health care spending stack up? Although recent data and policy innovations (see country-specific chapters later in this volume) present cross-national evidence of trends towards increased reliance on private mechanisms to fund later life incomes in many countries, evidence concerning privatizing trends in international health care expenditure data is decidedly mixed. Figure 1.3 graphically depicts the balance of public and private national health expenditures in 1990 and 2004 (the most recent year for which comparable data are available).[4] There are obvious differences in the public-private balance from country to country, but no dramatic changes over time. The share of total health expenditures designated as private sector in national accounts has increased slightly in Canada, Sweden, and Switzerland, and has declined slightly in Japan, Britain, and the United States. Public spending alone for health care in the United States exceeds the average level of public and private health spending combined for most other OECD countries. Even in the next most expensive countries' health care systems (Switzerland, Canada, and Germany), public and private health care spending together barely exceed public spending alone in the United States.

Recent changes in the public-private mix can also be examined for privatizing moments in health expenditure trends in either the short (2000–2004) or longer (1990–2004) term (see Table 1.2). However, no consistent trend away from public provision is readily apparent. Among the OECD countries for which data are presented in Table 1.2, the proportion of public spending for health care declined in over half of them from 1990 to 2000, averaging a 1 percent decline in public expenditure across all OECD countries. However, from 2000 to 2004, 18 countries recorded increases in the proportion of public spending on health. Over the entire period of 1990–2004, the largest declines in public shares of health care spending occurred

Table 1.2   Trends in health expenditures, 1990–2004

	US dollars calculated using Purchasing Power Parities				
	Percent public expenditure of total health expenditure per capita			Percent change in public share	Percent change in public share
	1990	2000	2004	1990–2000	2000–2004
Australia	67.1	68.9	67.5	0.5	–1.4
Austria	73.5	69.9	70.6	–2.8	0.8
Belgium	Na	75.8	71.1	Na	–4.7
Canada	**74.6**	**70.3**	**69.8**	**–4.7**	**–0.5**
Czech Republic	97.5	90.5	89.2	–8.3	–1.3
Denmark	82.7	82.4	Na	Na	Na
Finland	80.9	75.1	76.6	–4.3	1.5
France	76.6	75.8	78.3	1.7	2.5
Germany	**81.5**	**79.7**	**76.9**	**–4.6**	**–2.7**
Greece	53.7	52.5	52.8	–0.9	0.2
Hungary	89.2	70.8	71.9	–17.4	1.1
Iceland	86.6	82.6	83.4	–3.3	0.8
Ireland	71.9	73.3	79.5	7.6	6.2
Italy	79.1	72.0	75.1	–4.0	3.1
Japan	**77.6**	**81.3**	**81.5**	**3.9**	**0.2**
Korea	38.5	46.1	51.4	12.9	5.3
Luxembourg	93.1	89.3	90.4	–2.6	1.1
Mexico	40.5	46.4	46.4	5.9	–0.1
Netherlands	67.0	63.1	62.3	–4.8	–0.8
New Zealand	**82.4**	**78.0**	**77.3**	**–5.1**	**–0.7**
Norway	82.8	82.5	83.5	0.7	1.0
Poland	91.7	70.0	68.6	–23.1	–1.4
Portugal	65.4	72.5	73.1	7.7	0.6
Spain	78.7	71.6	70.9	–7.8	–0.7
Sweden	**89.9**	**84.9**	**84.9**	**–4.9**	**0.0**
Switzerland	**52.4**	**55.6**	**58.4**	**6.0**	**2.8**
Turkey	61.3	63.0	72.1	10.8	9.1
United Kingdom	**83.6**	**80.8**	**86.3**	**2.7**	**5.4**
United States	**39.7**	**44.0**	**44.7**	**5.0**	**0.7**
OECD average	73.1	72.0	72.0	–1.1	0.1
Switzerland	52.4	55.6	58.4	6.0	2.8
Turkey	61.3	63.0	72.1	10.8	9.1
United Kingdom	83.6	80.8	86.3	2.7	5.4
United States	39.7	44.0	44.7	5.0	0.7
OECD average	73.1	72.0	72.0	–1.1	0.1

Note: Data in bold typeface are from country cases covered in later chapters in this book.

Source: OECD Factbook (2007).

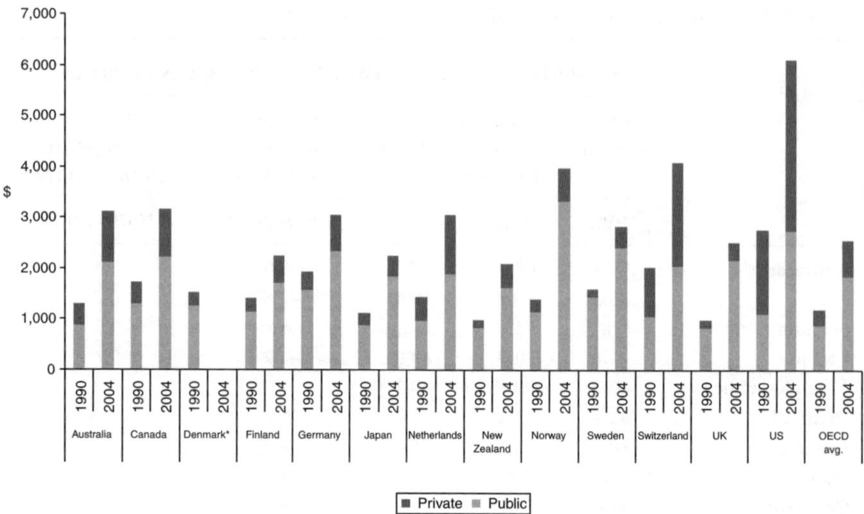

Figure 1.3   Public and private health care expenditures, 1990 and 2004 (US$ using PPP)

Note: *2004 data not available for Denmark.

in transitional Eastern European countries, such as Poland, Hungary, and the Czech Republic, where former state health systems were transformed into mixed systems.

Considering in more detail just the cases presented later in this book (bold typeface in Table 1.2), four countries (Canada, Germany, New Zealand, Sweden) have modestly smaller proportions of public health care provision in 2004 compared to 1990. All the above-mentioned four countries in 1990 spent above the OECD average of public expenditure for health care; by 2004, Germany, New Zealand, and Sweden still had public spending levels higher than the OECD average for public expenditures on health. Four other countries featured in this book had increased public expenditures on health care. Japan and Britain, among the least expensive health care systems in 1990, and the relatively expensive US and Swiss health care systems (with their traditionally higher reliance on private sector spending) all expanded public commitment to health care provision over the period. Regardless of small gains or losses in the individual nation-specific proportion of health expenditures designated as public in national health accounts, most of the change in the public-private balance across the eight countries occurred in the 1990s, with only marginal changes in the public-private mix since then.[5] Taken together, these trends may signal modest convergence across OECD countries towards a public-private health care expenditure balance, rather than any clear unidirectional move away from public provision (except in transitional economies, as noted earlier).

In contrast to the relatively small changes over the past decade and a half in the balance of most countries' public-private mix of health expenditure, changes in total health expenditures have been substantial for some countries. Thus, one trend persisting into the early twenty-first century from the last is the relatively steady increases in health care expenditures, whether measured as the proportion of GDP devoted to health care spending (Figure 1.4), or measured as per capita spending (Figure 1.5) using US$ purchasing power parity (PPP) to permit comparability. Total national health expenditures shown in Figure 1.4 are a measure of the final consumption of health care goods and services plus capital investment in health

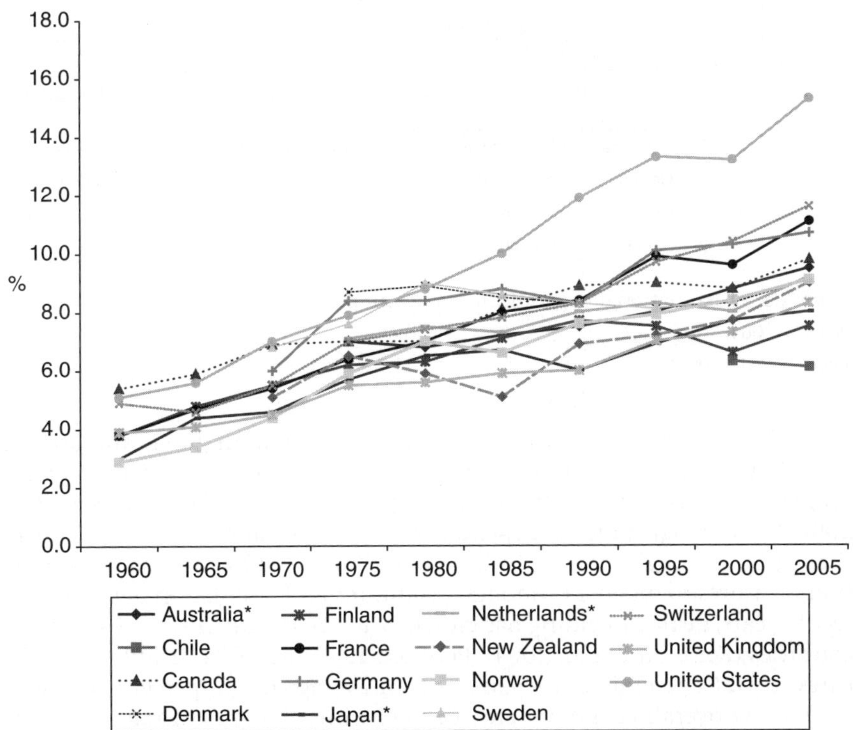

Figure 1.4   Total national expenditure on health as a percent of GDP
Note: * = 2004.
Source: OECD.

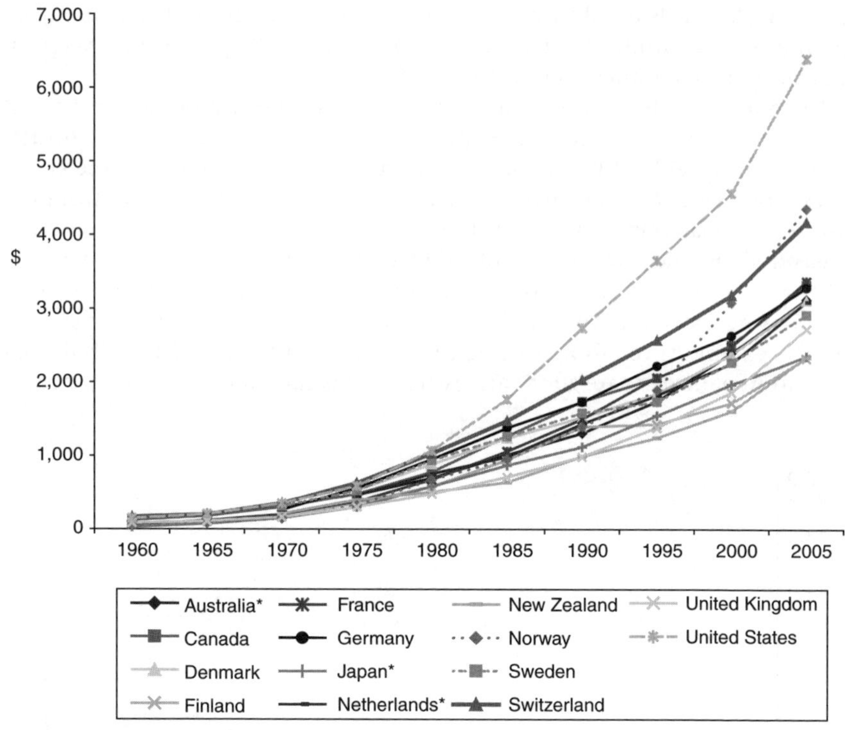

Figure 1.5   Total national expenditure on health per capita, US$ PPP
Note: * = 2004.
Source: OECD (2007).

care infrastructure. Total health expenditures cover both public and private spending on medical services and goods, public health and prevention programs, and the administration of medical faculties and programs (OECD 2006).[6] The magnitude of expenditure increases varies over time and is shaped by demand, medical inflation, and sensitivity of health consumption measures to broader economic conditions and population demands. In recent years, health spending has grown faster than GDP in almost all OECD countries (Reinhardt et al. 2004). Between 1997 and 2004, health expenditures in OECD countries increased by an average of 4.3 percent per year, double the overall economic growth rate, while the growth rate of health expenditure (2.6 percent) only slightly outpaced overall economic growth between 1992 and 1997 (OECD 2006). Other fluctuations in the proportion of health related to GDP are the result of broader economic conditions. The proportion of GDP devoted to health care is sensitive to annual estimates of national economies' expansions and recessions, because GDP is the denominator of the proportionate health care expenditure measure. For example, a country experiencing a short-term economic downturn, resulting in stagnant GDP and a "small" denominator, may appear to be suddenly spending more on health care if considered only in cross section. Yet the process driving the change is actually just the temporarily stagnant GDP, which exaggerates the apparent effect of health spending.

Taking a longer view, levels of national health care spending increased steadily from 1960 onward in most countries, measured as a proportion of national wealth. Figure 1.4 shows trends in total national health expenditures in five-year increments from 1960 to 2005. Most countries' total health expenditures were grouped similarly in 1960, with approximately 5 percent of GDP devoted to health care in most advanced industrialized countries. Japan was the 1960 outlier, spending substantially less than most other countries, at approximately 3 percent. Although Japan still spent less by 2005, it was clustered with several other relatively low-spending countries committing between 6 and 8 percent of national GDP annually to health care. In contrast, US health expenditures surged ahead of all others, particularly from 1980 onward, tripling the proportion of US GDP devoted to health care between 1960 and 2005. Although during the period all countries' health care spending increased, US health care expenditures exploded. The most obvious and robust trend in the cross-country comparisons is how much contemporary US spending outpaces all others.

Adjusting data for comparability, as is the case in the spending per capita data from 1960 to 2005 depicted in Figure 1.5, smoothes out some of the over-time data fluctuations seen in the GDP data of Figure 1.4. The starting point in 1960 for most counties' adjusted per capita spending was very similar, but that similarity is no longer reflected in current spending levels across the countries considered. Instead, countries such as the United States and Switzerland have growing gaps between their per capita spending and individual spending levels in other countries.

Welfare states, health care systems ... and the United States

The ideological component of the neoliberal moral economy is one foundation of the US health care system, which valorizes individual provision and the superiority of markets for meeting most social welfare, but which is not particularly attentive to unavoidable market flaws of the health care sector. This neoliberal ideology that the market should dominate economic and social life, while the state should restrict activities to a residual safety net, was most clearly expounded by Hayek (1960; 1982) and Friedman (1962; Friedman and Friedman 1980), and gained at least some political currency even in countries that had deeply entrenched, extensive social welfare programs. As political figures embracing this ideological perspective gained influence (most notably Reagan in the United States and Thatcher in the United Kingdom), concerns about the potential implication of demographic trends—particularly population aging—for national budgets contributed to neoliberal arguments that states will exceed their capacity to meet welfare needs, whether for the unemployed, the retired, or the sick, and that markets would provide more appropriately in any case (see Ginn et al. 2001).

Traditionally categorized liberal or residual welfare states (such as Britain, the United States, Canada, and New Zealand) are generally regarded as the sites where this individualistic policy ethos finds its most fertile soil. The Anglo-American models of welfare provision have most heavily relied on social welfare outcomes tightly linked to labor market participation, skeptical of Scandinavian or continental welfare states with their citizen-based or status-based systems of redistribution. If welfare state typologies are as sensitive to the particulars of health care arrangements as they are to income support program structures (whether unemployment or disability benefits, or pensions), or if liberal states are unusually vulnerable to retrenchment or privatizing initiatives, we would expect to see private sector involvement in health care delivery consistently highest in Anglo-American settings. Further, trends in the public-private character of health care expenditures and outcomes would logically track experiences in other domains, such as pensions, where reliance on private provision appears to be increasing (Ginn et al. 2001).

However, in some ways health care is the least discriminating policy domain, at least insofar as making crisp national distinctions about welfare state types are concerned. After all, as evidence provided earlier in this chapter shows, some countries in the traditional residual category, where reliance on private provision is expected to be highest, have among the most extensive and entrenched public health care systems. For example, Britain's National Health Service offers comprehensive cradle-to-grave health coverage for individuals, provided by medical professionals who are mainly public sector employees. In Canada, until a 2005 Supreme Court challenge to its constitutionality, private clinics or insuring medical procedures to Canadians for health care entitlements provided for under the Canada Health Act (1984) were illegal. This represented a strong legislative effort to guarantee a single-tier egalitarian system of health provision. Countries traditionally having more extensive institutional welfare arrangements, such as Sweden, match their more residual cousins such as Britain and New Zealand in terms of proportion of health care spending in the private sector. This private spending is typically for components of health care services regarded as desirable and health promoting, but which are not considered absolutely essential services even under otherwise relatively comprehensive health provision (see Figure 1.2).

Esping-Andersen (1990) noted that the particulars of health care arrangements were confounding factors in straightforward categorization of countries into the liberal category that appeared appropriate when considering other policy dimensions. Here the exception would be using the extent of reliance on private health care in the United States as evidence of its prototypically liberal welfare state status. Few scholars argue that dominantly market-based health arrangements similar to those in the United States are either efficient or equitable. Despite abundant evidence that health care represents a case of "abnormal economics" and inevitable instances of market failure (Hsiao 1995), over the past two decades neoliberal stakeholders around the world pushed an agenda to retrench social welfare expenditure, health care included. But privatizing policies, so far, have made only limited inroads into the reach of most countries' public health care systems (although there were notable policy initiatives seeking more substantive changes in recent decades) and none at all in the United States.

Several countries attempted to revamp components of health care systems using market or market-like models in the past several decades. For example, the introduction of internal markets to the British National Health Service (see Klein 1995) during the Thatcher-Major years (1979–97) was intended to transform health care provision based on market principles. This experiment ended, at least rhetorically, after the 1997 Labour landslide (Klein 2001). Other publicly oriented systems in Europe (such as Sweden: see Glennerster and Matsaganis 1994) also experimented with the introduction of some internal market-like mechanisms in attempts to improve health care system outcomes and satisfaction by making them more competitive and responsive to health care consumers. Exclusively private-pay, investor-owned hospitals have been permitted in Japan only since 2002, yet a handful of private hospitals is a far cry from a significant challenge to the primacy of publicly provided health care. Analysts are skeptical that they will ever gain acceptance in Japan's low-cost, egalitarian health care system (Ikegami and Campbell 2004). Developing countries, such as Chile, adopted—if not more enthusiastically, more thoroughly— the neoliberal prescription for minimal government social investment (Klein 2007) and pursued market-dominated health care policy trajectories that were more extensive than most other countries, albeit under different political conditions. After all, in the case of Chile it was not a liberal democracy expressing its neoliberal preferences, but rather a military dictatorship that imposed a newly privatized health system that covered only a third of its citizens. Nods in privatizing directions notwithstanding, public expenditure for health care outpaces private expenditure in almost all developed countries' health care systems, even the most "private" ones.

The routinely applied mantra, "the only advanced country in the world without a national health care system," places US health care arrangements in a league of its own. The United States is the unusual case among the countries we consider, both in the extent of reliance on private sector health care expenditures and the total amount of GDP devoted to health-related spending. The burgeoning scholarship on how and why the United States has such a different health care model has been something of a growth industry in recent years (Béland and Hacker 2004; Maioni 1998; Quadagno 2006) yet there is no evidence that the American system is arranged the way it is because it succeeds (Moran 1999; Tuohy 1999). The United States spends more than the OECD average of *total* public and private health care expenditures on its *public component alone*, yet the substantial extra spending does not appear to translate into much difference across most readily available health indicators. Those indicators show that the United States is typically either very similar to or lags behind other countries on measures ranging from health professionals per capita to ostensibly health-related outcomes such as infant mortality and life expectancy, despite a significantly larger investment in health care.

Health systems' performance can be measured in many ways, but there is no existing conventionally applied metric for accounting the merits and flaws of particular health care spending patterns and health system outcomes. Table 1.3 presents several indicators routinely used in international comparisons of health outcomes. In the first panel, the crudest measures of the healthfulness of a society, child mortality and life expectancy at birth, are shown. The second panel shows the density of two health occupations, physicians and nurses, as a rough indicator of how available basic health services might be, to the extent that they depend on supplies of health professionals to provide them. Finally, the third panel shows World Health Organization rankings of health systems' performance, including a score reflecting how fair the financing arrangements are, how responsive the health care system is, and an overall assessment of health system performance[7] from a landmark study in 2000. A high score for financial fairness indicates that access to care is compromised by ability to pay and that health care financing arrangements are regressive (proportionately more expensive for low-income than high-income individuals). Responsiveness indicates the capacity of the health care system to respond to consumer demands from individuals who have access to health care by providing choice and convenience for health care consumers. Responsiveness does not assess whether access to care is accomplished in the first place. Finally, a composite of several indicators including financial fairness, responsiveness, and several health outcome measures are combined to rank health care systems from best (low scores) to worst (high scores) in terms of overall health system performance.

Except for Chile, which is a developing country, the highest levels of infant mortality are in liberal welfare states. Despite spending less on health care than most other countries, life expectancy in Japan is the highest. In fact, life expectancy does not appear to be related to either total health care spending, or its particular public-private mix in any country in any straightforward way.

Table 1.3   Selected health-related indicators

	Population level health indicators (WHO 2006)		Health professionals (WHO 2006)		WHO health system rankings (WHO 2000) 190 countries ranked		
	Life expectancy at birth (in years, both sexes)	Child mortality/ 1,000 (children 5 and under)	Physician density per 1,000 in the population	Nurse density per 1,000 in the population	Financial fairness	Responsiveness	Overall performance
Canada	80	6	2.1	9.9	17–19	7–8	30
Chile	77	9	1.1	0.63	168	45	33
Germany	79	5	3.4	9.7	6–7	5	25
Japan	82	4	2.0	7.8	8–11	6	10
New Zealand	80	6	2.4	8.2	23–25	22–23	41
Sweden	81	4	3.3	10.2	12–15	10	23
Switzerland	81	5	3.6	10.8	38–40	2	20
United Kingdom	79	6	2.3	12.1	8–11	26–27	18
United States	78	8	2.6	9.4	54–55	1	37

Source: WHO World Health Report (2000, 2006).

Infant mortality is highest in liberal welfare states; yet it is being a liberal welfare state, not the particular public-private mix of health care expenditures, that appears to be associated with infant mortality. Sweden has the largest supply of doctors, Britain has the largest supply of nurses; each of these two countries has among the most publicly oriented health care systems and a relatively dense health professional supply.

Ranges of rankings for several macro-level system measures in the third panel of Table 1.3 show that the United States ranks quite low (among the 190 countries ranked) in terms of "fairness" of the financing arrangements that citizenries must use to gain routine access to health care, although the US system is nowhere near as unfair as Chile. The United States leads the way in its health care system responsiveness, a measure of how attentive its health care system is to consumer demands. The final column is a measure of overall system performance, using a formula that takes into account roughly comparable data on health outcomes, financing, and equity issues to create a single "score" or ranking (WHO 2000). Several very small, very wealthy countries rank higher in overall system performance than any of the countries considered in this book. Among those considered, Japan's relatively inexpensive health care system ranks highly in WHO rankings. New Zealand, with a relatively inexpensive but extensive public system ranks lowest among these countries in overall performance, but is ranked barely lower than the very expensive and the more private US system in this comparison. Neither the absolute amount of national health care expenditure nor the public-private mix appears to drive overall system quality in WHO rankings.

Another way to evaluate the perception of appropriate levels of health care expenditures and services, or the perceived adequacy of the public-private mix of any national health care system, is to assess the public's satisfaction with the health care system it confronts. Table 1.4 shows public satisfaction with health care systems in 17 countries. Clearly, satisfaction does not parallel directly the trends in the WHO "responsiveness" or consumer attentiveness measure shown in Table 1.3. For example, the United States (ranked 1) and Germany (ranked 6) had among the most responsive health care systems in the WHO ranking system, yet were not among the countries where citizens reported high levels of satisfaction with their health care systems. Countries ranked as substantially less responsive in the WHO data, such as the United Kingdom (ranked 26–27), are regarded as more satisfactory health care systems by their citizens.

Redistribution and the structure of the public-private mix

What makes health care such a distinctive case of social welfare policy and the assessment of its outcomes so complicated? Traditional welfare state typologies, such as Titmuss' classic residual-institutional provision distinction

Table 1.4   Satisfaction with health care system

	Percent saying they are fairly or very satisfied with their own health care system
Austria	83
France	78
Belgium	77
Denmark	76
Finland	74
Netherlands	73
Luxembourg	72
Sweden	59
United Kingdom	56
Germany	50
Ireland	48
Spain	48
Canada	46
United States	40
Italy	26
Portugal	24
Greece	19

Source: Blendon et al. (2001).

(Titmuss 1958) or Esping Andersen's (1990) more recent categorizations of social democratic, conservative-corporatist, and liberal, emphasize common characteristics for eligibility and the scope of social welfare policies. Such categorizations served as the springboard to even more elaborated typologies (for example, Castles and Mitchell 1991; Ferrera 1996; Sainsbury 1999). However national regimes are categorized, the families of rules and programs that constitute welfare state types usually create outcomes that predictably contribute to patterns of social inequalities in national populations. Alongside different types of institutional arrangements, varying ideologies provide foundational assumptions for particular types of welfare states. For example, citizens' collective rights to social welfare (broadly defined) are valued as a fundamental characteristic of the most extensive and institutionalized welfare states (the Scandinavian model). Conversely, expectations of individual self-reliance and a minimal safety net for market failures characterize most welfare domains in residual regimes (usually the Anglo-American countries).

Compared to other more consistently categorized domains of social spending, health care arrangements do not neatly conform to dominant welfare state typologies. Rather, health care systems vary substantially, even among countries whose welfare arrangements have traditionally been categorized similarly in the welfare state literature. There are no exclusively public or entirely private health care systems in advanced industrialized countries. Rather, health care systems are mixed public-private hybrids, arrayed on a continuum from more to less public (or private).

Understanding the public component of a nation's health care system and expenditures is not necessarily straightforward. All countries have some version of public health services, but a nation's public health system focuses on population health issues (such as safe water and food supplies, or issues such as fluoridation and epidemic surveillance), not individual access to health care. Consequently, it is not usually those agencies we consider when assessing the "publicness" or "privateness" aspects of health care systems except in discussion of national accounts. Instead, when considering the public-private mix in welfare states the focus is on how individuals manage to achieve routine access to health care when they need it due to their own ill health or accidents. This implicates both revenue and expenditures to support public programs, the sector within which health professionals and facilities are located, and any gaps in public provision that private arrangements must span. For example, even when individuals have publicly funded national health insurance, as in Canada, they receive the bulk of their health care in the private sector: in voluntary hospitals and from physicians who work as entrepreneurs in solo or group practices. Only the financing mechanism is public. In contrast, countries such as the United Kingdom implemented national health services whereby individuals sought care in state-owned health care facilities from health care professionals who were public sector employees.

Because so few systems have as extensive roles for private benefits as the United States does, typologies of modern health care systems generally describe public arrangements and fit within three broad categories:

1. ***Single-payer national health insurance systems***, such as Canada, Denmark, Norway, and Sweden, in which health insurance is publicly administered and most physicians are in private practice.
2. ***National health services systems***, such as Great Britain and Spain, in which salaried physicians predominate and hospitals are publicly owned and operated.
3. ***Highly regulated, universal, multi-payer health insurance systems*** such as those in Germany and France, where universal health insurance is delivered via sickness funds. In such multi-payer systems (also known as "all-payer" systems), sickness funds pay physicians and hospitals annually negotiated uniform rates (OECD 2006).

None of these systems is entirely public. In fact, the third category is "fuzzy" in that a public mandate requires private insurance, with a public substitute program for populations not eligible for the mandated private coverage.

Although the structure of each type of health care system is quite different, all of these systems share the common characteristic of providing universal health insurance coverage for individuals, regardless of age, gender, income, race/ethnicity, physical ability, or employment status.

Health care arrangements in the United States do not fit into any of these types of health care systems. In fact, scholars have characterized the United States as having a fragmented nonsystem (Davis 2003). The closest the United States comes to having a universal system component is Medicare, which entitles most US residents—65 or older—to health insurance coverage, automatically insuring more than 95 percent of elderly individuals against the costs of hospital stays (Medicare Part A), although even the physician component of Medicare (Part B) requires voluntary premiums and is neither mandatory nor universal. Other countries, even those with universal systems, do not have entirely comprehensive public health care. Instead, there are often "nonessential" health care gaps in universal programs, lacking such important health care components as prescription drug coverage, dental care, eye care, and hearing services. These services must typically be purchased with private out-of-pocket or third-party commercial insurance payments in otherwise comprehensive systems. Although many of these health services are important and seem critical to good health, they are not necessarily deemed so essential that they are covered for all citizens under public programs. Public programs may extend restricted coverage for some services only to low-income individuals who might otherwise go without. Examples include dental care provided at no cost to low-income citizens in the United Kingdom and provincial-level programs to subsidize prescription drug benefits for low-income and elderly Canadians. However, more affluent individuals are expected to pay privately for nonessential health-related goods and services, with such expenditures reflected in the private portion of total national health spending accounts.

The United States is unique in its safety net Medicaid program that uses means tests to establish eligibility for essential basic health care. Medicaid serves only some Americans, notably low-income pregnant women, poor and low-income children, individuals who are severely disabled, and impoverished elderly citizens in long-term care settings. For most working-aged Americans and their families, health insurance comes through a voluntary multi-payer system that links eligibility to employment, but without any of the regulatory or mandatory "all-payer" characteristics of Swiss or German multi-payer systems that place them in the category of universal public systems. For nonpoor, working-aged Americans who do not work at firms that offer group health insurance, most are uninsured. Point in time estimates are approximately 47 million uninsured (KFF 2007).

In common with other welfare state policy domains, most public expenditures for health care are redistributive and, as we have seen, often surpass pension systems in terms of the proportion of national GDP devoted to social welfare. In terms of redistribution, health care systems (depending on the particulars of revenue generation) generally redistribute from high income to low and from the healthy to the sick, progressive arrangements consistent with commitment to collective provision. If revenues are raised partially by contributions, whether insurance premiums or payroll tax contributions, then income-related redistribution is only somewhat progressive, since premiums are usually flat rate. Flat rate premiums consume a larger share of low-income individuals' incomes, and payroll contributions are usually capped at some maximum level, meaning the highest earning individuals are taxed on only a portion of their income, while earners below the cap are taxed on their entire income. For public systems whose resources are mainly from general revenues, whether income or consumptions taxes, the affluent subsidize a proportionately higher share of health expenditures than the less affluent, reflecting the general redistributive progressivity built into such systems.

Private health care spending, too, is often redistributive, although not necessarily in the same ways as public systems are. To give one example, in most systems that offer comprehensive publicly supported health coverage, such as Britain's National Health Service, affluent individuals have always been able to "buy over" standard coverage by consuming private care that they pay for themselves. When that happens, individuals purchasing private health services that are already insured actually maximize redistribution to the lower paid and less healthy, by paying their "share" of taxes to support the public system while removing themselves from it and consuming privately. The main risk of this particular form of private provision alongside a dominantly public system, however, is the creation of a two-tiered system of care. If the proportion of affluent individuals buying over the public system is sizeable, or opting out of receiving public services becomes routine and widespread, political support for the public system may deteriorate. Health care providers who would otherwise participate in public provision may be enticed into private practices unavailable for individuals with public insurance, degrading resources in the public system and restricting the most desirable forms of provision to the affluent (for example, avoiding waiting lines, having the most technologically sophisticated procedures, and so on). If buying into a more responsive tier, whether to avoid waiting lists or to receive care in more convenient and attractive settings than are widely available, becomes prevalent, there is significant risk of more affluent citizens revoking political support for a public system they no longer use and become unwilling to pay for. Wealthy individuals have always been able to purchase more, and more convenient, more discretionary health services than less affluent individuals. But as long as a parallel second tier remains relatively small, that would not necessarily threaten political support and resource streams for publicly provided services (see Tuohy et al. 2004).

However, when private health care depends on special tax arrangements to subsidize private health insurance coverage, conventional ideas about the appropriate direction of redistribution go out the window. Even staunch neoliberals would likely argue that if redistribution occurs at all, it should be towards those with the greatest need; that is, their preference would be for redistribution limited primarily to market failures served by means-tested programs. The practice of providing special tax breaks to accomplish social purposes, such as tax expenditures provided in the United States in return for the purchase of private health insurance, constitutes a practice that redistributes tax revenues from the uninsured to the insured, mainly from insecurely employed low-income workers in part-time or benefit-poor jobs, to the securely employed in occupations with a menu of employee benefits (see Myles and Street 1995).

This creates a type of perverse "upside down" redistribution (Sinfield 1993) whereby the unlucky (the unemployed, or those who work in jobs without health benefits) subsidize the private employment-based health insurance benefits of the lucky. In this case, the "fortunately" employed are actually bribed with public money (in the form of tax expenditures) to perceive self-interest in the for-profit private health care market as superior to collective welfare. Thus, when bolstered by state mechanisms, such as vouchers or tax expenditures designed to entice into or support private health care arrangements, redistribution is inevitable, albeit in less transparent and direct ways than public health care programs and in the opposite direction to most redistributive policies.

Tax-subsidized benefits do not inevitably result in perverse redistributive outcomes. Tax measures can be designed to maximize their redistributive effects in conventional ways, from the higher to lower income individuals, as is the case with the GIS component of the Canadian pension system or the Earned Income Tax Credit to low-income families in the United States (Howard 1997; Quadagno and Street 2006). However, particularly in the United States, the tax-subsidized redistribution associated with employment-based health insurance currently operates in the "wrong" direction, as Table 1.5 shows.

Considering the public-private aspects of the two main components of national health care systems underscores the blurred boundaries between the two sectors. Ensuring sustainable financing and efficient care delivery within health systems is critical for governments, as health spending as a share of GDP is projected to increase as health care prices continue to rise and demand is driven by national population aging. Given the complexities of even the simplest health systems, it is not surprising that public and private distinctions become blurred. In most OECD countries, the bulk of health care spending is financed through taxes, with 73 percent of health spending on average publicly funded in 2004 (OECD 2007). But even as sources of public funding vary, so do the outcomes accomplished with such

Table 1.5   Distribution of US tax-subsidized employee benefits by income level, 2005

Income range ($)	Percent of families with pension coverage	Percent of families with employer health insurance coverage	Estimated average tax savings from exclusion of employer health insurance coverage ($)
Less than 16,200	4.6	15.5	7.19
16,200–30,999	21.4	46.1	100.06
31,000–50,219	45.3	69.8	317.37
50,220–81,513	64.4	81.5	658.55
81,514 or more	74.3	86.1	1,482.17

Source: CRS (2006).

spending. Premiums, payroll taxes, and general revenue taxing mechanisms to support direct expenditure in public health care programs are easily categorized and available to public scrutiny by policymakers, the media, and citizens. In contrast, tax expenditures to support private health insurance are more complex and difficult to understand, as arcane components of the tax code are under-emphasized as expenditures in national accounts and are far from straightforward in their redistributive effects.

Health insurance and services can be arranged in ways that are decidedly more ambiguous. For example, Canadian employers often provide workers with supplemental health insurance policies that "fill the gaps" in public health coverage, providing "noncritical" vision, dental and hearing services, and prescription drug coverage. Such coverage is exclusively private. In contrast, employees and employers may pay premiums into sickness funds to guarantee health insurance coverage, as most German workers do. Because sickness fund coverage or an approved public program alternative is mandated in Germany and other countries with similar all-payer systems, expenditure is usually counted as public. This is because health insurance coverage is not voluntary, even though sickness funds are not government entities and may operate in the private sector. Finally, although tax expenditures to support private health care spending is usually overlooked in public accounts, it, too, is a form of public expenditure on health care, although the expenditure subsidizes voluntary commercial health insurance policies purchased exclusively in the private sector.

Health care delivery further complicates the crispness of any discussion of the public-private dichotomy. Whereas national health services are the quintessential form of public provision—publicly financed services delivered mainly by public sector employees in publicly owned institutions—national health services represent an ideal type rather than facts on the ground in many countries. Certain types of health services delivered to particular populations, such as those provided to active duty military personnel, also fit neatly into a public financing and public delivery rubric. This is often true of health care for other special populations, like prison inmates. However, publicly financed health care can be delivered entirely in the private sector. In national health insurance systems, the institutions (such as hospitals and clinics) where health care is delivered (but paid mainly through public means) are often private ones, and physicians and other health professionals often act as entrepreneurs in private practices. Some private institutions depend on market conditions for their survival as for-profit entities; others are community institutions in the private, voluntary, not-for-profit sector.

The consequences of the public-private mix for health care

Public components of health care systems, either insurance programs or national health services, relieve citizens of the necessity of making exclusively private health care arrangements. One benefit of universalist systems, then, is the security embodied by shared risk pooling in the event of ill health. Even the United States, with its large pool of uninsured citizens, has safety net programs that provide public services to some vulnerable subgroups of citizens like children and the elderly. However health services are arranged, combinations of the effects of population aging, long-term treatments of chronic diseases (such as arthritis, diabetes, and cardiovascular conditions) and expensive health care technology seem likely to challenge the capacity of public expenditure on health care to meet all citizens' needs. Yet only in the United States are working-age citizens, so far, expected to rely predominantly on private health care provision.

As with publicly funded pensions, public expenditures on health care redistribute resources within and between generations. The reasons for redistribution seem obvious: ill health and accidents are not entirely predictable, and insuring against them is most efficiently accomplished when risks are pooled, as they are in public systems. However, redistribution is not always associated with progressive goals of transferring resources to lower income and less healthy individuals. American-style tax expenditures that shore up a failing employment-based health insurance system actually redistribute towards the top end of income distributions, from strata below. This type of perverse redistribution, in fact, exacerbates existing inequalities that are implicated in health disparities.

Obviously, identifying the entirely public components and the entirely private components of a national health care system is hardly straightforward. Lack of precisely comparable data also complicates understanding of the public or private character of one or another type of health care spending. For example, do mandatory arrangements like those in the German health care system represent public health care expenditures because the expenditure (sickness fund participation) is mandated by the government and is not voluntary, even though sickness funds are not governmental organizations? Arguably, universal mandates constitute public guarantees, protecting the vulnerable and redistributing resources in the direction that enhances collective welfare. At the other end of the spectrum, how unambiguously "private" is employment-based group health insurance in the United States, in light of the substantial tax subsidies (from public funds) that are required to sustain them? Not so private after all. In this instance, public subsidies exaggerate the already existing inequalities implied by a voluntary health insurance "system" based on employee benefits. Differences in employer health insurance offerings constitute one source of inequality, with some offering bare bones policies and others offering comprehensive ones. That inequality is compounded because public funding subsidizes the differentially provided policies, regardless of their comprehensiveness and despite huge swathes of the employed population lacking any coverage at all. Thus, different definitions of public and private obscure clear boundaries across health care policy mechanisms, suggesting that apparently public activity has sometimes obscured private components that help make policies work, and vice versa.

Which health-related outcomes appear to be linked to the balance of public and private arrangements for health care? The most obvious is access to care in the first place, presumably a contributor to other health outcomes down the line. Dominantly public systems provide universal guarantees and minimum fiscal barriers to basic health services for entire populations. Larger shares of private health care expenditures in dominantly public systems carry the risk of tiered or stratified health care systems, in which affluent citizens have convenient and immediate access to high-quality care and advanced medical technology, and in which less affluent citizens have access to health care, but under less convenient circumstances, with longer waits and perhaps less access to the most recent medical innovations. Tiered systems, if the private component becomes too large (although there is surely debate over what "too large" would be), are at risk of losing political and fiscal support from citizens who no longer participate regularly in public systems. As Reinhardt and his colleagues (2004: 23) observe, "the debate over health care is less a pure macroeconomic issue than an exercise in the political economy of sharing."

Although definitive causal pathways to health disparities are still debated, they occur in all countries, regardless of the public-private mix in health care or the particulars of health care arrangements. Most of the evidence suggests that poverty, minority race, ethnic or cultural status, and immigrant status—aspects of social stratification linked to *relative* economic inequality—are all linked to health disparities in advanced industrial societies, however health care is arranged (Cooper 2002; Farmer and Ferraro 2005; Lantz et al. 1998; Link and Phelan 1995, 2005; Marmot and Wilkinson 1999). Gender inequalities in health status also persist, the public-private balance in health care notwithstanding. For example, although women have a mortality advantage over men—they outlive men in nearly all countries in the world—the social gradient in mortality is not as pronounced for women as for men (Soni and Kiri 1997). Older women, in contrast, have a morbidity disadvantage, with poorer self-reported health and more disabling and chronic health conditions than men (Arber and Ginn 1998). The fact that mortality and morbidity are stratified by major sources of inequality experienced by different demographic groups is not surprising. However, in systems in which private arrangements are most critical to timely access to care or high-quality medical services, market-driven health care systems may logically contribute to greater health disparities than in countries where there are fewer barriers to receiving routine care. Still, it is not only the political economy of a country that determines its mix and level of health spending. Culture and lifestyle practices and differences in the price, volume, and quality of medical goods and health care services consumed all lead to variations.

Conclusion

Throughout the world, developing countries with underdeveloped public infrastructures exhibit heavy reliance on the private sector health care for health care, but developing countries are also expanding their public sector health care systems at the most rapid pace (Hanson and Berman, n.d.). In a rather ironic turn of policy events, the prototypical developed country with the most extensive reliance on private sector health care, the United States, is also among the countries where the public health care sector has grown most recently. In part, recent growth in the public side of the US health care equation occurred because there was simply more room for public sector expansion in the United States than almost anywhere else in the developed world. It is a testament to the abnormal economics and the sheer extent of market failures in the private health sector that even under periods of neo-liberal, Republican political domination, the share of public expenditure on US health care has expanded. When the value of tax reliefs that bolsters the private health insurance market is considered, US public sector expenditure exceeds 50 percent of total health care spending.

To return to a question posed in the opening chapter: Is growing reliance on private benefits necessarily at odds with economic redistribution and the struggle against social inequality? In health care, it appears that policymakers in many countries think so, since private inroads into health care systems for fundamental health care have been limited so far. In countries with health care systems and welfare states as diverse as Sweden, Canada, Japan, and Britain, there is room within systems of universal care for private sector gap-filling coverage alongside dominantly public commitment. Although the structure of the health care system and political conditions favor the inertia that preserves its rather uniquely private sector reliance, even in the United States corrections to the health care system appear to be in the direction of a greater proportion of spending coming from public sources, and modest expansions of public commitment to health care for vulnerable populations. It seems unlikely that any country will ever create an entirely public health care system. Thus, the services that remain for the private sector to provide are a critically important component of health care systems in all developed countries.

One truism is that healthier and wealthier segments of the population must subsidize the less fortunate in any system of universal health care coverage (Savedoff 2007). The American system makes no pretense at universalism; so far, its heavy reliance on private funding for very expensive health care arrangements is rife with inequalities in terms of access to and quality of care. In other countries, where more institutional models of public provision dominate, universal coverage means fewer barriers to health care access. However, health inequalities related to poverty and other forms of social disadvantage still persist, if on a smaller scale than in more private systems. Further, public systems are not necessarily very nimble in the face of changing socio-demographic conditions. Cost-containment measures are regarded as the culprits that have compromised supply of care in a number of countries, evidenced by waiting lists for some health-enhancing procedures (Willcox et al. 2007). The residual model of private dominance and market competition, most closely associated with the US experience, fuels an innovative engine of health technology advances (Garber and Fuchs 2003; although see Light and Lexchin 2005) and concierge-style consumer attentiveness to some insured subsets of the population (NYT 2005).

Concern about the long-term sustainability of responsive, modern health care systems is *au courant* among stakeholders around the world. At one end of the welfare state spectrum, health care systems with dominant public roles traditionally provide generous and extensive social protection, but are sometimes unresponsive to consumer demands, perceived at risk of becoming financially unsustainable, or both. At the other extreme, residual social protection and dependence on voluntary private spending give little confidence that heavy reliance on health care markets offers more fiscal stability or consumer responsiveness, at least for most health care users. How policy-makers recently dealt with the strengths and weaknesses of their own nation's health care arrangements and plan for the future public-private balance of health care for its citizens is discussed in greater detail in country-specific chapters that follow.

Notes

1. The OECD is a voluntary organization with a membership of 30 countries "committed to democracy and the market economy," see http://www.oecd.org/pages/0,3417,en_36734052_36734103_1_1_1_1_1,00.html
2. Health expenditure per capita, converted to US dollars using purchasing power parities (PPP) can be used to compare the overall level of consumption of health goods and services across countries. The economy-wide PPPs for GDP are used, as these are the most available and reliable conversion rates.
3. As a non-OECD country, comparable Chilean data are scarce and for many indicators used in this chapter are not available.
4. Definitions of public and private are those used by the OECD to support standardization for cross-national comparisons. National spending allocations are as reported by member countries in their national accounts.
5. This may understate very recent trends towards increased private share in health care spending if substantial private development has occurred in the past three years. For example, the expanded private capacity in Canada in the aftermath of its 2005 Supreme Court decision would not be captured due to lags in the most recent available data.
6. Total health expenditures do not include expenditures on training medical staff, on research, and environmental health.
7. See the WHO report for information on how these measures were calculated, available at http://www.who.int/whr/2000/en/

References

Arber, Sara and Jay Ginn. 1998. "Health and Illness in Later Life." In David Field and Steve Taylor (eds), *Sociological Perspectives on Health, Illness and Health Care*, 134–53. Malden, MA: Blackwell Scientific.

Béland, Daniel and Jacob S. Hacker. 2004. "Ideas, Private Institutions and American Welfare State 'Exceptionalism': The Case of Health and Old-Age Insurance, 1915–1965." *International Journal of Social Welfare* 13(1): 42–54.

Blendon, Robert J., Minah Kim, and John M. Benson. 2001. "The Public Versus the World Health Organization on Health System Performance." *Health Affairs* 20(3): 10–20.

Castles, F. G. and D. Mitchell. 1991. "Three Worlds of Welfare Capitalism or Four?" *Luxembourg Income Study*, Working Paper 63. Luxembourg: CEPS/INSTEAD.

Congressional Research Service. 2006. *Tax Expenditures: Trends and Critiques*. Retrieved on July 2, 2008 from http://opencrs.cdt.org/document/RL33641

Cooper, Helen. 2002. "Investigating Socio-Economic Explanations for Gender and Ethnic Inequalities in Health." *Social Science & Medicine* 54(5): 693–706.

Davis, Karen. 2003. "Time for Change: The Hidden Cost of a Fragmented Health Insurance System." Invited testimony before the Senate Committee on Health, Education, Labor, and Pensions Hearing on "What's Driving Health Care Costs and the Uninsured?"

Drache, D. and T. Sullivan. (eds). 1999. *Health Reform: Public Success, Private Failure*. London: Routledge.

Esping-Andersen, G. 1990. *The Three Worlds of Welfare Capitalism*. Princeton, NJ: Princeton University Press.

Farmer, Melissa M. and Kenneth F. Ferraro. 2005. "Are Racial Disparities in Health Conditional on Socioeconomic Status?" *Social Science and Medicine* 60: 191–204.

Ferrera, M. 1996. "The 'Southern' Model of Welfare in Social Europe." *Journal of European Social Policy* 6(1): 17–37.

Figueras, Josep and Richard B. Saltman. 1997. "Building Upon Comparative Experience in Health System Reform." *European Journal of Public Health* 8(2): 100–2.

Friedman, M. 1962. *Capitalism and Freedom*. Chicago, IL: University of Chicago Press.

Friedman, M. and Friedman R. 1980. *Free to Choose*. London: Secker & Warburg.

Garber, Alan and Victor Fuchs. 2003. "Medical Innovation: Promises & Pitfalls." Brookings Institution. Retrieved September 2007 from http://www.brookings.edu/ articles/2003/winter_technology_fuchs.aspx

Ginn, Jay, Debra Street, and Sara Arber. (eds). 2001. *Women, Work and Pensions: International Issues and Prospects*. Buckingham: Open University Press.

Glennerster, H. and M. Matsaganis. 1994. "The English and Swedish Health Care Reforms." *International Journal of Health Services* 24(2): 231–51.

Gostin, Lawrence O. 2000. *Public Health Law: Power, Duty, Restraint*. Berkeley, CA: University of California Press, New York: The Milbank Memorial Fund.

Hanson, Kara and Peter Berman. n.d. "Private Health Care Provision in Developing Countries: A Preliminary Analysis of Levels and Composition." *Data for Decision Making Project, Department of Population and International Health*. Boston, MA: Harvard School of Public Health.

Hayek, F. 1960. *The Constitution of Liberty*. London: Routledge and Kegan Paul.

Hayek, F. 1982. *Law, Legislation and Liberty: A New Statement of the Liberal Principles of Justice and Political Economy*. London: Routledge and Kegan Paul.

Howard, Christopher. 1997. *The Hidden Welfare State: Tax Expenditures and Social Policy in the United States*. Princeton, NJ: Princeton University Press.

Hsiao, William C. 1995. "Abnormal Economics in the Health Sector." *Health Policy* 32: 125–39.

Ikegami, Naoki and John Creighton Campbell. 2004. "Japan's Health Care System: Containing Costs and Attempting Reform." *Health Affairs* 23(3): 26–36.

Institute of Medicine (IOM). 1988. *The Future of Public Health*. Committee for the Study of the Future of Public Health, Division of Health Care Services. Washington, DC: National Academy Press.

Institute of Medicine (IOM). 2003. *The Future of the Public's Health in the 21st Century*. Committee on Assuring the Health of the Public in the 21st Century, Board on Health Promotion and Disease Prevention. Washington, DC: National Academy Press.

Kaiser Family Foundation (KFF). 2007. *The Uninsured: A Primer. Key Facts about Americans Without Health Insurance*. The Kaiser Foundation on Medicaid and the Uninsured, October.

Klein, Naomi. 2007. *Shock Doctrine: The Rise of Disaster Capitalism*. New York: Metropolitan Books.

Klein, Rudolph. 1995. *The New Politics of the National Health Service* (Third Edition). London: Longman.

Klein, Rudolph. 2001. "What's Happening to Britain's National Health Service?" *New England Journal of Medicine* 345(4): 305–8.

Lantz, Paula M., James S. House, J. M. Lepkowski, David R. Williams, R. P. Mero, and J. Chen. 1998. "Socioeconomic Factors, Health Behaviors, and Mortality." *Journal of the American Medical Association* 279: 1703–8.

Light, Donald W. and Joel Lexchin. 2005. "Foreign Free Riders and the High Price of US Medicines." *British Medical Journal* 331: 958–60.

Link, Bruce G. and Jo C. Phelan. 1995. "Social Conditions as Fundamental Causes of Disease." *Journal of Health and Social Behavior* Extra Issue: 80–94.

Link, Bruce G. and Jo C. Phelan. 2005. "Fundamental Sources of Health Inequalities." In David Mechanic, Lynn B. Rogut, David C. Colby, and James R. Knickman (eds), *Policy Challenges in Modern Health Care*. 71–4. Piscataway, NJ: Rutgers University Press.

Maioni, Antonia. 1998. *Parting at the Crossroads: The Emergence of Health Insurance in Canada and the United States*. Princeton, NJ: Princeton University Press.

Marmot, Michael and Robert H. Wilkinson. 1999. *Social Determinants of Health*. New York: Oxford University Press.

Mau, Steffan. 2003. *The Moral Economy of Welfare States: Britain and Germany Compared*. Routledge/EUI Studies of the Political Economy of Welfare. London: Routledge.

Minkler, Meredith and Carroll Estes. (eds). 1999. *Critical Gerontology: Perspectives from Political and Moral Economy*. Amityville, NY: Baywood Publishing Company, Inc.

Moran, Michael. 1999. *Governing the Health Care State: A Comparative Study of the United Kingdom, the United States, and Germany*. Manchester: Manchester University Press.

Myles, John and Debra Street. 1995. "Should the Economic Life Course be Redesigned? Old Age Security in a Time of Transition." *Canadian Journal of Aging* 14(2): 335–59.

New York Times. 2005. "For a Retainer, Lavish Care by Boutique Doctors." Retrieved August 2007 from http://www.nytimes.com/2005/10/30/health/30patient.html?_r=1&oref=slogin

OECD. 2004. *The OECD Health Project: Private Health Insurance in OECD Countries*. OECD, Paris: The Organization for Economic Co-operation and Development.

OECD. 2006. *OECD Health Data 2006*. OECD, Paris: The Organization for Economic Cooperation and Development.

OECD. 2007. *Health at a Glance: OECD Indicators*. OECD, Paris: The Organization for Economic Co-operation and Development.

OECD. Factbook 2007. Economic, Environmental and Social Statistics. OECD, Paris. http://www.swivel.com/users/show/1004354

Quadagno, Jill. 2006. *One Nation, Uninsured: Why the U.S. Has No National Health Insurance*. New York: Oxford University Press.

Quadagno, Jill and Debra Street. 2006. "Recent Trends in U.S. Social Welfare Policy: Minor Retrenchment or Major Transformation?" *Research on Aging* 28(3):1–14.

Reinhardt, Uwe, Peter S. Hussey, and Gerard F. Anderson. 2004. "U.S. Health Care Spending in International Context." *Health Affairs* 23(3): 10–25.

Sainsbury, Diane. 1999. *Gender and Welfare State Regimes*. Oxford: Oxford University Press.

Saltman, Robert B., Josep Figueras, and C. Sakellarides. (eds). 1998. *Critical Challenges for Health Care Reform in Europe*. Buckingham: Open University Press.

Savedoff, W. D. 2007. "What Should a Country Spend on Health Care?" *Health Affairs* 26(4): 962–70.

Sinfield, Adrian. 1993. "Reverse Targeting and Upside Down Benefits: How Perverse Policies Perpetuate Poverty." In Adrian Sinfield (ed.), *Poverty, Inequality and Justice:* 29–48. Edinburgh: Edinburgh University Press.

Soni, Raleigh V. and Kiri V. 1997. "Life Expectancy in England: Variations and Trends by Gender, Health Authority, and Level of Deprivation." *Journal of Epidemiology and Community Health* 51: 649–58.

Titmuss, Richard M. 1958. *Essays on "The Welfare State."* London: Allen and Unwin.
Tuohy, Carolyn H. 1999. *Accidental Logics: The Dynamics of Change in the Health Care Arena in the United States, Britain, and Canada.* New York: Oxford University Press.
Tuohy, Carolyn H., Colleen M. Flood, and Mark Stabile. 2004. "How Does Private Finance Affect Public Health Care Systems? Marshaling the Evidence from OECD Nations." *Journal of Health Politics, Policy and Law* 29(3): 359–96.
Willcox, Sharon, Mary Seddon, Stephen Dunn, Rhiannon Tudor Edwards, Jim Pearse, and Jack V. Tu. 2007. "Measuring and Reducing Waiting Times: A Cross-National Comparison." *Health Affairs* 26(4): 1078–87.
World Health Organization (WHO). 2000. *The World Health Report 2000. Health Systems: Improving Performance.* Geneva: The World Health Organization.
World Health Organization (WHO). 2006. *The World Health Report 2006. Working Together for Health.* Geneva: The World Health Organization.

2
Orienting the Public-Private Mix of Pensions

Patrik Marier and Suzanne Skinner

Introduction

The history of pension policies is particularly interesting when it comes to the public-private mix. Originally, most states sought to encourage the establishment of voluntary pension plans while supporting some forms of pension schemes for their own employees. When private solutions failed to extend coverage and benefits to most citizens, states began to take more proactive stances. This intervention into the field of pensions increased substantially in the aftermath of the economic crisis of 1929 and World War II. Today, the ability of the state to act as the key provider of welfare benefits is being questioned in most industrialized countries, resulting in an increasing involvement of the private sector. In the field of pensions, the encroachment of the private sector is increasingly a reality. Numerous countries have extended the role of private pensions to compensate for the diminishing function of public pensions. Other countries have strengthened already potent private measures to encourage citizens to save more for their retirement income.

This chapter contributes to the emerging literature that concerns the roles of private benefits and actors within the welfare state (see Esping-Andersen 1990; Hacker 2002; Howard 1997; Ullman 1998) by tackling two important research questions. First, what is the impact of increasing reliance on private pensions? To answer this question, one needs to consider the traditional redistributive functions of the state and how private benefits reduce (or accentuate) their importance. For example, individuals with part-time employment and broken careers (mostly women) are less likely to thrive in pension systems that emphasize private benefits relative to full-time workers with uninterrupted careers.

Second, how do states promote the expansion of private social benefits? Do states achieve their objectives? The state possesses multiple tools to increase private retirement savings, which can be mandatory as well as voluntary. It can grant tax benefits, which is the case of the American 401(k) and Canada's Registered Retirement Savings Plans. It can introduce mandatory private schemes within its pension system, as in Sweden with the creation of the Premium Pension Authority in which individuals must choose pension funds for a fraction of their state contributions. Individuals may also be automatically enrolled in a private scheme managed by private actors, as in Finland, the Netherlands, and France. This is not an exhaustive list, but rather a snapshot of the multiple ways in which state interventions may alter private savings behaviors and the pension market in general.

This chapter is divided into four sections. First, a brief introduction to the relationship between the private and the public sectors is presented. The second section brings a closer look at the implications of this relationship for differences by gender and immigrant statuses. Third, the often-neglected role of taxation is analyzed. The conclusion discusses further avenues for research. It should be noted that this chapter does not seek to undertake a review of the ways in which pensions are being reformed, including the role of the private sector in facilitating reforms (see for example, Bonoli 2003; Myles and Pierson 2001; Peters 2005), but rather presents the consequences of increasing (or solidifying) the presence of private pensions within pension systems.

The public-private mix

In recent history, both private and public sectors have made crucial contributions to retirement income. Originally, very few workers expected to benefit from a lengthy retirement period when pension plans were first established in the late 1800s. Those fortunate enough to reach retirement age typically had inadequate financial resources, forcing a continued reliance on the labor market. Prior to their direct involvement in providing pensions for their citizens, many states promoted private savings rather than engage in the full responsibility of managing a public pension plan. In most cases, the state opted to support efforts undertaken by "friendly societies" and provided poor relief (Esping-Andersen 1990). In 1939, roughly 40 percent of those older than 65 received a pension in industrializing countries. Moreover, most pension schemes were not really generous, with only the United States (with only 5 percent coverage) and Denmark generating replacement rates above 20 percent of the average net wage (Esping-Andersen 1990, 99).

The generosity and coverage of both public and private plans grew rapidly after World War II. As stressed by Myles and Pierson (2001), the timing in which states opted to extend public provisions has played a key role in determining the size and place of private-sector pensions within pension systems. Among advanced industrialized democracies, Australia, Ireland, the Netherlands, New Zealand, Denmark, Switzerland, and the United Kingdom failed to establish a mature, public earnings-related scheme by the mid-1970s.

Alongside countries such as Canada and the United States, who created public schemes with limited replacement rate targets, they encouraged private solutions to provide a substantial replacement rate for retirement. In order to increase private savings, these countries often offer tax incentives, matching contributions (in part or in full), or legislate mandatory private schemes. As a result, in Australia, Canada, the Netherlands, and the United States more than 35 percent of all pension expenditures target private benefits (see Figure 2.1). In contrast, countries such as France, Germany, Sweden, Italy, and Belgium had matured public schemes by the 1970s with limited encouragement for private savings. In these countries, the share of private pensions rarely goes above 10 percent. Sweden is a significant exception due to its reformed pension system where 13.5 percent of new contributions are allocated to individual savings accounts.

Today, despite diversity in terms of coverage, replacement rates, and generosity, most pension policies across industrialized countries have two key similarities. First, all countries covered in this study provide public pensions that are not tied to contributions, but are usually financed by general

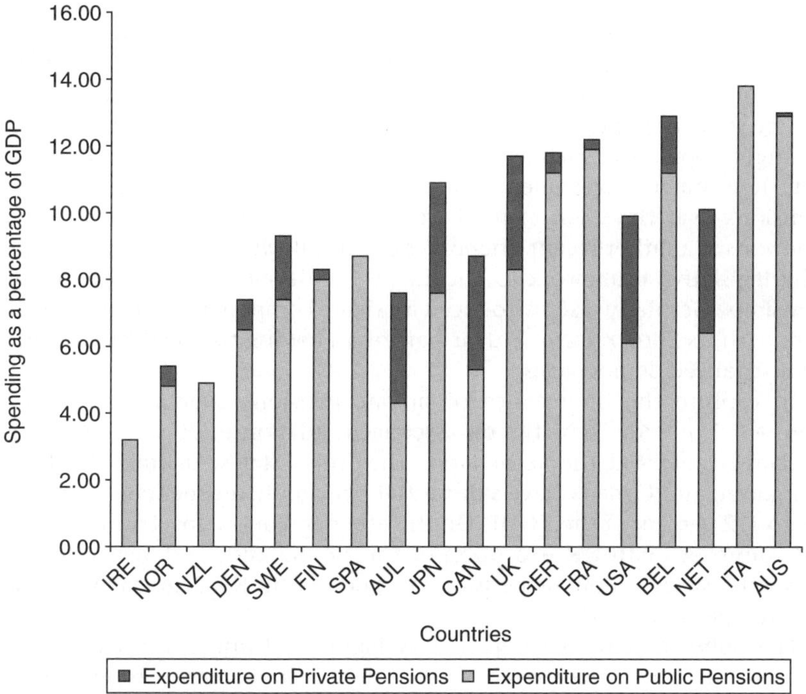

Figure 2.1   Spending on pensions in 2001
Source: Adema and Ladaique (2005).

taxation. All of them provide low-income retirees with some forms of social assistance and/or means-tested benefits. Many countries have also instituted either a basic (Canada, Denmark, Ireland, Japan, the Netherlands, New Zealand, and Norway) or minimum pension (Belgium, France, Portugal, Spain, Switzerland, and the United Kingdom), which usually benefits retirees who have low incomes. When it comes to these benefits, usually referred to as the first pillar of pension policies, the role of the private sector is non-existent. Second, most countries have a second pillar, composed of mandatory schemes (Ireland and New Zealand are the exceptions), that usually operate on insurance principles. The private sector has made significant inroads within this pillar with countries such as Australia, Denmark, the Netherlands, Switzerland, and Sweden setting up mandatory enrollment into private schemes (OECD 2005a: 22–5).[1] Denmark, Sweden, and Switzerland also have a public component. The other countries have adopted mandatory pension insurance schemes for all workers; these schemes are managed and administered by public authorities. The US Social Security is a good example of such public pension insurance scheme.

Before reaching conclusions on the basis of Figure 2.1, there are a few caveats to note. First, public pension expenditure provides benefits to current retirees whereas most private expenditure target future retirees. Second, aggregate figures do not indicate which income group benefits most from state intervention. Third, expenditure tends to be higher in countries with a large share of population over 65, such as Italy, as opposed to those with a younger population such as Ireland. Fourth, Figure 2.1 also does not indicate how much governments have been encouraging private and public pensions over time. For example, the involvement of Belgium in private pensions is a rather recent phenomenon. It follows the 2001 establishment of a legislative framework to encourage the development of occupational pensions. Germany also introduced a private component to its pension system with its 2001 reform. This is part of a growing trend within advanced industrialized democracies.

To capture the importance of private pensions over a longer period, Figure 2.2 provides statistics on asset accumulation in 20 states. Countries such as Switzerland, the Netherlands, the United States, Australia, the United Kingdom, and Canada have substantial pension investments ranging from 50 to 112 percent of their GDP. On the other end of the spectrum, continental countries (with the exception of the Netherlands and Switzerland) all rely extensively on public pensions and do not (in the aggregate) have substantial pension funds.

The public-private mix depicted by Figures 2.1 and 2.2 is supported by recent research on the source of retirement income among recent retirees. Using comparable LIS (Luxembourg Income Study (LIS) multiple years) data for an analysis of nine countries, Pedersen (2004) demonstrates that retirees in Canada, the Netherlands, the United States, and the United Kingdom

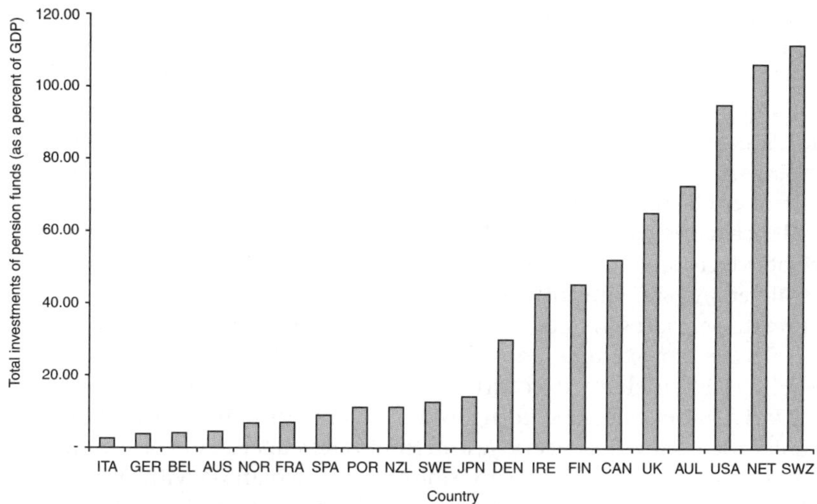

Figure 2.2   Size of pension funds relative to GDP, 2004

Source: Table 3, OECD Global Pension Statistics, OECD *Insurance Statistics Yearbook*; OECD (2006a).

gain more than 40 percent of their income from private sources.[2] States with generous public earnings-related schemes, such as Germany and Sweden, provide roughly 75 percent of individual retirement income, leaving 25 percent to private sources. The introduction of private components along with the expectation of a diminishing state role within these public schemes is likely to alter this ratio significantly (Rein and Schmahl 2004).

The consequences of relying strongly on private pensions

What are the consequences of relying strongly on private pensions and encouraging a shift in the public-private mix? A key element of most public pension systems has been the redistribution of resources between and within generations. This redistribution is pursued for multiple reasons such as accounting for shorter careers of immigrants and interrupted careers experienced by many women. Even in continental Europe, with public pensions structured on occupational status, redistribution still occurs. For example, Belgium grants fictive pension contributions for child care and provides a relatively generous minimum pension. We would expect a diminishing redistribution of resources with an increasing reliance on private resources given that higher retirement income from the private sector depends a great deal on one's fortune in the labor market, where groups such as women and immigrants tend to perform less well.

Analyzing the role of the private sector within the field of pensions is a complex challenge. First, what is a private pension? Compared to public schemes where pension points are earned in a more explicit fashion as part of a program, private savings for retirement can take multiple forms. Individuals can subscribe (voluntarily or not) to plans promoted by their employers, and they can invest privately in bonds, stocks, or other financial instruments. For example, they can decide to invest heavily into their own residence using the accrued value of the house to finance retirement. These private decisions are influenced by individual preferences in addition to employer and state incentives.

Private pension schemes also have various features resulting in a different set of risks. For example, most pension plans can be described as defined benefit (DB) or defined contribution (DC). In a DB plan, an employee receives a full pension according to the parameters stated in the plan, which usually includes years of service and final wages instead of contributions. In most cases, the managing responsibilities of the plan lie with the employer who must ensure sufficient funds to provide the benefit in question. Many American companies are currently facing difficulties in financing these pension plans. Retirees have been particularly vulnerable if they worked in industries where bankruptcies have been common (such as the steel industry) because they depend on the financial health of the enterprise to continue paying for their benefits (see Peters 2005). In DC plans, the value of a pension is a function of earlier contributions made by an individual and the accrued interests generated by those contributions. In this case, elements such as administration fees, the performance of the market, and the overall health of the economy play key roles in determining the value of one's pension. Thus, similar contributions do not necessarily generate similar pensions. For example, a study demonstrated that Americans who retired in 1972 experienced a ten-fold increase in their contributions compared to a four-fold increase for those who retired in 1974 (Hemming 1999: 21).

The numerous private pension instruments and tools lead us to the second challenge. The available data are sketchy due to an assortment of obstacles in their collection. Moreover, the data, once collected, are difficult to compare. The OECD has recently invested a lot of energy and resources into improving the knowledge of facts surrounding private pensions. Nonetheless, numerous challenges such as the diversity of tax systems, the strong involvement of regional governments, and a different understanding of what is a private pension make this exercise complicated.

It is with these caveats that we undertook our analysis of the consequences of relying strongly on private pensions and effects of public-private arrangements on groups such as women and immigrants. Although there has been a noticeable increase in studies analyzing gender and the welfare state, with Pierson (2000) referring to this strand as one of the three pillars of welfare state research, studies on immigration and the welfare state remain scarce. Relying primarily on LIS data and using the personal file, we have calculated the average net retirement wage for men, women, immigrants, and nonimmigrants and how much of their income comes from private sources. Within the LIS dataset, the variable immigrant was coded differently among the cases whether by year of entry, country of origin, or citizenship status. For our purposes the category of immigrant was conceptualized as being born outside of the country in question.[3]

We opted for the Person file (rather than the Household file) within the LIS databank in order to be able to look at pension outcomes at the individual level. The Person file presented some challenges with missing variables, as noted in the text above. However, this choice was essential in being able to conduct a gender analysis of pension earnings. Also, when looking at Finland and the Netherlands, note that the LIS data include their mandatory/statutory pension plans as second pillar, since they are only semi-directed by the state. As such, public pensions will be underestimated and private pensions will be inflated for these two countries.[4]

In order to ensure some level of comparability, we calculated national income as a proportion of net average earnings.[5] We calculate average earnings directly from the LIS dataset to avoid any problems associated with using the earnings of the "Average Production Worker" (APW). Although more conventional, a recent OECD report highlighted the problems with using the APW measure, including the decline of employment in the manufacturing sector, and the problem with using male earnings as the referent for the entire workforce (OECD 2005b). Finally, we assess impacts of home ownership on private pensions by analyzing data from Scanlon and Whitehead (2004). We suspect that higher rates of home ownership will result in lower private pension investments.

We have attempted to analyze the 20 advanced industrialized democracies that feature in many quantitative research studies on social benefits: the 18 countries found in Esping-Andersen's (1990) *The Three Worlds of Welfare Capitalism* (Australia, Austria, Belgium, Canada, Denmark, Finland, France, Germany, Ireland, Italy, Japan, the Netherlands, New Zealand, Norway, Sweden, Switzerland, the United Kingdom, and the United States), plus Portugal and Spain. However, an absence of data on private pensions in France and Ireland, and on immigration data in Finland, the Netherlands, and the United Kingdom, limited our number of cases in these areas. Furthermore, within the LIS dataset, data regarding any type of pension income in Switzerland are not available. For Germany, data limitations prevented us from calculating net benefits, which explains its omission from our results. Finally, LIS does not include Japan or New Zealand within their dataset. As a result, our number of cases ranges from 6 to 11. Accordingly, we have avoided relying on multivariate regressions and instead opted for more traditional tools such as bivariate regressions and comparative tables.

In addition, analyzing the LIS micro data we did not filter out pensioners who may still be earning wage income. It is important to note that the inclusion of wage earners in our sample actually changed the pension incomes very little. For more than two-thirds of our cases, the inclusion of pensioners who were also earning wage income changed average retirement earnings by less than 0.05 percent or nothing at all. Canada presents the most extreme case creating a mere 2.6 percent change. For this reason we felt confident in maintaining our sample with all pensioners, regardless of whether they were earning wage income.

Importantly, using the LIS personal file limited our ability to separate information on income from means-tested pension plans. Given that means-tested benefits are often determined based on household income thresholds, means-tested old-age supplements tend to be household level variables. In most cases, LIS uses the total household amount and divides this among members in the household. For this study, this is methodologically problematic since it does not accurately account for the dynamics in distributing income within the household. Furthermore, in most cases we are not able to differentiate between supplementary, means-tested benefits and basic, first pillar pension amounts. For most country datasets in the LIS, these figures are lumped together.

Clearly, means-tested benefits are important to disadvantaged groups in society, and even essential to maintaining a decent retirement income. Having access to this separate variable would be helpful in assessing the extent to which groups such as women and immigrants access such benefits. For example, in Canada the Guaranteed Income Supplement (GIS) is administered according to strict eligibility tests based on household income. As such, the receipt of GIS income is in itself an indicator of poverty. Recent research demonstrates that among women in the bottom income quintile, GIS consumption has increased by 44 percent between 1994 and 2004, compared to 4 percent for men. This suggests that despite a variety of gains made in terms of employment and education, vulnerable women in Canada actually experienced a rise in poverty (Marier and Skinner forthcoming: 16).

Importantly, means-tested programs that target certain types of individuals can be problematic. According to Schneider and Ingram, policies can socially construct certain target groups as dependent (1993: 337). Furthermore it can create "rigid class distinctions between the deserving and undeserving poor" (Quadagno 1994: 9). This type of stigmatization can restrain the recipients of these programs from maintaining lives of dignity and independence, especially if the program is not directly addressing the source of the inequality between groups (Schneider and Ingram 1993: 339). For example, that women have lower earnings than men is a reflection of the work they contribute to the household in the form of caring activities. Means-tested pensions, although an important addition to women's low pension earnings, do not directly address issues of childcare and wage-inequality for example, which would have more direct impacts on women's pension outcomes.

Although the lack of exclusive means-tested data are a challenge for this research, its presence in total pension outcomes illustrates the unequal distribution of social and private pensions across men, women, and immigrant groups. That is, despite the existence of means-tested programs, the disparities in basic pension outcomes between men and women, and between immigrants and nonimmigrants, are substantial. It is clear that most OECD countries have a long way to go before reaching equality in their pension distribution schemes.

Gender and retirement income

As a result of their caring activities, lower wages, longer life expectancy, and strong presence in part-time and/or contractual employment, we would expect women to receive less retirement income than men in countries relying strongly on private pensions. Despite the introduction of policy aimed at reducing the amount of caring activities, such as the introduction of day-care, women still devote proportionately and substantially more time performing these kinds of work than men (Esping-Andersen 1999). Thus, the long-term impact is likely to be a lower pension for women, especially if private components dominate. As stressed by Ginn (2003: 4) in a British study, a case where the reliance on private sources is strong, only 38 percent of women were obtaining private retirement income as opposed to more than 70 percent for men in the mid-1990s.

Figure 2.3 demonstrates clearly that men's pension earnings are linked to private sources more than women's. The private share of a man's retirement

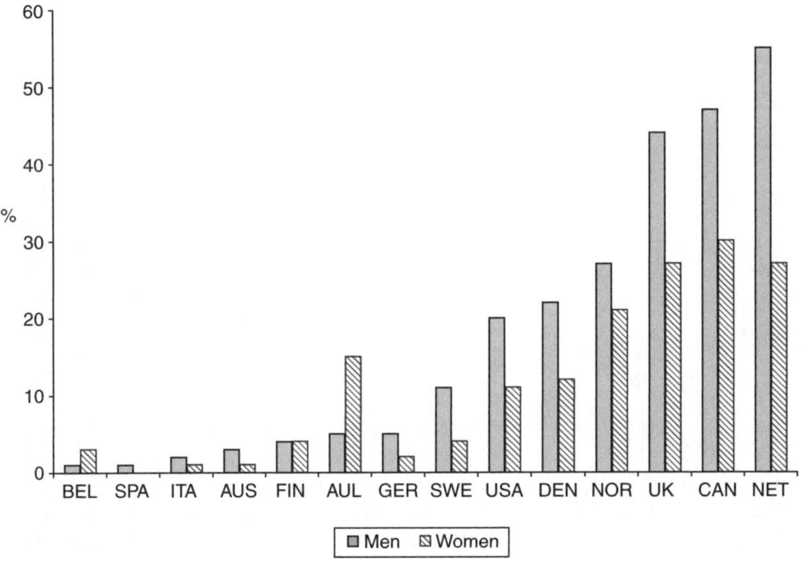

Figure 2.3 Private pension earnings of men and women, as a percentage of their total pension earnings

Note: Please note that all figures are gross except for Austria, Belgium, Italy, and Spain provided net figures.

Source: LIS (various years).

income is more than twice that of a woman's share in Australia, Austria, Germany, Italy, the Netherlands, and Sweden. In fact, on average the private pension revenues of men are more than three times those of women. Figure 2.4 shows the ratio of private pension earnings of men compared to those earned by women. The results demonstrate that regardless of the pension regime in place, men receive substantially more from private sources than women. A key exception is Belgium, which likely is a measurement discrepancy. Within the LIS dataset, the variable private occupational pensions includes private pensions and life insurance annuities (including both interests and capital) that are linked to the professional activity of the beneficiary or his or her spouse. We suspect that much of the private pension income of Belgian women is related to the private pension activity of their spouses and therefore skew the results.

This substantial gap between the private retirement income of men and women does not imply that women will necessarily receive a total lower income. Contrary to expectations, there is no relationship between the degree to which women depend on private sources and their total pension earnings. Two bivariate analyses were performed to address this issue and neither of them generated a statistically significant result. Moreover, the slope was near zero. There may be at least two reasons behind this outcome. First, public pension systems may also favor men, which is particularly the

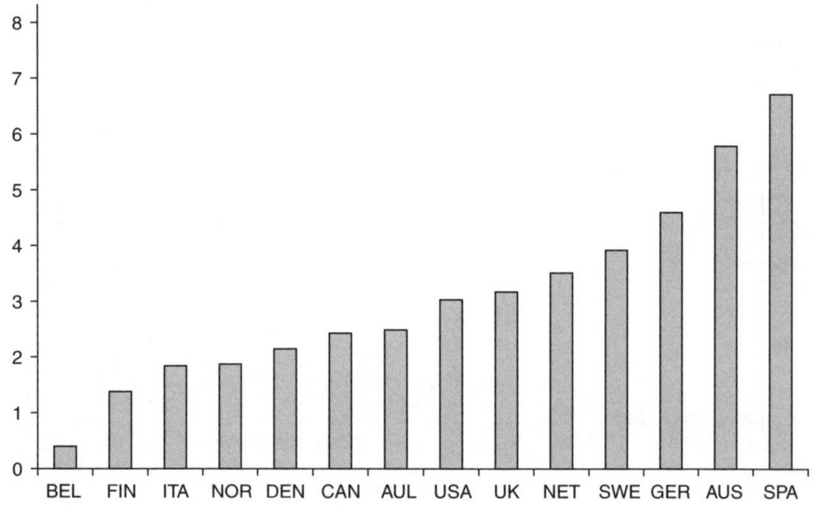

Figure 2.4   Ratio of men/women private pension earnings

Note: Please note that all figures are gross except for Austria, Belgium, Italy, and Spain provided net figures.

Source: LIS (various years).

case for public schemes that are organized along occupational lines, a key element in Continental Europe. This explains why retired men in Austria (191 percent), Belgium (184 percent), and France (177 percent) earn a net income substantially higher than women (Figure 2.5), despite a much lower reliance on private sources in those countries (refer to Figure 2.3). Second, many countries with a strong reliance on private sources have public mechanisms to counteract the ill-effects of the market. This explains why Canada (154 percent) and Sweden (158 percent) are so alike when it comes to promoting gender equality (Myles 2000; see also Korpi and Palme 1998). The Unites States (162 percent) is particularly interesting and demonstrates the effect of the tax system and social security in lowering the impact of gender in the provision of pensions. It must be noted, however, that the United States presents a relatively low replacement rate (see Figure 2.6).

We have established that the share of private pensions does not seem to be influencing lower pension results among women. However, we cannot conclude that public pension programs are necessarily alleviating poverty among elderly women. As stated above, the public schemes of Continental Europe are not likely to be women-friendly because benefits are linked to occupational status. In fact, there is substantive evidence that these types of public systems may counteract measures to combat inequality (see, for example, Hill and Tigges 1995). However, as stressed by Korpi and Palme (1998), the relationship between public programs and poverty is a complex

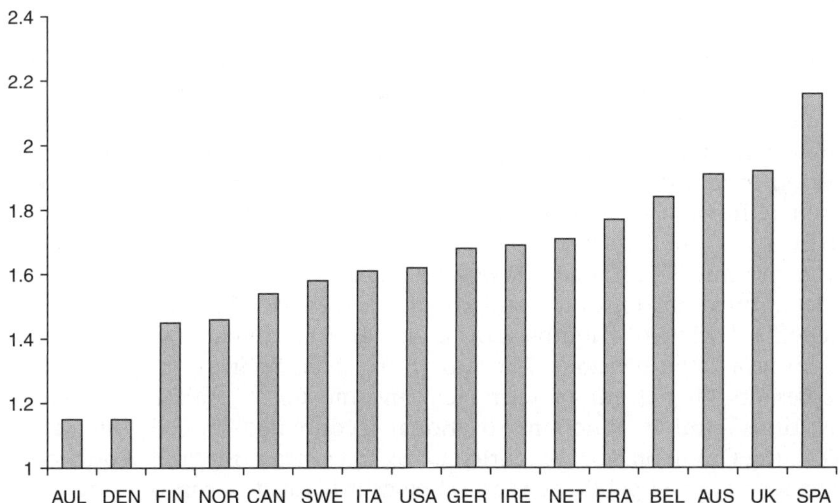

Figure 2.5 Ratio of men/women total pension earnings

Note: *All persons 65 years and older. All figures are net.

Source: LIS (various years) own calculations.

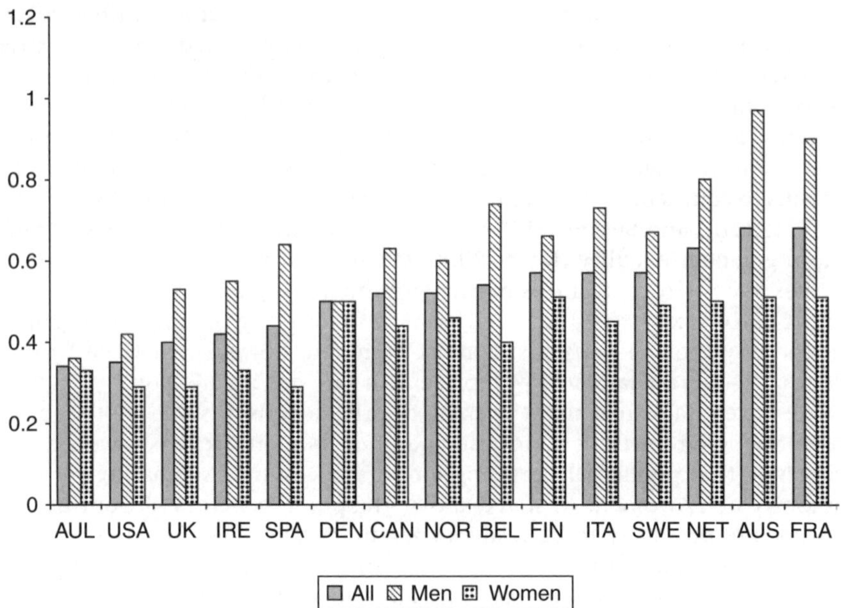

Figure 2.6   Average net pension replacement rates

Note: *All persons 65 years and older. All figures are net.

Source: LIS (various years) own calculations.

one. Even though means-tested programs are designed to lift individuals out of poverty, it is the public earnings-related pension schemes, which are not contingent on occupational status, that are more successful in preventing low incomes among women. In many countries, it is the active participation in earnings-related schemes that have enabled women to increase their retirement income and reduce the gap with men. For example, the maturity of public pension programs is responsible for the gains made by women retirees in Canada (Myles 2000). Active participation in earnings-related programs raises the redistributive potential of women's retirement benefits. These redistributive aspects only affect individuals who qualify for earnings-related pensions. The American Social Security program, which represents 90 percent of retirement income for 27 percent of women, performs similar functions (National Economic Council Interagency Working Group on Social Security 1998). In contrast, the stark reduction in generosity of the public pension schemes is blamed as contributing to the rising inequalities faced by women pensioners in the United Kingdom (Pensions Commission 2004).

Women have greatly benefited from key redistributive features of earnings-related public schemes, such as pension points for caring activities or additional (nonearned) points for low-income earners. Interestingly, it is these gender-friendly attributes that are currently being targeted for elimination by most pension reformers in efforts to strengthen the link between contributions and benefits. The 1998 Swedish pension reform, with its focus on the life income principle,[6] is a prime example. By granting a pension on the basis of one's performance in the market (the source of contributions), women are likely to have a much lower pension because of wage discrimination and the consequences associated with work stoppage for caring activities. Even though compensation for child rearing is accessible for upto four years, work stoppage reduces potential career growth. The consequences of shortened careers are lower lifetime earnings and accordingly, inferior pension earnings.

In order to test the relationship between the generosity of public benefits and women's retirement income, a bivariate regression was performed with Scruggs and Allen's Benefit Generosity Index for pensions in the year 2000 as an independent variable and women's pension earnings as a percentage of the average net earnings as a dependent variable (see Figure 2.7). Based on minimum and standard replacement rates, qualifying and contributive

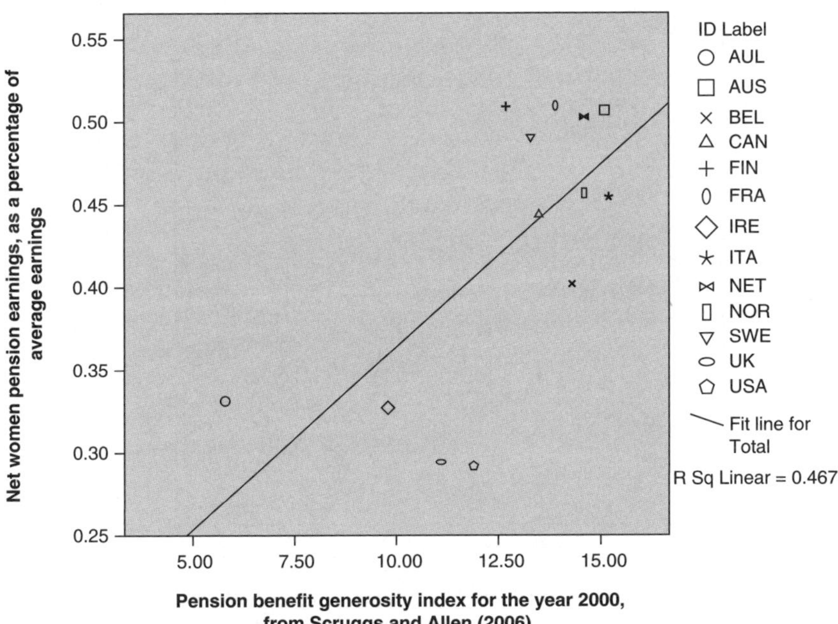

Pension benefit generosity index for the year 2000, from Scruggs and Allen (2006).

Figure 2.7   Women's pension income in relation to the generosity of public pension programs

Note: All persons 65 years and older.

Source: LIS (various years); Scruggs and Allen (2006).

periods, and coverage and take up rate, Scruggs and Allen (2006) developed a generosity index for 18 advanced industrialized countries, providing a welcome update and improvement of Esping-Andersen's (1990) decommodification index. The Pension Benefit Generosity Index ranges from 5.8 (Australia) and 15.2 (Italy). Despite having a low number of cases (13), a strong statistical relationship emerged with an R Square of 0.47 steep at the 0.01 level. However, the slope is not significant. An increase of 1 in the Benefit Generosity Index results in an increase of 0.022 in women's retirement income as a percentage of the average earnings. To illustrate what this means in practice, if the United States were to increase the generosity of their program by 1 (under the Scruggs and Allen scale), women would see their annual retirement income raised by \$198.

Interestingly, a similar relationship exists for men (with a strong R square of 0.59, statistically significant at the 0.01 level: see Figure 2.8). Continuing with our equation from above, an increase of 1 in the generosity index results in an increase 0.051 in men's retirement income as a percentage of average earnings. This would represent an annual increase in net pension

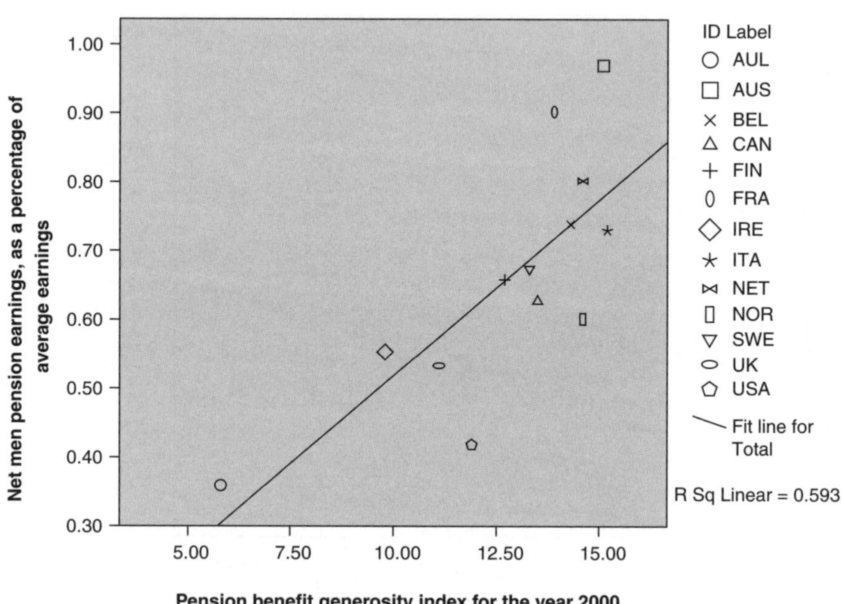

Figure 2.8   Men's pension income in relation to the generosity of public pension programs

Note: All persons 65 years and older.

Source: LIS (various years); Scruggs and Allen (2006).

income of $658 for men in the United States. That this increase is higher for men than women is not surprising due to the earnings-related component of many public pension schemes. As stated above, men are more likely than women to have higher wages, and full-year, full-time employment over their life courses. Women are more likely to have low earnings and work part-time due to their roles as caregivers. It follows, therefore, that the pension earnings of men would reflect this advantage in the labor market and result in higher earnings-related pensions. If we could examine basic public pensions without the earnings-related portion, we would expect that the slope linking pension income and the pension benefit generosity index would be much higher for women than it is for men. Unfortunately, due to data limitations, we are unable to disaggregate earnings-related pensions from the public pension total. Further analysis and more detailed data are needed to substantiate this claim.

This leads us to another question: are individuals likely to invest less in private pensions if the state provides a generous basic pension for its citizens? Figure 2.9 casts some serious doubts on this proposition.[7] The relationship is not statistically significant and the slope goes in a contrary direction,

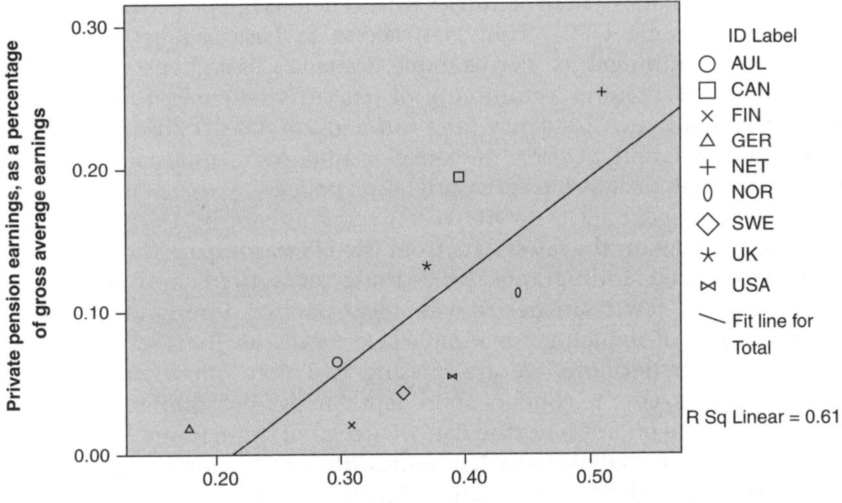

Figure 2.9 Relationship between private pension earnings and guaranteed minimum pension benefits

Note: All persons 65 years and older.

Source: LIS (various years); Scruggs (2004). Gross figures.

suggesting a possible relationship between higher private pensions and generous minimum benefits. Due to the limited number of cases and the complexity of this relationship, further analysis is required to provide a more definitive answer to this question.

Immigration and pension income

Like women, immigrants represent a highly vulnerable group when it comes to pensions. They have a high risk of having incomplete and broken careers combined with low wages. Indeed, the ability to build either social insurance benefits or private pensions is weakened for immigrants because they have migrated half-way through their life cycle (Ginn 2003: 42). Regardless of education levels, immigrants in most OECD countries have lower employment rates, and are more likely to be working in the unskilled services sector and in temporary jobs (OECD 2006b: 56–8). Reasons for this include a lack of recognition for foreign qualifications, discrimination, language problems, and a lack of domestic labor market experience (OECD 2006b: 69). Immigrant women are further disadvantaged in the labor market, as they face these problems in addition to those faced by most women. As a result, the earnings of immigrants tend to be lower than their native-born counterparts. Thus, we would expect immigrants to fare worse in countries relying on private pensions than in countries with generous public pension systems. However, in some OECD countries, access to basic public pensions is restricted for immigrants. For example, Canada's basic pension, Old Age Security (OAS), requires a minimum of ten years residency to collect any amount and 40 years residency for a full pension (OECD 2005a: 102). The study of immigrant pension outcomes is important, especially as many OECD countries turn to "proactive migration policies" as a response to ageing and skill shortages (OECD 2006b: 112).

We are relying on the latest data from the LIS to compare the retirement wage of retired immigrants with those of retired nonimmigrants. Unfortunately, few countries provide clear data on immigration, which has the effect of reducing our sample size significantly to seven or eight countries.[8] Furthermore, we are missing two very important pieces of information in order to conduct an in-depth analysis of immigrant pension trends. First, we do not have the date of arrival of immigrants for all cases. This variable would allow us to determine differences among immigrants by length of stay in their home country. Second, we are missing information on ethnicity. Knowledge of this variable would enable us to look at other issues that might limit immigrant pensions such as discrimination, language barriers, and so on. As such, the following analysis is an overview of general trends in immigrant pensions, subject to further analysis. Nonetheless, our dataset allows us to combine gender and immigration to present a picture of how these two dimensions interact.

Based on the retirement income of current immigrants and nonimmigrants, the share of private pensions is higher for the latter groups but the difference is not as substantial as one would expect (see Figure 2.10). The share of private pensions remains high in "private pension countries" such as Canada and the Unites States. In fact, these differences are close to nil when it comes to women, and higher for immigrant women in Belgium and Norway, meaning that both immigrant and nonimmigrant women rely on the same public-private mix. In the case of Belgium and Sweden this is less surprising due to the predominance of the public system and the low reliance on private pensions. Also, in Belgium, data sampling problems may be responsible for some of the surprising results. Nearly 70 percent of all immigrants in the Belgian dataset are originally from within the European Union. Given the large amount of EU employees in Brussels, we expect that we are dealing with a very specific type of immigrant, and thus not one that is representative of the "average" immigrant. The case of Norway is puzzling.

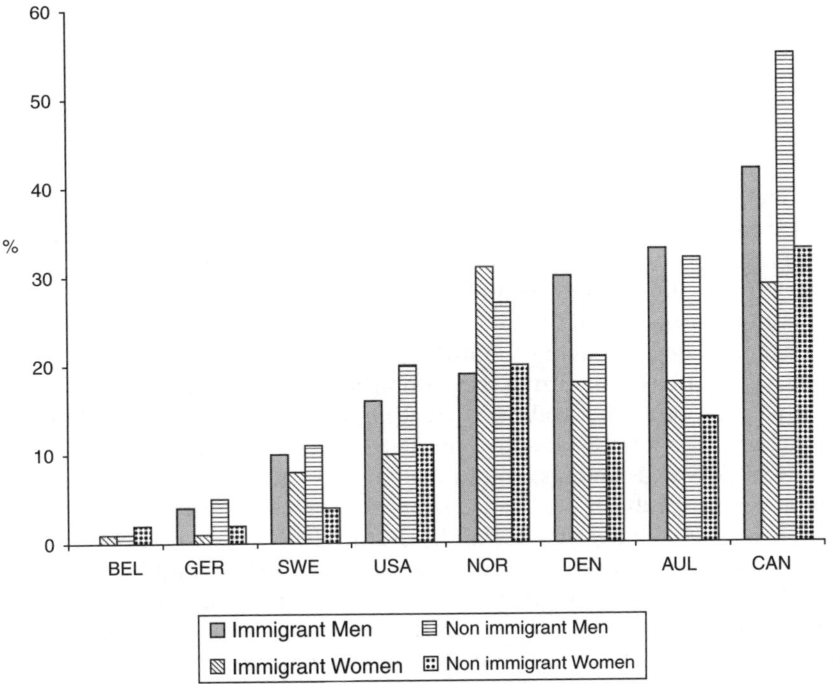

Figure 2.10   Immigrant and nonimmigrant private pension income as a percentage of their total pension income

Note: *All persons 65 years and older.

Source: LIS (various years) own calculations. All figures are gross except for Belgium.

One possible explanation would be that women immigrants would save more and be more likely to be beneficiaries of life insurance policies (probably the key reason in Belgium as well), since the public pension system clearly disadvantages them due to their limited careers. Another possible explanation is that immigrants save roughly the same amount or less than nonimmigrants, but their public pension earnings remain meager, leaving them with a much lower retirement income than their nonimmigrant counterparts. Also, it is important to note that immigrants in the Norwegian case represent just under 3 percent of our sample that identifies a potential measurement problem. Unfortunately, we are not able to speculate, as we did in the Belgian case, about the origins of these immigrants. This information was not available through LIS.

What is staggering about these results is the consistency in the gender-relationship across immigrant and nonimmigrant groups. In each case (except for the outlying cases of Norway and Belgium, as discussed above), the disparity between men and women in pension replacement rates is consistent among both groups: men do better (see Figure 2.11). Assuming that our immigrant samples include a variety of ethnic groups, this is consistent with Ginn's (2003: 42) conclusion that "gender differences outweighed those of ethnicity" in terms of advantages toward pension prospects.

The role of taxation

Despite repeated calls for a closer inspection of the role of taxation in social policy research, relatively few articles and books are devoted to this issue (for noticeable exceptions see Howard 1997; Sainsbury 1999). In relation to pension policies, taxation plays two important roles. First, in line with the literature stating that individuals underestimate the resources required for a pension and end up saving too little (see for example, Diamond 1977), the state is proactive by assuming this responsibility via the creation of mandatory pension programs and/or by creating incentives for individual saving. To achieve the latter's objective, numerous policies have been devised to increase personal savings among individuals and to encourage private employers to establish pension schemes for their workers. With the exception of Australia, Italy, New Zealand,[9] and Sweden, the countries analyzed in this chapter encourage the accumulation of pension savings by granting a tax deferral on the value of investments made into a personal (or occupational) retirement plan. The interest earned during the duration of the account is fully or partially exempt. However, citizens pay taxes when they withdraw their investment. Current examples include the US's 401(k) plan and Canada's Registered Retirement Savings Plans (RRSPs). Not only are these fiscal tools expected to increase retirement income, but economists often stress that an increased savings rate encourages economic growth. A recent Canadian publication stresses another potential side effect of

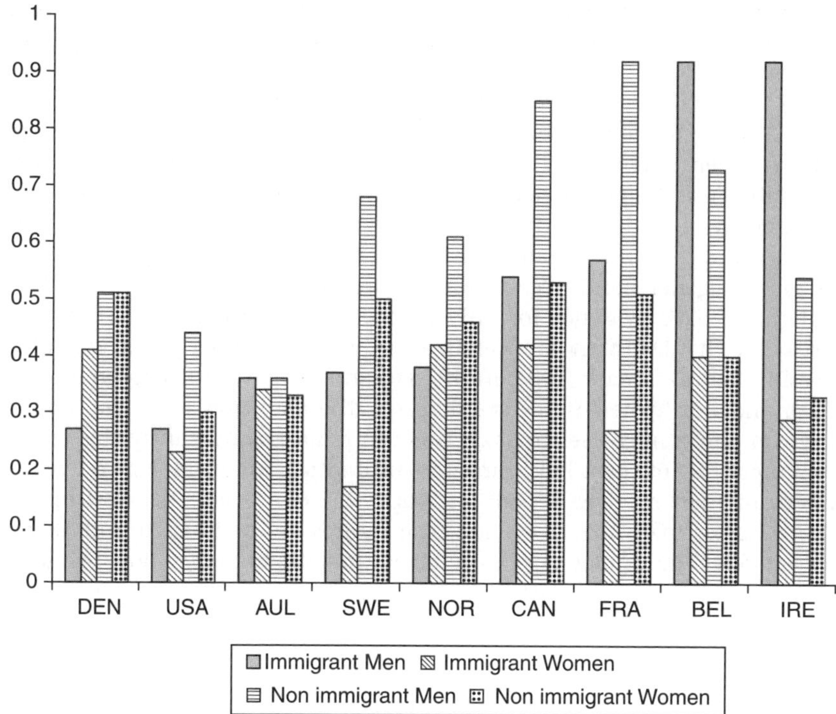

Figure 2.11   Average net pension replacement rate

Note: *All persons 65 years and older.

Source: LIS (various years) own calculations. All figures are gross except Austria, Belgium, France, Ireland, Italy, Spain are net.

deferring taxation on retirement savings. Retirement income originating from RRSPs is fully taxed as income, which can alleviate the economic impact of population ageing (Mérette 2002). Bluntly put, individuals with substantial RRSP income do not retire fiscally since they continue to pay taxes as if they were active in the labor force.

Second, taxation can also be used as an important redistributive tool. This is clearly demonstrated in Rothstein (2001) with his focus on the redistributive effect of the universal welfare state. With a basic fictive model, Rothstein shows how inequalities are starkly reduced via a flat income tax supplemented by universal transfers. For example, the high income earners group faces a reduction in net wage by 16 percent whereas the poorest group experiences an 80 percent net wage increase. The ratio between the highest wage earners and the lowest shrank from 5/1 to 2.33/1 (210–1). The LIS data allow us to do a similar exercise when it comes to the differential treatment of men and women retirees. High taxing countries can redistribute resources, via transfer or generous basic pensions, in ways that cannot be done by those with a lower tax base.

The LIS data set provides suitable tax information on seven cases.[10] It is interesting to notice that the disparities present among advanced industrial nations when it comes to taxing members of the labor market are also noticeable in retirement (see Figure 2.12). Surprisingly, tax rates do not vary much between workers in the labor market and retirees in Canada, Sweden, Finland, and the United States. Australian, Dutch, and Norwegian pensioners, on the other hand, receive a far more favorable tax treatment. Even though we have evidence for only nine countries (see Table 2.1), we can clearly see that Denmark reduces an already minor gender gap to zero after taxes. In fact, Denmark (100 percent), Finland (44 percent), Sweden (51 percent), and the United States (42 percent), the countries with the highest taxes on pensioners, use the tax system to reduce significantly the gender retirement income gap. This impact is substantial. For example, the average American man receives a pension worth $16,612 before tax and one of $12,897 after taxes. For a woman, the figures are of $10,276 and $8,993 respectively. The gender gap before taxes amounts to $6,336 but shrinks to

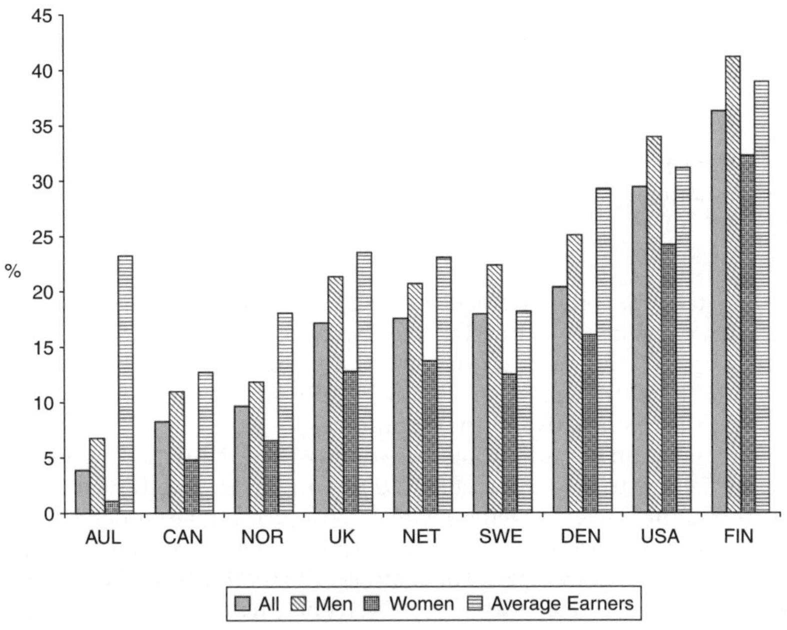

Figure 2.12 Average percentage of taxes paid by pensioners and average earners
Source: LIS (various years) own calculations.

Table 2.1   Impact of taxation on reducing the gender gap in retirement

Country	Gross total pensions, % of net average earnings			Net total pensions, % of net average earnings			Reduction of gender gap	Reduction in %
	Men	Women	Gender gap	Men	Women	Gender gap		
UK	0.6	0.31	0.29	0.53	0.29	0.24	0.05	17
NET	0.9	0.53	0.37	0.8	0.5	0.3	0.07	19
CAN	0.79	0.51	0.28	0.63	0.44	0.19	0.09	32
USA	0.54	0.33	0.21	0.42	0.29	0.13	0.08	38
AUL	0.38	0.33	0.05	0.36	0.33	0.03	0.02	40
NOR	0.76	0.52	0.24	0.6	0.46	0.14	0.1	42
FIN	0.88	0.61	0.27	0.66	0.51	0.15	0.12	44
SWE	1.02	0.65	0.37	0.67	0.49	0.18	0.19	51
DEN	0.85	0.74	0.11	0.5	0.5	0.0	0.11	100

$3,904 after taxes. The other countries do not fare as well, but the tax system still brings a reduction in the gender income gap. Taxation, like a public pension system, can play a determinant role in erasing, or at least reducing, inequalities among pensioners.

Conclusion

In spite of the numerous challenges faced by researchers seeking to analyze impacts of the public-private mix on social benefits, further analysis ought to be pursued to understand better the impact of the increasing presence of the private sector to provide social benefits. This paper hints strongly that the role of the state should be enhanced or altered with partial privatization. The share of private pensions is not the key element behind pension inequalities; rather, it is how the state complements private pensions via its public schemes and tax system. In some cases, the public schemes are causing more inequalities than private sector benefits. Before advancing clear and undeniable conclusions, however, key points need to be considered to shed light on the complexities surrounding these relationships.

First, better and comparable data need to be gathered. This is a formidable and, yet, important challenge. The number of ways in which private benefits can be obtained, especially in the case of pensions, accentuates the difficulties associated with this task. Nonetheless, it is imperative to comprehend how these instruments influence retirement income since national preferences may differ starkly. Second, it is important to increase our knowledge of the mechanisms behind pension and tax systems that produce retirement income. For example, what element(s) of the tax system is responsible for closing the gender gap? The answer to this question is essential if policymakers are to devise policies that seek to alleviate substantial difference among men and women retirees (or at least comprehend the consequences of tax reforms on retirees). Longitudinal research, despite its limitations, can provide a clear picture of how a reform affects individuals' behaviors. Longitudinal research may be critical to determining whether governmental programs aimed at aligning private and public benefits operate as planned.

Notes

1. Finland and France represent special cases since this pillar is managed and financed by social partners, but key elements are legislated.
2. Australia is slightly below this threshold. However, the survey data underestimates the size of occupational pensions, which often take the form of lump-sum payments (20).
3. Note that for the United States we regard persons born in Puerto Rico as immigrants.

4. See www.lisproject.org for more information.
5. Average net earnings includes cash wage and salary income, including employer bonuses, thirteenth-month bonus for all employed persons, aged 20–64. Samples were collected based on the respondent having earnings greater than zero and having reported some labor force activity during the reference year. Self-employment earnings are excluded since taxes and social contributions on this income may be different in some countries. Earnings from paid apprenticeships are excluded since in some countries this would be considered full-time education, not employment. Net figures are extracted directly through LIS for the following countries: Austria (2000), Belgium (2000), France (1994), Ireland (2000), Italy (2000), Spain (2000). Figures are calculated by subtracting average taxes based on the same criteria above, from gross earnings for the following countries: Australia (1994), Canada (2000), Denmark (1992), Finland (2000), the Netherlands (1999), Norway (2000), Sweden (2000), the United Kingdom (1999), the United States (2000).
6. The life income principle is the underlying philosophy behind the latest Swedish reform. It states that retirement income from the public system will be calculated in function of one's career contributions. Thus, if one works longer, he/she will receive a higher pension. This is in stark contrast to the previous system where any pension contributions made beyond 30 years did not result in additional pension income.
7. Private pension earnings (available in gross figures for most of our cases) are calculated as a percentage of gross average earnings. Cases providing net figures only were removed from the analysis.
8. Although the data were available, immigrants represented less than 1 percent of the sample for Austria, Ireland, Italy, and Spain. These cases were therefore eliminated due to insufficient numbers.
9. This practice has been changed recently with the introduction of the KiwiSaver program.
10. Please note that we did not take into account inheritance taxes due to a lack of data for most of these cases.

References

Adema, Willem and Maxime Ladaique. 2005. "Net Social Expenditure, 2005 Edition: More Comprehensive Measures of Social Support." *OECD Social Employment and Migration Working Papers*, No. 29, OECD Publishing.

Bonoli, Giuliano. 2003. "Two Worlds of Pension Reform in Western Europe." *Comparative Politics* July: 399–416.

Diamond, Peter A. 1977. "A Framework for Social Security Analysis." *Journal of Public Economics* 8: 275–98.

Esping-Andersen, Gøsta. 1990. *The Three Worlds of Welfare Capitalism*. Princeton, NJ: Princeton University Press.

Esping-Andersen, Gøsta. 1999. *Social Foundations of Postindustrial Economies*. Oxford: Oxford University Press.

Ginn, Jay. 2003. *Gender, Pensions and the Lifecourse: How Pensions Need to Adapt to Changing Family Forms*. Bristol: Policy Press.

Hacker, Jacob S. 2002. *The Divided Welfare State*. Cambridge: Cambridge University Press.

Hemming, Richard. 1999. "Should Public Pensions Be Funded?" *International Social Security Review* 52(2): 3–29.

Hill, Dana Carol Davis and Lean M. Tigges. 1995. "Gendering Welfare State Theory: A Cross-National Study of Women's Public Pension Quality." *Gender and Society* 9(1): 99–119.

Howard, Christopher. 1997. *The Hidden Welfare State: Tax Expenditures and Social Policy in the United States*. Princeton, NJ: Princeton University Press.

Korpi, Walter and Joakim Palme. 1998. "The Paradox of Redistribution and Strategies of Equality: Welfare State Institutions, Inequality, and Poverty in Western Countries." *American Sociological Review* 63: 661–87.

Luxembourg Income Study (LIS) Micro database. Multiple years, Wave V, Release 2. Harmonization of original surveys conducted by the Luxembourg Income Study, Asbl. Luxembourg, periodic updating.

Marier, Patrik and Suzanne Skinner. Forthcoming. "The Impact of Gender of Immigration on Pension Outcomes in Canada." *Canadian Public Policy*.

Mérette, Marcel. 2002. "The Bright Side: A Positive View on the Economics of Aging." *Choices* 8(1): 1–24.

Myles, John. 2000. La maturation du système de revenu de retraite du Canada: Niveaux de revenu, inégalité des revenus et faibles revenus chez les gens âgées. Ottawa: Statistics Canada.

Myles, John and Paul Pierson. 2001. "The Political Economy of Pension Reform." In Paul Pierson (ed.), *The New Politics of the Welfare State*: 305–33. Oxford: Oxford University Press.

National Economic Council Interagency Working Group on Social Security. 1998. *Women and Retirement Security*. Washington, DC: SSA.

OECD. 2005a. *Pensions at a Glance Public Policies across* OECD *Countries*. Brussels: OECD.

OECD. 2005b. "Special Feature: Broadening the Definition of the Average Production Worker." *Taxing Wages* 2003/2004: 33–42. Brussels: OECD.

OECD. 2006a. OECD Global Pension Statistics, Table 3. *OECD Insurance Statistics Yearbook*. Retrieved on March 18, 2008 from http://www.oecd.org/document/46/0, 2340,en_2649_34853_36091822_1_1_1_1,00.html

OECD. 2006b. *International Migration Outlook: Annual Report*. Brussels: OECD

Pedersen, Axel West. 2004. "The Privatization of Retirement Income? Variation and Trends in the Income Packages of Old Age Pensioners." *Journal of European Social Policy* 14: 25–39.

Pensions Commission. 2004. *Pensions: Challenges and Choices*. London: Department of Work and Pensions.

Peters, B. Guy. 2005. "I'm OK, You're (Not) OK: The Private Welfare State in the United States." *Social Policy and Administration* 39(2): 166–80.

Pierson, Paul. 2000. "Three Worlds of Welfare State Research." *Comparative Political Studies* 33(6/7): 791–821.

Quadagno, Jill. 1994. *The Color of Welfare*. Oxford: Oxford University Press.

Rein, Martin and Winfried Schmahl. (eds). 2004. *Rethinking the Welfare State: The Political Economy of Pension Reform*. Cheltenham: Edward Elgar.

Rothstein, Bo. 2001. "The Universal Welfare State as a Social Dilemma." *Rationality and Society* 13(2): 213–33.

Sainsbury, Diane. (ed.). 1999. *Gender and Welfare State Regimes*. Oxford: Oxford University Press.

Scanlon, K. and Whitehead C. 2004. *International Trends in Housing Tenure and Mortgage Finance*. London: The Council of Mortgage Lenders.

Schneider, Anne L. and Helen Ingram. 1993. "Social Construction of Target Populations: Implications for Politics and Policy." *American Political Science Review* 87(2): 334–47.

Scruggs, Lyle. 2004. "Welfare State Entitlements Data Set: A Comparative Institutional Analysis of Eighteen Welfare States." Version 1.1. Retrieved on March 18, 2008 from http://www.sp.uconn.edu/~scruggs/wp.htm

Scruggs, Lyle and James P. Allen. 2006. "The Material Consequences of Welfare State: Benefit Generosity and Absolute Poverty in 16 OECD Countries." *Comparative Political Studies* 39(7): 880–904.

Ullman, Claire F. 1998. *The Welfare State's Other Crisis: Explaining the New Partnership between Nonprofit Organizations and the State in France*. Bloomington, IN: Indiana University Press.

3
Extensive but Not Inclusive: Health Care and Pensions in the United States

Christopher Howard and Edward D. Berkowitz

Introduction

At first glance, the differences between health and pension policies in the United States appear stark. Lacking national health insurance—a trait often used to single out the United States among welfare states—the United States relies primarily on employers and individuals to finance medical care. Since some people are unemployed, others work for employers who do not offer health insurance, and few can afford to buy health insurance on their own, many Americans remain without coverage. The government fills in some of the gaps by offering health insurance to almost all of the elderly and many of the permanently disabled, children, and the poor. In contrast, the US government provides a retirement pension to virtually every senior citizen. Social Security, the core program, has been the single largest item in the national budget for years. Private pensions supplement, rather than replace, Social Security. Thus, although health care is largely private (but with the federal government being the largest single payer), pensions are fundamentally public (but with an accompanying, less developed private pension system).

Nevertheless, health and pensions in the United States share three striking similarities. First, a fuzzy line separates the public from the private in both domains. Through special provisions in the tax code, the US government provides substantial incentives for employers to offer health insurance and pensions to their employees. The government also regulates employer pensions and, to a lesser extent, health insurance. Public authorities routinely subsidize and shape "private" social benefits in the United States. Second, citizens' experiences vary by income. The poor and near-poor rely heavily on government for their health care and their retirement pensions, with Medicaid, Medicare, and Social Security essential to their well-being. The affluent depend on employment-based health insurance for much of their lives, and their private sources of retirement income often exceed their

Social Security benefits. Third, many analysts worry that public programs and private benefits in health insurance and in pensions will experience significant stress in the coming decades. Government programs may become prohibitively expensive, with resulting cutbacks in coverage and in the generosity of benefits, at just the time that employment-based benefits erode.

We intend this chapter as a primer that will help readers understand the public-private mix in health care and pensions. We will develop the similarities and differences mentioned above in order to convey a clear picture of who does what and who gets what in the United States. We will indicate how the public-private mix has changed over time. And we will draw out political implications of these policy choices. For example, if the more affluent members of society increasingly look to themselves and their employers for health insurance and retirement income, public programs may lose an important constituency and become vulnerable to cutbacks or privatization. At the same time, debates over health care and pensions in the United States do not always pit those who want more government against those who want less. Sometimes people argue over which policy tool—social insurance, grants, tax expenditures, or regulations—or which level of government (national, state, or local) should predominate in health care and pensions.

Health

Most Americans purchase health care rather than receiving it as an entitlement or matter of right. To finance that purchase, approximately two-thirds of citizens have private health insurance, typically provided through employment-based plans. Health insurance does not come cheaply. The average single worker in a company plan cost about $4,000 to insure in 2005, and an entire family cost almost $11,000 (Claxton et al. 2005).[1] Individuals who buy health insurance policies on their own pay even more.

Government insurance plans cover slightly more than one-quarter of the US population. Medicare and Medicaid, the largest of these plans, serve the elderly, the permanently disabled who have dropped out of the labor force, and those with end stage renal disease (Medicare), as well as several categories of poor Americans (Medicaid). Smaller public plans assist members of the military, veterans, low-income children, and injured workers (DeNavas-Walt et al. 2006). The level of government responsible for health care financing varies. The national government runs Medicare, with administrative assistance from local intermediaries such as private insurance companies. The national and state governments jointly run Medicaid and the closely related State Children's Health Insurance Program (SCHIP). Workers injured on the job receive their accident-related medical benefits from workers' compensation programs run by the individual states, with considerable variance in the program from state to state.[2] These arrangements apply to the financing, but not the delivery of health care, since the vast majority of Americans, even those covered by public insurance, are treated by private doctors in local community-based hospitals that operate as for-profit or nonprofit organizations.

Spending is almost evenly divided between the public and private sectors, even though more Americans have private health insurance than public health insurance. The public sector accounts for 45 percent of total health spending; employers and individuals pay the remaining 55 percent. One reason for the disparity between public sector spending and coverage is that the groups covered by government, such as people with disabilities and the elderly, often require more expensive medical care than the typical workers and their dependents covered by private employer-based plans. Although the national government spends the bulk of the public sector money, health care forms a large component of both national and state budgets (Smith et al. 2006; US Census Bureau 2005).

The fact the public-private spending mix in other affluent countries approaches 75/25 makes the United States a real outlier. Still, because the United States spends so much on health care—over 15 percent of GDP—even a secondary role for the government involves substantial sums of money. Public expenditure on health care in the United States is between 6 and 7 percent of GDP, much as it is in Australia, Canada, Italy, and the United Kingdom. The real difference is the level of private expenditure. In most of Europe, private health spending equals 2 to 3 percent of GDP. Greece and Switzerland, at 5 percent, are unusual. The comparable figure for the United States is over 8 percent of GDP (US Census Bureau 2005: Table 1323).

The private side of health care in the United States, however, is not strictly private. Governments at all levels help subsidize the construction and maintenance of private health care facilities, most prominently through the Hill-Burton hospital construction program. Governments support medical education through research and training grants and through aid for the construction of medical schools. The largest subsidy to the private sector works through the tax code. This technique, known as tax expenditure, is commonly used in the United States to make social policy. In this instance, employers can deduct the cost of health benefits from income that is subject to federal taxation. The idea is to make private health insurance more affordable for employers and thus more available to employees. Congress's Joint Committee on Taxation (2006) estimates that subsidizing employer health plans cost the national government almost $100 billion in lost revenues in 2006. The executive's Office of Management and Budget (2006), using somewhat different assumptions and techniques, puts the cost at approximately $135 billion. Either way, the level of support is significant.[3] If we add these indirect subsidies to the public side of health care spending, then the public-private mix in the United States is basically 50/50.

Apart from various direct and indirect subsidies, a patchwork series of state and federal laws affect the conduct of the health care industry. State governments attempt to control the supply of hospitals and nursing homes by requiring proof that new facilities are needed. In addition, state legislatures can and do mandate that certain services (for example, mental health care) or providers be included in health plans offered by commercial insurers that are sold in that state. At the national level, COBRA regulations (named after the 1986 budget act that created them and nearly always referred to in acronym form) allow workers to continue receiving health insurance after they leave their jobs, although, of course, these workers must pay for the privilege. Other regulations make it harder for private insurers to deny coverage to people with preexisting medical conditions (the Health Insurance Portability and Accountability Act), or for hospitals to deny emergency medical care to people without health insurance (the Emergency Medical Treatment and Labor Act). Perhaps the single most important federal regulation considerably *limits* the power of state governments. The 1974 Employee Retirement Income Security Act (ERISA) makes it difficult for state governments to regulate employers who choose to self-insure rather than purchase coverage from a commercial insurer. As one critic of ERISA notes, the law included "no funding or backup insurance requirements...no standards for coverage or minimum benefits...[and] no prohibitions against unilateral reduction or termination of benefits" (Hacker 2002: 257). Responding to the law's incentives, most employers who offer health benefits have since moved to self-insurance.

With such a patchwork structure and the lack of a basic entitlement to health insurance, it probably comes as no surprise that health care in the United States is riddled with inequities. Although the United States spends more on health care than any nation in the world, one out of every six Americans lacks health insurance, a total of almost 47 million people.[4] The odds of living without health insurance are greater for racial minorities (especially Hispanics), recent immigrants, and young adults. The chance of being uninsured is greater for part-time workers, nonunion workers, employees of small businesses, and the unemployed. Despite Medicaid and SCHIP, both targeted at the poor and near-poor, most of the uninsured have below-average incomes. At the other end of the spectrum, 99 percent of the elderly have health insurance because of Medicare and Medicaid. Affluent workers, often in professional and managerial occupations, are quite likely to be insured, as are those who work full-time for large corporations or the public sector (DeNavas-Walt et al. 2006; Fronstin 2005).

These inequities in coverage have real-world consequences. A lack of health insurance limits access to medical care. People without health insurance tend to put off visits to the doctor that would provide them with effective preventive care. As a result they encounter the health care system, often entering through hospital emergency rooms, only in catastrophic situations that lead to unpaid hospital bills and increases in the costs of private insurance for those with the means to pay the premiums. Numerous studies demonstrate that people without health insurance are more likely to forgo needed medical care than people who have health insurance (for example, Ayanian et al. 2000; Gorey 1999; Hadley and Cunningham 2005).

Some, but not all, government programs have the effect of reducing inequalities generated by the market. By covering many individuals who are excluded from the employment-based system of private health insurance, Medicare, Medicaid, and SCHIP serve the poor. Other government programs, particularly the tax benefits for employer health plans, lower the cost of health insurance for the affluent and do comparatively little for the poor. Sheils and Haught (2004) estimate that one-quarter of the tax benefits for health care go to families earning over $100,000 per year, and almost one-half to families earning over $75,000. Families earning less than $30,000 receive just one-tenth of the total tax benefits.[5]

In short, the US health care system resembles a patchwork quilt that has been assembled over a long period of time.[6] The system has a haphazard quality, the result of historical contingencies that reflect decisions made decades ago. A system that has accreted over time relies on many different levels of government, different policy tools, and different actors in the private sector. The United States did not consciously choose to spend so much on health care and at the same time leave so many people uninsured. Instead, yesterday's solutions have become today's problems, as a historical background reveals.

Historical development

Although the federal government ran hospitals for small groups such as indigent sailors from the very beginning of the Republic, most government involvement in financing and delivering medical care dates from the early decades of the twentieth century. The first group to receive help was injured workers. In the years before and after World War I, almost every American state enacted a workmen's compensation law that provided income support and medical care for eligible workers and their families.[7] Although some states ran their programs through state agencies to which employers were compelled to contribute, most states allowed companies to buy compensation policies covering the costs specified in the laws from commercial insurers or to self-insure. Thus, the program combined elements of social insurance and social regulation. Private insurance firms worked very hard to prevent states from creating government insurance funds, and they won more often than they lost. Over time, private insurance companies and public agencies responsible for workers' compensation developed a strong interest in keeping the program at the state level. Despite clear evidence that workers' compensation functioned badly, and despite periodic calls to nationalize the program or at least establish national standards, these interests preserved the status quo. The United States remains one of the very few countries in the world in which the national government does not run workers' compensation and in which private insurance plays such a key role (Berkowitz and Berkowitz 1984; Howard 2007).

At about the same time that workmen's compensation was taking root, national health insurance came up for debate.[8] Strong opposition from the insurance industry, lukewarm support from a labor movement that regarded government as a tool of management, coupled with a distrust of anything that seemed remotely German or socialistic proved too great an obstacle in the years following World War I. The social insurance movement of the progressive era stopped at workmen's compensation. The episode did, however, indicate growing public interest in health care, as opposed to disability pensions or payments for work-time lost due to illness, and private health insurance policies became more common in the 1920s and 1930s. At roughly the same time, groups representing hospitals and doctors created locally administered, nonprofit Blue Cross and Blue Shield plans. In 1935, when the Franklin D. Roosevelt administration surveyed the nation's existing social welfare programs and passed the pivotally important Social Security Act, it left health insurance alone. Health care received only indirect mention in the Act through federal grants for state infant and maternal health programs and crippled children's programs. Public retirement pensions presented fewer political obstacles because the private market had not developed as fully as it had for health insurance.

Harry Truman became the first president openly to advocate passage of national health insurance in 1946, and he renewed the battle in 1948. If his object was to pass such a program, rather than to frame an issue on which to run in 1948, then his timing was poor. Opponents in the American Medical Association (AMA) and the insurance industry pointed with pride to the high quality of American medicine and raised the specter of "socialized medicine," a potent label after Germany's defeat and the rise of the cold war. The AMA argued that public funding of medical care would lessen professional autonomy and hence the high quality of American medical care. The insurance industry maintained that the private sector was capable of handling the problem, and indeed private health insurance was becoming more commonplace. These two interest groups waged an expensive and ultimately successful campaign to defeat national health insurance. The fight was one-sided; little sentiment for national health insurance appeared to exist.

But the national government did not simply back away. Through laws tailored to particular interest groups, it increased both the supply and the demand for medical care. The Hill-Burton Act, promoting hospital construction and skewed in its distribution of funds toward southern states that had disproportionate influence in Congress, passed in 1946. That same year, the Veterans Administration began to reorganize its hospital system to serve the huge numbers of returning veterans better. Around 1948, workers gained the legal right to bargain collectively for fringe benefits, including health insurance. And by the mid-1950s, the Internal Revenue Service formally recognized health benefits as a legitimate tax deduction for employers. These last two steps were particularly important because they helped promote the spread of private health insurance during the 1950s and moved the center of the private system from the individual policy to the company plan. Doctors, hospitals, insurance companies, and now major employers and unions were heavily invested in the system of private health insurance.[9]

Beginning in 1950, public officials tried to fill in the most conspicuous gaps in the private system, in particular by allowing state welfare authorities to use federal funds to make direct payments to medical care providers on behalf of welfare beneficiaries. As it became increasingly clear that national health insurance was doomed, federal officials promoted the idea of paying for the hospitalization of Social Security beneficiaries who were, for the most part, retired individuals and their dependents. Doctors, at least those allied with the AMA, objected to these measures as the entering wedge for national health insurance. Insurers worried about losing a potential, if yet unrealized, market. Despite the creation of disability insurance in 1956, these interests succeeded in blocking health insurance legislation for retirees, which became known as Medicare, in 1957, 1960, 1962, and, despite Senate passage of the measure, in 1964. The assassination of President Kennedy and the election of 1964 marked a turning point for a measure that had been gaining momentum. As more urban liberals joined the key legislative committees, Medicare became law in 1965.

But nothing about Medicare disturbed the institutions that delivered medical care. On behalf of the elderly, the federal government agreed to pay the usual and customary fees to hospitals and doctors engaged in private practice. In other words, the government functioned similarly to private health insurance companies. As if to underscore that fact, the federal government contracted with regional Blue Cross and Blue Shield plans and with private health insurance companies to handle the processing of Medicare claims. If anything, passage of Medicare made payments to doctors and hospitals for services rendered to the elderly far more certain, and often more generous, than they had been previously.

Medicaid, created by the same law as Medicare, helped to pay the medical bills of the poor. Medicaid followed the federal structure of the American public assistance system: it took the form of federal grants to states and allowed states a great deal of flexibility to run the programs. Hence, the benefits for someone receiving Medicaid in New York differed substantially from the benefits for someone in Louisiana (and Arizona never even enacted a Medicaid law). This also meant that only certain categories of the poor—originally the elderly, dependent children, permanently and totally disabled, and the blind—would be eligible for Medicaid. Before passage of Medicaid, only the elderly poor received state-funded care on anything resembling a regular basis, and that care dated from a 1960 law that operated in only a few states.

Over the last four decades, Medicare and Medicaid have grown faster than any other spending programs. Rising costs of medical care more generally and such demographic factors as increases in the elderly population accounted for much of the growth. In addition, policymakers expanded the programs to include new groups and services. Liberals convinced Congress in 1972 to broaden Medicare so that it covered people with end stage renal disease and workers who qualified for Social Security Disability Insurance (although with a two-year waiting period from the onset of the disability). The same legislation broadened the entitlement to Medicaid through the creation of a new public assistance program, known as Supplemental Security Income (SSI), that, among other things, made it easier for children with disabilities to receive welfare benefits and Medicaid (even though 1972 legislators mistakenly thought that the elderly, and not people with disabilities, would be the main SSI beneficiaries). Between 1984 and 1990, Medicaid gradually expanded to cover all pregnant women and children up to and even somewhat above the poverty line. Congress added prescription drug benefits to Medicare in 1988, repealed them in 1989, and reestablished them in 2003. At the start of the twenty-first century, Medicare served over 40 million Americans at a cost of about $300 billion each year. Medicaid reached an even larger number of people for slightly less money. The combination of Medicare and Medicaid cost more than all the money currently spent on national defense (Howard 2007; Oberlander 2003; US Census Bureau 2005).

Despite its impressive size, Medicare does not cover all medical expenses. Dental, optical, and long-term care benefits are minimal, whereas co-payments and deductibles are substantial. In all, Medicare reimburses just under half of the elderly's medical costs ("Medicare At A Glance" 2006). Far from eliminating private health insurance coverage for the elderly, Medicare in fact has stimulated the development of a new private-sector health insurance product, known as supplemental or "medigap" insurance, to fill in the gaps. In this manner, the public and privately funded health care systems have become even more intertwined.[10]

Since the 1980s, calls for cost containment have been heard at least as often as calls for expansion, both among employers and government policymakers. Medicare adopted a prospective payment system in 1983, featuring a lengthy list of medical procedures and the amount of money the government would pay for each (known as diagnosis-related groups, DRGs). The idea was to set reimbursement levels for particular procedures in advance, rather than simply paying the accumulated costs of each hospital stay. Under the old system, doctors could run up the bill and hence their Medicare reimbursement essentially at their discretion—somewhat like sending someone to a hotel and allowing unlimited use of room service and the mini-bar. Under the new system, hospitals received a set amount which gave them an incentive to keep their costs below that set amount. The new system reflected the trend to put limits on the growth of Medicare, a process that played itself out in the late 1990s amid concerns over the size of the federal deficit. After the implementation of DRGs, Medicare's growth rate dropped by half.

What happened next was completely unintended. Doctors and hospitals started charging their private patients more to make up for the loss in revenues. Insurance premiums escalated, and employers became more sensitive to health care costs. They responded by shifting their workers from traditional fee-for-service plans to managed care, in which providers were supposed to have the incentive to keep workers healthy and health costs under control (Mayes 2004). In other words, private employers sought the same sorts of discounts on their health care costs that DRGs appeared to offer. The episode indicated yet another way in which private health care intersected with public health care.

At the national level, controlling Medicaid costs has sometimes meant trying to change the relationship between levels of government (Medicaid is a federal-state program). Ronald Reagan, a conservative president and a critic of big government, nevertheless proposed a national takeover of Medicaid, with all bills paid out of federal funds; in exchange, state governments would assume all welfare costs. He failed to interest Congress in this reform. After the historic 1994 elections, congressional Republicans tried to convert Medicaid from a budgetary entitlement to a block grant in which payments from the national government would be fixed in advance. A number of state governors worried that this plan would leave them responsible for even more Medicaid costs, and Republicans could not generate enough support to override President Clinton's veto. For their part, state governments have tried to slow down Medicaid's growth by limiting the number of optional services and optional populations that they cover (Moore and Smith 2005–06; Rowland 2005–06).

In the meantime, national health insurance remains an unrealized goal for proponents of fundamental reform of the health care system. The unsuccessful Clinton health plan (1993–94) would have forced all employers to offer health insurance to their workers or else pay into a public fund that would cover the uninsured. Organizations such as the National Federation of Independent Business strongly opposed the plan, fearing that small businesses would ultimately bear most of the costs of reform. Insurers and medical providers joined the anti-Clinton health plan coalition and played up its unpredictability, complexity, and potential to limit a patient's choice of doctor. They felt threatened by the proposed health purchasing alliances that were designed to hold down costs. All of this inner health care politics played itself out against the backdrop of traditional politics. Republicans seized upon opposition to the health care plan as a winning issue that would unite those conservatives who feared government control of a key industry such as health care and the more pragmatic party members who simply wanted to deny President Clinton a major legislative victory (Skocpol 1996). Instead of national health insurance, the Clinton initiative resulted only in modest changes in social regulation and tax expenditures that were designed to reinforce and expand private health insurance. Once again, the American health care system proceeded on its incremental way, with more patches being sewn on the quilt.

Recent changes have failed to stop the erosion of private health benefits. Coverage dropped from 75.5 percent of the US population in 1987 to 67.7 percent in 2005 (DeNavas-Walt et al. 2006).[11] Moreover, many employers who continue to offer health benefits have opted for less expensive plans with more limited benefits and more out-of-pocket costs for employees. A growing number of individual insurance policies cover catastrophic medical expenses but not routine care. As a result, the United States continues to witness not only inequities between those with and without health insurance but also inequities among those with health insurance.

Pensions

Scholars who write about the distinctiveness of American social welfare policy point to the absence of national health insurance, paid parental leave, and, in general, the limited reach of government. Public retirement pensions form a well-known exception (for example, Kingdon 1999). Social Security, the largest public program in the United States, remains one of the most popular. It paid out almost $450 billion in retirement and survivors benefits in 2005, to 40 million individuals (Social Security Administration 2006a). Almost everyone contributes to Social Security during his or her working years. Since benefits are loosely based on past earnings, the program creates a sense of entitlement among recipients that, at least until recently, has helped to fuel its political popularity and hence its expansion (Derthick 1979). Benefits for retirees are far more generous than other social programs for the poor or the unemployed.

For decades Social Security has remained the single most important source of income for the elderly. Currently, two-thirds of Americans age 65 and older depend on Social Security for at least half of their income. One-third of them rely on Social Security for at least 90 percent of their income. And one out of every five older Americans depends entirely on Social Security. Of course, some of the elderly depend more on Social Security than others. Unmarried individuals (single, divorced, or widowed), racial minorities, women, and the very old all tend to derive more of their income from Social Security than do other subgroups among the elderly.[12] For example, Social Security represents less than 20 percent of the income received by the most affluent quintile of older Americans. Although these senior citizens no doubt look forward to their monthly benefit checks, they have other sources of income to fund their retirement (Social Security Administration 2006b).

Many senior citizens rely heavily on Social Security, yet benefits come nowhere near to replacing all of a retiree's previous wages. Public officials refer to Social Security as one part of the "three-legged stool" of retirement income, along with private pensions and asset income. A little over half of all older Americans have asset income such as dividends from stocks or interest on savings. About 40 percent receive a pension other than Social Security, either from their employer (or from a private occupational pension scheme, such as a very large one for teachers and university professors known as TIAA) or an individual retirement account (IRA). These individuals tend to be more affluent than the typical retiree, in large part because their private sources of retirement income are so large (Social Security Administration 2006b).

In the area of pensions, therefore, public provision outstrips private provision. Social Security comes closest among American social welfare programs to universal coverage. At the same time, older Americans as a group receive more income from private than public sources. The combination of private pensions, asset income, and earnings accounts for about 60 percent of aggregate income for the elderly, and various public benefits the remaining 40 percent. This pattern resembles that of Australia, Canada, and the United Kingdom, where government pensions provide 40–50 percent of retirees' income, and differs from that of the Scandinavian countries, where public pensions account for approximately two-thirds of the total (Brown and Prus 2003; Social Security Administration 2006b).

The public-private mix has profound implications for poverty and inequality. The pattern among nations is clear: in most cases, the greater their reliance on private sources of retirement income, the more poverty and inequality among senior citizens. Although elderly Americans have a lower poverty rate than the US average, they are more likely to be poor than the elderly in other affluent democracies. Moreover, although the income of the average retiree is larger in the United States than elsewhere, income inequality among the elderly is higher in the United States. Those who rely exclusively on Social Security run a real risk of living in poverty; those who supplement Social Security with employer pensions, IRAs, and the like live quite well. It comes as no surprise that poverty rates for elderly black Americans are three times those of elderly whites. The percentage of elderly blacks with asset income is less than half that of whites, and whites retain a sizable lead when it comes to private pensions (Brown and Prus 2003; DeNavas-Walt et al. 2006; Social Security Administration 2006b; Whitehouse 2005).

Once again, the terms "public" and "private" do not define distinctive realms. The US government spends billions of dollars subsidizing private sources of retirement income. Employers can shield pensions from income taxation just as they can health benefits. The Joint Committee on Taxation

(2006) estimates that tax expenditures on pensions cost over $100 billion each year in lost revenues. Similar benefits for IRAs (individual retirement accounts) amount to at least $10 billion. For those who hold financial assets, tax breaks for dividends and long-term capital gains total over $90 billion annually. Some authors suggest that tax expenditures for homeowners provide a crucial source of support for the elderly: the less they have to pay for housing, the more they can spend on food, medical care, and other necessities; and homes are their largest assets (for example, Castles 1998; Conley and Gifford 2006). Tax expenditures for home owners, notably the home mortgage interest deduction, easily exceed $100 billion each year.[13]

Companies that take advantage of tax expenditures for retirement pensions must comply with a vast array of rules governing their eligibility, financing, investment, and disclosure. These ERISA rules, designed to promote the reliability, availability, and portability of private pensions, require hundreds of pages in the Internal Revenue Code to explain. The 1974 ERISA legislation also created the Pension Benefit Guaranty Corporation (PBGC), designed to insure many employer pension plans against bankruptcy. The PBGC covers over 30,000 plans and 44 million individuals. Almost 700,000 people now receive pensions from PBGC, and another 500,000 have qualified for aid and will receive pensions when they retire. The main claimants come from the steel and airline industries (Howard 1997; Pension Benefit Guaranty Corporation 2006).

When the US government helps older Americans directly, as with Social Security, it distributes benefits widely and helps reduce inequality. Almost all senior citizens collect Social Security. Although higher wage earners receive larger Social Security pensions than lower wage earners, the Social Security replacement rate is greater for low-wage workers than for high-wage workers. A hypothetical low-wage worker, earning a little less than half the national average, could expect Social Security to replace a little over half (54 percent) of her preretirement earnings in 2007. A hypothetical high-wage worker could expect Social Security to replace one-third of previous earnings. The average replacement rate for all workers that year was 40 percent (Board of Trustees 2007).

In contrast, the more indirect forms of assistance—tax expenditures and insurance—go disproportionately to the middle and upper-middle classes, which does little to stem inequality. The Congressional Budget Office estimates that only 20 percent of workers earning below $20,000 per year participate in a tax-favored retirement plan, either through their employer (for example, 401(k)s) or as individuals (for example, IRAs). In contrast, 80 percent of workers earning over $80,000 have a private pension. Most doctors and lawyers have private pensions; most couriers do not. People who work for a big business such as Microsoft are more likely to have such pensions than people who work for a small landscaping company. And even if a courier or landscape worker does have a private pension, it will usually be much smaller than that of a well-paid professional. Similarly, the insurance offered by the PBGC is helping well-paid airline pilots and steelworkers afford retirement more than it is helping waitresses or clerks (Congressional Budget Office 2007; Howard 2007). At the individual level, the best means of remedying this situation is for a person to shift occupations, a more likely event than an overhaul of the public pension system in favor of the poor.

Many observers have noted how much the US government helps the elderly, especially through Social Security and Medicare. This trend becomes even more pronounced when we include the relevant tax expenditures and the Pension Benefit Guaranty Corporation. Yet doing more does not mean accomplishing more, at least if one objective of social policy is reducing inequality. The less traditional forms of public support limit government's ability to reduce the gap between haves and have-nots.

Historical development

Retirement pensions, be they public or private, were rare in the United States prior to the 1930s. Retirement itself represented a modern social construction, for most people in the nineteenth and early twentieth centuries worked until they died or were seriously disabled (and even then many remained as docile figures on the farm or workplace) (Haber and Gratton 1994). The process of industrialization, however, made it harder for workers to retain their jobs in old age, even as it improved the general standard of living. A need developed to force workers to use some of the newly generated wealth to save for the contingencies of old age. What the English called friendly societies and the Americans tended to call fraternal orders met some of the new need, but these voluntary, small-scale efforts provided only enough money for burial expenses, the one contingency of old age that was certain. Private insurers also entered the market through the door-to-door sale of "industrial" life insurance in urban areas. This form of insurance involved high transaction costs and amounted to little more than burial insurance.

Toward the end of the nineteenth century, a few companies started offering pensions to their workers. Although the Treasury Department and Congress created tax incentives for company pensions between 1914 and 1926, pensions spread very slowly. At most 5 percent of all workers had some reasonable chance of receiving such a pension by the first decades of the twentieth century. Beginning in 1911, several states passed laws that permitted local counties to pay pensions to poor, elderly citizens—a development very much parallel to the initiation of old-age benefits in England. The initial impact of these pensions, few in number and small in size, was quite limited (Berkowitz and McQuaid 1992; Hacker 2002; Howard 1997; Lubove 1986; Quadagno 1988).

Although state-level pensions expanded in the 1920s and into the 1930s, they did little to counter the disastrous effects of the Great Depression. The elderly, many of whom owned their own homes, fared no worse than the other victims of the Depression (Haber and Gratton 1994). Nonetheless, the plight of the elderly, cut off from their assets in banks that were going out of business and unable to depend on their hard-pressed children, became a national concern in the early years of the New Deal. Self-proclaimed advocates for the elderly, such as Francis Townsend, started organizations composed entirely of elderly members and lobbied for national old-age pensions modeled loosely on pensions paid to the veterans of foreign wars. The elderly, they argued, had served the nation in the same manner as its soldiers and deserved recompense for a hard-earned life. At the same time, the elderly would serve as a vehicle for economic recovery by putting the money from their pensions into general circulation and boosting the level of economic activity. This agitation, combined with the more orderly bureaucratic politics within the Roosevelt administration, culminated in the 1935 passage of the Social Security Act, which became the centerpiece of America's welfare state (Amenta 2006).

The Social Security Act contained two different pension programs for the elderly. The first program (old-age insurance), which came to be called Social Security and which was administered by the national government, depended on payroll taxes to finance individual, wage-related pensions. The second program (old-age assistance), which was administered by the state governments with matching federal grants, relied on general revenues to finance pensions for the elderly who could prove to state authorities that they were poor (Béland 2005; Berkowitz 1991; Hacker 2002; Howard 1997).

In the intertwined American welfare state, the introduction of public pensions helped the spread of private pensions. During the Congressional debate over the Social Security Act, interests representing private pension plans tried to sell Congress on a measure (the Clark Amendment) that would have allowed employers with private pensions to opt out of Social Security. This measure passed in the Senate, and legislators paid a great deal of attention to it in the conference committee that ironed out differences between the House and Senate versions. In the end, the Roosevelt administration managed to pull the measure back for further discussion, and the Social Security Act passed without it. Employers soon learned to think of their pensions as supplements to Social Security. As more workers could expect a public pension, private pensions could be targeted more easily at top officials and senior staff. Some of the inequities we see today in the distribution of retirement income thus date back to the 1930s and 1940s. The Act also changed public expectations. According to one historian, the Social Security Act made Americans more "security conscious" and stimulated the sale of private pensions (Klein 2003; see also Béland 2005; Hacker 2002).

Between 1935 and 1950, Social Security did relatively little to help retirees. Many occupations, such as small businesses and farms, were excluded from the program, and the fact that benefits were linked to contributions kept the benefit levels low and, in the cases of people already old, nonexistent. Old-age assistance, targeted at the poor, functioned as the key public program during these years. It grew fast enough that some members of Congress, particularly those in agricultural districts with few Social Security beneficiaries, argued that Social Security did not need to be expanded. Advocates for expansion managed to add family and survivors benefits to Social Security in 1939—in large measure due to financing problems that had developed in the program, rather than broad-scale support. Other measures, such as disability insurance, went nowhere in a manner analogous to the fate of national health insurance (Béland 2005; Berkowitz 1991; Derthick 1979; Hacker 2002).

The period between 1950 and 1975 represented a golden age for pensions, public and private. Congress expanded eligibility for Social Security, beginning with agricultural and domestic workers and self-employed business-men in 1950 and later including most professions. By 1960, Social Security approached universal coverage. Beginning with women in 1956 and men in 1961, early retirement became an option. Social Security benefits rose, first gradually and then swiftly. Between 1968 and 1973, Congress approved annual benefit increases of 13, 15, 10, 20, and 7 percent. In 1972, simultan-eously with the 20 percent increase, Congress indexed benefits to the rate of inflation, a feature which took effect in 1975. In 1956, meanwhile, the United States initiated a program of disability insurance that allowed impaired, functionally limited, or seriously ill workers to retire before the normal retirement age. With the expansion of coverage, increased range of benefits (including disability), and more generous benefits, Social Security replaced old-age assistance as the foundation of public retirement pensions in the 1950s, and it helped move millions of older Americans out of poverty in the 1960s and 1970s. Yet even the old-age assistance program became more generous, particularly after the creation of SSI in 1972. SSI combined the state welfare programs for the blind and permanently and totally disa-bled and the aged into one big federal program. Although policymakers expected many beneficiaries to qualify both for Social Security and SSI, the Social Security benefit increases, particularly indexing Social Security to the inflation rate, prevented that development from occurring. Social Security benefits were now large enough to move most of the elderly above the income thresholds for SSI. In an unintended development, one of many in America's welfare state, SSI essentially became a program for people with disabilities rather than for the elderly (Béland 2005; Derthick 1979, 1990).[14]

Private pensions started to spread in the 1940s and took off after the Supreme Court ruled in 1949 that pensions could be subject to collective bargaining. Organized labor, which grew tired of waiting for Social Security to expand, pushed hard for pension and health benefits in the 1950s and 1960s. American companies could afford to expand these benefits because the United States was the dominant economic power in the world. Moreover, the growth of the income tax around World War II gave companies and their workers an incentive to find compensation that could be shielded from income taxation. Between 1940 and 1970, the percentage of American workers covered by private pensions tripled (Hacker 2002; Howard 1997).

Such rapid growth came with a price. As company pensions spread, so did instances of mismanagement, fraud, and bankruptcy. The reality of pensions sometimes fell short of workers' expectations. The most famous case was the termination of the Studebaker pension plan in 1963, which went bankrupt as the auto maker itself went bust. Congress debated a variety of pension reforms, some modest and some comprehensive, before passing ERISA in 1974. Interestingly, the rapid growth of Social Security in the late 1960s and early 1970s helped make comprehensive reform possible. A number of moderate and conservative legislators finally embraced ERISA as a way of reducing pressures to enlarge Social Security. They hoped that expanding one part of government would hold another part of government in check. A robust network of private pensions, subsidized and regulated by government, might diminish the need for bigger public pensions (Howard 2007; Wooten 2004).

The same policymakers who thought they needed to assure the solvency of private pensions gave much less attention to the question of whether Social Security would be able to meet its long-term obligations. That condition changed during the mid-1970s when it became clear that Social Security was dangerously close to insolvency. Indexing benefits to inflation had the effect of greatly raising the promised level of the benefits in the future, particularly after the inflationary episodes of the 1970s. High unemployment, another feature of that period, exacerbated the problem by decreasing the number of people who paid into Social Security and increasing the number of workers who applied for disability benefits. Demographic trends, notably the baby boom after World War II followed by a "baby bust," meant fewer workers supporting more retirees in the future. In an important policy shift that occurred in the mid-1970s, the question changed from how to expand Social Security to how to sustain it (Berkowitz 2003, 2006).

In the short run, the defenders of Social Security got the better of the argument. In 1983 the Reagan administration acquiesced to legislation that, although it delayed the payment of a cost of living adjustment by six months and accelerated the introduction of higher tax rates that had been legislated in 1977, essentially preserved the basic nature of the program. The Social Security rescue legislation, as it was known, kept the program out of controversy for the rest of the 1980s. The financial pressure on the program eased, in part because of the economic recovery and lessening of inflation after 1982, in part because of the increased revenues and program savings generated by the 1983 amendments, and in part because of the low birth rate in the 1930s. In 1989 one prominent Social Security advocate told Congress that the trust funds were "building at an astonishing rate" (Robert Ball quoted in Berkowitz 2003: 344). The serious fiscal crisis of the early 1980s was, however, a sobering experience for program advocates who had constantly to reassure members of the large baby boom birth cohort that the program would be there for them when they began to retire in large numbers starting around 2010.

How would a program, already under severe pressure, be able to accommodate the retirement of the baby boom? This question gave a new legitimacy to what became known as the forces of privatization. They argued that a defined-benefit program needed to be converted to a defined-contribution program and that the private sector would garner a larger return for people than would the old public sector program, with all of its hidden subsidies for less advantaged, poorer, or disabled groups. The exuberant bull stock market of the 1990s, combined with the relatively high Social Security taxes of the same period (10.6% without disability insurance), gave the impression that money invested in the stock market brought a far better return than did worker and employee contributions to Social Security. At the same time, financial stresses on private pensions and a spate of bankruptcies that undermined the continuity of private pension programs created pressure among private employers to switch from defined-benefit to defined-contribution programs. As workers learned how to manage their own retirement accounts through such devices as 401(k) plans, the idea of a defined-contribution benefit plan gained more legitimacy in both the public and private sectors.

Hence a new sort of proposal that harked back to older proposals in the progressive era made its way to the bargaining table—federally mandated, privately provided pensions, with a core benefit being provided through the public sector. The idea was for the federal government to continue to pay a smaller guaranteed benefit and for the worker to be able to add to this benefit through private but federally monitored savings plans. Talk of a long-term funding crisis in Social Security, such as a reported long-term shortfall of 2.13 percent of payroll in 1994, gave the appearance to some that to privatize Social Security was to save it. Privatization advocates pointed out that, using 1995 data, the trust funds would be exhausted in the year 2030. That meant that those retired or retiring after that date would have to depend on revenue collected in payroll taxes on a year by year basis to fund their retirements. Actual benefits would be significantly smaller than promised benefits. A defined-benefit plan meant nothing if the benefits could not actually be paid, according to this argument. It was more realistic and humane and generous to switch to a defined-contribution program. Privatization advocates bolstered this argument by pointing out that even the 2030 date depended on the questionable ability of the federal government to collect a surplus in the Social Security trust fund until the baby boom cohort began to retire, and then to spend the interest on that surplus to shore up benefits to the promised level before even that remedy was exhausted in 2030. President George W. Bush emphasized this argument in his privatization proposal of 2004 (Béland 2005).

This proposal, like so many others in the history of social welfare provision in America, illustrated how intertwined the public and private sectors were. Even a reform of a public program designed to privatize that program required the legislative authority of the federal government, and no one seriously considered abandoning the federal role. Nothing would happen to SSI, for example, if a privatization plan were to pass. Indeed, it might be strengthened to accommodate those who might be made worse off by the privatization scheme. The private plan would be closely monitored by the federal government to make sure that private companies kept accurate records and, more importantly, that private companies maintained the necessary solvency to serve as the stewards of publicly mandated funds. Privatization, therefore, implied increased federal regulation with no end to ultimate federal responsibility for the pension system. The entire mechanism of privatization, furthermore, depended on favorable tax treatment for the money collected.

Conclusion

We therefore conclude this survey by noting that the public sector has assumed more responsibility for old-age pensions than it has for health insurance in the United States. In both areas of endeavor, however, the line between the public and private sector remains blurred. Actions in one sector influence the actions in another sector in a complicated, intertwined system. A remarkably wide variety of organizations, some with significant political power, have a stake in the status quo. The diverse nature of policy tools and the federal nature of the US political system contribute to this complexity.

The convoluted mix of public and private helps to explain why comprehensive reform remains so elusive. As problems facing pensions and health care have mounted, calls for "entitlement reform" have become more commonplace (Peterson 2004; Samuelson 2007). In this context, reform usually means retrenchment, and the main targets are Social Security, Medicare, and Medicaid. Typically, such calls have had minimal impact. President Clinton established a Bipartisan Commission on Entitlement Reform in the mid-1990s, and its reports did little except collect dust. During his State of the Union message in January 2006, President George W. Bush proposed a similar commission, but as of the summer of 2008 he and Congress had failed to appoint a single member. Clinton's attempt to overhaul the health care system and Bush's pension privatization initiative met similar fates.

Incremental reform is still possible. Policymakers in recent decades have found ways to slow down the growth of spending on Social Security, Medicare, and Medicaid; to expand coverage and benefits in select cases; and to counter partially the erosion of pension and health benefits in the private sector. Increasingly, however, modest changes cannot mask major problems. The nation's capacity to solve problems has not kept pace with the severity of those problems, and no burst of activity, in the manner of the New Deal or the Great Society, appears to be on the horizon. The health care crisis remains pressing as Americans continue to lose coverage, either partly or completely, and as health care costs escalate far beyond general inflation. Although the problems facing pensions may be comparatively smaller, they are likely to grow.

Our hope is that Americans, not satisfied with the occasional episode of modest reform, will instead make significant changes in the ways that public agencies and private organizations deal with health care and pensions. We know that such changes are technically and politically daunting. Economics, politics, and the simple contingencies of history force social policy into an incremental mode in which the past constrains the present. Nonetheless, the problems remain real and create their own sense of urgency, as this examination of America's intertwined public and private social provision for health care and retirement pensions demonstrates.

Notes

1. Although employers typically pay most of these costs, economists believe that the burden is ultimately borne by workers in the form of lower wages.
2. The financing varies as well. Medicare is funded by a combination of payroll taxes, income taxes, and individual monthly premiums. Programs for veterans and active military are financed largely by income taxes. Medicaid and SCHIP are funded by a combination of income taxes at the national level and income and sales taxes at the state level.
3. Sheils and Haught (2004) offer a much higher estimate, primarily because they include foregone payroll tax revenue (for Social Security and Medicare) as well foregone income tax revenue.
4. The sum of privately insured, publicly insured, and uninsured exceeds 100 percent in the United States because some people (especially retirees) have private and public insurance.
5. Social regulations can have a similar effect. The COBRA rules, for example, only benefit those who already have health insurance, and those who can afford to pay the full premium.
6. Indeed, calling health care a "system" may imply more coherence than actually exists.
7. The more gender-neutral term "workers' compensation" didn't come into wide usage until the 1970s.
8. The following discussion of health care between the 1910s and 1960s is based primarily on Hacker (2002), Quadagno (2005), and Starr (1982).
9. Public and private merged in other ways during this period. The United Mine Workers Welfare and Retirement Fund – on the surface the creation of a private labor union that, among other things, constructed hospitals in the coal-producing areas of West Virginia – was in fact heavily influenced by professional advice from and personnel imported from the federal government (Berkowitz 1980; Krajcinovic 1997).

10. Such policies may become less common now that prescription drug benefits have been added to Medicare. Even so, the structure of the drug program guarantees that private companies will play a central role in delivering this benefit.
11. The numbers of uninsured would have increased dramatically during this period had not Medicaid been expanded and SCHIP been created.
12. In addition, the government helps a small fraction of the elderly, most with low incomes, through Food Stamps, Supplemental Security Income (SSI), and veterans' benefits.
13. Clearly, many people who are not elderly receive capital gains and own a home. The JCT does not apportion the cost of these tax expenditures by age, so it is impossible to know exactly how much older Americans benefit.
14. Although Derthick (1979) attributes the growth of Social Security to a small network of dedicated bureaucrats and powerful legislators, Béland (2005) emphasizes the role of demographic and economic factors, as well as electoral competition.

References

Amenta, Edwin. 2006. *When Movements Matter: The Townsend Plan and the Rise of Social Security*. Princeton, NJ: Princeton University Press.

Ayanian, John Z., Joel S. Weissman, Eric C. Schneider, Jack A. Ginsburg, and Alan M. Zaslavsky. 2000. "Unmet Health Needs of Uninsured Adults in the United States." *Journal of the American Medical Association* 284: 2061–9.

Béland, Daniel. 2005. *Social Security: History and Politics from the New Deal to the Privatization Debate*. Lawrence, KS: University Press of Kansas.

Berkowitz, Edward D. 1980. "Growth of the US Social Welfare System in the Post–World War II Era: The UMW, Rehabilitation, and the Federal Government." In Paul Uselding (ed.), *Research in Economic History* 233–47. Greenwich: JAI Press.

Berkowitz, Edward D. 1991. *America's Welfare State: From Roosevelt to Reagan*. Baltimore, MD: Johns Hopkins University Press.

Berkowitz, Edward D. 2003. *Robert Ball and the Politics of Social Security*. Madison WI: University of Wisconsin Press.

Berkowitz, Edward D. 2006. *Something Happened: A Political and Cultural Overview of the Seventies*. New York: Columbia University Press.

Berkowitz, Edward D. and Kim McQuaid. 1992. *Creating the Welfare State: The Political Economy of 20th-Century Reform* (Revised edition). Lawrence, KS: University Press of Kansas.

Berkowitz, Edward D. and Monroe Berkowitz. 1984. "The Survival of Workers' Compensation." *Social Service Review* 58: 259–80.

Board of Trustees, Federal Old-Age and Survivors Insurance and Federal Disability Insurance Trust Funds. 2007. The 2007 Annual Report of the Board of Trustees of the Federal Old-Age and Survivors Insurance and Federal Disability Insurance Trust Funds. Washington, DC: Government Printing Office.

Brown, Robert L. and Steven G. Prus. 2003. Social Transfers and Income Inequality in Old-Age: A Multi-National Perspective. Luxembourg Income Study Working Paper no. 355. Retrieved on July 2, 2008 from www.lisproject.org

Castles, Francis. 1998. "The Really Big Trade-Off: Homeownership and the Welfare State in the New World and the Old." *Acta Politica* 33: 5–19.

Claxton, Gary, Isadora Gil, Benjamin Finder, Jon Gabel, Jeremy Pickreign, Heidi Whitmore, and Samantha Hawkins. 2005. *Employer Health Benefits: 2005 Annual*

Survey. Menlo Park, CA and Chicago, IL: Kaiser Family Foundation and Health Research Educational Trust.

Congressional Budget Office. 2007. *Utilization of Tax Incentives for Retirement Saving: Update to 2003*. Washington, DC: Congressional Budget Office.

Conley, Dalton and Brian Gifford. 2006. "Home Ownership, Social Insurance, and the Welfare State." *Sociological Forum* 21 (March 1): 55–82.

DeNavas-Walt, Carmen, Bernadette D. Proctor, and Cheryl Hill Lee. 2006. *Income, Poverty, and Health Insurance Coverage in the United States: 2005*. Washington, DC: US Census Bureau.

Derthick, Martha. 1979. *Policymaking for Social Security*. Washington, DC: Brookings Institution.

Derthick, Martha. 1990. *Agency under Stress: The Social Security Administration in American Government*. Washington, DC: Brookings Institution.

Fronstin, Paul. 2005. "Sources of Health Insurance and Characteristics of the Uninsured: Analysis of the 2005 Current Population Reports." *EBRI Issue Brief no. 287* (November).

Gorey, Kevin M. 1999. "What Is Wrong with the US Health Care System? It Does Not Effectively Exist for One of Every Five Americans." *The Milbank Quarterly* 77: 401–7.

Haber, Carole and Brian Gratton. 1994. *Old Age and the Search for Security: An American Social History*. Bloomington, IN: Indiana University Press.

Hacker, Jacob S. 2002. *The Divided Welfare State: The Battle over Public and Private Social Benefits in the United States*. New York: Cambridge University Press.

Hadley, Jack and Peter J. Cunningham. 2005. "Perception, Reality, and Health Insurance: Uninsured as Likely as Insured to Perceive Need for Care but Half as Likely to Get Care." Center for Studying Health System Change Issue Brief no. 100 (October).

Howard, Christopher. 1997. *The Hidden Welfare State: Tax Expenditures and Social Policy in the United States*. Princeton, NJ: Princeton University Press.

Howard, Christopher. 2007. *The Welfare State Nobody Knows: Debunking Myths about US Social Policy*. Princeton, NJ: Princeton University Press.

Joint Committee on Taxation. 2006. *Estimates of Federal Tax Expenditures for Fiscal Years 2006–2010*. Washington, DC: Government Printing Office.

Kingdon, John W. 1999. *America the Unusual*. New York: St. Martin's/Worth.

Klein, Jennifer. 2003. *For All These Rights: Business, Labor and the Shaping of America's Public-Private Welfare State*. Princeton, NJ: Princeton University Press.

Krajcinovic, Ivana. 1997. *From Company Doctors to Managed Care: The United Mine Workers' Noble Experiment*. Ithaca, NY: Cornell University Press.

Lubove, Roy. 1986 (1968). *The Struggle for Social Security, 1900–1935*. Pittsburgh, PA: University of Pittsburgh Press.

Mayes, Rick. 2004. "Causal Chains and Cost Shifting: How Medicare's Rescue Inadvertently Triggered the Managed-Care Revolution." *Journal of Policy History* 16: 144–74.

"Medicare at a Glance." 2006. Menlo Park: Henry J. Kaiser Family Foundation. Retrieved on July 2, 2008 from http://www.kff.org/medicare/upload/1066–09.pdf.

Moore, Judith D. and David G. Smith. 2005–06. "Legislating Medicaid: Considering Medicaid and Its Origins." *Health Care Financing Review* 27: 45–52.

Oberlander, Jonathan. 2003. *The Political Life of Medicare*. Chicago, IL: University of Chicago Press.

Office of Management and Budget. 2006. *Analytical Perspectives, Budget of the United States Government, Fiscal Year 2007.* Washington, DC: Government Printing Office.

Pension Benefit Guaranty Corporation. 2006. *Pension Insurance Data Book 2005.* Washington, DC: Pension Benefit Guaranty Corporation.

Peterson, Peter G. 2004. *Running on Empty: How the Democratic and Republican Parties Are Bankrupting Our Future and What Americans Can Do about It.* New York: Farrar, Strauss and Giroux.

Quadagno, Jill. 1988. *The Transformation of Old Age Politics: Class and Politics in the American Welfare State.* Chicago, IL: University of Chicago Press.

Quadagno, Jill. 2005. *One Nation, Uninsured: Why the US Has No National Health Insurance.* New York: Oxford University Press.

Rowland, Diane. 2005–06. "Medicaid at Forty." *Health Care Financing Review* 27: 63–78.

Samuelson, Robert J. 2007. "Entitled Selfishness: Boomer Generation Is in a State of Denial." *Washington Post.* January 10, 2007: A13.

Sheils, John and Randall Haught. 2004. "The Cost of Tax-Exempt Health Benefits in 2004." Health Affairs web exclusive. Retrieved on 25 February from http://www.healthaffairs.org/

Skocpol, Theda. 1996. *Boomerang: Health Care Reform and the Turn Against Government.* New York: W. W. Norton.

Smith, Cynthia, Cathy Cowan, Stephen Heffler, and Aaron Catlin. 2006. "National Health Spending in 2004: Recent Slowdown Led by Prescription Drug Spending." *Health Affairs* 25: 186–96.

Social Security Administration. 2006a. *Fast Facts & Figures about Social Security, 2006.* Washington, DC: Social Security Administration.

Social Security Administration. 2006b. *Income of the Aged Chartbook 2004.* Washington, DC: Social Security Administration.

Starr, Paul. 1982. *The Social Transformation of American Medicine.* New York: Basic Books.

US Census Bureau. 2005. *Statistical Abstract of the United States: 2006.* Washington, DC: Government Printing Office.

Whitehouse, Edward R. 2005. *Testimony before the United States House of Representatives, Committee on Ways and Means, Sub-Committee on Social Security Reform* (June 16, 2005). Retrieved on July 2, 2008 from http://www.oecd.org/dataoecd/35/45/35004104.pdf

Wooten, James A. 2004. *The Employee Retirement Income Security Act of 1974: A Political History.* Berkeley, CA: University of California Press.

4

The Canada Paradox: The Public-Private Divide in Health Insurance and Pensions

Gerard W. Boychuk and Keith G. Banting

Introduction

In recent years, academic attention has returned to an issue highlighted by Richard Titmuss half a century ago: the intersection of public and private social benefits (Titmuss 1958). This renewed interest in the public-private divide reflects an understanding that the structure of private benefits can have a significant impact on the development of public programs. It also reflects a growing realization that the balance between public and private benefits is critical to the distribution of risk in contemporary society, and that current changes in private benefits in many countries are triggering a privatization of risk that is not being offset by public benefit programs.

Recent research on the politics of the public-private divide has tended to focus on the experience of the United States. This chapter focuses on Canada, another liberal welfare state. The primary purpose is to examine the evolution of the relationship between public and private benefits in health care and pensions, focusing on two distinct stages of development: the initial setting of the public-private balance, and its evolution in the decades that followed. In addition, the chapter highlights important contrasts between the developmental patterns in Canada and those in the United States, in order to contribute to the comparative analysis of the deep embrace between public and private social benefits.

The basic Canadian pattern can be summarized succinctly. In the case of health insurance, private benefits were well developed before public benefits emerged. Nevertheless, in two major steps, the state simply displaced private benefits, establishing a virtual public monopoly in core hospital and medical services, in some cases taking over private organizations to deliver the new public programs, and relegating private benefits to a supplementary role. In the case of pensions, however, the state was the first mover and had the field largely to itself for at least four decades. Yet private pensions eventually expanded to become an equal pillar in the retirement income system.

These contrasting starting points had a powerful impact on the trajectory of development in the decades that followed. Dominated by public programs, the field of health insurance has been remarkably stable, following a pattern of "punctuated equilibrium," with major changes being followed by a long period of lock-in and relatively little change. Pensions, where private benefits have played a much larger role, have followed a different trajectory. Although there has been impressive stability in public programs, there has been more scope for incremental change which—paradoxically—has tended both to entrench the historic public-private balance more firmly and to facilitate the redistribution of risk within the private sector in worrying ways.

Canadian experience thus stands in contrast to that of the United States. In the United States, the prior existence of private benefits strongly constrained the development of public programs, helping to explain the dominant role of public pensions and the supplementary role of public health insurance in that country. By this standard, the Canadian case presents a paradox. Public health care benefits came to dominate where private benefits were already strong; but public pensions have come to share the field with private benefits which did not expand significantly until well after the introduction of public programs.

The comparison of the subsequent policy trajectories in Canada and the United States is slightly more complex, revealing both similarities and contrasts. Pensions in Canada have seen some of the dynamics that characterize US experience: policy drift, policy conversion, and subterranean policy shifts. But health care has seen much less incremental change, pointing to powerful limits on such processes in public-dominated systems.

To develop this analysis, the chapter proceeds as follows. The second section provides a brief summary of the existing literature, especially that dealing with the United States, to identify key points for comparison. The third section turns its attention to Canada, examining the public-private divide in health insurance, both in the early decades and through its later evolution. The fourth section provides a similar analysis of the field of pensions. Finally, the fifth section summarizes the findings about Canada, and reflects on their implications for comparative analysis.

The literature on the public-private divide

Recent research on US experience has generated an interesting set of propositions regarding the relationship between private and public benefits at the inception of public programs. A related literature emphasizes the importance of the relationship between private and public benefits to the evolution of policy over time.

In the United States, the scope of private benefits at the inception of public programs is argued to have had a strong role in determining whether public programs predominated or were relegated to a supplementary role. Hacker provides the fullest statement of this interpretation in regard to pensions and health insurance:

> Divergence emerged between the two areas, however, because of the relative timing and sequence of public and private developments in the two areas. The passage of Social Security before private plans were widespread…created strong path-dependent processes in favor of the program…. In contrast, the failure of health insurance during the New Deal and then after World War II created a path of policy development far less conducive to the eventual expansion of public authority. Subsidies for employment-based health benefits and for high-technology medicine created an expensive, fragmented system of health care finance and delivery that undercut the constituency for reform while raising the political and budgetary costs of policy change. (Hacker 2002: 277–78).

In the US context, public programs which emerged after private benefits had come to play a core role in social protection were "…more likely to be limited to subsidizing private social provision and filling the gaps it creates" (Béland and Hacker 2004: 47). In contrast, public benefit programs implemented in the absence of a strong system of private benefits were more likely to be comprehensive and universal. Private benefits are argued to have constrained public programs in at least three ways: they fostered vested interests, they shaped public expectations, and they embedded institutions of private provision (Béland and Hacker 2004: 43). Private benefits created vested interests both among providers (leading to the rise of organized interest groups) and beneficiaries (due to their habituation to private benefits). Private benefits shaped not only public expectations but also "policymakers' governing conceptions of the appropriate shape and scope of *public* social programmes" (Béland and Hacker 2004: 47). Finally, a direct challenge to private benefits, which have become a core source of social protection, "entails large social dislocations and fiscal costs" (Béland and Hacker 2004: 47).

A second literature has extended this work by tracking the public-private divide over time. This literature proposes an alternative to the "punctuated equilibrium" model of policy change, which emphasizes path-dependency and the locking-in of policies for long periods of time. Drawing on Thelen's evolutionary models of institutional change (Thelen 2004), this literature focuses on incremental policy change, identifying ways in which policy can shift even in the context of relative program stability. Such changes can occur through *policy conversion* (where existing programs are reoriented toward new policy ends without major program reconstruction), *subterranean policy shifts* (where changes in regulation and tax subsidization of private benefits result in major shifts without fundamental redesign of public benefits), and *policy drift* (where the effects of major public programs are deliberately allowed to fade by failing to adjust the programs in response to changing conditions). Hacker draws on US experience to make a "strong case" that policy drift and subterranean policy shifts are important and have likely been overlooked in other national contexts (2004: 244).

This chapter also takes up this challenge, and explores more fully the factors that define the scope for such evolutionary change. Although Hacker demonstrates the importance of policy conversion, subterranean policy changes, and policy drift, he does not identify the circumstances under which these processes are likely to occur. Our expectation is that the initial public-private divide is critical in defining the scope for such evolutionary policy change. The greater the reliance on private benefits, the greater the potential for subterranean policy shifts in regulatory standards and subsidization through tax expenditures (see Howard 1997, 2006). Similarly, the larger the role of private benefits, the more sensitive the field is to changes in private decision-making, especially decisions by employers. As Hacker and others have demonstrated, such processes increase the venues for pursuing retrenchment. Moreover, if such trends are not offset by concomitant changes in public benefits, the result can be a growing privatization of risk.

However, fields strongly dominated by public programs are unlikely to create the same opportunities for evolutionary change. The difficulty of retrenching major public programs even in the face of strong pressures for change is now widely recognized (Pierson 1996). But the dominance of public programs also forestalls processes of evolutionary change that depend on the role of private benefits. Without substantial private benefits, there is simply less scope for subterranean shifts in the regulation and subsidization of private benefits, and less sensitivity to changes in employers' approach to private benefits. As a result, policy fields dominated by public programs are likely to approximate the model of punctuated equilibrium, with episodic periods of major change being followed by long periods of relative stasis.

To test these expectations, this chapter examines the relationship between private and public benefits in health insurance and pensions in two phases: the period in which major public programs were first implemented, and the subsequent period of evolution of the public-private balance.

Health insurance

Setting the initial public-private divide: displacing private benefits

A national system of public health insurance was introduced in Canada in two major steps, with the introduction of a federal cost-sharing program for universal hospital care insurance in 1957 and the introduction of a similar program for medical care insurance in 1966.

From the outset, the federal system conditioned the development of health insurance, with provincial governments establishing precedents for federal action. The social-democratic government of Saskatchewan implemented a program of universal hospital insurance in 1947 and, shortly afterwards, British Columbia implemented a similar plan. Both provinces then launched campaigns for a national initiative that would provide federal financial support for their programs. Federalism thus magnified the importance of the ideological trends developing in these provinces. In Maioni's classic statement of this argument, the federal system not only "encouraged the formation of a social-democratic third party" (the Cooperative Commonwealth Federation which would later become the New Democratic Party) but also provided opportunities to innovate at the provincial level, and thereby "enhanced its efficacy in promoting health policy reform" (1998: 6).

Although much attention has rightly been paid to developments in Saskatchewan, the politics of the public-private divide in Ontario, the largest province, were also critical. The federal government was only willing to implement a national plan if the program included a majority of the provinces representing a majority of the Canadian population—thus effectively requiring the participation of Ontario. Although the scope of private benefits for health services was significant across Canada, this was especially the case in Ontario. On the eve of the advent of a national program in 1956, 70 percent of the population of Ontario had hospital insurance coverage (see Figure 4.1). Private benefit plans constituted just under half of all hospital revenues (46 percent), making private benefits a much larger source of hospital revenue than either government funding (22 percent) or out-of-pocket payments (29 percent).

Crucially, the existence of private benefits in Ontario did not forestall the province's support for a national public program. The growth of private benefits had certainly created commercial interests that were strongly opposed to universal public hospital benefits. But the Conservative premier of the province, Leslie Frost, did not seem particularly concerned with their opposition and took several opportunities to publicly challenge the industry.[1] Indeed, in several ways, the existence of a well-established set of private benefits in Ontario facilitated the adoption of a system of public benefits.[2] First, it established public acceptance of the collective insurance principle. Second, it created a ready-made revenue source as the Ontario government viewed private premiums as a preexisting self-imposed tax. Third, the extent of private benefit coverage assuaged concerns on the part of policymakers about compliance and achievement of universal coverage. The Ontario government proceeded in the belief that the large portion of the population that was already covered could be easily moved over to public coverage—resolving, in advance, the problem of

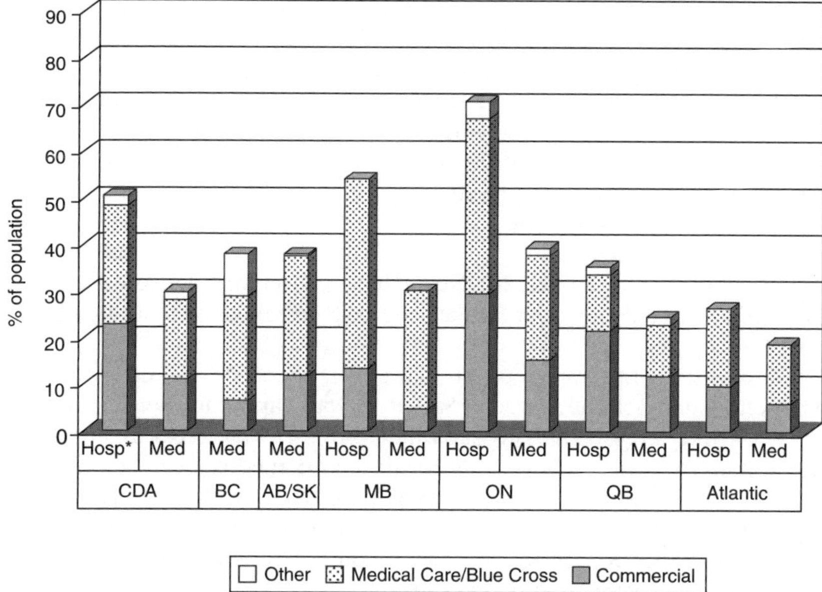

Figure 4.1 Private hospital benefit coverage, by plan type, Canada and provinces, 1955

Note: *Average hospital coverage for Canada includes the six provinces without an existing public hospital insurance plan—Manitoba, Ontario, Quebec, New Brunswick, Nova Scotia and Prince Edward Island.

Source: Canada National Health and Welfare, 1955.

adverse selection. Finally, private benefits helped address the critical issue of administrative capacity as the province simply converted the largest nonprofit voluntary insurance plan (Blue Cross) into the public agency responsible for administering the new public program. Had Ontario faced a relatively clean slate in terms of private benefits as had Saskatchewan in 1947, the obstacles to moving ahead would have been much more difficult (Taylor 1978: 119–20).[3] It is therefore not surprising that hospital insurance developed earlier than medical insurance for doctors' services, despite the fact that private hospital coverage was much higher than private medical coverage (see Figure 4.1). In 1955, Ontario announced its support for a national public insurance program, and the federal government acted soon afterwards. "By assuming leadership of those pressing the federal government in 1955..., the Ontario government was clearly the determinative force that brought the nationwide system we now have" (Taylor 1978: 158).

A universal public program for medical care, including physician services, did not emerge until the 1960s, by which time private benefit coverage had reached levels comparable to those for hospital care at the inception of national hospital insurance. Once again, federal-provincial dynamics mattered. Because Saskatchewan already had its own hospital insurance program, the advent of federal cost-sharing for hospital insurance provided Saskatchewan with a large financial windfall which allowed the province to move ahead on public medical care insurance. Doing so required confronting the medical profession and expropriating its major revenue source—its near-monopoly control of private medical care benefits which in 1960 extended coverage to just under 40 percent of the Saskatchewan population through plans directly controlled by the Saskatchewan College of Physicians and Surgeons (Taylor 1978: 328). Nevertheless, after an intensely bitter confrontation and strike by doctors, Saskatchewan established a public medical care plan.

In this case, conservative provincial governments tried—unsuccessfully in the end—to block the spread of Saskatchewan's approach across the country. The three largest English Canadian provinces (Ontario, BC, Alberta), which had the highest levels of surgical and medical care coverage in Canada, almost immediately introduced plans that would rely primarily on employer-provided medical care insurance and subsidized (or government offered) insurance for those with low incomes—thus incorporating a very strong role for private benefits in conformity with the positions of both the medical profession and insurance industry (Taylor 1978: 328). With this level of provincial support, it appeared that the private benefit model would dominate: "With three of the four most powerful provincial governments adopting CMA-CHIA policy, the odds in favour of the market economy approach and against the political economy philosophy...had shifted most favourably" (Taylor 1978: 348).

In the end, however, the federal government opted for universal public insurance, and that choice predominated. A variety of factors tipped the federal choice. The interaction between developments in pensions and health insurance was crucial, with the province of Québec playing a catalytic role. Québec, home to the vast majority of Canada's French-speaking minority population, had embarked on an aggressive program of asserting provincial dominance in social policy. As discussed in the next section, Québec announced its intention to build a separate provincial pension program at a federal-provincial conference in September 1963. This decision was perceived as a major loss for the federal government and raised serious concerns about the integrative capacity of national social policy. When combined with related decisions on other programs, Québec was effectively opting out of all major national universal social programs including youth allowances, pensions, and hospital insurance.[4] However, opting out need not necessarily apply to new programs, and a national system of public medical care insurance provided a new opportunity to help redress the perceived imbalance between provincial and federal predominance in social policy. Under a federal shared-cost program, the link with individual citizens would be indirect but, nevertheless, a universal program certainly reflected the idea of pan-Canadian social rights of which the federal government could cast itself as guarantor. It was in this context that the federal government announced its intention to move forward with medical care insurance in the Speech from the Throne in April 1965. Legislation was to be passed in 1967 and came into effect in 1968. By 1971, all provinces had opted in to the universal program.

Thus, in the crucial case of the debate over hospital insurance in Ontario in the 1950s, private benefits, rather than having constraining effects, contributed to the development of public hospital insurance benefits. In the 1960s debate over medical insurance, such constraints seemed to be emerging, as the three provinces with the highest levels of private benefits pushed to preserve a much larger role for the private sector. But the opposition was trumped by the federal government's desire to use medical care insurance as a tool of nation-building. As a result, the public-private divide in health insurance in Canada emerged in a much different form than in the United States.

The public-private divide over time: stability and limited drift

The centrality of public programs in health insurance established in the 1950s and 1960s has represented a powerful anchor, limiting the impact of evolutionary processes that have been critical elsewhere. There has been remarkably little drift in response to changes in private benefits, and subterranean shifts in the subsidization and regulation of private benefits have been limited.

Public consolidation without expansion

In the decades following adoption, the Canadian system of universal hospital and physician care insurance was consolidated. The *Canada Health Act, 1984 (CHA)* tightened the existing principles adding the principle of accessibility (provincial plans must provide reasonable access to health services) as well as imposing nondiscretionary penalties for provinces allowing user fees or extra-billing.[5] This legislation was essentially a federally imposed mechanism to stem a drift at the provincial level to allow private funding in the form of user fees and extra-billing to increasingly permeate the public system.

Consolidation, however, took place without expansion either of national programs or in the scope of public expenditures relative to private ones. Although public benefits increased rapidly as a proportion of total expenditures after the implementation of national programs, the trend did not continue (see Figure 4.2). More importantly, public insurance at the national level has not been extended to other expanding areas of health provision such as prescription drugs and long-term care.

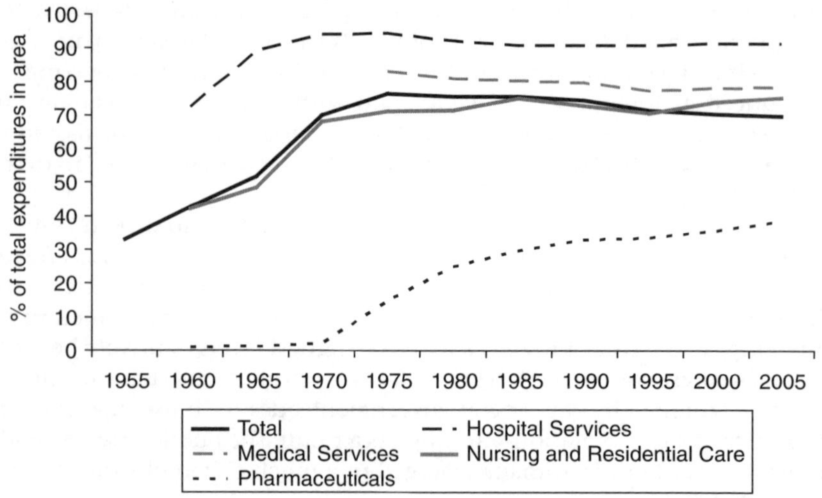

Figure 4.2   Public health expenditure as proportion of total expenditure, by area of provision, 1955–2005

Notes: Pharmaceuticals include prescription drugs as well as other personal health nondurables. A breakdown in public-private funds for medical services is not available prior to 1975.

Source: Canada, National Health and Welfare (1955); OECD (2006).

Public unresponsiveness in these areas cannot be attributed primarily to the existence of private benefits. Private insurance plans do cover about one-third of expenditures on pharmaceuticals but are nonexistent in long-term care (see Table 4.1). Yet there has been no expansion of universal public insurance coverage in either area, despite prolonged and numerous debates especially in the 1990s and early 2000s. Clearly, the prevalence of private benefits provides little explanatory leverage on this shared fate. Even in the case of pharmaceuticals, where private benefits are significant, the primary source of the blockage to an expansion of public insurance has been fiscal constraints and intergovernmental relations. Provincial governments are very reluctant to enter into expensive new programs without a significant federal financial contribution. For its part, the federal government is reluctant to make open-ended spending commitments, especially as it faces heavy pressure from the provinces to make large infusions of funds for existing health programs (see Boychuk 2002, 2003, 2005, 2006, 2007). As a result, provincial governments have responded primarily with nonuniversal programs targeted on specific groups such as social assistance recipients. Thus, although private benefits undoubtedly have some effect in dulling pressure for the expansion of public insurance, their constraining role is not the central explanation for the failure of national programs to expand.

Table 4.1 Private health insurance benefit payments and Out-of-Pocket Payments (OPP) as a proportion of total health expenditures, 1988–2005

		1988	1990	1995	2000	2005
Hospital Accommodation	Private Expenditure (% of Total)	9.3	9.4	9.3	8.7	8.7
	OPP (% of Total)	2.5	2.2	2.2	1.9	1.6
	Private Insurance (% Total)	1.3	1.4	1.7	2.3	2.4
Nursing Home Care and Other Accommodations	Private Expenditure (% of Total)	26.8	27.5	29.5	27.6	28.1
	OPP (% of Total)	26.8	27.5	29.5	27.6	28.1
	Private Insurance (% Total)	0.0	0.0	0.0	0.0	0.0
Physician Care	Private Expenditure (% of Total)	1.0	1.0	1.0	1.4	1.1
	OPP (% of Total)	1.0	0.9	1.0	1.3	1.1
	Private Insurance (% Total)	0.0	0.0	0.0	0.0	0.0
Prescription Drugs	Private Expenditure (% of Total)	54.4	53.2	54.5	54.6	54.0
	OPP (% of Total)	24.2	23.1	22.8	21.8	19.6
	Private Insurance (% Total)	30.2	30.1	31.8	32.9	34.4
Dental Care	Private Expenditure (% of Total)	91.0	90.7	92.3	94.1	95.3
	OPP (% of Total)	45.5	42.4	41.6	41.6	40.9
	Private Insurance (% Total)	45.5	48.3	50.6	52.5	54.3
Eye Care	Private Expenditure (% of Total)	84.7	83.9	89.1	91.1	91.7
	OPP (% of Total)	74.0	71.7	72.2	72.3	75.5
	Private Insurance (% Total)	10.7	12.3	16.9	18.9	16.2
Other Practitioners	Private Expenditure (% of Total)	58.5	58.7	64.7	67.4	76.7
	OPP (% of Total)	38.9	39.5	40.1	39.4	56.0
	Private Insurance (% Total)	19.7	19.2	24.7	28.0	28.4

Note: Prescription drugs as reported here do not include drugs administered in hospitals. http://secure.cihi.ca/cihiweb/dispPage.jsp?cw_page=statistics_nhex_definitions_e.

Source: Data supplied to author by CIHI courtesy of Daniela Panait. Available from author upon request.

Limited drift within existing public programs

The failure to expand public coverage has created space for a limited amount of policy drift, with private insurance benefits coming to represent a larger portion of total health expenditures. This drift has primarily resulted from the growing significance of pharmaceuticals. From the early 1970s until the mid-1980s, spending on pharmaceuticals remained constant at approximately 10 percent of total health expenditures; and during this period there were significant increases in the proportion of expenditures borne by public (primarily nonuniversal) programs. From 1985 to 2005, however, the proportion of total health expenditures devoted to pharmaceuticals more than doubled to over 20 percent, but related public spending grew more slowly. As a result, the overall growth in pharmaceuticals in health spending has had an effect on the overall public-private expenditure mix. A second trend has been in the mix of private spending itself: private insurance benefits have come to make up a larger proportion of prescription drug expenditures relative to private out-of-pocket expenditures (see Table 4.1).

The overall result of these two trends has been the increasing significance of private insurance expenditures in the overall health system (see Figure 4.3). Although out-of-pocket payments remained at exactly the same level between 1988 and 2005, the proportion of total health expenditures comprised by private insurance payments almost doubled from

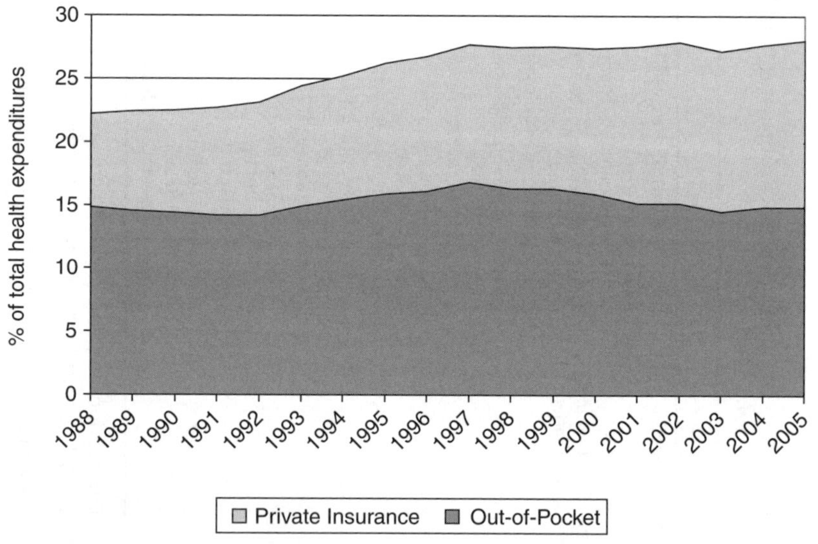

Figure 4.3   Sources of private expenditure (as % of total health expenditures), 1988–2005

Source: OECD (2006).

1988 (7.4 percent) to 2005 (13.2 percent). In the absence of the expansion of public programs, this represents a modest policy drift and a modest privatization of risk.

Subterranean policy change and policy conversion

Subterranean policy change both in terms of public regulation and subsidization of private benefits has also been limited. Provincial regulation of private insurance has not dramatically altered to encourage greater private insurance coverage. The Canada Health Act does not actually require provinces to prohibit third-party insurance for otherwise publicly insured services. Nevertheless, all provinces regulate private benefits to a much more stringent degree than is actually required under the CHA, and private benefits have, in most cases, not developed even to the degree allowed by provincial legislation. To be sure, the public-private boundary in health insurance has been actively contested and the federal and provincial governments have been the central antagonists in these battles. Intense politics and considerable intergovernmental brinkmanship have revolved around the issue. However, the challenge has not been generated by the existence of private benefits. Rather, most of these issues have revolved around the use of private financing to access publicly insured services (for example, user fees or extra-billing). There has been much less contestation over the role of third-party insurance coverage for otherwise publicly insured benefits.

One exception to this pattern emerged in 2005, when the Supreme Court challenged Quebec's blanket ban on private insurance for publicly insured services.[6] The Supreme Court highlighted a gap in the Canadian system caused by the combination of regulatory prohibitions on private insurance in areas ostensibly covered by public insurance on one side, and insufficient public provision, often resulting from funding restraints and retrenchment, on the other. The result is the potential for gaps between what is publicly provided and what private insurance is allowed to cover. These gaps manifest themselves in terms of unmet needs or private out-of-pocket expenditures that are covered by neither public nor private benefits—a potentially important form of subterranean policy change.[7]

In response to the court's judgment, Québec accepted a greater role for private insurance for a limited number of procedures such as joint replacement, cataract surgery, and cardiac care. However, the Québec response seems unlikely to presage a wholesale shift in the role of private benefits for several reasons. First, third-party insurance is only allowed for these procedures. Second, the public health sector is trying to improve its performance by adopting a maximum wait-time guarantee for these procedures, reducing the appeal of private insurance. Finally, the new Québec law requires that private insurance cover the full cost of the entire medical intervention, allowing no scope for public benefits to subsidize private provision.

The potential for subterranean policy shifts through changes in tax policy is also circumscribed due to the limited overall role of private insurance in the Canadian health care system. There simply is no large hidden welfare state underwriting private health insurance coverage in stark contrast with the US example (for the latter, see Howard 1997; 2006). The minimal public subsidization of private benefits through tax expenditures that does occur takes two forms: the exemption of premiums for employer-provided health insurance from the calculation of personal income tax; and a personal income tax deduction for private insurance premiums and medical expenses. In the latter case, these costs must comprise 3 percent of net income to qualify for tax exemption, and comparatively few Canadians benefit from the provision.[8] Moreover, these tax exemptions for health care have also not been liberalized. Indeed, they were reduced in the mid-1960s and the mid-1980s.[9]

Despite the fact that tax provisions have not been liberalized, tax expenditures have been growing as a proportion of total health expenditures because private insurance expenditures have grown. (Figure 4.4 sets

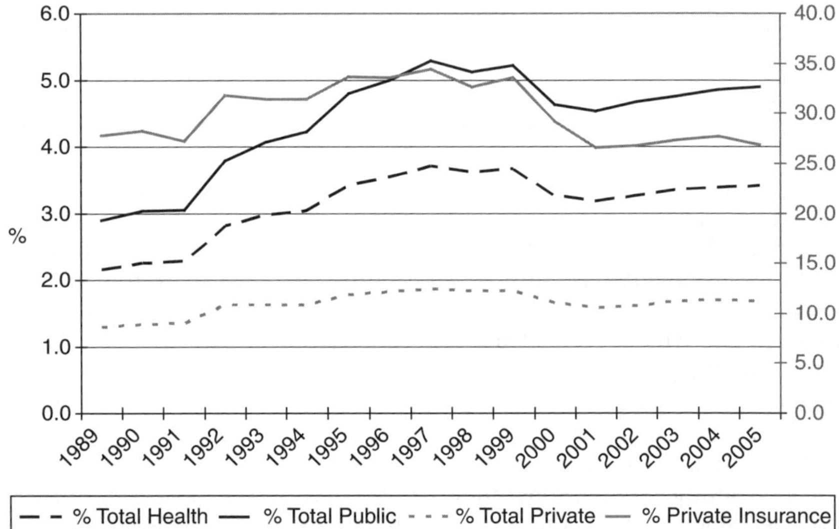

Figure 4.4   Tax expenditures as percent of total health expenditures, total public health expenditures, total private health expenditures and private insurance expenditures, Canada, 1989–2005

Note: Provincial tax expenditure calculated by author.

Source: Department of Finance. *Tax Expenditures*. Ottawa: Department of Finance (various years); Canadian Institute for Health Information, online database, OECD (2006) for total private health insurance expenditures.

out the general pattern.) Tax expenditures relative to private insurance expenditures were actually slightly lower in the mid-2000s than they were in the early 1990s. However, due to growth in overall private insurance expenditures, tax expenditures increased from just under 3 percent of direct public outlays to nearly 5 percent in 2005. Nevertheless, tax expenditures remain small relative to the overall system. In 2005, tax expenditures comprised roughly 3.5 percent of total health expenditures. Because their scope is limited, policy conversion or drift in tax expenditures is unlikely to lead to significant change in the overall public role in the provision of health benefits.

Summary: limits on the privatization of risk

Public benefit programs have been impressively resistant to retrenchment efforts. Governments have struggled to ratchet down the rate of growth in public expenditures. But they have not widely delisted services (which has occurred only at the margins), changed the eligibility criteria away from universal access, or expanded the role of extra-billing or user fees. The basic pattern has been expenditure restraint within the existing policy model. Thus, the privatization of risk has been limited. There has not, for example, been any sustained trend toward higher levels of out-of-pocket payments over the past 30 years.

There are undoubtedly conflicting pressures on the future balance between private and public benefits. On one side, the growth of prescription drugs as a tool of medical interventions and as an expensive component of the health care system will generate greater pressure to expand public coverage. On the other side, federal-provincial fiscal arrangements have created counter pressures. Although health care is not consuming a dramatically greater proportion of GDP than in the past, the increased costs have been primarily borne at the provincial level due to the idiosyncrasies of federal-provincial fiscal arrangements (Boychuk 2004), generating increasing pressure on provinces to allow a greater privatization of health risk. Similar conflicting pressures surround the gaps in coverage which emerge when provinces simultaneously restrict the provision of health services though budgetary restraint while continuing to prohibit private insurance from filling the gap. How this set of pressures is resolved remains to be seen. Whether the recent reinjection of public funds into provincial health care systems and efforts to reduce wait times will be sufficient to address these demands is not yet clear. If not, there will be significant pressure to allow a greater role for private funding through private insurance.

Despite all of these theoretical possibilities, the striking reality is that the existing system and the current public-private divide have been impressively resistant to change. To this point, a major shift in the balance between private and public benefits does not seem imminent. But if such change does come, it is more likely to represent a case of punctuated equilibrium than steady evolutionary change.

Pensions

Setting the initial public-private divide: preserving space for private benefits

In the early stages of pension politics, a private pension industry barely existed. Private pensions were available to a tiny minority of employees, and those that did exist were "top hat" benefits for senior executives. When the state moved into the pensions field, it entered a largely empty terrain. The first step came in 1926–27, with the introduction of the Old Age Pension (OAP), a means-tested pension of $20 per month for those 70 years of age and older. Full implementation took time. The OAP was a federal-provincial program and provincial adoption took nine years to produce country-wide coverage, with many poorer provinces joining only after 1931 when Ottawa raised its contribution from 50 to 75 percent. By the late 1930s, however, a national system was in place, with reasonably comparable benefits prevailing across the country as a whole (Banting 1987; Orloff 1993).

Despite the smallness of this first step, which targeted only the poorest and oldest, the expansion of private pensions remained slow. A survey in 1938 suggested that less than 10 percent of the labor force enjoyed some form of private pension (Industrial Relations Centre 1938). The terrain was still largely unoccupied in 1951 when the public sector took its second step. A constitutional amendment gave the federal government authority to provide old-age pensions directly to citizens, and the government introduced Old Age Security (OAS), a universal, flat-rate pension of $40 per month paid to all citizens aged 70 and above, funded through general tax revenues.

The final step, which came in the mid-1960s, sparked more intense political conflict. OAS did not fully meet the income-replacement needs of the middle class, which was expanding rapidly in the postwar era. Coverage of the labor force by private pensions expanded during the 1950s and early 1960s, especially after changes in prevailing interpretations of tax regulations provided greater flexibility (Latimer 1964). Figure 4.5 tracks growth in coverage by various forms of private pensions. As many covered individuals had multiple forms of savings, it seems unlikely that the proportion of the labor force with some type of private benefit in 1965 was much greater than a quarter (Bryden 1974). Nevertheless, a private pensions industry was emerging, and the days of uncontested state action were over.

Returning to power at the federal level in 1963, the Liberal Party was committed to the introduction of a contributory pension plan, which would be layered on top of the universal Old Age Security. Their proposal was supported by organized labor, a wide range of social groups, and the social-democratic New Democratic Party, whose support the government needed

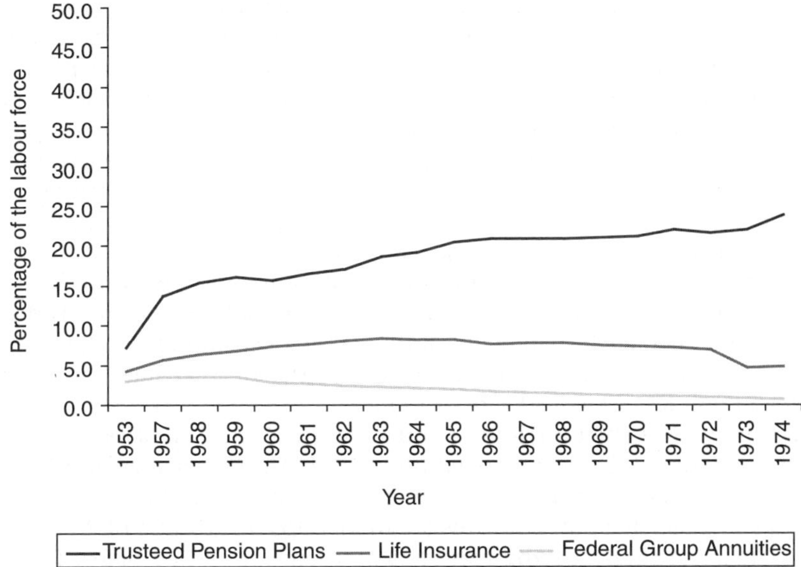

Figure 4.5 Members of private pension plans as percent of labor force, 1953, 1957–77

Source: Data on memberships in private plans from Dominion Bureau of Statistics (1952–1974); data on the labor force from Urqhart (1965) and Statistics Canada (1980).

to maintain a majority in the House of Commons. However, the federal government also faced two powerful challenges. First was opposition from a conservative alliance consisting of the business community and its provincial allies. Business opposition was led by representatives of the financial and insurance industries, but received substantial support from general business organizations (Banting 1985; Bryden 1974). Throughout this battle, industry's most important ally was the government of Ontario, which was governed at the time by the Conservatives. The province was also home to the headquarters of much of the insurance and finance industry, and industry representatives were deeply involved in Ontario's planning. In contrast to the Liberal's emphasis on a public program, Ontario advocated a private-sector strategy, which would require employers above a certain size to provide occupational pensions, massively expanding the role of the private sector in the retirement income system.

As full contributory public pensions required an additional constitutional amendment for which Ontario's support was essential, the province was in a strong position. In the end, however, the provincial government recognized that the federal proposal was popular both with Ontario voters, and accepted that contributory pensions of some sort were inevitable. But the province and the financial industry held out for a limited plan that left ample scope for private pensions and minimized redistribution by relating individual contributions and benefits closely. In addition, the province insisted on a formula governing future changes in the plan which would give the government of Ontario a veto.

The second major challenge came from the province of Quebec, which chose to invoke its constitutional paramountcy in the field and introduce its own contributory plan. Implementing its own pension program not only enhanced the province's role in social policy. It also gave the Quebec government control over pension funds which it would use powerfully in shaping economic development in the province. As a result, the Quebec Pension Plan (QPP) operates in parallel with the Canada Pension Plan (CPP). As we saw earlier, the symbolism of this move was crucial in setting the stage for the later politics of medical care insurance.

The politics of their birth shaped the design of the Canada and Quebec Pension Plans, which began operation in 1966. The C/QPP are contributory programs financed through employer and employee contributions. Benefits are earnings-related but, critically, are limited to a maximum of 25 percent of average earnings, leaving considerable room for private plans. In addition, as a result of the original federal-provincial agreement, changes in the CPP require the consent of the federal government and two-thirds of the provinces representing two-thirds of the population of the country, a requirement which is more demanding than the amending formula for most parts of the Canadian Constitution. Critically, as just noted, the formula gives the province of Ontario a veto.

The introduction of the new contributory plans was accompanied by related enrichment of public pensions. Critics of the contributory pensions argued that they would do nothing for those already retired or about to retire, and the federal government responded in two ways. First, the universal OAS was increased, the benefit was indexed for future changes in the cost of living, and the age of eligibility was reduced in a series of steps from 70 to 65. Second, the government introduced the Guaranteed Income Supplement (GIS), an income-tested supplement that is added to the OAS payment for elderly citizens with middle- and low-incomes. The GIS supplement is, in effect, a guaranteed income for the elderly with a 50 percent tax-back rate: the benefit is reduced by 50 cents for every dollar of other income beyond the OAS itself. At the time, the GIS was widely seen as a provisional program, which would naturally wither away as the contributory C/QPP matured and started to pay significant pensions. As we shall see, however, its introduction was to have substantial, unexpected consequences for the public-private balance in retirement income.

Thus, despite the first mover status enjoyed by the public sector for almost half a century, the pension system that emerged was relatively "liberal" in nature. In combination, the universal OAS and the maximum contributory benefit from the C/QPP replace approximately 40 percent of earnings for the average wage earner, a modest amount by European standards (Béland and Myles 2005). Consistent with this liberal ethos, the strength of the Canadian system is at the bottom of the income distribution, and the replacement rate is much higher for low-income workers (Brown and Ip 2000). The primary constraint on the development of public benefits was first posed by the complications inherent in the Canadian constitutional division of powers, and only later did the presence of private benefits expand to rival public benefits.

The evolving public-private divide: conversion, drift and risk

The evolution of pensions in Canada since the mid-1960s has more closely followed the incrementalist patterns evident in health insurance and pensions in the United States. Efforts at bold reform of public pensions in Canada have been regularly defeated, and change in the field has tended to be evolutionary. Although the balance between the private and public sectors has changed little, incremental shifts have had important and some-times unexpected consequences.

Stability in contributory public programs

In the years following the introduction of the C/QPP, the public plans and the private sector settled into a relatively stable equilibrium. Private plans adapted to the introduction of the C/QPP fairly speedily. Existing plans moved to a two-tier formula, with a lower level of private benefits and con-tributions up to the C/QPP ceiling and a higher level of benefits and contri-butions on earnings over the ceiling. Thereafter, the public and private sec-tors fell into self-sustaining balance. On one side, the introduction of the public plans slowed the formation of new private ones. As the trend line in Figure 4.5 confirms, the expansion of coverage in the early 1960s stalled with the introduction of the C/QPP in 1966 and stagnated for the following decade. On the other side, the existence of private plans also constrained efforts to expand the role of the public programs, and the two sectors have remained locked in a relatively stable embrace

The constraints on the dramatic *expansion* of public programs became clear during the Great Pensions Debate of the 1970s and early 1980s (Banting 1985). In 1975, the Canadian Labour Congress, supported by pensioners groups, women's organizations, and social bodies such as the National Welfare Council, launched a campaign for such an expansion. Their pro-posal would have ensured that, in combination, the universal OAS and the contributory C/QPP would provide 75 percent of preretirement earnings for average income earners. The main element of the proposal called for a dou-bling of the C/QPP benefit levels, making it the basic retirement income vehicle for the bulk of the population.

The private sector spearheaded the opposition to the proposal. All segments of the private sector—businesses which sponsor plans and the financial industry which manages them—united in the fight, and proposed an alternative strategy based on improvements in private pensions. Initially, they had difficulty in finding consensus on a specific package of reforms. The financial institutions strongly supported the extension and enrichment of private plans, making them compulsory if necessary. Not surprisingly, however, the businesses that actually contribute to such plans were much more cautious about increasing their pension costs. Agreement was further complicated by the large gulf between large and small business over such critical issues of the day, such as mandatory coverage and inflation protection.

These difficulties, however, were more than offset by powerful reinforcement from the veto-wielding government of Ontario. The formidable alliance of business and Ontario was able to stall the expansionist campaign during the 1970s. By the 1980s, economic recession and an increasingly conservative political climate led all governments to oppose expansion of the C/QPP. In August 1982, nine business organizations agreed to a common package of marginal improvements in existing pension plans: earlier vesting, compulsory spousal benefits, and improvements in portability. In its 1984 budget, the federal government explicitly deferred expansion of public programs and settled for a similar set of improvements in private plans and tax changes designed to improve personal retirement savings through Registered Retirement Savings Plans (RRSPs). The outcome of the Great Pensions Debate thus stabilized the role of the private sector.

The next phase of the political cycle in the late 1980s and 1990s revealed equally powerful constraints on dramatic *retrenchment* in public programs. In keeping with the theory of the "new politics" of the welfare state, public expectations and electoral sensitivity protected the OAS-GIS program (Pierson 1996). In 1985, the newly elected Conservative government proposed partial deindexation of the universal OAS, but backed down quickly in the face of angry voters. A decade later, the Liberal government proposed to replace the OAS and GIS with a new, enlarged income-tested program called the Seniors Benefit, but the proposal faced attacks from both the left and the right. From the left, women's groups and the social-democratic New Democratic Party objected to the family based income-test for the proposed program; in contrast to the universal OAS, many women's payment from the Seniors Benefit would have been reduced or terminated in light of their husband's income. From the right, investment brokers worried about eroding the incentive to save for retirement through a larger income-tested benefit. Not surprisingly, the proposal was dropped. The only change that survived was a more stealthy measure to "claw back" OAS from high-income seniors through the tax system. However, the measure affects barely 5 percent of seniors (Battle 2001).

Contributory pensions were protected by the same electoral sensitivities, reinforced by the consensus-driven, incremental logic inherent in joint federal-provincial control (Banting 2005). During the 1990s, actuarial reports raised questions about the long-term financial status of the C/QPP, triggering extensive rhetoric about unsustainability in the media and political debate. However, intergovernmental politics took substantial cuts off the table. The province of Québec announced that it would not consider significant reductions in benefits, a position supported by NDP governments in Saskatchewan and British Columbia. In the end, the federal and provincial governments agreed to accelerate increases in contribution rates from 5.5 to 9.9 percent of earnings over a ten-year period, and to invest the additional revenues in the equities market. There was a modest trimming of some benefits, especially disability benefits, and the two NDP governments refused to sign the final agreement. But governments did not even try for more dramatic retrenchment, such as an increase in the retirement age, and the final changes largely stabilized the role of contributory pensions in the retirement income system (Béland and Myles 2005).

Although both major expansion and major retrenchment of public benefit programs were both off the table, the pension sector has seen evolutionary changes through policy conversion, policy drift, and subterranean policy shifts.

Policy conversion and the GIS

The income-tested benefit, the GIS, has undergone a process of unintended policy conversion. During the 1960s and 1970s, political parties regularly competed for seniors' votes with pension promises. However, the provincial vetoes governing contributory plan deflected these expansionist pressures away from the C/QPP toward the exclusively federal GIS. In 1972, both the OAS and the GIS were indexed to increases in consumer prices. But promises for additional boosts in the GIS became a central feature of electoral politics, with increases preceding or following virtually every federal election. Moreover, when automatic indexing of the OAS was suspended for several years in the mid-1980s, the government maintained full indexing of the GIS. As a result, the GIS rose steadily in real terms. By the mid-1980s, the maximum GIS payment was considerably larger than the OAS payment which it was meant to supplement, and its reach crept further up the income scale.[10] At that time, close to half of retired Canadians were receiving a full or partial payment. The role of such income-tested benefits was further extended in the 1980s with the introduction of the Spouses Allowance for the spouses aged between 60 and 65 years who were married to retired individuals.

This development reinforced the existing public-private divide, constraining change in both sectors. On the private side, the rise in the real value of the GIS generates a disincentive for modest-income earners to save for retirement, as the value of any additional private retirement income would be partially offset by reductions in the GIS payment they otherwise would receive. As we have seen, this disincentive effect explains why the financial industry opposed the proposal for an even larger income-tested benefit, the Seniors Benefit, in the late 1990s. As a result, the GIS forestalls any effort to revive the idea of mandatory private pensions, which Ontario favored in the 1960s. However, the same logic applies on the public side. The benefit of a significant increase in the C/QPP system, such as that advocated by organized labor in the 1970s, would be mitigated by reductions in the GIS benefit received by many of the very people organized labor worries about. In effect, the GIS creates a political wall surrounding low- and modest-income Canadians, reducing both the incentives for private savings and the benefits of an expansion to the C/QPP for these groups.

Subterranean policy and private benefits

Although incremental change led to an unplanned outcome in the case of the GIS, successive federal governments since the 1980s have deliberately tried to encourage the growth of private retirement benefits through regulatory and tax policies. In contrast to debates over changes to major public pension programs, which mobilize social movements and the wider public, debates over the regulation of private plans tend to be an elite conversation between industry representatives and public officials, with media coverage limited to the business pages of major newspapers. Although significant changes in regulatory legislation are normally debated publicly within this community, the ongoing process of interpreting and refining regulations made pursuant to legislation tends to be a largely "subterranean" process, to borrow Hacker's apt phrase (Hacker 2002: 43).

Changes in regulations have certainly led to improvements in pension standards. With the exception of a small number of industries falling under federal jurisdiction, regulation of private pensions is a provincial responsibility. The province of Ontario led the way in introducing pension standards as part of its larger campaign to enhance the role of the private sector during the 1960s. Its Pension Benefits Act of 1965 imposed minimum requirements for vesting and locking-in of pension benefits, and set rules governing the funding and investment of pension funds. Legislation soon followed in other major provinces. In the words of an experienced commentator, "the pioneer days were over" (Cloward 1969: 4). By the end of the decade, legislation covered 90 percent of pension plan members in the country, and refinements in technical regulations have occurred in successive waves since then.

Governments have also relied on tax policy to stimulate the expansion of private pensions and personal retirement savings, and the process here is even more secretive. In the Canadian policy process, changes in tax provisions flow from a particularly closed process. Consultations are limited and highly formalized; policy development is dominated by the Department of Finance; decisions are made by the Minister of Finance and the Prime Minister, usually with little discussion even with other members of cabinet; changes are announced in the Minister's annual budget statement; and in a majority parliament the enabling legislation is passed without amendment. The contrast to the politics of changing major public pensions is dramatic.

Tax support flowing through this process has been important to both occupational plans, known as Registered Pension Plans (RPPs), and personal tax-assisted retirement savings accounts, known as RRSPs. As early as 1917, employer contributions to pension plans became deductible as business expenses, and deductibility was extended to employee contributions in 1919 (Statistics Canada 2004). In 1957, RRSPs were introduced, initially to provide a parallel tax-assisted vehicle for self-employed people to save for their retirement. Changes in these provisions, especially increases in the ceiling on the total amount individuals can contribute to their RPP and/or RRSP each year, have taken place regularly.[11] In 1991, the government restructured its approach in order to equalize treatment of the two private vehicles. As Table 4.2 indicates, however, the reforms also significantly increased the combined deduction limit. The initial 1991 proposal also planned to raise the ceiling in a series of steps to $15,500 by 1995 and then introduce automatic indexation of the ceiling (Cloward 1991: 143). The intense fiscal pressures generated by the federal government's massive debt in the mid-1990s set back the schedule, and the ceiling was actually lowered and frozen for six years. But with the return of federal financial health, the original policy reasserted itself in 2003, and

Table 4.2 Deduction limits for RPPs and RRSPs, 1990–2005

	RPPs		RRSPs
1990	7,000*	1990	7,500
1991–92	12,500	1991	11,500
1993	13,500	1992–03	12,500
1994	14,500	1994	13,500
1995	15,500	1995	14,500
1996–02	13,500	1996–03	13,500
2003	14,500	2004	14,400
2004	15,500	2005	15,500
2005	indexed	2006	indexed

Note: *Until 1990, the deduction limit for RPPs was split equally between employer and employees at $3,500 each. Beginning in 1991, the equal division was eliminated.

Source: Statistics Canada (2004).

the ceiling was indexed to changes in average wages and salaries in 2005. In addition, changes to RRSPs allowed recipients to use the funds for a wider range of purposes. In the aftermath of the increase in 1991, contributions to RRSPs in particular grew significantly as a proportion of earnings. These tax provisions provide a major subsidy to the sector, and the resulting tax expenditures represent a significant and rapidly growing public commitment, as Figure 4.6 confirms.[12]

However, enhanced subsidization has had limited success in expanding the overall role of private retirement vehicles, especially in recent years. As Table 4.3 records, overall membership in private pension plans (RPPs) has been in decline since the late 1970s, especially in the case of men. Women's participation followed a separate trajectory, converging to the male rate in the 1980s, but then stagnating and declining gently thereafter. So far, the decline in RPPs has largely been offset by the growth in contributions to RRSPs. But the overall role of private sector has been stable.

Thus, the main story is the stability in the overall balance between private and public benefits in the retirement income system. One indicator of this is the sources from which elderly Canadians derive their income. The maturation of both public and private programs set in place in the postwar era has changed the flows *within* each sector, as Figure 4.7 confirms. But

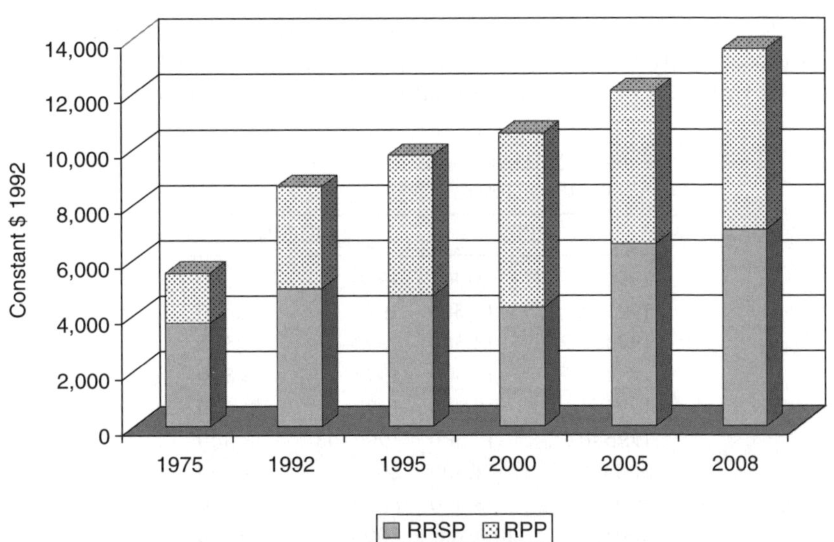

Figure 4.6 Tax expenditures; deductions for contributions to registered pension plans and registered retirement savings plans, 1975–2008, millions of dollars, constant 1992 dollars

Source: Department of Finance (various years).

Table 4.3 Proportion of the labor force covered by a Registered Pension Plan (RPP), 1979–2003

Year	All %	Men %	Women %
1979	38.3	43.5	30.2
1985	35.3	39.9	29.0
1991	36.7	38.9	34.0
1997	33.5	34.1	32.7
2003	32.7	32.3	33.2

Source: Statistics Canada (2004).

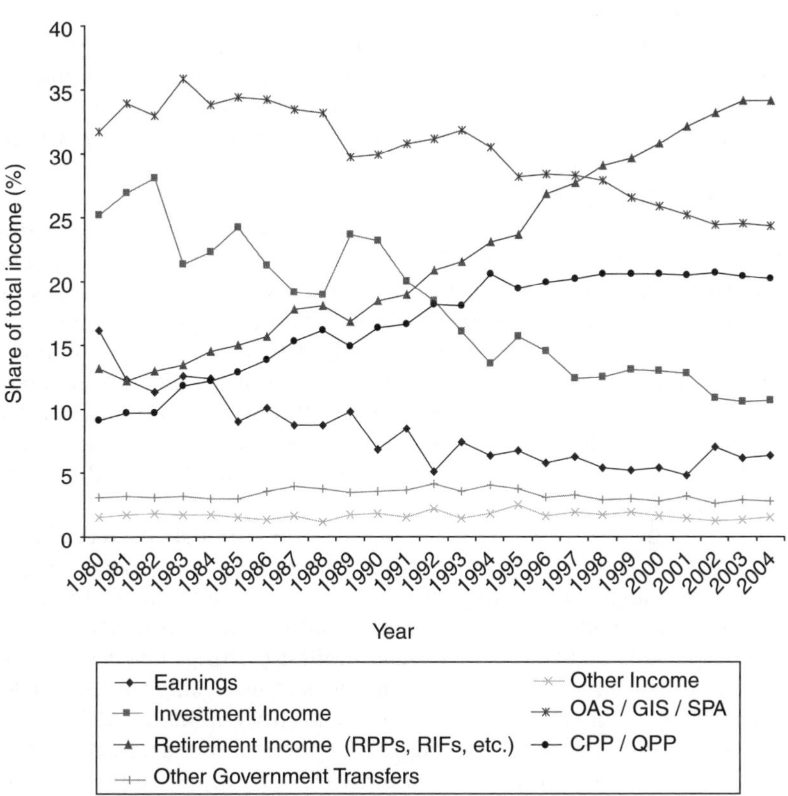

Figure 4.7   Income sources of the elderly, as a percent of total income, 1980–2004
Source: Based on data from Statistics Canada CANSIM, Table 202-0407.

the division of the overall retirement income system *between* the public and private sectors remains equal. The C/QPP, which paid out its first pensions in 1976, has raised its share to about 20 percent of all retirement earnings; in combination with the OAS/GIS/SPA, public programs provided about 45 percent in 2005. Private instruments, RPPs and RRSPs,[13] have risen to be the largest single source of income at almost 35 percent. When combined with other investment income, private instruments also represent about 45 percent of total income.

Conversion, policy drift, and the privatization of risk

This overall pattern of stability obscures conversions *within* the private sector, which are generating a slow but clear trend toward the privatization of risk. One conversion is drift from private pensions to individual savings. As we have just seen, the decline in RPPs has been largely offset at the aggregate level by the growth in RRSPs. However, RRSPs lack the protection of collective pooling of risk inherent in pension plans. Individuals relying on RRSPs bear the risk of poor investment returns, as well as the uncertainty about the strength of the annuity that can be purchased at the time of retirement. Increasing life expectancy is deepening these risks: on one hand, greater longevity increases the costs of life annuities; on the other hand, where retirement savings are not annuitized, longevity increases the chances of an individual outliving his or her savings.

A second conversion is a shift among private pensions from defined benefit (DB) plans to defined-contribution (DC) or money-purchase plans. DB plans promise a specific pension benefit for each year of service, and normally any shortfall in the funds necessary to finance the promised benefits is the responsibility of the plan sponsor. Under DC plans, the contribution rates of the employer and employee are defined, but the benefit is determined only at retirement, based on an annuity that may be purchased with the accumulated contributions and associated investment income. Figure 4.8 suggests that the drift to DC plans is relatively moderate, but the direction of change is clear.

These two conversions represent a privatization of risk in retirement income, with the burden being highly concentrated in Canada. High-income earners have the resources to secure their retirement years; low-income Canadians benefit from the redistributive strength of the public programs, especially the GIS. It is those at modest earnings levels that face the greatest vulnerabilities. Modest-income earners, especially those who do not have an RPP, are at the greatest risk of not saving enough in RRSPs.

This privatization of risk has not triggered a public response. In combination, these shifts in the private sector and the lack of a robust response from the public sector represent a classic instance of policy drift. The ethos of social insurance and the collective pooling of risk that characterized postwar thinking about social policy have faded, and Canadian policymakers seem

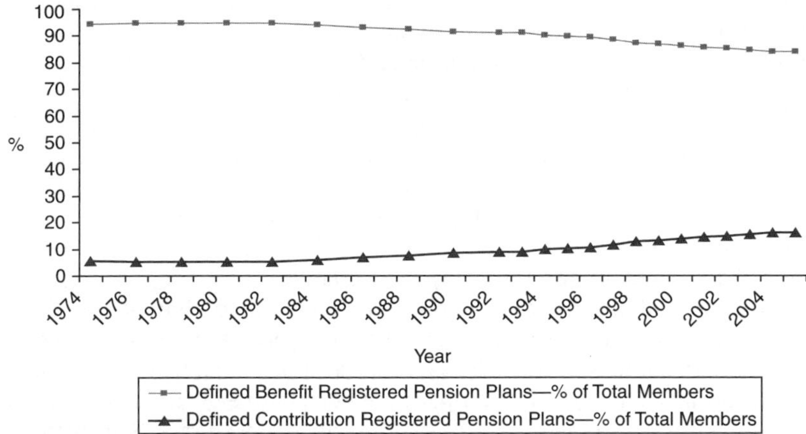

Figure 4.8   Defined contribution versus defined benefit pension plans, number of members as percent of total plan membership

Source: Statistics Canada, CANSIM Table 280–0012.

content with a world in which individuals bear the growing risks inherent in a turbulent global economy. This approach has never been formally announced in a major policy statement, or introduced as a new policy initiative. Rather the shift has emerged quietly through an evolutionary process marked by policy conversion and drift.

Conclusions

Canadian experience in health insurance and pensions presents a paradox. In the field of health insurance, private benefits were well developed before public benefits emerged. Nevertheless, the state simply displaced private benefits, establishing a virtual public monopoly in core hospital and medical services, in some cases taking over private organizations to deliver the new public programs, and relegating private benefits to a supplementary role. In the case of pensions, in contrast, the state had the field largely to itself for at least four decades. Yet private pensions eventually expanded to become an equal pillar in the retirement income sector. Hence the Canadian paradox: public benefits dominate in the field where private benefits had already emerged strongly before the state entered; and private benefits expanded most in the field in which the public sector was unrivalled for close to half a century.

These contrasting starting points shaped the developmental pattern of the two fields, setting them off on different trajectories. The pension field, where private benefits play a larger role, has seen significant evolutionary change. Despite impressive stability in the major public programs, the scope of private benefits has created room for subterranean policy shifts and policy drift. Although these processes of evolutionary change have actually reinforced the balance *between* the public and private sectors in the retirement income system, they are redistributing risk *within* the private sector in worrying ways. Health insurance, however, presents a different pattern. The dominance of public programs has limited the scope for subterranean policy change and policy conversion. Overall, health insurance benefits have been remarkably stable, following a pattern of "punctuated equilibrium" in which the major changes of the 1950s and 1960s have been followed by a long period of lock-in and relatively little change.

Clearly, Canadian experience stands in contrast to that of the United States, where preexisting private benefits did constrain the expansion of public benefits, and both health insurance and pensions have been marked by evolutionary change. The comparative perspective on the two countries generates a number of qualifications about the role of the public-private divide in social policy.

First, strong preexisting private benefits do not always constrain public benefits. The introduction of hospital insurance in Canada demonstrates that preexisting private benefits can actually spur rather than limit the expansion of public programs. Of course, the Canadian history also reveals instances when the existence of private benefits did constrain the expansion of public benefits. But whether private benefits stimulated or constrained public action was not determined by the nature of the relationship between public and private benefits, independently of the larger institutional and political context in which they operate. Politics and context could trump, and in the Canadian case, dynamics embedded in the federal system were critical. During the battle over the introduction of medicare in the 1960s, the three conservative provinces whose populations had strong preexisting private coverage fought hard against universal public insurance, but they lost. Their concerns were washed away by broader political realities. In the end, the federal government was driven by the interaction between health and pension policy and the imperative to use health insurance as a mechanism of nation-building.

Second, Canadian experience reminds us that there are multiple constraints on the expansion of public benefits, and we should be careful about over-emphasizing the role of private benefits. In the case of pensions, the constraining effects of federalism were considerable even where public programs faced a relatively open terrain. That powerful constraints existed even in the absence of private benefits serves as a reminder that other constraints may be at work in cases where private benefits do exist. In the case of health insurance, the failure to expand coverage to include newer and expanding medical needs cannot be laid exclusively at the door of the private sector. That failure flowed more directly from a history of fiscal pressure on Canadian governments and the peculiarities of federal-provincial fiscal relations. Attributing the limited development of public benefits primarily to the existence of private benefits would seriously overestimate their effects.

Third, the public and private sectors are not always locked in a competitive struggle to occupy policy terrain. The Canadian case highlights the emergence of medical gaps, where both the state and the private sector tread with caution. Neither governments nor private insurers are moving strongly to meet the need for long-term care insurance. Similarly, the weakening of public benefits, in the form of lengthening waiting times, has so far not triggered an aggressive movement of private insurers into the core hospital and medical care sectors. The existence of such gaps is a reminder that the politics of social policy are shaped by factors beyond the public-private divide.

Finally, Canadian experience adds to our understanding of evolutionary processes of change. Hacker draws on US experience to emphasize the importance of policy drift, policy conversion, and subterranean policy shifts, and correctly suggests that these phenomena have often been overlooked in other national contexts (2004: 244). However, the contrast between health insurance and pensions in Canada suggests that it is precisely where private benefits are more central—as in pensions in Canada and both health insurance and pensions in the United States—that one would expect the high levels of drift, conversion and subterranean shift. Rather than being endemic in all welfare states, the degree of policy drift which Hacker discovers in the United States may be a result of its own distinctive features. In Canada, the more mixed nature of the welfare state results in the more mixed applicability of this model of policy development. Considering the role of private benefits in shaping the development of the public-private divide remains important. In countries and policy areas where private benefits play a substantial role, there is more scope for evolutionary processes. But in countries and policy areas where public programs strongly dominate, shifts in public benefits are likely to remain the primary driver of social policy change, with punctuated equilibrium the most likely pattern of development.

Notes

1. Although Frost was philosophically predisposed toward private market options, he was particularly inimical to health insurance carriers after two of his own personal health insurance policies were cancelled. See Taylor (1978, esp. 154).
2. The following draws from Taylor (1978: 110–24).
3. These factors mattered less in Saskatchewan because of its small size and strong municipal system which could be used to collect premiums.
4. 'Opting out' of established federal programs and running separate provincially defined programs was an option which the federal Liberal Party had espoused while in opposition in the early 1960s.
5. Penalties for provincial breach of the five national principles (universality, comprehensiveness, accessibility, portability, and public administration) are

discretionary. Although there have been numerous penalties levied under the nondiscretionary clauses related to user fees and extra-billing, no province to date has been penalized for breach of any of the five principles even though there have been violations by individual provinces.
6. *Chaoulli v. Quebec* (Attorney General), [2005] 1 S.C.R. 791, 2005 SCC 35.
7. This is the basic issue addressed in *Chaoulli v. Attorney General (Québec)*.
8. For example, only 10 percent of Canadian tax-filers claim the medical expenses credit (see Smart and Stabile 2005: 349). Smart and Stabile estimate that 26 percent of higher-income filers (over $50,000) are eligible for the medical tax credit with only 6 percent actually claiming it (2005: 363).
9. Unfortunately, the value of tax expenditures associated with the nontaxation of premiums for employer-provided insurance and the medical expenses tax credit are not available on a reliably comparable basis prior to the late 1980s.
10. In 2002, for example, the monthly OAS payment was $442.66 and the maximum GIS for a single person was $526.08.
11. For details of the changes in the deduction limits for both RPPs and RRSPs, see Statistics Canada 2004: 47–50 and 83–4.
12. In part, the tax treatment of RPPs and RRSPs can be thought of as a tax deferral device, as the income is taxed at the time of withdrawal from the plan. However, beneficiaries' tax rates are normally lower during retirement and considerable tax assistance still results.
13. RRSPs are converted into Registered Income Funds (RIFs) when they begin to pay out benefits.

References

Banting, Keith. 1985. "Institutional Conservatism: Federalism and Pensions." In J. S. Ismael (ed.), *Canadian Social Welfare Policy: Federal and Provincial Dimensions*. Montreal: McGill-Queen's University Press.

Banting, Keith. 1987. *The Welfare State and Canadian Federalism* (Second Edition). Montreal: McGill-Queen's University Press.

Banting, Keith. 2005. "Canada: Nation-Building in a Federal Welfare State." In Herbert Obinger, Stephan Leibfried, and Frank G. Castles (eds), *Federalism and the Welfare State: New World and European Experiences*. Cambridge: Cambridge University Press.

Battle, Ken. 2001. "Relentless Incrementalism: Deconstructing and Reconstructing Canadian Income Security." In Keith Banting, Andrew Sharpe, and France St-Hilaire (eds), *Review of Economic Performance and Social Progress: The Longest Decade: Canada in the 1990s*. Montreal: Institute for Research on Public Policy.

Béland, Daniel and Jacob S. Hacker. 2004. "Ideas, Private Institutions and American Welfare State 'Exceptionalism': The Case of Health and Old-Age Insurance, 1915–1965." *International Journal of Social Welfare* 13: 42–54.

Béland, Daniel and John Myles. 2005. "Stasis Amidst Change: Canadian Pension Reform in an Age of Retrenchment." In Giuliano Bonoli and Toshimitsu Shinkawa (eds), *Ageing and Pension Reform Around the World: Evidence from Eleven Countries*. Cheltenham: Edward Elgar.

Boychuk, Gerard W. 2002. "Federal Spending in Health … Why Here? Why Now?" In G. Bruce Doern (ed.), *How Ottawa Spends 2002–2003: The Security Aftermath and National Priorities*: 121–36. Don Mills: Oxford University Press.

Boychuk, Gerard W. 2003. "The Federal Role in Health Care Reform: Legacy or Limbo?" In G. Bruce Doern (ed.), *How Ottawa Spends 2003–2004: The Legacy Agenda*: 89–104. Don Mills: Oxford University Press.

Boychuk, Gerard W. 2004. "The Changing Economic and Political Environment." In Greg Marchildon, Tom McIntosh, and Pierre-Gerlier Forest (eds), *The Fiscal Sustainability of Health Care in Canada*: 320–39. Toronto: University of Toronto Press.

Boychuk, Gerard W. 2005. "How Ottawa Gambles: Rolling the Dice and the Politics of Health Care Reform in 2004." In G. Bruce Doern (ed.), *How Ottawa Spends, 2005/6: Mandate Change in the Paul Martin Era*: 41–57. Kingston: McGill-Queen's University Press.

Boychuk, Gerard W. 2006. "The Chrétien Non-Legacy: The Federal Role in Health Care Ten Years On, 1993–2003." In Steve Patten and Lois Harder (eds), *The Chrétien Legacy*: 234–54. Kingston and Montreal: McGill-Queen's University Press.

Boychuk, Gerard W. 2007. "Patience!...Wait Time Guarantees: Harper and Health Care." In Bruce G. Doern (ed.), *How Ottawa Spends, 2007/8*. Kingston and Montreal: McGill-Queen's University Press.

Brown, Robert and Jeffrey Ip. 2000. "Social Security—Adequacy, Equity and Progressiveness: A Review of Criteria Based on Experience in Canada and the United States." *North American Actuarial Journal* 4(1): 1–19.

Bryden, Kenneth. 1974. *Old Age Pensions and Policy-Making in Canada*. Montreal: McGill-Queen's University Press.

Business Council on National Issues. 1982. Testimony before the Ontario Select Committee on Pensions. *Proceedings* (January 21): 23.

Canada National Health and Welfare. 1955. *Health Care in Canada: Expenditures and Sources of Revenue, 1953*. Ottawa: National Health and Welfare.

Canadian Institute for Health Information. 2008. *National Health Expenditure Database*. Retrieved on 25/03/08 from http://secure.cihi.ca/cihiweb/dispPage. jsp?cw_page=spend_nhex_e .

Cloward, Laurence. 1969. "Recent Pension Developments." In National Trust, *A Study of Canadian Pension Plans* (Third Edition). Toronto.

Cloward, Laurence. 1991. *Mercer Handbook of Canadian Pensions and Welfare Plans*. Don Mills: CCH Canadian Limited.

Department of Finance. Various years. *Tax Expenditures*. Ottawa: Department of Finance.

Dominion Bureau of Statistics. 1952–1974. *Trusted Pension Plans in Canada*. Ottawa: Dominion Bureau of Statistics.

Hacker, Jacob S. 2002. *The Divided Welfare State: The Battle over Public and Private Social Benefits in the United States*. Cambridge: Cambridge University Press.

Hacker, Jacob S. 2004. "Privatizing Risk without Privatizing the Welfare States: The Hidden Politics of Social Policy Retrenchment in the United States." *American Political Science Review* 98(2): 243–60.

Howard, Christopher. 1997. *The Hidden Welfare State: Tax Expenditures and Social Policy in the United States*. New Jersey, NJ: Princeton University Press.

Howard, Christopher. 2006. *The Welfare State Nobody Knows: Debunking Myths about US Social Policy*. Princeton, NJ: Princeton University Press.

Industrial Relations Centre. 1938. *Industrial Retirement Plans in Canada*. Kingston: Industrial Relations Centre, Queen's University.

Kingdon, John. 1984. *Agendas, Alternatives and Public Policies*. Boston, MA· Little Brown.

Latimer, William. 1964. "Pension Plans and Income Tax." In Laurence Cloward (ed.), *Pensions in Canada*. Don Mills: CCH Canadian Ltd.

Maioni, Antonia. 1998. *Parting at the Crossroads: The Emergence of Health Insurance in the United States and Canada*. Princeton, NJ: Princeton University Press.

Organisation for Economic Cooperation and Development. 2006. *OECD Health Data 2006* [CD-ROM]. Paris: OECD.

Orloff, Ann. 1993. *The Politics of Pensions: A Comparative Analysis of Britain, Canada, and the United States, 1880–1940*. Madison, WI: University of Wisconsin.

Pierson, Paul. 1996. "The New Politics of the Welfare State." *World Politics* 48(2): 142–79.

Smart, Michael and Mark Stabile. 2005. "Tax Credits, Insurance and the Use of Medical Care." *Canadian Journal of Economics* 38(2): 345–65.

Statistics Canada. 1980. *Historical Statistics in Canada*. Ottawa: Statistics Canada.

Statistics Canada. 2004. *Pension Plans in Canada 2003*. Ottawa: Statistics Canada.

Taylor, Malcolm. 1978. *Health Insurance and Canadian Public Policy: The Seven Decisions that Created the Canadian Health Insurance System and Their Outcomes*. Montreal and Kingston: McGill-Queen's University Press.

Thelen, Kathleen. 2004. *How Institutions Evolve: The Political Economy of Skills in Germany, Britain, the United States and Japan*. Cambridge: Cambridge University Press.

Titmuss, Richard. 1958. *Essays on the "Welfare State"*. London: Allen and Unwin.

Urqhart, M. C. 1965. *Historical Statistics in Canada*. Toronto: Macmillan.

5
New Zealand: The Expansion of the State in a Liberal Welfare Regime

Toni Ashton and Susan St John

Introduction

Internationally, New Zealand and Australia are often coupled together in some kind of an Antipodean version of the British welfare system. Yet, although they may be placed within the same "liberal welfare regime" camp, and both countries share a commonwealth heritage that has informed the development of their welfare states, there are significant differences in policy objectives, policy design, and institutional structures (St John 2004). In contrast to Australia's federal system of government, New Zealand has a unicameral government that, until 1993, was elected via a first-past-the-post electoral system.[1] This system of government proved conducive to extreme policy swings and allowed some unusual experiments to be undertaken in both economic and social policy, including attempts to use private mechanisms to achieve public objectives. Although there is now some evidence of a trend toward convergence in some components of social policy across the two countries (McClelland and St John 2006), New Zealand remains unique and worthy of examination in its own right. Accordingly this chapter focuses primarily on New Zealand in the belief that its particular experience of the public-private dichotomy may be of interest to other countries. Some comparisons are drawn with health and pensions policies in Australia to illustrate the rather different approaches to social policy that have been taken in these neighboring countries.

In the 1980s and 1990s New Zealand pursued neoliberal economic policies that opened up markets to the forces of globalization by removing barriers to trade, liberalizing the financial sector, and deregulating the labor market. The guiding principle was that of economic efficiency, to be attained by freeing the market from interference by the state. By the early 1990s the principles of social security that had given New Zealand a reputation of being "a cradle-to-grave" welfare state had been replaced by maxims of individual responsibility, freedom of choice and welfare "only for the poor."

In this period, which followed the election of a conservative National government, welfare benefits were cut, and user fees were introduced to health, housing and education policies, along with a radical deregulation of the labor market (Boston et al. 1999).

Unlike in Australia, where traditions of collectivism remained strong, the social policy reforms of the early 1990s in New Zealand increased rather than ameliorated inequality and poverty, especially among families (McClelland and St John 2006). By the end of the 1990s there was a clear equity-efficiency imbalance and the newly elected "Third Way" Labour government began a softening of the free-market approach.[2] In particular there were significant policy reversals in state housing, the labor market, the health sector, and accident compensation.

This chapter focuses on the specific changes that occurred in health care and pensions policy during the welfare state reforms and economic transformation of the 1980–2006 period, and the effect that these policy changes had on the roles of the public and private sectors. The general conclusion is that, in a country where economic liberalization has been taken further than most comparable countries, the role of the state has remained surprisingly strong, at least in pensions and health. Moreover, until recently the lines between the public and private sectors have generally remained more clearly defined in New Zealand than in Australia and other countries which have liberal welfare regimes.

Health

A notable feature of health care in New Zealand has been that, in spite of 15 years of almost continuous reorganization and reform—including a period of major restructuring aimed at introducing market solutions into the public health system—the public-private mix in both funding and provision of health services has remained largely unchanged (Ashton et al. 2005; Mays and Devlin 2005). This remarkable endurance of the configuration of the public-private sectors throughout a period of major organizational turbulence is a tribute to the resilience of an institutional framework that first evolved following efforts by the first Labour government in 1938 to establish a fully funded, integrated, national health service. The aim of the government at that time was to provide a wide range of health services free of charge for all residents regardless of their income. The focus was to be on prevention, with general practice services being funded on a capitation basis rather than by fee-for-service (Gauld 2001). The medical profession saw these proposals as a threat to their professional autonomy and vigorously opposed them (Gauld 2001). They were especially opposed to becoming what they regarded as employees of the state, without the freedoms associated with private practice. After a lengthy stand-off between the government and the medical profession, a compromise was struck and a hybrid system emerged in which the public and private sectors operated in tandem, with hospital services being fully publicly funded and publicly provided while general practice services were only partially publicly funded and almost entirely privately provided. The profession retained the right to work in both public and private practice. In the case of general practice, payment of the new subsidies by capitation was rejected in favor of fee-for-service, and general practitioners (GPs) retained the right to charge patients a fee over and above the government subsidy. Patients wishing to pay for their own health services privately out of their own pocket or (later) through private health insurance could do so although they would still be eligible for publicly funded services. These are the broad arrangements that remain in place today.

The neoliberal economic policies that New Zealand pursued during the late 1980s and early 1990s triggered the most far-reaching changes to the public health system since 1938 (Easton 2002; Gauld 2001). The central feature of these reforms was the introduction, in 1993, of a "quasi-market" in which the roles of purchaser and provider were separated in an effort to introduce market-like incentives for efficiency. Four regional public purchasing authorities were established and provided with funds to contract for services from either public or private providers. Although akin to (and possibly influenced by) the internal market reforms that had been introduced in the United Kingdom in 1991, this was in fact an external market in which both public and private providers would compete for funds. Public hospitals were structured as for-profit organizations, charged with a statutory objective "to be as successful and efficient as comparable businesses that are not owned by the Crown" (Health and Disability Services Act 1993: S11d). Although the government retained its role as the dominant funder, a new system of targeted subsidies together with income-related user charges was introduced for patients, now called "clients." This included the rather radical policy of introducing co-payments for services provided in public hospitals in 1992.

The first coalition government (led by the national party which is traditionally conservative) was formed in 1996 following prolonged negotiations by a minority third party (New Zealand First) with each of the two main parties. New Zealand First was opposed to the quasi-market structure. One outcome of this political tussle was therefore a reorientation of the health system away from the ideas of competition and markets, back toward a public service focus. Although the purchaser-provider split was retained, the four regional purchasers were replaced by a single central purchasing agency. The for-profit objective of public hospitals and the competitive tendering for services were replaced by principles of "public service" that had traditionally underpinned the public health system. The user charges for hospitals were also short-lived. Public opposition to these charges was strong and many people simply refused to pay. The co-payments for inpatient services therefore became the first casualty of the reforms: they were abolished in 1993 after only 13 months. The co-payments for outpatient services survived a little longer but they too were eventually abolished in 1997. In the same year, the government increased subsidies for general practitioner (GP) services for children to a level that allowed GPs to provide free consultations for children under six years of age (Mays and Devlin 2005). This marked the beginning of a progressive shift away from the targeted regime back toward universal subsidies for primary health care.

Overall, these efforts to introduce market-based principles and practices into the publicly funded health system during the 1990s proved difficult to implement. Many of the key aspects of the original proposals were not put into place (Finlayson 2001) and, of those that were, a number of adjustments were subsequently made (Gauld 2001). Thus, in spite of the rhetoric of markets, competition and choice, the government remained the dominant funder and public hospitals maintained their regional monopolies throughout this reform period (Mays and Devlin 2005).

In 1999 the preelection campaign of the Labour Party included a renewed commitment to the public health system with a focus on "cooperation, rather than competition" and on "patients, rather than profits" (New Zealand Labour Party 1999). The key feature of the round of reform initiated by the Labour-led coalition government was the decentralization of decision-making to 21 locally elected district health boards (DHBs). These boards own the public hospitals and are responsible for either providing health services through what has become known as their "provider arm," or purchasing services from nongovernment providers. Funded according to a population-based formula, the DHBs are responsible for assessing the needs of the people living within their district and for planning services and allocating health funds accordingly. Their budget covers all personal health services (hospital care, community services, pharmaceuticals, and so on) and also social care for older people.[3] However, the DHBs are by no means autonomous: they operate under strong government control. The government has developed a national health strategy which specifies a set of objectives and priorities for the DHBs and for the public health system overall (King 2000).

Each DHB owns at least one public hospital and most also provide some community-based services (especially community nursing services). Some of the larger DHBs also provide public health services such as health protection and environmental health services. All other services are provided by a range of (for-profit and not-for-profit) private providers. These include self-employed general practitioners (most of who work in a group practice), community-based pharmacies and laboratories, community-based mental health services, physiotherapy and other allied health services, and long-term care. Secondary services are also provided by private specialists and private hospitals. Most of the revenue of these private providers comes from private patients, although DHBs and previous public purchasers may purchase from private providers if they wish. Within the private hospital sector (and also long-term care), the current trend is toward for-profit, corporate ownership, away from not-for-profit, religious organizations.

The sector now has the appearance of relative stability. However, as we shall see, a number of the planned policy changes are likely to have quite profound impacts on the configuration of the public and private sectors in the longer term.

The public health system

In 2004, public funding accounted for 77.2 percent of total health expenditure and 6.6 percent of GDP. Of these public funds, the large majority (87 percent) comes from central taxes. Most of the rest is raised through a compulsory social insurance scheme (Accident Compensation Corporation—ACC) which provides funds for the prevention, treatment, and rehabilitation of accident-related injuries (Ministry of Health 2007).

All residents are eligible for services funded by the public health system. In addition, any nonresidents who have an accident in New Zealand are entitled to medical treatment funded by ACC. Table 5.1 summarizes the level of coverage of public funds, together with any specific limitations on eligibility.

Anybody requiring emergency care or urgent treatment will normally receive this care immediately in the public system. However as in most other tax-funded systems, waiting for nonurgent care is common, especially for specialist assessments and surgical procedures. The line between urgent and nonurgent care is by no means clear, and access to nonurgent procedures varies significantly across regions and over time.

In an effort to define the boundaries of the publicly funded health system more clearly, in the early 1990s, the government set up a committee which attempted to identify a set of "core" services that are publicly funded (Cumming 1997; National Advisory Committee on Core Health and Disability Services 1993; National Advisory Committee on Core Health and Disability Support Services 1992). Although this attempt did not succeed, it triggered a series of other activities directed toward more explicit decision-making about who gets access to which services, and under what circumstances. In particular, attention turned toward methods for prioritizing the public funding of health services (Ashton et al. 1999; Health Funding Authority 1998) and to developing tools for assisting clinicians to decide which patients should be given priority to elective surgery (Dew et al. 2005; MacCormick et al. 2004).

More recently, the government has set a number of performance indicators for the 21 DHBs in an effort to improve the certainty and timeliness of

Table 5.1 Coverage of public funding for health services

Type of service	Level of public funding	Comments
Primary care	Co-payments $0–$30	Higher subsidies apply for special groups, including children up to 6 years. Co-payments are set by providers.
Pharmaceuticals	In hospital, pharmaceuticals are 100% publicly funded. Co-payments of $0–$15 apply for drugs prescribed in the community	Some drugs attract an additional surcharge because manufacturers are unwilling to accept the reference price paid by the government in full payment for their drug.
Laboratory tests	100%	
Diagnostic imaging	100%	Public funding only applies to services carried out in public hospitals.
Secondary and tertiary care	100%	Requires a GP referral.
Mental health	100%	
Maternity	100%	
Physiotherapy	In hospital, services are 100% publicly funded. In the community, co-payments (or full-charges) normally apply.	Access to public funding to physiotherapy depends on a number of factors, including cause of health problem, method of referral, and duration of treatment.
Dental	100% up to 18 yrs Nil for adults	Public funding for adult dental care is available in emergencies, but is income-tested and is only provided in public hospitals.
Optometry	Nil	
Long-term residential care	100%. For those aged under 65 years, subject to a needs test, and income and asset tests.	The threshold of assets to which the asset test applies is now being progressively raised with the aim of gradually removing the asset test completely (see text).

treatment and to cut waiting lists for nonurgent surgery. These indicators include:

- all patients referred to hospital by their GP should be seen for a first specialist assessment within six months;

- all patients given a commitment to getting treatment should receive that treatment within six months.

The general approach of what has become known as the "booking system" is for clinicians to use a common set of assessment criteria for prioritizing patients for treatment. The level of funding available for each service then determines how many patients can be treated within the six-month period. These patients should then be booked in for treatment on a specific date. Patients falling below the priority threshold are referred back to their GP to be cared for in the community. These people must either wait until their condition has worsened and then apply to be reassessed in the public system, "go private" by paying for their own care from a private specialist or hospital, or go without surgical treatment. Although the booking system and the setting of targets are not without problems,[4] this approach has increased the certainty with which people will (or will not) be treated within the public health system.

The private health system

Although approximately one-third of the population is covered by private health insurance, this source of funding accounts for only 5.0 percent of total health spending. A further 17 percent is paid directly by users (Ministry of Health 2007). The apparent mismatch between expenditure on and coverage of private health insurance reflects the fact that private insurance is not comprehensive but provides a supplementary role to the public health system. Acute services are explicitly excluded from most insurance plans, plus many services (for example, chronic care, treatments for medical conditions including chemotherapy, many mental health services) are only available through the public health system.

Most insurance plans are purchased by individuals, although some employees (usually at the executive level) are offered health insurance as part of their employment package. The main reason for purchasing private insurance is to get more rapid access to nonurgent surgery which is provided in private hospitals. More comprehensive policies also cover co-payments for publicly funded services (mainly GP services and pharmaceuticals), and sometimes services that are not publicly funded such as dental and optometry services. Private insurance also provides people with access to their choice of specialist, and to treatment at a time that suits their personal lives. The population covered by private insurance is, on average, of higher socio-economic status than those who are uninsured (Blumberg 2006). Those aged 35–64 years are more likely to be insured than those in other age groups.

The general trend has been toward reduced private insurance coverage both in terms of proportion of population covered and the comprehensiveness of the plan. During the 1990s, the proportion of the population covered by insurance declined from almost a half to the current level of one-third (Health Funds Association of New Zealand 2006b; Ministry of Health Various years). Although overall coverage now seems to have stabilized, the current recent trend is away from comprehensive coverage to hospital only coverage (Health Funds Association of New Zealand 2006c). One possible reason for this is that some companies have moved away from community rating of premiums to age-banded risk rating and this has increased the price of premiums quite significantly for older people.

No special tax treatment applies to private health insurance. Premiums are not tax deductible, and premiums paid by employers are subject to a fringe benefit tax which applies to all nonmonetary benefits provided to employees.[5] Private health insurance is also not subject to any special regulations, other than the usual regulations that apply to insurance and commercial activities more generally. Thus benefits, prices, and all other aspects of an insurance package are set by individual insurers. The industry is keen to maintain this situation and is developing a method for voluntary self-regulation through an accreditation scheme (Health Funds Association of New Zealand 2006a). The scheme will provide standards for solvency, risk management, governance, consumer information and selling practices, and management of complaints.

Current trends

A number of changes are occurring in the mid- to late 2000s that are likely to shift the boundaries between the public and private systems. Most of these changes will result in a greater role for the public health system, although some will reduce it.

One major initiative that will increase public funding quite significantly is the Primary Health Care Strategy, a key aim of which is to reduce the financial barriers to primary health care (King 2001). Toward this end, increases in public subsidies for GP consultations and pharmaceuticals were rolled out between 2005 and 2007, with a shift away from the targeted regime toward universal subsidies for all of the population. This resulted in a fall in co-payments for these services—most particularly for higher-income people (Centre for Health Services Research and Policy 2004). Additional public funding has also been directed toward improving primary health care for various special needs groups, such as those with chronic conditions.

Public funding is being increased for long-term care of the elderly where subsidies are income and asset tested. In July 2005, the threshold to which the asset test applies was raised as a first step toward the progressive removal of the asset test over time (Dyson 2004). This policy is expected to triple the cost of long-term residential care to the government over the next 15 years (Ministry of Health 2001, 2002). The ageing of the population will further add to these costs.

One policy change that is reducing rather than increasing public funding is funding of laboratory services. Traditionally, patients referred for laboratory tests by private specialists have been entitled to free tests funded by the government. However, from November 2006, one DHB began charging private patients for these tests. This practice is likely to be introduced nationwide, with the associated costs being shifted from the public to the private sector.

As far as the provision of services is concerned, the public-private mix is being affected by technological and social developments which are resulting in a shift away from hospital-based care toward care in the community (see Figure 5.1). Because most community-based services are provided privately in New Zealand, this trend implies an extension of the role played by private sector providers. It could also imply increased private funding because some community-based services attract co-payments whereas most hospital-based services are fully subsidized (see Table 5.1). However, to date most of this shift has occurred within those services that are fully publicly funded (such as mental health services). The shift toward universal subsidies for primary care described above will also counteract the potential for deinstitutionalization to shift costs to the private sector.

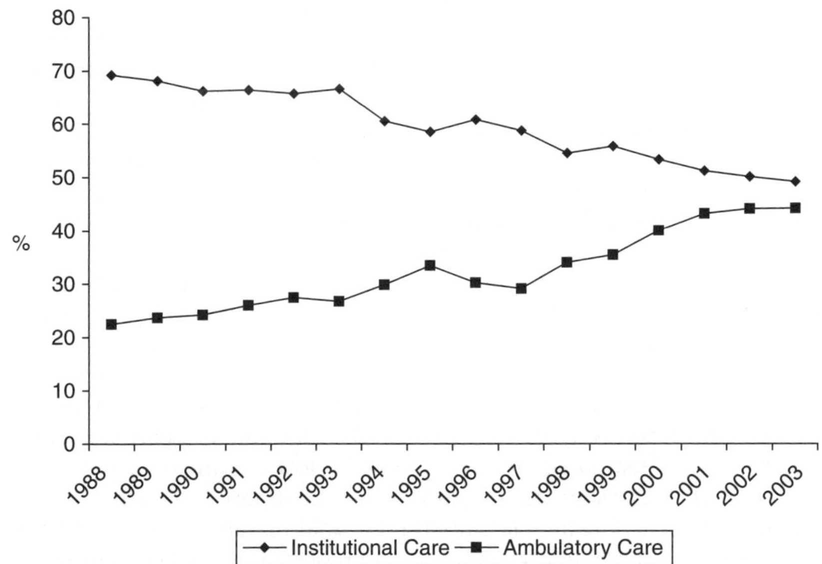

Figure 5.1   Percentage of total health expenditure spent on institutional and ambulatory care

Source: Ministry of Health (various years).

A final point of interest in the public-private mix is that there has been a long-term shift toward the private provision of nonclinical services. During the 1980s, services such as cleaning and catering in public hospitals were contracted out to private providers. Some public hospitals are now also choosing to purchase some clinical support services, particularly diagnostic services, from private providers rather than providing them in-house. A potential future trend is for DHBs to purchase more clinical services (especially nonurgent surgery) from private providers rather than providing these services directly themselves.

In summary, New Zealand has now turned its back on the quasi-market health reforms of the 1990s and the government is increasing its investment in the public health system in a number of ways, particularly in primary health care. For its part, the private sector is calling for greater collaboration between the public and private sectors (Health Funds Association of New Zealand 2006a). Proposals from private health insurers have included tax rebates for private health insurance, the provision of elective surgery in private hospitals for publicly funded patients, and the colocation of hospitals (Southern Cross Healthcare Group 2005). Although none of these proposals have met with any clear response from the government, some political parties have expressed their support for a greater role in the provision of health services by the private sector.

The proposals being put forward by the private insurers in New Zealand appear to have been inspired by recent reforms in Australia where, in contrast to the laissez-faire approach that New Zealand has taken to date to the private sector, an explicit goal of the Australian government is to support the private sector as a means of taking pressure off public hospitals and providing greater choice of health services. This support includes direct subsidies both to private hospitals and private health insurance within a system that, like New Zealand, is predominantly publicly funded with all residents entitled to free public hospital treatment.

There has been a long tradition in Australia of state support to private hospitals, with 75 percent of the scheduled fee for medical services provided in a private hospital being reimbursed by the public system (Medicare) (Healy et al. 2006). In the case of private health insurance, concerns about declining coverage during the 1980s and early 1990s led to the introduction of a three-stage strategy. First, in 1997, an income-tested rebate was offered to make private insurance more affordable for low-income people (Hall and Savage 2005). At the same time, a surcharge was imposed on Medicare levies paid by higher-income people who did not hold private insurance. In 1999, the income-tested rebate was removed and replaced by a 30 percent subsidy available to everybody, paid in the form of a tax rebate or a reduced price on premiums. In addition, from 2000, anyone who purchases health insurance before they are aged 30 years is entitled to Lifetime Health Cover under which they pay a base rate of premium as long as they maintain continuous coverage. These policies (but most especially Lifetime Health Cover) were extremely effective in extending insurance coverage, which increased from 32 percent to 45 percent of the population (Hall and Savage 2005). They also appear to have been effective in increasing the use of private hospital beds (Moorin and Holman 2007; Walker et al. 2007). However, this has not led to the desired concomitant reduction in the use of public hospitals beds. Moreover, these policies have come at a price, leading some analysts to argue that the money would be better spent directly on public hospitals rather than on subsidies to private health insurance (Duckett and Jackson 2002).

Overall, relationships between the public and private sectors are considerably more complex in Australia than they are in New Zealand. Some private patients are treated in public hospitals and some public patients are treated in private hospitals. Although private insurance in Australia enjoys significant public subsidies, the insurance industry is also more tightly regulated than in New Zealand. In addition, because responsibility for hospital care lies with the six states and two territories, funding and administrative arrangements vary considerably from state to state. In health services, therefore, the line between the public and private sectors is less clear in Australia than it is in New Zealand.

Pensions

In the 1990s, radical reforms to social welfare, in health care as described above, and in other social provisions produced a residual welfare state in which the numbers in poverty mushroomed (Ministry of Social Policy 2001). Against this background, the story about pensions is a remarkable one. New Zealand has emerged in the twenty-first century as one of the few countries, either developed or developing, with a fully universal pension (Willmore 2007). This pension, called New Zealand Superannuation (NZS), is set at a level well above subsistence so that few of the elderly are in poverty, and has enjoyed a remarkable level of political and public support (St John 2005b; Starke 2005). Supplementation of the state pension has been a matter of choice, and until very recently government itself played very little role in private saving. Throughout the period of reform housing remained a tax-advantaged savings vehicle contributing to the high home ownership of the elderly and this in turn to their relatively higher living standards compared to others on comparable incomes (Ministry of Social Development 2006).

Since 1990 private pensions in New Zealand have been remarkably free of the institutional legacies that shape other countries' policies. The hidden role of the state in providing subsidies to private saving for retirement was first placed under intense scrutiny in the neoliberal reforms of the late 1980s. In a dramatic package of changes to the tax system, all tax incentives for private saving were removed, virtually overnight.[6] The reform process managed to eschew the power of the vested interests of insurance and superannuation companies (St John 2005a). The "first-past-the-post" political system of the time facilitated a purist approach to comprehensive income tax reforms, in which the drive for economic efficiency was paramount. In this exercise, the tax scale was substantially flattened with a top rate of 33 percent and the base broadened by the exclusion of most rebates and exemptions, the inclusion of fringe benefits and full imputation for company dividends.

In pensions, more than in any other social area, it was clear what could be expected of the state and what individuals should do for themselves. Nevertheless the sharp public-private dichotomy had started to blur by the mid-2000s. In 2007, a new quasi-compulsory, tax-subsidized saving scheme called KiwiSaver was introduced.[7] Thus, the role of the state in private provision has now been extended in the murky and hard-to-measure ways used by other countries (St John, 2007). Australia and New Zealand have always had very different approaches to retirement saving with New Zealand taking a far more hands-off approach to private saving. The 2007 changes will have the effect of bringing New Zealand closer to Australia where there is both tax-subsidized voluntary and compulsory saving. In terms of the basic pension, Australia has a means-tested aged benefit. It remains to be seen whether New Zealand will ultimately also follow that track with the generous, universal NZS.

The public pension system[8]

The modern public pension, NZS, had its origins in the mid-1970s when a fledgling compulsory, defined-contribution, funded saving scheme managed by the state was abolished and a universal pension for all at age 60 was introduced (Ashton and St John 1988). This taxable pension was initially set at 80 percent of the average wage for a married couple, and was sufficient to enable poverty problems among the old to all but disappear.

The generosity of this scheme was put under pressure in the leaner economic times of the late 1970s and 1980s. To save costs, a surcharge on "other income" was introduced in 1985 to claw back the pension from better-off superannuitants. The surcharge and the taxable nature of the pension provided a mild degree of income testing in which only the top 6 percent of superannuitants lost all of their entitlement (Periodic Report Group 1997).

The benefit formula was changed to one of providing a floor of 65 percent of the net average wage for a couple and over time by indexation to prices, not wages, the relative level of the pension fell toward this floor. At the same time, the progressivity of the tax system was reduced in the 1980s through a flattening of the tax scale. In most respects, the effect of the surcharge was simply to provide a higher degree of progressivity in the tax structure, albeit only for those over 65 (St John and Ashton 1993).

In 1990, the incoming National Government was faced with a dilemma. They had promised to remove the surcharge, if elected, thus restoring full universality, but they also had an agenda of sweeping welfare reform. Other welfare benefits were to be severely cut under their agenda, so that universal entitlement to a pension for all at age 60 at a level above other welfare benefits did not sit well. To resolve this they announced in the 1991 budget, that, in essence the state pension would also become a welfare benefit subject to the same rigorous means-testing that applied to other benefits (Shipley 1991).

The approach envisioned by National would have given New Zealand the most extreme neoliberal approach to pensions in the OECD: a means-tested welfare payment for the poor, and voluntary unsubsidized private saving. But, unlike other sectors affected by the notorious 1991 budget (known as the "mother of all budgets"), the political power of the elderly was able to block and reverse these changes. In late 1991 the pension was restored, however the surcharge was retained and its provisions made less generous. The age of entitlement was raised from 60 to 65 over the ten years from 1992–2002 (St John 1992).

One of the legacies of the 1991 budget reversals was a heightened antipathy to the surcharge. More people were affected by it because the exemption had been lowered. It could be argued however, that fully universal pensions only made sense when taxes were quite progressive. Once the top tax rate had been reduced to 33 percent, if the pension was universal, better-off pensioners could have effectively retained 67 percent of the gross payment. Nevertheless the political pressures around this issue led to the abolition of the surcharge in 1998.

Price indexation caused the pension to breach the 65 percent floor in 1999, and to save costs the National-led coalition government attempted to lower the floor to 60 percent. At the end of 1999, the incoming Labour-led coalition government acted quickly to restore the floor and to legitimize the 65 percent of the net average wage for a couple at 65 in the NZS Act 2001.

The parameters of the NZS are set out in Part 1 of the Act. Although the retirement income system in New Zealand has been subject to intense political debate over many years, this part of the Act now enjoys wide political support. NZS is payable at age 65 years to all New Zealanders living in New Zealand who meet the minimal residency requirements of 10 years residency since the age of 20 years and not less than 5 years residency since attaining the age of 50.

The net rate of payment for a couple is legislated to be within the band of 65 percent and 72.5 percent of net Average Ordinary Time Weekly Earnings (AWE).[9] For each married person this means a floor of 32.5 percent of AWE is guaranteed. Each year there is an annual adjustment to reflect movements in the Consumer Price Index, unless the floor of 65 percent is breached at which point wage indexation restores the floor.[10] The rate for a single pensioner who shares accommodation is 60 percent of the married rate, or a minimum of 39 percent of AWE. The rate for pensioners living alone is 65 percent of the married rate or a minimum of 43.25 percent of AWE. Each person is taxed in their own right as an individual on total gross income including the gross pension, so that with mildly progressive income tax rates, the top income pensioner effectively receives a pension worth approximately 72 percent of the pension of the lowest income pensioner.

NZS is a pay-as-you-go (PAYG) tax-funded scheme. No contributions records are needed and the pension is paid for from general taxation. In essence it provides a secure basic income on which people can build their own extra income privately from working or saving. Far from a minimal role, the state involvement in NZS allows for several attractive and unusual features:

- The pension recognizes both paid and unpaid contributions to society equally. This is particularly beneficial for women who tend to spend less time in the paid workforce (St John and Gran 2001).
- Each person over 65 is treated as an individual and receives the pension in his or her own right. Although there are different rates depending on marital status, each individual is taxed as an individual and there is no account taken of a spouse's income.
- The payment is indexed to living standards by the provision of a floor-related to average wages so that protection is afforded not only for inflation but also for a growth in living standards generally.
- The pension protects against the longevity risk.
- The pension is very simple to understand and apply for.

The NZS has advantages to New Zealand society as well:

- As social insurance, the scheme does not require any guarantee period or return of capital on death.
- The general tax base is wider than wage income, as it includes taxes on investment income and on consumption. Thus some of the burden of the PAYG scheme is spread from the working-age population to include tax contributions from the old as well.
- The level has been largely effective in preventing poverty in the elderly. In 2004 only 4 percent reported living in severe or significant hardship compared to 15 percent of the entire population or 26 percent of all children (Ministry of Social Development 2006).
- Administration costs are minimized and there are no inherent disincentives to work or save because the pension is not means-tested.

In terms of sustainability, the net cost of paying NZS is currently 3.6 percent of GDP and expected to increase to approximately 7.5–8 percent of GDP by 2051.[11] Although the fiscal pressures of an aging population are real, the size of the problem seems modest in comparison with other OECD countries, many of which already face much higher pension/GDP ratios. It must also be remembered that other countries provide subsidies in the form of tax expenditures for private provision that are not reflected in pension/GDP ratios. Ireland for example has a regime of tax expenditure for retirement incomes that, if counted as part of the state's pension costs for 2000–1, would increase the pension/GDP ratio by 1.7 percentage points (Hughes 2005). Thus it may be argued that the lack of tax incentives assists in the affordability of the relatively generous tax-funded universal NZS.

NZS has never had a contributory basis as do the social insurance schemes of most European countries, nor does it provide earnings-related pensions. Yet NZS itself is much more than a first tier, poverty prevention tax-funded provision that other countries may provide. It can be regarded as a sophisticated variant of social insurance in which there is a social contract between the generations to provide wage-linked pensions to all older citizens.

The New Zealand Government has also begun to prefund NZS by setting aside part of the fiscal surplus each year to provide a buffer against the needed increase in taxation. The Fund enables the state to be fiscally prudent and to resist pressures for immediate tax cuts by ring fencing these assets on its balance sheet. It is managed at arms length using best private practice by an independent board. To date this Fund has performed above the market average (Eriksen 2004) and the position of NZS looks secure.

Private provision

New Zealand has had a simple system of voluntary, unsubsidized supplementary provision for retirement saving. In theory one could save in any way that is appropriate, whether that be in acquiring equity in housing, repaying debt, investing in financial assets, or even in furthering one's own education or that of one's children.

The removal of all tax incentives for retirement saving between 1988 and 1990 sent shock waves throughout the financial community. All schemes were restructured to conform to the Tax/Tax/Exempt model, so that just as saving money in the bank, all contributions were made out of taxed income, earnings in the fund were fully taxed but the final withdrawal was tax-free. Treasury had found tax incentives, as is the case in other countries, hugely favored the better-off, not only because the better-off are on higher tax rates but also because they save the most anyway. Tax incentives made little sense because they encouraged shifts from nontax favored saving into tax-favored saving with scant evidence that saving actually improved overall. They noted the large hidden cost to the government in tax foregone, that either reduced public saving or forced average taxes to be higher. Treasury was also adamant that tax favored savings vehicles diverted scarce capital into inappropriate investments at the cost of reducing economic growth (St John and Ashton 1993).

New Zealand has a relatively low level of private pension saving compared to Australia where there is a large, compulsory, private, defined-contribution savings scheme. Coverage in private employment-based superannuation schemes fell to a low of about 14 percent of the employed labor force in 2002 recovering somewhat to 14.7 percent by 2005 as a new scheme for state employees attracted members (Government Actuary 2006).

As in other countries, defined-contribution schemes have been replacing defined-benefit schemes so that far fewer people start retirement with either an annuity or a private pension.[12] New Zealand's tax neutral approach has precluded the right to regulate private retirement saving for social purposes. This means there is no potential, for example, to legislate for the purchase of an annuity from the accumulated retirement lump-sum.

New developments

The dichotomous policy environment described above was sharply challenged by the Labour government in 2005. Rather than leave it up to the individual to save if they so choose, a new savings scheme, KiwiSaver, was introduced in 2007 to encourage the "savings habit." The preamble to the Act sets out the purpose:

> The purpose of this Act is to encourage a long-term savings habit and asset accumulation by individuals who are not in a position to enjoy standards of living in retirement similar to those in pre-retirement. The Act aims to increase individuals' well-being and financial independence, particularly in retirement, and to provide retirement benefits (KiwiSaver Act 2006).

KiwiSaver is a voluntary, work-based savings scheme for employees over 18, administered by the Inland Revenue Department using the existing PAYE (pay as you earn) tax system. An up-front $1,000 and a small annual subsidy to help meet the managed fund's fees are provided by the government. New employees must be automatically enrolled into KiwiSaver when they start a new job with eight weeks to "opt out."[13] Deductions from wages are at a rate of 4 percent or 8 percent of gross pay. As first announced, KiwiSaver could have voluntary, matched, tax-free contributions by employers of up to 4 percent. The tax-free nature of the employer contribution was not part of the detailed scrutiny of the Bill at the Select Committee stage but appeared in the final legislation, seemingly as part of a political agreement with coalition partners. It was clear that the tax concession would create immediate pressure for the government to extend similar tax concessions for existing employee-sponsored schemes that were not part of KiwiSaver. Indeed, in a little noticed move just before Christmas 2006, the extension was made, with little apparent analysis or debate.

Savings are primarily for retirement and "locked in" (that is, will not be accessible) until the age of eligibility for NZ Superannuation, currently 65 years, except in cases of: financial hardship, permanent emigration, or after a minimum of three years to contribute toward a deposit on a first home. However, savers can stop contributions for up to five years at a time by applying for a "contributions holiday." Contributions resume at the end of the five years unless the individual applies for a further "contributions holiday."

Withdrawal of an individual's own and employer contributions may be made after three years of saving to provide a deposit for a first home. There is a subsidy of $1,000 per year of membership in the scheme, up to a maximum of $5,000 for five years subject to an income test and a cap on the value of the home.

This first version of KiwiSaver greatly extended the role of the state in pensions. It was clear, however, that there would be more to come, especially once the slippery slide toward providing tax concessions had begun. The 2007 Budget announced further tax credits for those who join: a matching $20 a week for the first $20 contributed and a phased in compulsory employer contribution of 4 percent, matched by a tax credit to employers of up to $20 a week.

Associated with the introduction of KiwiSaver the government sought to overcome some of the penalties that have arisen for individuals who saved in superannuation schemes under the tax neutral treatment introduced with the tax changes in the late 1980s. The problem was that the original reforms envisaged a flat tax under which it would not have mattered if the fund earnings were taxed within the fund as that would have been at the marginal tax rate of the individual.

Until the recent changes, both the employer contributions and the earnings in the fund were taxed at 33 percent. Those tax payers on a 21 percent tax rate were over taxed, whereas those on the top rate of 39 percent were under-taxed. Under the changes associated with KiwiSaver, fund earnings that qualify (called Portfolio Investment entities) are taxed at either 19.5 percent for low-income tax payers or at 30 percent for higher-income tax-payers. The tax on fund earnings is a final tax so there is no reconciliation at the end of the year. Ironically, the tax regime for private saving is now favorable to those on the top tax rate of 39 percent and may provide a mechanism whereby some income can escape the income test for income-based family assistance (Retirement Policy and Research Centre 2007).

The initial government "sweetener" of $1,000 did not suffer from the regressivity of tax incentives, and the neutral tax treatment of saving was not seriously challenged. The matching, tax-free, employer contributions to 4 percent, the member tax credit subsidy, and $20 a week tax credit to offset the employer contribution, are of quite a different order of cost and distributional impact. They favor older workers and wealthier individuals who can shift existing savings into the tax-favored forms.

Future developments

In shifting the public-private mix in the manner outlined above, New Zealand no longer holds the moral high ground on tax concessions. This in turn leaves open the possibility of further change. For example there is now no particularly good argument for not making the employee contribution to the KiwiSaver scheme also tax-free. The matching employer contribution, with a phase-in period to 2011, is compulsory for those employees who join, making remuneration policy much more complex. It is likely, therefore, that at some time in the future the employer contribution to the KiwiSaver scheme will be made compulsory, as it is in Australia, perhaps in some kind of trade-off for an income tax rate cut.

The loss of the unique characteristics of the NZ private pension arrangements also has implications for the retention of the tax-free nature of the final payouts from saving schemes, including KiwiSaver. Currently there is no restriction on taking KiwiSaver funds as a tax-free lump-sum, yet it can be argued that the provision of an income stream in retirement is one of the only justifications for tax concessions.

Indeed, there has been little discussion on how retirement saving should be used in retirement to contribute to the costs of old-age care and other health costs (Ashton and St John 2005). Residents of long-term care facilities are expected to contribute their state pension to their care costs and are means-tested for top-up subsidies. Despite a liberalization of the means-test detailed above, there has been an explosion in family trusts set up to avoid this test (Briggs 2006). The absence of requirements on the use of KiwiSaver funds may add further to this avoidance and allow the state's role to expand at the expense of the working-age, tax-paying population.

It is inevitable that as more people retire with tax-subsidized private savings, there may be pressure to income and/or asset test the currently universal state-funded pension. Thus, although there is no current evidence of an intention to establish this test, it is possible that the New Zealand system will come to resemble the Australian system much more closely over time.

Discussion and conclusion

An influential view in contemporary scholarly debates on social policy is that, in "liberal" welfare regimes such Australia and New Zealand, a common recent trend has been toward a withdrawal of the state from direct welfare provision, and a concomitant shift toward greater use of market-based social protections, usually with some kind of state support. Although there was a clear contraction of the welfare state in New Zealand during the 1980s and

1990s, in neither pensions nor health care could it be argued that overt government spending was replaced by some kind of "hidden welfare state." This has meant that, until recently, the public-private dichotomy in New Zealand was neither "fuzzy" nor "ambiguous" (Rein and Schmähl 2004), at least with respect to health and pensions policies.

During the 1980s and 1990s, the neoliberal approach to economic policy in New Zealand was manifested in changes to the funding of pensions and health care in two key ways. First, means-testing was introduced for primary health care subsidies and for the state pension, indicating a shift away from universal provision toward targeted welfare payments. Second, changes were made to the tax treatment of private health insurance and private pensions so that any kind of tax incentives for private provision were effectively removed in an effort to create a level playing field across all forms of income and savings. In addition, market-style solutions were introduced into the public health system in an effort to capture some of the efficiency-enhancing incentives that are assumed to flow from these types of arrangements.

In the last decade there has been something of a reversal of efforts to introduce market mechanisms into both health care and pensions in New Zealand and there is now no evidence of welfare state retrenchment in either of these sectors. Indeed, the trend now is, if anything, in the opposite direction. The means-testing of benefits is being (or has been) removed for both health care and pensions, and the state is moving in the direction of a significantly larger role in encouraging private savings. In pensions, the expanded role of the state in private provision has not been promoted as a means to reduce the costs of the public pension, or at least not yet.

These policies signal some important new directions for social policy in New Zealand. First, the provision of significant state support to private savings schemes through KiwiSaver marks a shift away from the hands-off approach to the private provision of health and pension benefits that has been a central feature of both of these sectors since the mid-1980s. The new scheme blurs the line between the two sectors, and aligns New Zealand more closely with Australia which has had a long tradition of state support for private health insurance and private hospital care as well as private pensions.

Second, recent changes in both health and pensions favor those who are better-off rather than poorer people. The distribution of benefits from KiwiSaver is clearly regressive, and the main beneficiaries of the increased subsidies for primary health care and long-term residential care are middle- and higher-income people. This seems both ironic and unfortunate, given that New Zealand has experienced the fastest growth in inequality in the OECD (Förster and d'Ercole 2005). The new policies will, if anything, further widen this gap.

Third, unlike many other countries, the absence of state support for private benefits has meant that the work place has not historically been a significant source of health and pension benefits for most New Zealanders. Being a work-based model, the KiwiSaver scheme again marks something of a shift in policy direction. Although open to workers and nonworkers alike, the main point of access to the scheme and to the maximum tax credits is through employment. Moreover, workers also enjoy higher levels of state support via tax-free employer contributions.

Interestingly, unlike many other countries, private interest groups have not generally featured as major influences in these policy changes. Calls from the private health insurance industry for greater state support and cooperation with the private sector have so far gone unheard, and the pressure for KiwiSaver to have tax concessions also did not really come from private vested interests and lobbying. Nevertheless, these interventions in pensions have been largely welcomed by the industry. They gain an increase in fund management business and will enjoy state subsidies on costs. It is also not hard to foresee that the political temptation to emulate Australia and make the scheme fully compulsory may be hard to resist in the future.

Perhaps, appropriate to the New Zealand experience, is the recognition that, under a coalition government, it is politics that creates policy. Compromises on principle on political grounds are not only possible but are often the price of forming a government and/or staying in power. This is being played out in pensions just as it has been in health. The result of this is that the dichotomous line between purely public and purely private is becoming blurred in New Zealand in line with trends in Australia and other liberal welfare regimes.

Notes

1. The first-past-the-post electoral system was replaced by Mixed Member Proportional representation following a referendum in 1993. In large part this was in response to a perception that the first-past-the-post system had failed to reflect the diverse views of the electorate and had allowed governments to push through policies even in circumstances where they did not have a majority of the total electoral vote.
2. Labour governments in New Zealand since 1984 have not conformed to the social democratic model. The fourth Labour government 1984–1990 was a reforming government with economic efficiency as a core value. The fifth Labour government elected in 1999, has been largely a Third Way "enabling state" with work and social provision associated with employment as a core values.
3. In 2008, the Ministry had retained responsibility for distributing funds for public health services (such as health promotion and health protection services) and social care services (such as home care) for people aged under 65 years. However, these funds may also be devolved to the District Health Boards over time.
4. Problems have included

- the potential for subjective interpretation of the clinical assessment criteria by clinicians and for gaming (MacCormick et al. 2004; Seddon et al. 2006).
- insufficient resources for elective surgery and assessments, causing DHBs to decline to see or treat some patients who are deemed to be in need clinically (Johnston 2006).
- a tendency on the part of DHBs to over-promise, given the level of resources available. In 2006, this resulted in an estimated 20,000 people being dropped from surgical or outpatient waiting lists in order to meet the deadline to meet the six-month targets (Kiong 2006).

5. The introduction of the Fringe Benefit Tax in 1985 may account for the decline in private insurance coverage during the 1990s.
6. Some reforms to the tax system, such as flat tax did not survive.
7. For current details see www.ird.govt.nz
8. This section is based on (Preston 2001; St John 2005a, 2005b)
9. AWE is weekly earnings averaged for male and female.
10. An agreement with New Zealand First Party, a minor political party, raised this minimum to 66 percent in 2005.
11. See http://www.retirement.org.nz/
12. An annuity is an annual income stream purchased from a Life Office with an individual's lump sum. Annuities can be paid for life (life annuities) or for a fixed term (term annuities). Pensions are group annuities paid from company, government or group retail schemes.
13. Self-employed people, those under 18 and beneficiaries can join but need to make payments directly to Inland Revenue. Savers can select their own fund and can change fund providers, but can only have one provider at any time. Those who do not specify a fund are randomly allocated to a default provider.

References

Ashton, Toni, Jacqueline Cumming, and Nancy Devlin. 1999. *Prioritising Health and Disability Support Services: Principles Processes and Problems*. Wellington: National Health Committee.

Ashton, Toni, Nicholas Mays, and Nancy Devlin. 2005. "Continuity through change; the rhetoric and reality of health reform in New Zealand." *Social Science and Medicine* 61: 253–62.

Ashton, Toni and Susan St John. 1988. *Superannuation in New Zealand. Averting the Crisis*. Wellington: Institute of Policy Studies.

Ashton, Toni and Susan St John. 2005. *Financing of Long Term Residential Care in New Zealand: Swimming against the Tide*. Paper Presented at the Fifth World Congress of the International Association of Health Economists, Barcelona, July 10–13.

Blumberg, Linda. 2006. *The Effect of Private Health Insurance Coverage on Health Services Utilisation in New Zealand*. Wellington: The Ian Axeford New Zealand Fellowship in Public Policy.

Boston, Jonathon, Paul Dalziel, and Susan St John. (eds). 1999. *Redesigning the Welfare State in New Zealand: Problems, Policies, Prospects*. Auckland: Oxford University Press.

Briggs, Phil. 2006. *Family Trusts*. Paper presented at the Household Saving Workshop Reserve Bank of New Zealand.

Centre for Health Services Research and Policy. 2004. Reducing Co-payments for General Practice: Health Policy Monitor.

Cumming, Jacqueline. 1997. "Defining Core Services: The New Zealand Experience." *Journal of Health Services Research and Policy* 2(1): 31–7.

Dew, Kevin, Jacqueline Cumming, Deborah McLeod, Sonya Morgan, Eileen McKinlay, Anthony Dowell, and Tom Love. 2005. "Explicit Rationing of Elective Services: Implementing the New Zealand Reforms." *Health Policy* 74(1): 1–12.

Duckett, Stephen and Terri Jackson. 2002. "The New Health Insurance Rebate: An Inefficient Way of Assisting Public Hospitals." *Medical Journal of Australia* 172: 439–42.

Dyson, Ruth. 2004. Government Increases Aged Care Funding.

Easton, Brian. 2002. "The New Zealand Health Reforms of the 1990s in Context." *Applied Health Economics and Health Policy* 1(2): 107–12.

Eriksen, Jonathan. 2004. *Report: The Guardians of New Zealand Superannuation Fund*. Wellington: Eriksen & Associates Limited.

Finlayson, Mary. 2001. "Policy Implementation and Development." In Peter Davis and Toni Ashton (eds), *Health and Public Policy in New Zealand*: 159–80. Auckland: Oxford University Press.

Förster, Michael and Marco Mira d'Ercole. 2005. *Income Distribution on Poverty in the OECD Countries in the Second Half of the 1990s*. Paris: OECD.

Gauld, Robin. 2001. *Revolving Doors: New Zealand's Health Reforms*. Wellington: Institute of Policy Studies.

Government Actuary. 2006. *Report of the Government Actuary for the Year Ended 30 June 2006*. Wellington: Ministry of Economic Development.

Hall, Jane and Elizabeth Savage. 2005. "The Role of the Private Sector in the Australian Healthcare System." In Alan Maynard (ed.), *The Public-Private Mix for Health*: 247–78. Oxford: Radcliffe Publishing.

Health Funding Authority. 1998. *How Shall We Prioritise Health and Disability Support Services? A Workshop Background Paper*. Wellington: Health Funding Authority.

Health Funds Association of New Zealand. 2006a, April 24. *Cover Stories: Health Insurance News*. Wellington: Health Funds Association of New Zealand.

Health Funds Association of New Zealand. 2006b. Health Insurance Statistics July 2006 (Electronic Version). Retrieved on November 17, 2006 from http://www.healthfunds.org.nz/Downloads/Health%20Insurance%20Statistics%20July%2020061.pdf

Health Funds Association of New Zealand. 2006c. *Fact File—Health Insurance in New Zealand*. Wellington.

Healy, Judith, Evelyn Sharman, and Buddhima Lokuge. 2006. "Australia: Health System Review." *Health Systems in Transition* 8(5). Copenhagen: European Observatory on Health Systems and Policies.

Hughes, Gerry. 2005. "Pension Tax Reliefs and Equity." In J. Stewart (ed.), *For Richer, for Poorer. An investigation of the Irish Pension System*. Dublin: Betaprint Limited.

Johnston, Martin. 2006. "Waitemata Health Still Turns Away Heart Cases." *New Zealand Herald*. June 1, 2006: A2.

King, Annette. 2000. *The New Zealand National Health Strategy*. Wellington: Ministry of Health.

King, Annette. 2001. *The Primary Health Care Strategy*. Wellington: Ministry of Health.

Kiong, Errol. 2006. "Most Health Boards Cull Waiting Lists." *New Zealand Herald*. September 30, 2006: A5.

KiwiSaver Act. 2006. Retrieved on November 10, 2006 from http://taxpolicy.ird.govt.nz/publications/files/200640.pdf

MacCormick, Alistair, Macmillan A., and Brian Parry. 2004. "Identification of Criteria for the Prioritisation of Patients for Elective General Surgery." *Journal of Health Services & Research Policy* 9(1): 28–33.

MacCormick, Alistair, Tan Chuan P., and Brian Parry. 2004. "Priority Assessment of Patients for Elective General Surgery: Game on?" ANZ *Journal of Surgery* 74(3):143–5.

Mays, Nicholas and Nancy Devlin. 2005. "The Public-Private Mix in Health Services in New Zealand." In Alan Maynard (ed.), *The Public-Private Mix for Health*: 219–47. Oxford: Radcliffe Publishing Ltd.

McClelland, Alison and Susan St John. 2006. "Social Policy Responses to Globalisation in Australia and New Zealand 1980–2005." *Australian Journal of Political Science, Special Issue Jennifer Curtin, Francis G. Castles and Jack Vowles (Guest editors), Globalising the Antipodes? Policy and Politics in Australia and New Zealand* 41(2).

Ministry of Health. Various years. *Health Expenditure Trends in New Zealand.* Wellington: Ministry of Health.

Ministry of Health. 2001, 2002. Assorted discussion papers on asset testing for long-term care. Released to S. St John in May 2003 under the Official Information Act.

Ministry of Health. 2007. *Health Expenditure Trends in New Zealand 1994–2004.* Wellington: Ministry of Health.

Ministry of Social Development. 2006. *New Zealand Living Standards 2004.* Wellington: Ministry of Social Development.

Ministry of Social Policy. 2001. *The Social Report 2001. Indicators Of Social Well-Being in New Zealand.* Wellington: Ministry of Social Policy.

Moorin, Rachel and Cashel D'Arcy Holman. 2007. "Does Federal Health Care Policy Influence Switching between the Public and Private Sectors in Individuals?" *Health Policy* 79(2–3): 284–95.

National Advisory Committee on Core Health and Disability Services. 1993. *The Best of Health 2: How We decide on Health and Disability Support Services We Value Most.* Wellington: National Advisory Committee on Core Health Services.

National Advisory Committee on Core Health and Disability Support Services. 1992. *The Best of Health. Deciding on the Health Services We Value Most.* Wellington: National Advisory Committee on Core Health and Disability Support Services.

New Zealand Labour Party. 1999. *Focus on Patients: Labour on Health.* Wellington: New Zealand Labour Party.

Periodic Report Group. 1997. *1997 Retirement Income Report: A Review of the Current Framework—Interim Report.* Wellington.

Preston, David. 2001. "Retirement Income in New Zealand: The Historical Context." Retrieved on November 10, 2006 from http://www.retirement.org.nz

Rein, Martin and Winfried Schmähl. (eds). 2004. *Rethinking the Welfare State: The Political Economy of Pension Reform.* London: Edward Elgar.

Retirement Policy and Research Centre. 2007. *The Tax Implications of Pay, Salary Sacrifice, KiwiSaver and PIEs* (Briefing Paper No. 06/07): RPRC.

Seddon, Mary, Joanne Broad, Sue Crengle, Dale Bramley, Rod Jackson, and Harvey White. 2006. "Coronary Artery Bypass Graft Surgery in New Zealand's Auckland Region: A Comparison between the Clinical Priority Assessment Criteria Score and the Actual Clinical Priority Assigned." *New Zealand Medical Journal* 119(1230): U1881.

Shipley, Jenny. 1991. *Social Assistance: Welfare That Works.* Wellington: Government Printer.

Southern Cross Healthcare Group. 2005. *Paper on Health Care in New Zealand.* Auckland: Southern Cross Healthcare Group.

St John, Susan. 1992. "National Superannuation: Or How Not to Make Policy." In Jonathon Boston and Paul Dalziel (eds), *The Decent Society. Essays in Response to National's Economics and Social Policies.* New Zealand: Oxford University Press.

St John, Susan. 2004. "Redesigning the Welfare State in New Zealand." In Catherine Jones Finer and Paul Smyth (eds), *Social Policy and the Commonwealth. Prospects for Social Inclusion.* Hampshire: Palgrave Macmillan.

St John, Susan. 2005a. *Pensions Taxation and Retirement Incomes in New Zealand.* (Seminar paper No. SP2005–08). Dublin: The Economic and Social Research Institute.

St John, Susan. 2005b. "Retirement Income Policy in New Zealand." *The Economic and Labour Relations Review* 15(2): 217–39.

St John, Susan. 2007. New Zealand's Experiment in Tax Neutrality for Retirement Saving. *The Geneva Papers 32*: 532–52.

St John, Susan and Ashton Toni. 1993. *Private Pensions in New Zealand: Can They Avert the Crisis?* Wellington: Institute of Policy Studies.

St John, Susan and Brian Gran. 2001. "The World's Social Laboratory: Women Friendly Aspects of New Zealand Pensions." In Jay Ginn, Debra Street, and Sara Arber (eds), *Women, Work and Pensions.* Buckingham: Open University Press.

Starke, Peter. 2005. Resilient or Residual? From the Wage Earners' Welfare State to Market Conformity in New Zealand (Transtate Working Paper No. 022). Bremen: TranState Research Center. Retrieved on November 17, 2006 from www.state.uni-bremen.de

Walker, Agnes E., Richard Percival, Linc Thurecht, and Jim Pearce. 2007. "Public Policy and Private Health Insurance: Distributional Impact on Public and Private Hospital Usage." *Australian Health Review* 31(2): 305–14.

Willmore, Larry. 2007. "Universal Pensions for Developing Countries." *World Development* 35(1): 24–51.

6

Much Noise, Little Progress: The UK Experience of Privatization

Peter Taylor-Gooby and Lavinia Mitton

Introduction

Since the 1970s, UK governments in common with those of other welfare states have faced a dilemma: pressure on social spending due to population aging and a changing labor market, and at the same time, strong pressures to contain taxation as international competition intensifies, capital becomes more mobile and electorates resist a greater tax-take. The United Kingdom stands out in its use of the private sector and introduction of market forces. Under the Thatcher (1979–1990) and Major (1990–1997) governments, the "marketization" of welfare involved two strands. One was encouraging individuals to finance their own welfare, for example, by saving for their own pension or taking out private health insurance. The other concerned the promotion of "quasi-markets" linking "public" and "private" in the welfare field (Deakin and Walsh 1996). This involved a new form of welfare state organization: private commercial or voluntary providers alongside public providers. The assumption was that this process would use competitive pressure to promote greater efficiency and responsiveness to the needs of those using the services, most notably in the area of health (Le Grand 1990; Le Grand and Bartlett 1993). Services from social housing to refuse collection, from social care to running prisons were contracted out to private and voluntary sector agencies (Vincent-Jones 2006).When Tony Blair became Labour leader he rejected both right-wing promarket approaches and traditional left support for public ownership of state services in favor of a Third Way, between the state and the market (Blair 1998). Consequently, the party was renamed New Labour. Since coming to power in 1997 the New Labour governments have not taken apart the reforms of their Conservative predecessors, but have built on them. A 1999 policy document Modernising Government explained their approach:

> This Government will adopt a pragmatic approach, using competition to deliver improvements. This means looking hard but not dogmatically at

what services government can best provide itself, what should be contracted to the private sector, and what should be done in partnership (Prime Minister and Minister for the Cabinet Office 1999).

Central government typically retains regulatory powers and sets performance targets for public services that are delivered by a range of separate providers, often operating in competition. The assumption is that this will widen choice and drive down costs. In this chapter, we examine recent policies in health care and pensions in the United Kingdom to see what lessons can be drawn from this experiment in welfare privatization and quasi-markets.

The UK health system

Introduction

In a nutshell, the UK health services can be described as mainly publicly financed, although moving toward greater use of private suppliers in a bid to lower costs by bringing in free market influences.

The National Health Service (NHS) was created in the immediate aftermath of World War II, as one of a package of welfare reforms which also included improved social insurance and pensions. The government in any case had to take over the organization of hospital services during the war, and this paved the way for state takeover of private and charitable hospitals.

The overriding reason for its popularity with the voting public was that it provided free visits to doctors and free treatment for everyone based on clinical need and not ability to pay. Treatment had always been free for those on the lowest incomes, so the NHS was beneficial for the middle class in particular, who under the previous system had to pay. The British show enduring attachment to the concept of an NHS available to everyone and free at the point of use. The only charges are means-tested charges for medicines, and some optical and dental treatment. Exemptions—for pensioners, children, disabled people, those living in Wales or Scotland, those with certain medical conditions, and those on low incomes—mean that 85 percent of NHS prescriptions are in fact dispensed free of charge. The rest are charged at a flat rate of £6.85 (April 2007). On the other hand the vast majority of optical and dental treatment is paid for privately (Sihota 2003). To the extent that the NHS is funded out of general taxation and transfers from the national insurance fund (effectively a form of taxation), the risk pool consists of the entire population rather than a restricted group. Tax finance also means that the HM Treasury is better able to control spending than in countries where numerous agencies reimburse medical fees charged by diverse providers (Glennerster 2003).

Right from the outset, costs rocketed above those that the wartime planners had anticipated. Since then, the NHS has endlessly been shaken up every few years in yet another bid to reduce expenses, as improvements in medication and medical technology have driven up costs and expectations.

One consequence of these developments is that although the care provided is free, the NHS rations resources according to priorities. An independent body called the National Institute for Health and Clinical Excellence (NICE) provides guidance to encourage "evidence-based" (that is, cost-effective) prescribing. People with quite serious needs may be denied treatment because the cost is greater than the estimated likely benefit. For example, the legal battle by myeloma sufferers in England and Wales denied the drug Velcade, and that of breast cancer patients seeking treatment with Herceptin, reveal the heartbreaking value for money decisions facing the NHS. Private health insurance and cash payment for private treatment are relatively uncommon. This means that for most people, the quality of care they receive is constrained by limited public funding.

It should also be noted that despite the principle of a universal health service, different socioeconomic groups do not succeed in gaining equal access to the NHS. Tudor-Hart labeled this the "inverse care law"—the groups in greatest need are least likely to receive the level of health services they require (Tudor-Hart 1971). Despite the aspiration of its founders to secure a comprehensive health service, provision has always been patchy, a particular problem for the most disadvantaged. For example, fewer general practitioners (GPs) serve deprived areas (HM Treasury and Department of Health 2002), perhaps because of personal preferences not to live and work there. London has some of the best teaching hospitals in the world, but ironically, it can be difficult to register with a GP. There is evidence that disadvantaged people are more likely to receive treatment as an emergency and not at the early stages of disease (HM Treasury and Department of Health 2002). The impact is that the NHS does not adequately compensate for the relationship between poverty and ill health. This is partly because the disadvantaged do not receive as much health care in relation to their needs, but mainly because it does not address access to other services that promote well-being, such as food shops, social and leisure activities.

The NHS can be divided into a number of different branches. Primary care is that provided by a family doctor (GP), dentist, optician, or pharmacist. Community nursing, occupational therapy, NHS Walk-in Centers, and the phone helpline NHS Direct are also branches of primary care. If a GP cannot deal with a problem themselves, they refer a patient to a hospital consultant with specialized knowledge. In Britain a patient must always be referred by a primary care practitioner before attending hospital as an inpatient or outpatient (except for emergencies). Thus, the GP acts as "gatekeeper" to limit access to the rest of the NHS. This principle is one explanation for why the United Kingdom has traditionally spent less on health care than most other advanced economies. The United Kingdom spends only about 8.3 percent of its gross domestic product (GDP) on health;

Germany spends 10.9 percent, and the United States 15.3 percent (OECD 2006), although the government is currently committed to increasing real spending on health care to the EU average level of 9 percent (HM Treasury 2006b). The bulk of expenditure on the NHS goes to hospitals, although contact with primary care accounts for some 90 percent of NHS activity (DoH 2003).

Most NHS services are provided either within a so-called NHS Primary Care Trust (PCT) or NHS hospital trust. In England, the central government Department of Health sets overall policy and a lower tier of 150 or so locally based NHS PCTs run the NHS in their particular geographical area. The PCTs are statutory bodies, responsible for delivering health care and health improvements to their local area. They have their own budgets and set their own priorities, within the constraints of those set by the Department of Health. They directly provide funding for a range of community health services such as general practitioners and prescription medicines. They also "commission" (that is, purchase) hospital and mental health services on behalf of the patients in their area, either from NHS hospital trusts or from the private sector. The local government has no involvement in the running of the NHS, and since the boundary of the local government is not always contiguous with the boundary of a PCT, problems can arise in coordinating cross-cutting policies such as social care provision.

An important aspect of policy affecting governance is the increased devolution of some aspects of social policy to the "home countries": England, Wales, Scotland, and Northern Ireland. The result has been significant divergence in health policy, despite the so-called "national" health service (Greer 2004; Talbot-Smith and Pollock 2006; Woods 2004). For brevity, this chapter will focus on England. In future, research at the level of the devolved administrations will be increasingly necessary.

In what follows, we discuss the blurring of the public-private boundary in health care by the use of contracting out, the "internal market", the Private Finance Initiative and efforts to introduce a consumer-focused market ethos into the service. Lastly, we describe the privately financed sector.

1979–1997: The NHS under the Conservative governments

In order to understand health policy today, it is necessary to understand how the NHS has developed in the last 25 years. In the 1970s the NHS was run according to a traditional model of state finance, state provision, and strong trade unions, and health professionals were trusted to run all aspects of the service. Unhappily, the tension between increasing demand and limited resources meant that by the mid-1980s waiting lists were growing. Reforms by the Conservatives in response were based on the notion that the NHS would be more cost efficient if it was reorganized along more market-like principles. Their first reforms included putting out catering, cleaning, and laundry services to tender to private contractors, which was contentious, especially in circumstances where it did not result in the hoped-for cost savings or led to a poorer quality of service, or pay cuts and job insecurity for workers.

A little later the NHS was overhauled by the far-reaching NHS and Community Care Act 1990 which introduced the so-called "internal market." The central innovation was a split between purchaser and provider, which was aimed at bringing about incentives to control costs. In establishing the internal market, "purchasers" (health authorities and some family doctors known as "GP fundholders") were given budgets with which to "shop around" to buy health care from "providers" (hospitals, and even private providers). NHS hospitals became independent trusts, with their own managements, competing with each other. It should be emphasized that it was managers in the health authorities and GP fundholders who were doing the choosing and purchasing, not individual patients.

The internal market improved value for money in the NHS and reduced waiting times. Yet the experiences also demonstrated that whether or not the introduction of markets in public services delivers improvements depends on the precise market structure. In the case of the NHS, the competition encouraged between providers led to unnecessary doubling-up of services (for example, where two nearby hospitals both bought MRI scanners which were not fully utilized). Another problem was that for an internal market to work as intended, alternative providers must exist, that is, there must be contestability. This means that it must be made easy for new providers to enter the market, and merger of existing providers should be discouraged. At the same time, failing providers must go out of business. However, the government lacked the political nerve to force hospitals in the red to close, so the extent of true market discipline was limited. Finally, although the internal market may have been successful at cutting cost, it is less clear whether rewards existed for improving the quality of care.

The NHS since 1997

In this section we discuss the ongoing contracting out of service provision to the private sector, and the use of private investment to finance capital building projects.

New Labour claims to have removed the internal market created by Conservatives. In a 1997 document, New Labour proposed to hold on to what it felt had worked previously, but to move away from encouraging outright competition to a more collaborative approach (DoH 1997). New Labour's 2000 NHS Plan also dismissed the value of competition between hospitals, on the grounds that it resulted in variable standards, and because most local areas lacked competition anyway as they were served by only one or two general hospitals (NHS 2000). In fact the main elements of the internal market were retained—the purchasing role of local health authorities (now called Primary Care Trusts) and the provider trusts.

Another reorganization took place in 2002, with the publication of "Reforming NHS financial flows: Introducing Payment by Results" (DoH 2002). This revived competition between NHS hospitals. In England, cash is allocated from the center, which the Primary Care Trusts use to "commission" (buy) hospital care. However a fundamental modification is that under payment by results, the prices PCTs pay for a medical procedure are regulated by a national tariff based on average costs, instead of the former locally negotiated block contracts which prevailed under the internal market. This earlier system led to variation across the country in the prices charged, reflecting the local hospitals' actual costs instead of rewarding efficient providers. The new system is designed to sharpen competition between hospitals by offering them a financial incentive to draw patients by improving their services, and to boost their "profits" by lowering their costs below the nationally fixed price.

The Labour government has switched its position on the use of the private sector since it made its first pronouncements: it has now committed to a major expansion in its use of the private sector. As far as it is concerned, it no longer matters who provides health care on behalf of the NHS, so long as it is free to the patient at point of use and of high quality. The Wanless Report on health costs, which the government accepted, explicitly endorsed collaboration of the public and private sectors (HM Treasury 2002b).

The government's change of strategy can be explained, in part, by its failure early on to drive down waiting times, a key concern of the voting public. In response, not only was a large increase in resources announced (HM Treasury 2000), but where waiting times are deemed too long, the NHS can now use public finance for a patient to be treated faster at one of the forty-or-so Independent Sector Treatment Centres (ISTCs). These are run by private companies, some of which are based overseas. ISTCs are additional to, rather than in competition with, the NHS. As many use overseas staff they have been successful at cutting waiting times for common routine operations (for example, cataract surgery, hip and knee replacements) by increasing capacity.

The new ISTCs are controversial for a number of reasons. There have been concerns that employees will be poached from NHS hospitals which are already struggling to retain staff. Others have warned that the centers could "cherry-pick" simpler operations: many NHS hospitals depend on the income from more straightforward treatments to subsidize other more expensive treatments. Yet for the government the use of ISTCs is an article of faith, and there is a commitment to expand such provision sharply.

Further, the government wants to see a range of providers running community NHS services too. The first GP surgery for NHS patients run by a commercial private company opened in 2006. However, despite these developments, the private sector will add only a small contribution to total NHS clinical activity for the foreseeable future. Another model of public-private partnership is an arrangement first seen in 2007 in which an NHS Primary Healthcare Center was opened within a branch of the Boots pharmacy retail chain located in a shopping center. The PCT and the pharmacy concerned "are seeing this as a way to inform future developments not only locally but potentially nationally as well" (Wright 2007: 101).

Contracting out of NHS services has continued. For example, in 2006 the services delivering medical supplies provided by the internal nonprofit organization NHS Logistics were outsourced to the private commercial company DHL/Novation. The Unison trade union and employees protested, believing that to use even more private firms is a step toward full privatization of the health service which will erode public sector ethos—the "goodwill" and dedication among workers. As well as a diversity of providers, and in some tension with this policy, national targets for acceptable waiting times and quality now pervade the health service (set out in DoH 2004). National standards have been put in place to ensure minimum standards throughout the service for particular client groups (DoH 2006). There is also a highly centralized process of audit and performance review by the Healthcare Commission. A major—and controversial—aspect of private-sector involvement in the NHS is that investment in new hospitals is now paid for by the private finance initiative (PFI), in which the private sector designs, builds, manages, and sometimes operates facilities that are then rented to the NHS, which continues to provide all clinical services. The PFI provides a way of funding major capital investments, as an alternative to adding to public sector borrowing. The 1997 document Partnerships for Prosperity set out the Government's support for PFI (Treasury Taskforce 1997). From 1997 onwards, nearly all major hospital schemes—either complete hospitals or major extensions—have been financed and built under the PFI, delivering 185 new or refurbished health care facilities (HM Treasury 2006a). The aim of this approach is to capitalize on the private sector's innovation and entrepreneurial managerial skills. It is also argued that the PFI, under the right circumstances, yields greater value for money than projects wholly dependent upon the public sector for finance and management. The basis of the PFI is risk transfer. For example, in the case of price risk the parties negotiate a fixed price for construction of a hospital. If during construction the cost of building that hospital increases, under a traditional procurement route, any extra outlay would be passed on to the health authority. Under the PFI the private sector has to meet these costs. However, the contractor is entitled to any profits that it can generate. By requiring the private sector supplier to put its own capital at risk and to deliver strict levels of service, it is argued that the PFI helps to deliver high quality public assets that are delivered on time and to budget. The government argues that PFI has allowed a massive and much needed capital investment in the NHS. The government has been able to make a much more rapid improvement to NHS buildings than would be possible if dependent only on the limited public funding to be had from the Treasury. But the PFI has been problematic (Ruane 2000). Allegations of profiteering have been thrown at the scheme (see Unison 2001). Another problem is that when companies have let them down, the penalty clauses in their contract are sometimes nonenforceable, leaving the government no option but to use the same contractors to resolve the problems they created. Critics say the PFI is overly expensive and will burden the NHS with high lease costs for decades because the private sector charges a premium for operating and maintaining facilities for up to 30 years for a fixed cost.

Private companies are also building primary care facilities by competitive tendering in partnership with local health services. Under this scheme, although there is private-sector involvement, the health center premises are not wholly privately owned. Although it has been criticized for putting profit before patients (for instance, by Unison 2006) the government sees this development as an effective procurement mechanism (National Audit Office 2005). In summary, in the traditional understanding of the welfare state in Britain, it was assumed that the state would provide the finance and act as the front-line delivery agency. The role of central government has increasingly become one of regulation (price-per-case tariffs, targets) rather than management (Klein 2005). The day-to-day management of welfare services is partly in the public sector and partly in the hands of commercial and not-for-profit voluntary organizations. Yet despite the constant reorganizations of the NHS over the last 20 years, the basic concept of a publicly funded service, available to everyone and free at point of use, has been preserved.

Private health care

There have always been private physicians, pharmacy, dental, and optical services alongside the NHS. There are also private care homes, although they will not be considered here. Nevertheless, in the past, private medicine was only attractive to a relatively small number of patients. In the United Kingdom, 14 percent of health spending was funded by private sources in 2004, below the average of 27 percent for OECD countries (OECD 2006). The share of private spending has decreased from approximately 20 percent in 1998, reflecting the government's commitment to increasing NHS spending (rather than a slowing in private-sector growth). The Thatcher government promoted private health care as an alternative to NHS provision. Compared to the 3.6 million people covered by private medical insurance in 1980, there were approximately 6.4 million adults and children covered in 2001 (Emmerson et al. 2001). Although the Labour government is substantially increasing NHS spending, it has no ambitions to expand private health insurance. In fact, it abolished the tax relief for private medical insurance for over-60s and relief against national insurance contributions for employer-provided medical insurance introduced in 1990. Despite this, its importance has grown. Observers have predicted a further increasing role for the private sector as the NHS continues to struggle with ever-increasing demands, despite the significant increases in funding and the British electorate's reluctance to move to a two-tier system.

Some people are insured by their employer as an occupational benefit; some insure as individuals. There is also a significant market in direct cash financed private health care for those who do not have insurance. Sixty-five percent of the private-sector revenue comes from private medical insurance, 22.5 percent from self-pay, 7.5 percent from NHS patients in private facilities and 5 percent from foreign patients (Salter 2004). Private health care is sometimes provided in separate private hospitals employing their own staff; however it can be provided in NHS "paybeds." The Healthcare Commission regulates the independent health care sector through registration, annual inspection, monitoring complaints, and enforcement. However, it does not provide a performance rating comparable to that applied to NHS hospitals, because of the commercial sensitivity of such data (Crinson 2005). Only 12.5 percent of the UK population are covered by private insurance (Emmerson et al. 2000). However, there are some sectors where private funded treatment is considerably higher than this, for example abortion services of which 33 percent were privately financed in 2001 (Salter 2004). Users of private health care in the United Kingdom are richer and have other linked characteristics, being predominantly middle-aged and male (Burchardt and Propper 1999; Emmerson et al. 2000). But use of the private sector is not restricted to this specific group: although 40 percent of those in the top decile are insured, 5 percent of those in the bottom 40 percent are too (Emmerson et al. 2000). Those in the higher-income groups are more likely to have their insurance paid for by their employer as an employee benefit. The group with the highest level of coverage are those still in education (and therefore covered by their parent's policy). There are many private insurance providers. Basic, standard and comprehensive policies are available, covering a different range of diagnostic tests and varying levels of inpatient or outpatient treatment. In order to keep the contributions down, the kind of cover which is offered tends to be limited. Chronic or preexisting conditions are often not covered. Therefore, even those with private health insurance rely on the NHS. It has been argued that those with private medical insurance are less likely to support the NHS, although Propper and Green (2001) find no evidence for this. Primary care has overwhelmingly remained within the NHS even though a number of private Medicentre GP practices have opened. Emergency care has also remained within the NHS, which is another reason why there is extensive overlap between users of the NHS and private care. Staff also flows between sectors: even in private hospitals, many of the clinical staff received their training and experience in NHS hospitals and have jobs in the NHS alongside their private practice (although the amount of private practice NHS doctors may undertake is regulated). Private medicine diverts staff who would otherwise work in the NHS while making a negligible contribution to costs of their training.

A perceived advantage of private health care is that it may enable a patient to receive faster treatment. Another concern which has increased the appeal of private health care is the perception that private hospitals are clean. Advertising by the private health insurers plays on the fears of catching secondary infections such as MRSA and C.Diff in public hospitals. There is evidence from the UK that the quality of the NHS is associated with demand for private medical insurance, though not with the use of the private sector (Burchardt et al. 1999).

The United Kingdom has one of the most progressively financed systems of health care (Glennerster 2003; Sefton 2002). The pro-poor bias of the NHS partly derives from the source of finance—progressive general taxation—and is reinforced by the use of private medicine by the better-off, who essentially pay for their health care twice.

Future issues

Policies to widen patient choice and further increase the role of the private sector have created a much more businesslike environment for the NHS since 1997. Demands for more spending on health care are being met mainly by increased public spending, although a further spread of private health insurance could change the public-private balance in the future. New Labour Third Way policies, public-private partnerships, and a "what matters is what works" philosophy means that there will be an even further blurring of the boundaries of the public and private sectors. It therefore does not make sense to think of a public-private dichotomy.

Commentators argue that the right form of public-private partnerships can deliver better public services (Commission on Public Private Partnerships 2001). However, the government's commitment to using the private sector has stirred up concerns that range from outright hostility toward profit-making in health care, to clinicians' worries that the transfer of the most straightforward cases to private centers will make it harder to provide suitable training to doctors.

Under "payment by results" it is unclear what will happen if a hospital gets into financial trouble. It might cross-subsidize from their profit-making side. However, they might cut costs in the loss-making area, putting quality considerations in jeopardy. They might shed some types of treatment altogether, if they cannot provide them competitively. This could provoke controversy if cherished local services start to disappear. This is already happening. The established trend is for hospitals to specialize so they can develop into centers of expertise, but the public have reacted vehemently against the inevitable cuts and closures this policy requires. An indication of the strength of feeling against such rationalization of services was the highly unusual election in 2001 to Parliament of a single-issue candidate, a doctor opposed to NHS "reconfiguration" who stood as "Independent Kidderminster Hospital and Health Concern."

Yet market-influenced policies will certainly continue. One is that of offering patients choice, which forms an important plank of current health policy referred to as the "patient-led NHS." From December 2005, all patients referred by their GP for a specialist consultation for nonemergency treatment at a hospital have been offered a choice of at least four hospitals, both NHS and private. Yet arguably, people care less about having a choice of hospitals than they do about being treated by good doctors, without a long wait and without having to travel long distances (Appleby and Alvarez-Rosete 2005). Some people are skeptical that offering patients more choices will make the outcomes that they really care about happen.

The choice agenda raises numerous issues. In order for it to really work consumers need to know what is in their best interests. But do they? Consumer-patients will need access to practical information and advice on which to base their choice. Will loss-making hospitals be forced to close or merge? Will patients be willing to travel to a hospital with a shorter waiting time? Early research findings suggested that middle-class groups may tend to gravitate toward what they perceive as the better health services, leading to a possible widening of health inequalities (Crinson 2005; Lewis 2005). Those without cars, who are elderly or generally more unwell will not be able to exercise choice as freely as others. However, if some patients opt to go further from home for treatment, this might relieve the demands on local providers and so improve access for other patients less willing to travel.

This scenario may not improve the quality of local care; indeed, it may even reduce it, as the provider's reputation may fall further, prompting further "middle-class flight" (Exworthy and Peckham 2006). Thus, the diversity and choice agenda is likely to lead to inequality in access to services.

The other issue is providing public accountability as a means of promoting service improvement where choice and market-based strategies are not an option. Service users are involved by satisfaction surveys, panels, and patient forums. For instance, in a bid to add to the now existing forms of consumer power in health services, a Patient and Public Involvement Forum (PPIF) made up of local volunteers for every NHS Trust and Primary Care Trust in England has been set up.

When they were in opposition, the Labour Party criticized the Conservative's creation of an "internal market" for health care. Yet ten years on, New Labour have embraced the private sector and the power of market discipline. However, the pace of improvement is slow and practical problems may obstruct further implementation (Lewis and Gillam 2003). New Labour has increased spending on health at a record rate because of the high political profile of the NHS. UK health spending as a proportion of GDP is projected to reach 9.4 percent by 2007–08 (HM Treasury 2002a). Despite the fact that much of this increased expenditure has gone toward improving the pay and conditions of doctors and nurses, hospitals have been refurbished under the PFI, staff numbers have increased and there have been substantial improvements in waiting times. Unfortunately, the pay-off for the government has been abysmal: staff morale is low and even though most patients say that their recent personal experience has been good, half the voters nevertheless perceive that the NHS is getting worse (24dash.com 2006).

The UK pension system

Introduction

In the UK pensions system, public and private provision is so entangled that it is difficult to separate the two areas as independent schemes. The range and quality of public provision affects the market for the private sector, and government carries a responsibility to ensure that private pensions are organized so that they contribute to effective overall pension provision for the citizens of the United Kingdom. Any pension settlement must take both sectors and their interaction into account. The UK experience illustrates the problems in trying simply to substitute private for public welfare as welfare states move toward a system of greater individual responsibility in response to pressures from globalization, slowing growth rates, population aging and family change, which bear particularly heavily on pension provision (Pierson 2001).

Basic structure: state and private pensions

The public pension system in the United Kingdom has been described as one of the most complex in the world (Pensions Policy Institute 2004). It consists of four main elements:

1. A flat-rate national insurance pension payable to UK citizens who have contributed the relevant number of contributions (in most cases equivalent to a 40-year working life). The pension is at a relatively low level (£84.25 for a single person, £134.75 for a couple in 2006). People with no source of support other than this benefit will also often be entitled to means-tested supplementation. This pension is financed through a notional fund into which contributions from workers and employers are paid. However, the system has been subject to supplementation from direct taxation and is best thought of as a pay-as-you-go system. This scheme is compulsory for all workers.

2. A second-tier, earnings-related state pension. The original State Earnings Related Pension, established in 1979 was phased out seven years later by the market-oriented Conservative government, so that relatively few people have an entitlement under it. More recently, the 1997 New Labour government established a State Second Pension, directed at lower- and middle-income people. The formula is complex and redistributive, effectively flat rate for the lower paid. The scheme is contribution financed but with relatively generous

direct payment by government of contributions for disabled people and those with child or elder care responsibilities. Since the scheme was only introduced in 2002, pensions have not yet built up. These pensions are compulsory for all employees, but those with approved private pensions, typically the better-off half of the population, may be contracted out.

3. Private, tax-subsidized pensions. These schemes are voluntary. Private pension schemes that meet various requirements are exempt from tax on contributions or on the surpluses generated by funds and are thus advantageous savings vehicles for old age. There are two main varieties: occupational pensions, negotiated typically between employers and unions, and private personal pensions, arranged by an individual with an insurance company. Most of the original occupational schemes provided defined-benefit pensions (often at a proportion of final salaries) and mostly covering middle-class and professional groups and state-sector workers. At one time they were seen as the "gold standard" of provision, since they could provide good pensions for the most influential groups of workers, and cost the state little directly. Membership peaked in the late 1970s with over 12 million active members, drawn equally from state and private sector. The schemes have come under pressure from increasing life expectancy. In many cases the risk has been transferred from providers to users by a switch to defined-contribution entitlements. Membership has declined below 10 million, with some three-fifths in the state sector, and current negotiations will probably reduce that number further (GAD 2005).

The private personal pensions were established by the Conservative government with preferential tax arrangements and initially direct state subsidies. After a rapid expansion in the mid- and late 1990s (which led to a scandal about misselling by unscrupulous private-sector agents), the schemes ceased to grow. The New Labour government remodeled them as Stake-Holder Pensions with stringent requirements as to transparency, low management charges, and uprating and stronger regulatory arrangements. Taken together, the two main forms of private personal schemes, private individual and stake-holder pensions, cover only a relatively small group—some 15 percent of men and 9 percent of women employees and less than half of self-employed people by 2001–2 (PPI 2003). They have proved unattractive to both providers and the public and have failed to grow.

4. The means-tested state Pension Credit. Last-resort tax-financed provision has recently been redesigned and strengthened and the new scheme consists of two components. For those who fall below a defined income level there is an income component (the Guarantee Credit element of Pension Credit) which would in 2006 bring the weekly income of a single pensioner up to a minimum of £114.05 a week, a modest but adequate level standard of living. A further component (the Savings Credit element of the Pension Credit) is intended to soften the disincentive to private savings resulting from means-testing. It pays 60p for every £1 of private income over the

means-test level up to a maximum of about £20 a week. It is estimated that only 60 to 69 percent of entitled households claim the pension credit (DWP 2004).

Pension finance

In the United Kingdom, pension finance has four main features. First, the relatively low level of pensions implies that the associated tax and contribution demands are moderate. The United Kingdom spent 5.5 percent of GDP on public pensions in 2000, less than any other EU member country and about half the EU average of 10.4 percent. It is estimated that, if current trends continue, the percentage will fall to 4.4 percent by 2050, whereas average EU spending will rise to 13.3 percent (Pensions Commission 2004).

Second, the weakness of pension spending has implications for a shift toward means-testing. Current projections indicate that without a new policy direction the percentage of pensioners entitled to supplementation from means-tested pension credit will increase sharply. According to DWP, entitlement to credit will rise from roughly half of pensioners at present to about two-thirds by 2050. According to the independent Institute for Fiscal Studies the proportion may exceed four-fifths (Pension Policy Institute 2003).

Third, the fact that the pension system is under the direct and immediate control of a centralized government, rather than at arm's length as in more corporatist countries such as France and Germany, means that responsibility for pensions is brought home to government directly and unavoidably.

The tax arrangements imply a substantial government subsidy to the private sector. Since private pensions tend to be taken out more by middle-class groups this is effectively an upwards redistribution. In general these groups live longer than the population average, so they also gain disproportionately from entitlement to the state flat-rate pension. The current pattern of increases in life-expectancy whereby the longevity advantage of privileged groups is sustained and slightly increased will extend upward redistribution. The net cost of tax relief on private pensions is estimated at 1.8 per cent of GDP (Pensions Policy Institute 2004). This is equivalent to one-third of current direct spending and is concentrated upwards on higher-income groups. Some 60 percent of the relief goes to higher rate tax payers, who make up 11 percent of all tax payers.

Fourth, pension saving is simply inadequate. The state schemes provide cheap, low-standard pensions. About half of workers have no voluntary personal or employers' schemes to top up what the state offers. Occupational pensions are in fact in decline, as pointed out earlier. Private pension contributions for each worker have stalled, peaking at 7.8 percent of National Average Earnings in 2000 (PPI 2003). Young people are starting to save later in life, and younger workers are less likely than older workers to be members of a nonstate scheme. Sixty-eight percent of 45–54 year olds were members in 2001 as against 56 percent of 25–34 year olds (PPI 2003).

UK pension provision faces severe problems. Many people will be entitled to low benefits and be forced to rely on means-tested supplementation, whereas a privileged minority will benefit from generous state subsidies delivered mainly through tax exemptions. These problems are made hard to solve by the balance of forces in the United Kingdom, with a weak state sector and a private sector that is very large, but does the majority of its business with particular groups.

Pension actors

The range and complexity of the current system gives rise to a range of actors, pressures for change and identified problems. Five groups are of importance: current pensioners; current workers, who are both contributors and tax-payers; employers who cofinance and have interests in the work incentives associated with the system; the government; and the private insurance industry. The United Kingdom has one of the largest private pension systems in the world and an extremely powerful financial sector in the city of London. The last-named player is of greater relevance here than in many other countries.

The interests of current pensioners are divided. The UK pension system is highly class and gender related. Private pensions are almost entirely directed to middle-class workers, predominantly male. The class divisions sharpen the political tensions surrounding pension reform.

Current workers save for pensions through compulsory state schemes and through private personal and employers' schemes. Almost all commentators agree that the rate of saving by whatever system is inadequate to provide viable pensions in the future. Although projections of a rising dependency ratio imposing greater stress on pensions have been available in the United Kingdom as elsewhere for a considerable period (see the review in the Pensions Commission report 2003), savings rates fail to rise.

Employers have responded to pressures on existing occupational schemes by cutting back on provision so that over half of defined-benefit schemes were closed to new entrants by 2004. By that year, membership of defined-benefit schemes had declined from 6 million in 1979 to 3.5 million, while defined-contribution has risen from 0.1 million to about one million (GAD 2005). The substitution of defined-contribution for defined-benefit schemes transfers risk from employers to workers. A further development involves the failure of employers' contributions to keep up with the demands on the defined-contribution schemes. Between 2002 and 2005 employers' contribution to the more advantageous defined-benefit schemes rose from 11.5 to 16.5 percent of earnings; for the defined-contribution schemes the rise was from 5.1 to 5.9 percent (ACA 2002, 2005). This will have a major impact on the value of benefits provided by schemes and is not simply a result of demographic imbalance. It implies that total remuneration packages for those groups weakest in the labor market are subject to erosion. This is one outcome of the shift in the balance of power away from labor associated postindustrialism to economic globalization.

The pensions industry has a strong interest in maintaining and if possible strengthening the position of nonstate pensions, which are supported by tax-exemptions and by the demand generated by the weakness of state alternatives. The position of the national finance sector is an important element in policymaking in the United Kingdom and a powerful constraint on the capacity of government to develop new radical solutions.

The government wishes to demonstrate commitment to a viable pension scheme, since pensions are highly popular—far and away the most important element in social security according to repeated annual rounds of the British Social Attitudes survey since 1983. Current patterns of provision appear unsatisfactory. At the same time pensions are a major cost and one that is likely to grow greater in the future. However, tax rises are unpopular in the United Kingdom and there is ample evidence that many voters fail to make the link between valued public services and the unwelcome taxation necessary to provide them. On the other hand, pension costs are likely to impinge on labor costs and damage the competitive position of the United Kingdom in increasingly globalized international markets. This point is highly relevant in competition with countries such as Japan where social security spending is 11 percent of GDP or South Korea where it is 2.4 percent, against 13 percent in the United Kingdom (OECD 2005).

A further consideration is the series of scandals surrounding the misselling of the personal pensions introduced by the Conservative government which damaged public confidence in the private pension industry and combined with a series of high profile bankruptcies which resulted in workers losing pension rights they had paid for as well as their jobs (Goode 1994; Waine 1995). Recently, government has established a mandatory last-resort coinsurance fund for private pensions on the US model. This currently has sufficient resources to meet less than half the losses of pensioners in bankrupt schemes (Cohen 2006).

The outcome of the interaction of these complex and disparate structures is a conflict between pension affordability, pension adequacy, and pension security in public policy. Government wishes to keep pensions cheap in terms of tax, which implies a transfer of responsibility to the private sector. However, it is also reluctant to intervene strongly in the private sector, because it values individual responsibility and because it is committed to maintaining the freedom of the powerful UK finance industry. Official policy under both Conservative and Labour governments has been to increase the scope of the private sector in pensions from 40 to 60 percent. Due to the unattractiveness of what is on offer (both limited and expensive private pensions from the viewpoint of citizens, and new lower-income and less profitable groups of private customers, from the viewpoint of the industry), little headway has been made in this direction.

However, government also wishes to be able to guarantee security and adequacy to pensioners, which implies greater intervention, with a means-tested last line of defense. Current policy includes the limited State Second Pension, and a strengthening of means-tested Pension Credit to fill the obvious gaps in provision. The better the state provision, the more difficult it is to sell private pensions, so the commitment to the private sector by the UK government indicated by the resources foregone in tax relief, and the obvious power of the City of London now raise serious issues for the future of pensions. The sharp end of this point emerges in the debates about means-tested pensions which are often seen as eroding individual incentives for private saving (Pensions Commission 2004).

Emerging issues

The reform of pensions has been high on the policy agenda for some time. The conflict of interest between the various parties involved, most importantly between pensioners, finance capital and government, means that policy consensus is difficult to achieve. Since all have power resources but exert them in very different ways, it is difficult for government to promote a solution that imposes substantial obligations on UK capital without damaging its own economy, or to pursue a direction that is unacceptable to pensioners and workers whose votes are essential to its continued authority.

The Conservative government attempted to introduce a settlement in the late 1980s that decisively shifted the balance toward the private sector. This was unsuccessful. Insufficient numbers of individuals were willing to purchase the private pensions on offer and the scandals over misselling and poor value for money strengthened this reluctance and effectively discredited a solution led by lightly regulated private pensions. The government has cut back the state earnings-related schemes to save money and reinforce incentives for private saving. The result is that pensioners face a bleak future and the political demands for a solution have grown more pressing. The problem is exacerbated by the decline of the occupational schemes, increasingly affecting the position of middle-class voters, who are a particularly vocal and influential group.

Government initially procrastinated through a series of reports, none of which was implemented in any thorough-going way. The current state of play is that the recommendations of a major and authoritative commission led by Lord Turner, a leading figure in the finance sector, and strengthened by the participation of major academic figures, have been largely accepted by all relevant parties as a way forward (Pensions Commission 2005). The key elements are

1. Automatic enrollment of all workers into a national system of funded personal pensions, from which they may exercise the right to opt out.

2. Mandatory employer contributions, matching employee contributions, up to three percent of salary.
3. Reduction of the number of contribution years required for the basic state pension to 30, a move that benefits those with interrupted working lives, particularly women.
4. A continued basic state pension increased annually uprated by the earnings rather than the prices index, to be introduced by 2015 at the latest.
5. A gradual increase in state pension age in line with rising life expectancy, starting in 2020—with a rise to 66 sometime in the 2020s.

The proposals meet the security and adequacy requirements by linking the basic flat-rate pension to earnings rather than prices (although the date at which this link will be implemented is some way off and may well be deferred to 2012 or even later), and topping it up from compulsory nonstate pensions for the vast majority of people. Government will support provision for parental and care-related needs. The private sector retains a buoyant middle-class market on top of this relatively ungenerous framework of state managed provision.

The issues that arise are

1. The proposal to increase pension age to counter the extra cost of longer lives. Further working years bear more harshly on those for whom work is more burdensome and this may reproduce some of the social class inequalities surrounding pensions. Separate proposals to make the tests for disability benefits more stringent will intensify this division.
2. Proposals that private companies should manage the national accounts. The experience of personal pensions indicates that this will lead to differences in pay-out and cream-skimming that will strengthen inequalities, and also loss of the economies of scale available to a national scheme. This issue is at present unresolved.
3. The proposal leaves the existing private sector and the subsidies that support it largely untouched. At the same time, the extra compulsory savings by the whole population through the automatic enrollment scheme will reduce the scope and cost of the directly financed means-tested benefits. It is probably that the perverse redistribution bias of UK pensions will be strengthened.
4. Proposals to extend the basic scheme so that it became a citizen scheme available to all and financed through contributions from workers and employers have been ignored. This would have the advantages of simplicity, cheap administration, and virtually universal coverage, leading to the eradication of almost all old-age poverty. The element of compulsion required appears to be unacceptable to a government committed to market freedom and anxious to protect opportunities for the private sector. Some 30 percent of pensioners are likely to be poor enough to qualify for means-tested supplementation when the scheme matures.

Future prospects

The proposed settlement has been criticized as too little, too late. Despite the delay that will do nothing to resolve the problem of insecure and inadequate pensions for the current age-cohort of pensioners, the proposals appear to represent a solution that will be acceptable to the major policy actors. Finance capital will continue with its protected and subsidized market, pensioners will receive better and more stable pensions, financed mainly by workers with a contribution by employers, and government will be able to claim it has dealt with the pension crisis in way that keeps UK labor costs low in comparison with other EU countries. Realism triumphs over redistribution in a welfare settlement that allows a substantial but not overwhelming role to the private sector.

Conclusion

The United Kingdom has the largest private sector of any European welfare state and has been at the forefront of the recent expansion of nonstate provision. Experience in this country indicates that the gains to be made by movement in this direction are limited and require very careful regulation and monitoring of the part played by nonstate actors. Here there are difficult problems. In both health care and pensions, private providers strive to cherry-pick particular groups of service users. Attempts to encourage the private sector to take on pension responsibility for those on middle- and lower incomes have been largely unsuccessful. The ambitions of government in the 1980s and 1990s to expand the scope of private provision could only be pursued through extensive and damaging deregulation. Independent health care providers and insurance companies that operate within a relatively narrow range of largely predictable kinds of treatment are keen to pursue contractual arrangements that ensure that it is government that deals with risk.

Government often assumes that, as the institution with a monopoly on legislative and fiscal authority, it determines what happens. In practice, private players, particularly those with large resources, such as the UK insurance industry, or multinational drug companies, health insurers or hospital groups, have considerable success in influencing the design of tax subsidy policies (in pensions) or prescribing policies or the division of labor between NHS and competing ITSCs (in health care) to suit their own balance sheets. It is difficult for a government which relies on the private sector to meet the expanding demand for health care and pensions to exert strong controls over this sector, for fear of choking off the supply of services. A simple division between state and private sector as alternative suppliers of welfare services ignores the dimension of political power. In an increasingly globalizing world, the balance of power shifts increasingly toward private capital.

References

24dash.com. 2006. Half of voters think NHS has "got worse since 1996." Last updated: 1 November. Retrieved on November 2 from http://www.24dash.com/health/12427.htm

ACA. 2002, 2005. Pension Trends Surveys. ACA London.

Appleby, J. and Alvarez-Rosete. 2005. "Public Responses to NHS Reform." In A. Park et al. (eds), *British Social Attitudes*. London: Sage.

Blair, T. 1998. *The Third Way*. Fabian Society.

Burchardt, T. and C. Propper. 1999. "Does the UK Have a Private Welfare Class?" *Journal of Social Policy* 28(4): 643–65.

Burchardt, T., J. Hills, and C. Propper. 1999. *Private Welfare and Public Policy*. York: Joseph Rowntree Foundation.

Cohen, N. 2006. "Pension Fund Faces £1billion in Potential Claims." *Financial Times*. November 8, 2006.

Commission on Public Private Partnerships. 2001. *Building Better Partnerships*. IPPR.

Crinson, I. 2005. "The Direction of Health Policy in New Labour's Third Term." *Critical Social Policy* 25(4): 507–16.

Deakin, N. and K. Walsh. 1996. "The Enabling State: The Role of Markets and Contracts." *Public Administration* 74(1): 33–48.

DoH (Department of Health). 1997. "The New NHS: Modern, Dependable": Cm 3807.

DoH (Department of Health). 2002. "Reforming NHS Financial Flows: Payment by Results."

DoH (Department of Health). 2003. "Chapter 7 Activity, Performance and Efficiency." In Departmental report 2003: CM 5904.

DoH (Department of Health). 2004. "National Standards, Local Action: Health and Social Care Standards and Planning Framework 2005/06–2007/08."

DoH (Department of Health). 2006. National Service Frameworks (NSFs). Retrievedon July 2, 2008 from http://www.dh.gov.uk/PolicyAndGuidance/HealthAndSocialCareTopics/HealthAndSocialCareArticle/fs/en?CONTENT_ID=4070951&chk=W3ar/W

Emmerson, C., C. Frayne, and A. Goodman. 2000. "Pressures in UK Healthcare: Challenges for the NHS." IFS Commentaries: C081.

Emmerson, C., C. Frayne, and A. Goodman. 2001. "Should Private Medical Insurance Be Subsidised?" *Health Care UK* (Spring): 49–65.

Exworthy, M. and S. Peckham. 2006. "Access, Choice and Travel: Implications for Health Policy." *Social Policy and Administration* 40(3): 267–87.

GAD Government Actuaries Department. 2005. "Occupational Pension Schemes, 2004."

Glennerster, H. 2003. *Understanding the Finance of Welfare*. Bristol: The Policy Press.

Goode Committee. 1994. "Pensions Law Reform": Cm 2342–1, HMSO.

Greer, S. 2004. *Territorial Politics and Health Policy*. Manchester: Manchester University Press.

HM Treasury. 2000. "Chapter 5: Fairness for Families and Communities." In Budget 2000.

HM Treasury. 2002a. "Chapter 6: Delivering High Quality Public Services." In Budget 2002.

HM Treasury. 2002b. "The Wanless Report: Securing Our Future Health: Taking a Long-Term View."

HM Treasury. 2006a. "PFI: Strengthening Long-Term Partnerships."

HM Treasury. 2006b. "Pre-Budget Report 2006: Investing in Britain's Potential: Building Our Long-Term Future."

HM Treasury and Department of Health. 2002. "Tackling Health Inequalities: Cross-Cutting Review."

Klein, R. 2005. "Transforming the NHS: The Story in 2004." In M. Powell, L. Bauld, and K. Clarke. (eds), *Social Policy Review 17: Analysis and Debate in Social Policy, 2005.* Bristol: The Policy Press.

Le Grand, J. 1990. "The State of Welfare." In J. Hills (ed.), *The State of Welfare: The Welfare State in Britain since 1974.* Oxford: Oxford University Press.

Le Grand, J. and W. Bartlett. (eds). 1993. *Quasi-Markets and Social Policy.* London: Macmillan.

Lewis, R. 2005. "More Patient Choice in England's National Health Service." *International Journal of Health Services* 35(3): 479–84.

Lewis, R. and S. Gillam. 2003. "Back to the Market: Yet More Reform of the National Health Service." *International Journal of Health Services* 33(1): 77–84.

National Audit Office. 2005. *Department of Health: Innovation in the NHS: Local Improvement Finance Trusts, HC 28 2005–2006.* London: The Stationary Office.

NHS. 2000. "The NHS Plan: A Plan for Investment, a Plan for Reform": Cm 4818-I.

National Statistics and DWP (Department of Work and Pensions). 2007. Pension Credit: Estimates of take up in 2005–06.

OECD. 2005. *OECD in Figures.* Paris: OECD.

OECD. 2006. *OECD Health Data 2006: How Does the United Kingdom Compare.*

Pensions Commission. 2004. *Pensions: Challenges and Choices (The First Report).* London: Stationery Office.

Pensions Commission. 2005. *A New Pension Settlement for the 21st Century (Second Report).* London: Stationery Office.

Pensions Policy Institute. 2003. *The Pensions Landscape.* London: Pensions Policy Institute.

Pensions Policy Institute. 2004. *The Pensions Primer.* London: Pensions Policy Institute.

Pierson, P. 2001. *The New Politics of Welfare State.* Oxford: Oxford University Press.

Prime Minister and Minister for the Cabinet Office. 1999. "Modernising Government: Cm 4310."

Propper, C. and K. Green. 2001. "A Larger Role for the Private Sector in Financing UK Health Care: The Arguments and Evidence." *Journal of Social Policy* 30(4): 685–704.

Ruane, S. 2000. "Acquiescence and Opposition: The Private Finance Initiative in the National Health Service." *Policy & Politics* 28(3): 411–24.

Salter, B. 2004. *The New Politics of Medicine.* Houndmills: Palgrave.

Sefton, T. 2002. "Recent Changes in the Distribution of the Social Wage." CASE Paper 62. Centre for the Analysis of Social Exclusion, London School of Economics.

Sihota, S. K. 2003. "Creeping Charges." National Consumer Council.

Talbot-Smith, A. and A. M. Pollock. 2006. *The New NHS: A Guide.* Houndmills: Routledge.

Treasury Taskforce. 1997. "Partnerships for Prosperity: A New Framework for the PFI."

Tudor-Hart, J. 1971. "The Inverse Care Law." *Lancet* 1: 406–12.

Unison. 2001. Refinancing: Profiteering from Public Services.

Unison. 2006. In The Interests Of Profit: At The Expense Of Patients.

Vincent-Jones, P. 2006. *The New Public Contracting: Regulation, Responsiveness, Relationality.* Oxford: Oxford University Press.

Waine, B. 1995. "A Disaster Foretold? The Case of Personal Pensions." *Social Policy and Administration* 29(4): 317–34.

Woods, K. J. 2004. "Political Devolution and the Health Services in Great Britain." *International Journal of Health Services* 34(2): 323–40.

Wright, M. 2007. "Pharmacy Opens Doors to GP Services." *The Pharmaceutical Journal* 278(7436): 101.

7
Sweden: Markets within Politics

Karen M. Anderson, Paula Blomqvist, and Ellen M. Immergut

Introduction

The Swedish welfare state is regularly praised (or maligned) as the prototype of publicly organized and provided welfare. No matter how you slice it, the public sector is among the largest in the OECD, with public sector spending totalling 54 percent of GDP in 2005; the tax levels required to finance these extensive public commitments are similarly high (Statistiska centralbyrån 2007: 31). As in most other advanced industrial countries, pensions and health care are the two largest categories in the public budget, and governments have faced strong economic and political pressures to reform both programs. The public pension and health care systems have undergone substantial change during the past two decades, but both programs remain firmly within the public sector. However, the role of "markets within politics" has increased substantially.

Today's reformed pension system is more market-conforming in terms of its actuarial fairness than the old "ATP" system it replaced. Indeed, the introduction of the individual pension accounts in the new system (the "premium reserve") defies the public-private distinction because it represents a quasi-private scheme administered by a public sector agency. The health care sector has experienced a similar set of changes. Internal markets have been introduced, and private providers are now permitted to compete with public ones. Thus, the central conclusion of this chapter is that public dominance prevails, but the role of markets and other mechanisms usually associated with private provision has increased markedly. Politicians have introduced market mechanisms into pensions and health care in order to improve efficiency, cut costs, and stave off calls for more radical privatization initiatives. These shifts in the structure and financing of pensions and health care have far-reaching implications for the *politics* associated with pensions and health care. The reformed pension system is designed to function without political interference, thus taking much of the politics out of public pension provision (Anderson 2005). And the further decentralization of health care means that local governments take the heat for slow service delivery and increasing out-of-pocket expenses. In sum, developments in both sectors are marked by the partial retreat of the state—the public pension operates autonomously and most health care decision-making is in the hands of local government.

The public-private mix in health care

The Swedish health care system is dominated by public provision. The central government provides substantial public funding (from tax revenues) and sets the regulatory framework, and the 21 county councils (*landsting*) administer the system. The county councils are obligated to provide equal access to quality health care for all of their residents, and despite central regulation, they have considerable autonomy in their role as health care providers. Health care outcomes are among the best in the world. Life expectancy for women was 82.8 in 2005 and 78 for men, and infant mortality is very low.[1]

Sweden spends about 9 percent of GDP on health care (Socialstyrelsen 2005: 17), which is close to the OECD average. Health care financing relies on a mix of local taxation, state grants, and user charges. About 70 percent is financed by local taxes, 16 percent by the state, 3 percent is covered by patient charges, whereas the remaining 10 percent comes from other sources.[2] About 90 percent of health care costs are publicly financed; the fifth highest level (behind Luxembourg, the Czech Republic, the Slovak Republic, and the United Kingdom) in the OECD in 2004. As noted, county councils have much freedom, so it is not uncommon for public hospitals to purchase private health care services. According to OECD data, public health spending in Sweden has decreased as a share of GDP by 5 percent between 1990 and 2004.[3]

Patient fees are comparatively low, although they have risen in recent years. A doctor's visit typically costs SEK 100–150, and there is a small charge per day for hospital stays. A high cost limit (per year) means that no one pays more than SEK 900 per illness per year and SEK 1,800 per year for prescription drugs. Unlike other national health care systems, patients usually do not need a referral to visit a specialist.

The Swedish health care system is strongly decentralized. Its current organization dates to 1862, when the regional political units called county councils (*landsting*) were created and given the responsibility of operating the hospitals, which had been state owned since the Reformation in the sixteenth century. In 1955, national public health insurance was introduced, obligating the counties to provide care to all citizens at heavily subsidized cost. Over the following decades, the system was gradually transformed into an NHS-type system, financed primarily through local income taxes levied by the counties. In this process, most of the remaining private providers in the outpatient sector disappeared as their financial conditions deteriorated (Immergut 1992). Thus, until very recently, Swedish health care could be described as a system of virtually all publicly provided services, managed directly by elected county council politicians and their staff of civil servants. Services were available to all citizens, and private health insurance in Sweden was rare. Elections to the political assemblies of the 21 county councils (functioning like regional parliaments) are held every fourth year, on the same day as elections to the national parliament and municipal level. Since Sweden is a unitary state, the central government retains an overriding political responsibility for the health of the population and can adopt national laws governing aspects of the health care system, such as basic patient rights or regulations regarding contagious diseases. Through the National Board of Health and Social Welfare (*Socialstyrelsen*), an expert agency, the government can also issue guidelines regarding medical practice and evaluate developments at county council level.

In recent decades both policymakers and researchers have been more concerned with the governance of the system. This can be attributed both to harsher economic conditions and increasing interest in new public management. Reforms implemented during this period have generally been oriented toward decentralizing political power within the system and making the county councils more autonomous. In the 1970s and 1980s, the national legislation regulating the health care tasks of county councils was replaced by so-called discretionary laws, which stipulated overriding goals and values of the system, rather than detailed rules. During the 1970s, such decentralization reforms were primarily driven by the desire to strengthen the democratic character of the system by allowing for more localized decision-making and local community involvement. In the 1980s, the continued decentralization policies in the health care area became framed in the "management by objectives" philosophy that had gained influence among Swedish policymakers at the time (Montin 1997). At this point, it was stated that the role of the county council politicians should be to set goals for administrators and professionals within the system but leave its actual management to these groups. This meant a departure from the previous emphasis on detailed local planning, whereas provider units (hospitals, clinics, primary-care health centers) became more self-governing.

In the early 1990s, the economic situation of the counties deteriorated, both because of local unemployment (generating less tax revenue) and reductions in central government grants to the health care sector (which constitute about 15 percent of total health care expenditure). The need to contain costs reinforced within the counties the existing interest in market-oriented organizational reforms. Guided by the ideals of the "new public management" (NPM) movement, the counties began to experiment with organizational models that separated purchaser and provider functions and allowed for privatization and competition on the provider side (for example, Hood 1991). Apart from promoting economic efficiency and cost awareness, a stated objective behind these NPM reforms was to strengthen the role of the political representatives within the system. These reforms were made possible by changes in national legislation that removed some of the remaining barriers to fully independent health care provision at county council level by making it legal, for the first time, for the county councils to contract out the provision of services to private, including for-profit, actors. By the end of the 1990s, a majority of the county councils had introduced purchaser/provider splits and private contracting practices. The 1990s also saw a reinforced political emphasis on the rights of patients, both at the national political level and among the county councils themselves (Department of Social Affairs 1999).

During the 1980s and 1990s political and administrative power within this system was further decentralized. In recent years, waiting lines and poor coordination between different health providers have led to a critical debate about the functioning of the system and the performance of the county councils. Since the late 1990s, the government has made some attempts to strengthen its control over the system, but, so far, these efforts do not appear to have been very successful. In addition, some observers believe that the country councils are too small to provide efficiently all types of specialized care within their geographical areas.[4] As a result, Swedish health care today is characterized by ongoing discussions about the future of the country councils and their degree of independence from the central government.

The key political decision-making bodies within the Swedish health care system are the county councils, as they provide over 90 percent of all services. The small share of health care provided by nonpublic actors (about 9 percent) is typically regulated and, to an overwhelming degree, financed by the county councils as well. The county councils are also the employers of most health care personnel in Sweden, including the vast majority of doctors. Although the central government formally retains political responsibility for ensuring that health services are available to all citizens, the actual task of providing the services (including dental care) has been delegated to the county councils.

The most important national legislation underpinning the system is the Health and Medical Services Act of 1982. This Act is framework legislation so it sets out general objectives and does not regulate the system in detail. Thus it gives the county councils much freedom in organizing the provision of services. The county councils enjoy considerable financial autonomy from the central government as well because they have the right to levy local taxes. Central government block grants make up about 20 percent of the system's total finances.

In 1991, the Local Government Act further extended the already substantive political autonomy of the county councils by removing existing regulations regarding their internal organization and giving them the right to contract out service provision to nonpublic actors, including profit-making enterprises (Montin 1992). This led to locally initiated reforms in many county councils, the most common of which was the division of purchasing and provision and the expansion of patient choice. Local reforms during the second half of the 1990s often also included elements of decentralization, such as making provider units more organizationally independent or delegating the purchasing of services to local boards (Anell 1996). During the same period, responsibility for long-term and home-based health care, and later outpatient psychiatric services, were transferred from the county councils to the 290 municipalities who are traditionally the providers of social services for the elderly and handicapped. This added a new set of actors to the health care system, whose jurisdictions and responsibilities are not always clearly separated from those of the county councils.

The main role of the central government in the highly decentralized Swedish system is to formulate the overriding political goals and values guiding it. The government can also propose more detailed regulations regarding matters of national interest, for instance patient rights or contagious disease prevention. The government supervises the system through its expert agency, the National Board of Health and Welfare (*Socialstyrelsen*). Among the tasks of the Board is collecting data from the county councils to monitor their performance, evaluate policy outcomes, and provide treatment guidelines and other kinds of medical information to health care providers.

It should be noted, furthermore, that in practice health policy in Sweden is often formulated through largely informal contacts between the main actors of the system, that is, the government (represented by the Ministry of Social Affairs), the Board of Health and Welfare and the organization representing the county councils at the central level, and the National Federation of County Councils (*Landstingsförbundet*). The predominantly cooperative and consensual nature of these relations may at least in part be attributed to the dominant position of the Social Democratic Party in postwar Swedish politics, which resulted in Social Democratic governance at the central, regional, and local political levels during most of this period.

A prominent goal behind the far-reaching decentralization of political power to the county councils in the 1980s and 1990s was to strengthen the democratic character of the health care system. Reformers sought to bring the decision-making process within the system closer to the population and create new opportunities for active community involvement. Above all, it was hoped that their democratic accountability would be enhanced. Free choice of care provider in combination with a "money follows the patient" system of reimbursement was another reform measure employed to empower health consumers and democratize the system further (Blomqvist 2002).

Did these reforms have the intended effects? Reform outcomes have generally been hard to measure, given the plurality and vagueness of the stated goals (which were also related to the value of economic efficiency), but evaluations indicate that community involvement in health policymaking has reached state goals in at least some communities. Patient organizations appear to have become more actively involved in trying to influence processes of local health services purchasing. Other examples of community involvement include participation in health policy study groups and meetings with county council politicians (Bergman and Dahlbäck 2000). The introduction of health services purchasing has also led to more active attempts on part of policymakers to establish local medical needs and preferences, for instance through public surveys. In some county councils, such as Östergötland, there have also been moderately successful attempts to involve the local community in priority-setting, for instance through polls and discussion groups (Garpenby 2002). Among providers, the introduction of patient choice and performance-related payments has stimulated a new interest in measuring and evaluating patient satisfaction.

Patient choice of provider is probably the one reform measure that has received the most public attention. Patients now enjoy the right to choose their provider freely, both at primary- and secondary-care levels and across county borders. So far, patient flows between county councils remain marginal, however, and there is some indication that bureaucratic obstacles prevail when people seek care outside the previous "catchment areas" of, for instance, individual hospitals. Recent research indicates that another reason for persistently low patient mobility may be related to the attitudes of medical professionals, whose role in informing patients about their right to provider choice for further treatment is crucial for implementing this part of the reform (Winblad-Spångberg 2003).

Whether political accountability within the system has increased as a result of the decentralization reforms is hard to determine as well. There are some indications that local politicians have become more directly involved in the planning and purchasing of health services, thus "taking back" some power from the civil servants (Bergman and Dahlbäck 2000). Political accountability within the system may also have been enhanced by a different factor: increased media attention to health care issues in recent years. This has resulted in local politicians being exposed to a greater level of public scrutiny. At the same time, the organization of health care provision has become more complex since the introduction of contracting and more "market-like" relations between actors within the system. The increasingly complex web of contracts between the county councils and a multitude of different providers tend to create diffuse lines of accountability and make the system less transparent. This problem is further complicated by the recent transferral of responsibility for long-term care and outpatient psychiatric services from the county councils to the municipalities, a change that sometimes has left patients confused about who is responsible for providing various services.

At present, questions of central-local relations and responsibility for various health services are highly salient in Swedish politics. As stated above, the government has attempted recently to reassert its influence over developments within the system, both through legislation and negotiated agreements with the county councils. Evaluations of these efforts demonstrate, however, that governmental attempts to influence policy priorities often fail (National Board of Health and Welfare 2004). Partly in response to what has come to be regarded as an overly complex system, with overlapping lines of jurisdiction between different public bodies, the government appointed in 2003 an investigative committee to review the overall structure of and division of responsibilities within the health care system (Ministry of Finance 2003).[5] Since then, several political interest groups, including the conservative (*Moderaterna*) and liberal (*Folkpartiet*) parties, the Swedish Medical Association, (*Sveriges läkarförbund*) and the main union federation, the LO (*Landsorganisationen*) have openly advocated the abolition of the county councils. These recent political developments illustrate the fact that power struggles within the nearly all-public Swedish health care system often have constituted themselves along the lines of central-local relations.

Whether the market-orienting reforms and the decentralization of powers to the county councils have actually strengthened the political governance of the Swedish health care system remains unclear. That the county councils have become more autonomous vis-à-vis the national government during this period is obvious, which can be said to have reinforced the local democratic character of the system. By the same token, regional variation within the system has increased significantly, making broad characterizations of developments within it increasingly difficult. The few postreform evaluations of the democratic governance of the system show that efforts have indeed been made in many counties to involve local communities in decisions regarding purchasing priorities. However, it has been difficult to create the kinds of institutions that would promote the required level of citizen-politician interaction for this (Bergman and Dahlbäck 2000; Garpenby 2001; Pettersson 1998). In many counties, the "purchaser side" has often been too weak to bargain effectively with providers, and the politicians have tended to lose influence to civil servants and professionals in the often complicated and technical negotiations that purchasing of health services entails. A further complicating factor for democratic governance within the system is increased provider choice available to patients. This can be said to strengthen the system's democratic character, but it also makes priority-setting and planning within the system more difficult.

It is clear that the increased autonomy of the county councils in recent years has resulted in attempts by national authorities to regain some control over the system. For example, the central government passed legislation to prohibit the sale of hospitals to for-profit firms in 2002, formulated national guidelines for prescribing drugs and choosing treatment methods, and adopted a new, national "action plan" (*nationella handlingsplanen*) in 2001 to promote governmental (Social Democratic) health priorities. The emerging power struggle between regional and national levels of government has been reinforced by local party politics. Many county councils are governed by different parties than those in the national government (this phenomena is explained by voters "splitting their ticket" between the national and county council elections, which has become more common).

At the same time, the continued need for cost containment and rationalization in the health care system has made local policy choices more controversial and exposed county council politicians to public discontent, in some cases even death threats. This is especially the case when hospital closings are announced. Dissatisfaction with the county council political leadership in many regions, not least among medical professionals, has fueled demands that the county councils be reorganized or even abolished. Other critics have argued that the county councils are too small to plan health care provision effectively; or that outpatient care should be localized even further and transferred to the municipal level. Hence, at this time, the future of the county councils is uncertain and structural reforms reformulating their tasks cannot be ruled out.

The emphasis on further decentralization within the already decentralized Swedish health care system over the last two decades has reinforced the tradition of local democratic governance. At the same time, however, this trend has exposed the system to far-reaching changes initiated by local reformers. Continuing budget constraints in many county councils also means that local policymakers will have to continue to search for new ways to contain expenditure. This makes it likely that regional differences within the system will increase further, as political priorities come to reflect differing regional circumstances and value orientations.

Despite productivity gains, waiting lists continue to plague the system. In 2005 the Social Democratic government and the county councils introduced a "care guarantee" setting the maximum wait at three months.[6] The ongoing process of European integration has added an international dimension to the issue of timely access to care. A recent decision by the European Court of Justice confirms patients' rights to seek treatment abroad, and this has potentially far-reaching implications for the Swedish health care system.

The public-private mix in pensions

Historical background

Sweden was one of the first countries to legislate a universal public pension. Before the breakthrough of full parliamentary democracy in 1921, Liberal groups in the two-chamber Riksdag vied for control of the "social question" with influential farmers and the nascent Social Democratic Party. Farmers' opposition to Bismarckian-style social insurance delayed the introduction of public pensions until 1913, when the government led by Liberal Prime Minister Karl Staaff introduced a universal old-age and invalidity pension scheme. The design of the new scheme satisfied agricultural and labor interests, and passed easily.[7] The 1913 Law provided for a contribution-based pension (*avgiftspension*). Invalids were eligible for a means-tested supplement (*pensionstillägg*). Total pensions were low, and in 1935 this "premium reserve system" (*premiereservsystemet*) was replaced by the flat-rate basic pension (*folkpension;* Elmér 1960: 50–51, 66ff.). By the end of World War II, the Social Democrats had become the dominant party in the Riksdag, and the party soon embarked on its so-called "Harvest Period" during which the major programs of the postwar welfare state were introduced. A key component of this strategy was a substantial increase in the basic pension so that it covered basic living costs. By the early 1950s, the size of the pension equaled about 30 percent of average industrial wages (Ackerby 1992).

With the basic pension firmly in place, political actors turned their attention to earnings-related pensions in the 1950s, ushering in perhaps the greatest political conflict of the postwar period: the "ATP Struggle" (*ATP-striden*). In the 1950s, public employees and white-collar workers enjoyed generous occupational pensions while the majority of households only had access to the basic pension. Metalworkers, later supported by the Trade Union Confederation, LO, were the first blue-collar group to demand earnings-related pensions on equal terms with white-collar workers. With blue-collar workers pushing hard for legislation on supplementary pensions, the Social Democratic-Farmers coalition government appointed several commissions to study the issue, but agreement with the nonsocialist parties (backed by employers) was elusive. To break the deadlock, an advisory referendum was held in 1957. The Social Democratic proposal received a plurality, followed by the Liberal-Conservative proposal and the Agrarians' proposal. The Social Democrats went ahead with their proposal, prompting the break-up of their coalition with the Farmers' Party. The legislation passed by a razor-thin margin in 1959 and the Social Democratic government called early elections to consolidate their gains.[8]

The new national supplementary pension scheme (ATP, in force since 1960) provided earnings-related pensions to all wage-earners, including the self-employed. Collectively negotiated white-collar pensions were retained, and in 1971 LO members got their own collective pensions (Ståhlberg 1993: 13). A key element of the ATP reform, and the Social Democrats' new "wage-earner strategy," was the inclusion of the white-collar workers in the ATP scheme on favorable terms. ATP's benefit formula was based on the best 15 of 30 years of labor market participation, and this was specifically designed to gain white-collar workers' support (Svensson 1994).

The ATP was closely integrated with the existing basic pension. Together with the basic pension, a full ATP pension would provide 65 percent of previous income (the best 15 of 30 years) up to the ATP ceiling (equal to average earnings). According to the generous transition rules, the system would approach maturity by the early 1990s. The ATP system also included provisions for disability pensions (*förtidspensioner*) and family pensions (*familjpensioner*), which provided coverage to widows and orphans.

In the 1960s and 1970s, Social Democratic governments, now firmly in control of government, improved public pensions with the support of the opposition. In 1969, the pension supplement (*pensionstillskott*) was introduced for those who were not included in ATP or who had few ATP points. After a series of increases, the supplement equaled about half of the basic pension by the early 1990s. Between 1970 and 1972, eligibility rules for disability pensions were relaxed so that it could also be awarded for so-called labor market reasons.[9] In 1974, sickness and unemployment insurance were made taxable and eligible for pension points. In 1976, the pension age was reduced from 67 to 65, and the partial pension (*delpension*) was introduced. Workers aged 60–64 who switched to part-time employment became eligible for the partial pension[10] until they reached retirement age. In 1982, the basis for ATP contributions was increased to include the entire wage sum even though only incomes up to a specified ceiling earned pension points. Since 1982, the care of small children has also been eligible for ATP pension points. Throughout the 1970s and 1980s, employer contributions to both the basic pension and ATP pension system were raised several times.

Prelude to reform

In the mid-1970s, welfare state reform reached the political agenda in Sweden as it did in many other West European countries. The oil shocks and the emergence of stagflation rattled the foundations of the Swedish welfare state because generous social policy and high tax rates presupposed steady economic growth and full employment. The nonsocialist parties governed Sweden from 1976 to 1982 but made little progress on welfare state reform. The Social Democrats returned to power in 1982 and promptly started a debate about how to modernize the welfare state. Pension reform was slated to be part of this debate, so the government appointed an official commission of inquiry to pinpoint areas in need of reform (SOU 1990: 76).[11] Despite the participation of major stakeholders (unions, employers, political parties, and other experts), and nearly ten years of work, the commission could not agree on significant reform proposals. The commission's work, however, did set in motion a period of serious debate about the direction of reform. Before the Social Democrats could take any concrete steps, the nonsocialist parties won the September 1991 election, so the initiative was now in their hands. The new government wasted little time. The Minister of Social Affairs (Liberal Party) recruited the opposition parties to negotiate on pension reform. After several years of deliberations in a closed parliamentary working group, the nonsocialist coalition government adopted framework legislation in the spring of 1994 with the support of the opposition Social Democrats.[12] The Social Democrats returned to office in September 1994, so they presided over the passage of detailed legislation in 1998.[13] The reform has been implemented in steps between 1995 and 2001, and the new system was fully operational starting in 2003.

Briefly, the reformed pension system breaks with the old system in several important ways. First, benefits are based on lifetime earnings rather than the best 15 of 30 years of labor market participation. Second, the earnings-related pension includes mandatory individual accounts (the "premium reserve"). Third, a pension-tested "guarantee pensions" replaces the old basic pension. Finally, wage earners pay individual contributions into the system, and the state (or relevant social insurance agency) pays contributions for pension credits earned for child-rearing, military service and spells of sickness, unemployment, and disability.

The new public pension system consists of three parts: the guaranteed pension (*garantipension*), the income pension (*inkomstpension*), and the premium pension (*premiepension*). This system replaced the basic pension (introduced in 1913) and the ATP pension (adopted in 1959).[14]

The guarantee pension covers residents with insufficient earnings-related benefits. For those born before 1938, the old basic pension (*folkpension*) continued to pay a flat-rate benefit until 2003 when it was converted into the "transitional guarantee pension." Those with income from employment (including the self-employed) are covered by the new income pension and the premium pension. There is no separate scheme for civil servants or the self-employed.

The National Insurance Office (*Försäkringskassan*) administers the guarantee pension and the income pension.[15] The Premium Pension Authority (*Premiepensionmyndigheten*, PPM), a state agency, administers the premium pension. The PPM was set up in 1998 to administer contributions to the individual accounts (the premium reserve) and to manage contracts with the fund managers whose products are part of the premium pension catalogue. In 2004 wage earners could choose from 600 investment funds, including a public default fund, the Premium Savings Fund (*Premiesparfonden*) for those who do not make an active fund choice.[16]

General revenues finance the guarantee pension, a clear break from previous policy in which employers paid an earmarked contribution (6.75 percent of payroll) that covered about 52 percent of basic pension costs in 1993. This contribution was eliminated in 1998. Earmarked pension contributions finance both the income pension and the premium pension. Of the 18.5 percent total pension contribution, 16 percentage points are allocated to the income pension and 2.5 percentage points to the premium pension. Another novelty in the reformed system is that wage-earners pay 7 percent of their eligible earnings up to a ceiling of 8.07 "income base amounts."[17] In the old system, employers paid the entire contribution. In 2004 the contribution ceiling was SEK 42,300, and it is indexed to increases in average earnings. Employers pay 10.21 percent contribution to the earnings ceiling, and half of this for earnings above the ceiling. The latter is called a "tax" rather than a pension contribution.

The reformed system breaks with past policy by eliminating unfunded liabilities. This does not necessarily mean that all pension promises are backed up by money in the bank. It does mean that all pension rights are backed up by contributions, whether these are paid by wage-earners, employers, or the state. General revenues finance the entire contribution for "child years"[18] and those in military service. For claimants of unemployment insurance or sickness benefit, the state pays the employer share of the contribution (10.21 percent), and the individual pays her contribution as if she were working. In 2002 state payments for those receiving social insurance benefits or those not working were 12 percent of all revenues in the income pension scheme (Riksförsäkringsverket 2004: 32).

Like the old system, the new pension system operates largely on a pay-as-you-go basis, with "buffer" funds to compensate for economic and demographic shifts. However. the scope and function of the buffer funds in the new system are much different from that of the old system.[19] Under the old pension system, the AP[20] Funds functioned both as buffer funds and as a source of capital for infrastructure such as public housing (see Pontusson 1992a). At their peak in the 1980s, assets in the AP Funds equaled about 40 percent of GDP, enough to cover pension payments for more than seven years without contributions. In the reformed pension system, the buffer funds are smaller and play little role in terms of an active investment strategy. Over time, the assets in the premium reserve will exceed those in the AP Funds.

The introduction of automatic stabilizers is another important and innovative feature of the new pension system. The "automatic balancing" mechanism requires the National Insurance Office to calculate the notional assets and liabilities of the system every year. Notional assets are 90 percent of total assets and are the sum of all pension contributions (16 percent of qualifying income).[21] AP Fund assets make up the remaining 10 percent of financial assets. Notional liabilities are the sum of pension promises to current workers and retirees. If the ratio of assets to liabilities, the balance ratio (*balanstal*), falls below one, the balancing mechanism is activated. Both pension rights and benefit payments are indexed at a lower rate until the system returns to balance (Riksförsäkringsverket 2000).[22]

All social insurance benefits in Sweden are based on a bookkeeping device called the base amount (*basbeloppet*), which was introduced with the ATP reform in 1959. In the old pension system, there was a single base amount indexed to inflation. The full ATP pension was equal to 6.5 base amounts, which combined with the flat-rate basic pension of 1 base amount, added up to a pension of 7.5 base amounts. This level was approximately equal to average wages, at least in the first two decades of the ATP's existence. The reformed pension system breaks with this principle by introducing three kinds of base amount: the "price base amount" (*prisbasbelopp*), the "increased price base amount" (*förhöjda prisbasbeloppet*), and the "income base amount" (*inkomstbasbeloppet*). The new "price base amount" replaces the old base amount, and it is the basis for calculating the guarantee pension and several other social insurance benefits. The "increased price base amount" is also indexed to inflation, but when it was introduced in 1998 its initial value was set higher than the price base amount. The "increased price base amount" is used to calculate supplementary pension rights for those born between 1938 and 1953 who are covered by the old ATP system and the new pension system. Finally, the "income base amount" is indexed to increases in pension-carrying income, and is the basis for calculating the income ceiling for income pensions (7.5 "income base amounts") as well as the notional pension assets (*avgiftsunderlag*) in the new pension system. In 2006 the price base amount is SEK 39,700, the increased price base amount is SEK 40,500, and the income base amount is SEK 44,500.

Residents with insufficient income from the income pension system have the right to the guarantee pension starting at 65.[23] The guarantee pension replaces the basic pension, pension supplement, and the special tax deduction for pensioners. A novel aspect of the guarantee pension is that it is taxable (the old basic pension was not). The size of the guarantee depends on the level of pension rights in the income pension system, so the amount varies. In 2006 the guaranteed minimum is 2.13 price base amounts, or SEK 86,149 annually. Married pensioners receive 1.9 price base amounts (SEK 76,820) each. The premium pension, private pension income, and occupational pension income do not affect the level of the guarantee pension. To qualify for the maximum benefit, 40 years of residence from age 25 is required. For those who do not meet this requirement (usually immigrants), there is a special maintenance allowance. Low-income pensioners are also eligible for the pensioners housing supplement (BTP). The guarantee pension is payable to those born 1938 or later.[24]

One of the most distinctive features of the reformed pension system is that earnings-related benefits are based on "notional defined contributions" (NDC). This does not mean that pensions are prefunded and backed up by 100 percent capital coverage as in a true defined-contribution scheme. Instead, the income pension scheme emulates a prefunded defined-contribution scheme by estimating an internal rate of return for accumulated pension contributions. The new system counts lifetime contributions, and the monthly benefit is calculated based on (gender-neutral) life expectancy at the time of retirement. The National Insurance Office administers individual NDC accounts. The notional balance in individuals' accounts is indexed annually to an "income index" (*inkomstindex*) based on changes in average pension-carrying income for wage-earners aged 16–64. At retirement, an individual's notional assets are converted to an annuity using the "annuitization divisor" (*delningstal*) which is the expected remaining life expectancy for an individual's cohort plus an internal rate of return of 1.6 percent. The reformed pension system permits flexible retirement, starting at age 61. Thus later retirement increases the pension benefit because the divisor decreases and pension assets increase. The reverse is true for earlier retirement. The notional assets of those who die before retirement are credited to her birth year cohort. Administrative costs are deducted annually. Benefit payouts are indexed to the adjustment index (*följsamhetsindex*) which is the income index minus 1.6.[25]

Another innovative component of Sweden's reformed pension scheme is the "premium reserve": 2.5 percentage points of the 18.5 percent income pension contribution are placed in a defined-contribution, individual investment account. Individuals currently choose from about 600 investment funds. The PPM, a state agency, administers premium pension accounts and manages contracts with investment funds. All fund balances are annuitized at the time of retirement and can be paid out either as a fixed annuity with a minimum rate of return of 3 percent or as a variable annuity. Premium pensions cannot be inherited; and the individual bears all investment risk. The premium pension is payable from age 65.[26]

The reformed pension system is being gradually phased in. Those born between 1938 and 1953 receive pensions according to the old and new systems.[27] Every person with pension rights in Sweden receives an annual pension statement from the National Insurance Office, the so-called "orange envelope," that contains estimates of future pension benefits (for both the income pension and premium pension) based on current individual employment and different economic growth scenarios.

Several factors account for the adoption of one of the most radical pension reforms in the OECD. First, Sweden experienced a deep economic crisis in the early 1990s that prompted across-the-board cuts in government spending. Between 1990 and 1993, Sweden went from budget surplus to recording a deficit of 12.3 percent of gross domestic product (GDP). During the same period, open unemployment rose from 1.7 percent to 8.2 percent (Huber and Stephens 1998; Pontusson 1992b). Second, the historic defeat of the Social Democrats in the 1991 election meant that the nonsocialist government coalition managed the crucial initial stages of the pension reform negotiations. The Social Democrats had already come out in favor of major pension reform in their 1990 budget, and the party's opposition role in the Riksdag certainly made it easier to overcome some of the opposition within the party and among blue-collar union members. Finally, crucial aspects of the existing policy structure facilitated a strategy of "rationalizing redistribution." (Anderson and Meyer 2003). Specifically, the capital in the AP Funds (about 30 percent of GDP in the early 1990s) could be used to finance the transition to the new system. Moreover, reform advocates could credibly claim that the introduction of the lifetime earnings benefit formula was more fair than the old 15/30 rule that benefited mainly white-collar workers.

The Swedish reform is all the more remarkable when we consider that politicians faced a popular, universal, and nearly mature pension system. The "lock-in" effects of pension policy development dictated that reform would have to take place within the structure of the existing system. The nonsocialist parties recognized this, but the large capital reserves in the AP Funds provided an opening for fundamental change. The role of the AP Funds in facilitating the transition to the new pension system can hardly be exaggerated. By 2004, the AP Funds had transferred SEK 350 billion (about € 38 billion) to the government budget to compensate the state for increased costs resulting from the reform. This made it possible to devote a larger share of contributions (16 percent of qualifying income) to income pensions, (compared to 12 percent of qualifying income in the old system) and to devote 2.5 percentage points to the new funded accounts. Thus the reform means that more resources flow to earnings-related pensions while the state assumes the noninsurance functions of the old pension system (basic security, survivor's pensions, disability pensions). The financial cushion provided by the AP Funds gave reformers a degree of maneuvering room that simply does not exist in other public pension systems (Anderson and Immergut 2007; Anderson and Meyer 2003).

The role of the AP Funds is important for another reason as well. As assets accumulate in the new premium reserve, it will eventually replace the AP Funds as a source of investment capital. Although this aspect of the reform would not affect the level of benefits, it was a major victory for the nonsocialist parties because they succeeded in the partial privatization of very large publicly controlled pension funds. Finally, the reform was an opportunity to "rationalize redistribution" (Anderson and Meyer 2003; Myles and Pierson 2001) because the existing benefit formula (the 15/30 rule) was considered unjust. This feature of the old system was repeatedly criticized by reformers, and given the very high levels of female labor force participation, the rationale behind the old rules was hard to justify.

In sum, retirement provision remains overwhelmingly public, despite the sweeping reforms of the 1990s. Most Swedes' retirement packages rely heavily on public pensions, topped up by occupational pensions bargained as part of collective wage agreements.[28] Individual private pension savings accounts have become more popular in the last decade, but remain fairly insignificant in comparison to public and occupational coverage. Thirty-eight percent of those aged 20–64 have individual accounts, with an average value of about SEK 6,000 in savings (about \$800; www.scb.se). Despite the growing importance of contractual and private provision, the public system provides the bulk of retirement income. Income inequality in retirement is likely to increase, however, because future pension income will more closely mirror employment income as well as variable investment returns for the premium pension.[29]

Comparing the public-private dichotomy in pensions and health care

The pace of reform in both health care and public pensions since the early 1990s has been dramatic. Both systems remain firmly within the public sector, but the role of the state has changed substantially. Internal markets now permeate the health care system, and most decision-making has been decentralized. Despite enduring public dominance, the state has retreated in favor of local government (health care) and autonomous public agencies administering more or less self-sustaining programs (pensions). These changes mean that the state is less implicated in the *politics* surrounding both programs. The reformed pension system operates on "auto-pilot," so decisions about raising or cutting benefits emerge from the built-in automatic stabilizers. In short, the state makes no promise about the level of future (earnings-related) pension benefits. So far, the potentially negative effects of the new system remain untested; benefits have been indexed at least as much as they would have been in the old system, and those who "lose" under the new pension system have adequate time to adjust their labor force and savings behavior in order to compensate for their losses. The retreat of the state is similar in health care. The decentralization reforms of the 1990s mean that the county councils face any hard decisions about the allocation of resources. To be sure, the state remains the central financier and regulatory player, but county councils have considerable leeway in organizing health care delivery.

The wave of reforms during the last two decades has redrawn the lines of conflict characteristic of both sectors and has led to the emergence of new actors as the state has retreated. The central line of potential conflict in health care is between local government and the central state. In pensions, the potential for conflict is much diminished because of the automatic features of the new pension system. Notional defined contributions and automatic stabilizers mean that if pensions decrease, it is because of economic and demographic trends and not because of a specific political decision.

Private providers are the main new actors in health care, whereas investment funds have entered the world of public pensions because of the introduction of the premium pension. Assets in the premium reserve at the end of 2006 totaled about SEK 230 billion (\$30 billion). In 2007 wage earners could chose from more than 600 investment funds. Since the premium pension was introduced in 2003, assets have increased in value by 29.2 percent (PPM 2007). Since all wage earners participate in the scheme, all now have a stake in financial markets, even if one chooses the state-run default fund.

Swedish membership in the European Union (since 1995) has potentially important implications for both health care and pensions policy because of the rules governing the internal market. Recent European Court of Justice rulings establish the right of patients to seek (and be reimbursed for) health care outside of their home country. It is too early to tell what the full ramifications of these rulings will be, but the NHS-style health care systems in the EU, including Sweden, now face the previously unthinkable prospect of residents seeking care in other EU member states in order to avoid waiting lists or to seek treatment not offered at home. This development obviously threatens the sovereignty of national health care systems like Sweden's at the same time that it increases the pressure to expand care options and improve access to care.

These European developments notwithstanding, national politics will continue to dominate pensions and health care. Both systems—their creation, consolidation, and recent reform—have been heavily influenced by the political dominance of the Social Democratic Party. The victory of the nonsocialist parties[30] in the September 2006 election marks the end of more than a decade of Social Democratic rule. It is important to note that the Conservatives remade themselves as the "party of workers," signaling their acceptance of public dominance in welfare. But the nonsocialists want a different kind of public dominance than the Social Democrats. The toughest reforms have already been adopted, so the current and future issue concerns which political block (the nonsocialists or the socialists) will dominate the process of further consolidation. Fiscal austerity, at least in the short-term, is not a pressing issue because the budget is in surplus, and the pension system is now largely self-financing. However, aging will continue to create challenges for both the health care system and the elder care system. Thus, the pension challenge may be "solved" but the care-related implications of aging have yet to be effectively dealt with.

Notes

1. Sweden had the fourth lowest infant mortality in the world in 2003 behind Iceland, Japan, and Finland (Socialstyrelsen 2005: 33).
2. Most Swedes only pay local income tax, which averages about 30 percent of taxable income. High income earners pay an additional 20 percent in state income tax. The municipalities and country councils share the local revenue.
3. www.oecd.com.
4. The size of the county council areas varies between 60,000 and 1.8 million people.

5. In 2007 the committee released a detailed report recommending that large regional municipalities (*regionkommuner*) of relatively equal size take over most of the county councils' responsibilities in health care. The committee also recommended simplification of national governance arrangements and substantial improvements in patient rights (SOU 2007: 10).
6. After three months the patient has the right to be treated elsewhere at the cost of his/her home county council.
7. See Heclo (1974) and Baldwin (1990).
8. For discussions of the ATP reform, see Heclo (1974: 246).
9. This change was intended to help wage-earners between the ages of 60 and 64 in poor health or with physically taxing jobs.
10. The partial pension paid 65 percent of lost income without reducing the amount of pension points earned until retirement age.
11. Sweden is known for its forward-looking investigative commissions that are often or usually appointed to study reform needs and propose policy change.
12. Initially, the Left Party and the New Democracy Party participated in the negotiations but both quickly left the group, complaining that the committee's work was undemocratic.
13. See Anderson and Immergut (2007) and Lundberg (2003) for the politics of the reform process. See Palme (2003) and Palmer and Wadensjö (2004) for analyses of the effects of the reform.
14. All citizens were entitled to the basic pension while ATP provided benefits based on previous income from work. In addition, the partial pension (*delpension*) and disability pension (*förtidspension*) provided benefits for early retirees. The relevant reports from official commissions of inquiry are Ds 1992: 89; Ds 1995: 41; SOU 1994: 20; and SOU 1997: 131.
15. The National Insurance Office (Försäkringskassan) took over this function from the National Social Insurance Board (*Riksförsäkringsverket*) in 2005.
16. On the premium pension see Weaver (2003/04).
17. The pension contribution is not pension-carrying, so 93 percent of 8.07 income base amounts is 7.5 income base amounts (100 percent–7 percent fee = 93 percent).
18. The amount of the pension credit is calculated according to the most favorable of three methods and goes to the mother unless the parents apply for the father to receive the credit. One of the calculation methods is to award the pension credit for income equivalent to one "base amount," or euro 4,500. Sixty percent of women are eligible for a higher credit (See *RFV redovisar* 1999: 12. Den nya allmänna pensionen).
19. In the new system, AP Funds 1–4, and 7 are the buffer funds. In the old system, AP Funds 1–4, 6, and 7 were the buffers.
20. AP stands for "Allmänna pensionsfonderna" or national pension funds that are part of the public pension system. There are currently seven AP Funds.
21. Ds. 1999: 43; Proposition 2005/06: 01. *Ålderspensionssystemet vid sidan av statsbudgeten.*
22. In 2004, the balance ratio was 1.0014. Notional assets were SEK 5,607 billion, and financial assets in the AP Funds were SEK 646 billion, for a total of SEK 6,263 billion in assets. Liabilities were SEK 6,244 billion.
23. The ceiling is 3.16 price base amounts for singles and 2.8275 price base amounts for spouses.
24. Those born earlier fall under the old system, so they received the old basic pension (and possibly supplements) until 2003, when a transitional guarantee

pension was introduced for this particular group. The transitional guarantee pensions pays the same net amount as the old basic pension and pension supplements that the retired person was entitled to before 2003.

25. For example, if the income index is 2.0, the economic adjustment index is 2.0–1.6 = 0.4. 1.6 percent is deducted because the same percentage rate of return is applied to the notional annuity at retirement. Thus the annuity is front-loaded and this is compensated for afterwards by the construction of the economic adjustment index.
26. On the premium pension, see R. Kent Weaver (2003/2004) and SOU (1997: 131).
27. The calculation is proportional. For example, someone born in 1940 receives 13/16 of his/her pension from the old system and 3/16 from the new.
28. Four sectoral pension schemes top up public benefits, covering about 90 percent of wage earners. For most wage earners, these schemes add about 10 percent to public benefits. The amount is higher for higher-income earners.
29. In 1997, income inequality in Sweden was among the lowest in Western Europe (Jansson 2000: 8) despite a slight increase in the 1990s.
30. Conservatives, Center Party, Christian Democrats, and Liberals.

References

Ackerby, Stefan. 1992. *Pensionsfrågan. Bilaga 12 till Långtidsutredningen 1992.* Stockholm: Ministry of Finance.

Anderson, Karen M. 2005. "Sweden: Radical Reform in a Mature Pension System." In Giuliano Bonoli and Toshimitsu Shinkawa (eds), *Ageing and Pension Reform around the World.* Cheltenham: Edward Elgar.

Anderson, Karen M. and Ellen M. Immergut. 2007. "Sweden: After Social Democratic Hegemony." In Ellen M. Immergut, Karen M. Anderson, and Isabelle Schulze (eds), *The Handbook of West European Pension Politics.* Oxford: Oxford University Press.

Anderson, Karen M. and Traute Meyer. 2003. "Social Democracy, Unions, and Pension Politics in Germany and Sweden." *Journal of Public Policy* 23(1): 23–55.

Anell, A. 1996. *Decentralization and Health Systems Change: The Swedish Experience.* IHE Working Paper. Lund: IHE.

Baldwin, Peter. 1990. *The Politics of Social Solidarity: Class Bases of the European Welfare State, 1875–1975.* Cambridge: Cambridge University Press.

Bergman, S.-E. and Dahlbäck, U. 2000. *Sjukvård –en svårstyrd verksamhet. En studie över styr–och ledningsformer i svensk sjukvård.* Stockholm: Landstingsförbundet.

Blomqvist, P. 2002. *Convergence and Policy Reforms. Health Care Reforms in the Netherlands and Sweden in the 1990s.* Doctoral dissertation, Columbia University, New York.

Department of Social Affairs (*Socialdepartementet*). 1999. *Vård på lika vilkor,* SOU 1999: 66. Stockholm: Fritzes.

Ds. 1992: 89. *Ett reformerat pensionssystem—Bakgrund, principer och skiss. En promemoria av Pensionsarbetsgruppen.*

Ds. 1995: 41. *Reformerat pensionssystem.*

Ds. 1999: 43. *Automatisk balansering av ålderspensionssystemet.*

Elmér, Åke. 1960. *Folkpensioneringen i Sverige.* Lund: C. W. K. Glerups Förlag.

Garpenby, P. 2001. *Medborgaren i prioriteringsprocessen.* Report 2001: 1. Linköping: Prioriteringscentrum.

Garpenby, P. 2002. *Samtalsdemokrati och prioritering: utvärdering av ett försök med medborgaråd.* Rapport 2002.3, Prioriteringscentrum. Linköping: Landstinget i Östergötland.

Heclo, Hugh. 1974. *Modern Social Politics in Britain and Sweden. From Relief to Income Maintenance.* New Haven, CT: Yale University Press.

Hood, Christopher. 1991. "A Public Management for All Seasons?" *Public Administration* 69(1): 3–19.

Huber, E. and Stephens, J. D. 1998. "Internationalization and the Social Democratic Model. Crisis and Future Prospects." *Comparative Political Studies* 31: 353–97.

Immergut, E. 1992. *Health Politics: Interests and Institutions in Western Europe.* Cambridge: Cambridge University Press.

Jansson, K. 2000. "Sverige har jämnast inkomstfördelning." *VälfärdsBulletinen* 1: 6–8.

Lundberg, Urban. 2003. *Juvelen i kronan. Socialdemokraterna och den allmänna pensionen.* Stockholm: Hjalmarson & Höberg.

Ministry of Finance. 2003. Kommittédirektiv. Dir 2003: 10. See also additional direktives issued in 2004. Tilläggsdirektiv till Ansvarskommittén. Dir 2004: 93.

Montin, S. 1992. "Privatiseringsprocesser i kommunerna." *Statsvetenskaplig tidskrift* 95(1).

Montin, S. 1997. "Citizenship, Consumerism and Local Government in Sweden." *Scandinavian Political Studies* 18(1).

Myles, John and Paul Pierson. (2001). "The Comparative Political Economy of Pension Reform." In Paul Pierson (ed.), *The New Politics of the Welfare Atate.* Oxford: Oxford University Press: 305–33.

National Board of Health and Welfare. 2004. *Den nationella handlingsplanen. Årsrapport 2004.* Stockholm: Socialstyrelsen.

Palme, Joakim. 2003. "Pension Reform in Sweden and the Changing Boundaries between Public and Private." In Clark Gordon L. and Whiteside Noel (eds), *Pension Security in the 21st Century. Redrawing the Public-Private Debate.* Oxford: Oxford University Press.

Palmer, E. and E. Wadensjö. 2004. "Public Pension Reform and Contractual Agreements in Sweden: From Defined Benefit to Defined Contributions." In Martin Rein and Winfried Schmähl (eds), *Rethinking the Welfare State.* Cheltenham: Edward Elgar.

Pettersson, H. 1998. *Styrsystem och demokrati.* Lund: Department of Political Science.

Pontusson, Jonas. 1992a. *The Limits of Social Democracy. Investment Politics in Sweden.* Ithaca, NY: Cornell University Press.

Pontusson, Jonas. 1992b. "At the End of the Third Road: Swedish Social Democracy in Crisis." *Politics and Society* 20: 305–32.

Premiepensionsmyndigheten. 2007. "Tolv procents värdeökning för PPM-fonderna år 2006." Press release, January 9, 2007.

Proposition. 2005/06: 1. *Ålderspensionssystemet vid sidan av statsbudgeten.*

RFV. 2000. "Automatisk balansering av ålderspensionssystemet—redovisning av regeringens beräkningsuppdrag." *RFV Analyserar* 2000: 1.

Riksförsäkringsverket. 2004. *Pensionssystemets årsredovisning 2004.* Borås.

Riksförsäkringsverket. 2005. *Pensionssystemets årsredovisning 2005.* Borås.

Socialstyrelsen. 2005. *Hälso- och sjukvårdsrapport.* Stockholm: Edita Norstedts tryckeri.

SOU. 1990: 76. *Allmän pension.*

SOU. 1994: 20. *Reformerat pensionssystem.*

SOU. 1997: 131. *Lag om premiepension.*

SOU. 2007: 10. *Hållbar samhällsorganisation med utvecklingskraft.*

Ståhlberg, Ann-Charlotte. 1993. *Våra pensionssystem.* Stockholm: SNS Förlag.

Statistiska centralbyrån. 2007. *Public Finances in Sweden.* Örebro: SCB-Tryck.

Svensson, Torsten. 1994. *Socialdemokratins dominans. En studie av den svenska social-demokratins partistrategi.* Uppsala: Acta Universitatis Upaliensis.

Weaver, R. Kent. 2003/04. "Design and Implementation Issues in Swedish Individual Pension Accounts." *Social Security Bulletin* 65(4): 38–56.

Winblad-Spångberg, U. 2003. *Från beslut till verklighet. Valfrihetsreformer i svensk sjukvård.* Doctoral dissertation, Uppsala University, Uppsala.

8

Germany: The Public-Private Dichotomy in the Bismarckian Welfare Regime

Sven Jochem

Introduction

The German welfare state has undergone fundamental reforms over the past three decades. Since the early 1980s, various governments changed the programmatic contours of German social policies. Beyond the question of how various national governments could push through these reforms under the conditions of federalism, divided government ("joint-decision trap"; Scharpf 1988, 2006), corporatism, and increasing party competition, this chapter focuses on the changing contours of the public-private mix in health and pension policies. The argument of this chapter is that privatization, understood as a "risk shift" (Hacker 2004, 2006), has taken place in the German welfare state. However, because this welfare state was, and largely remains, a highly interwoven social insurance state in which the state and social partners (for example, labor and business organizations) coincidentally finance and regulate important welfare programs, these reforms do not imply that the federal government lost its prominent role in social policy. Rather, the national government still strongly regulates benefits, contributions, and other programmatic features of public and private social policies.

As a result of these reforms, the relationship between the state and market forces in Germany has become even more complex, and the boundaries between "public" and "private" social policies increasingly blurred. This German case study provides broad evidence in favor of the argument that the analytical distinction between "public" and "private" is a "murky terrain" (Rein and Rainwater 1986: 203). Instead of the traditional, clear-cut analytical distinction between "public" and "private," one can speak of a continuum that opens new perspectives to investigate the fuzzy interplay between the "market" and the "state" in social policies.

Three main sections comprise this chapter. First, after a brief discussion concerning the development of the German welfare state, developments in health politics and policies are reported, the analytical perspective being to trace shifts in the public-private mix. Second, the development of pension politics and policies is discussed. In this policy area, major shifts in the public-private mix were triggered by "red-green" (that is, Social Democratic and Green coalition) governments. The final section discusses future challenges and possible reforms.

Notes on the German welfare state

The German welfare state is a prototype of a "social insurance state". Public social security schemes are financed mainly through payroll contributions. Employees and employers are obliged to contribute to the financing of the welfare state (albeit to different degrees and with important exceptions). In most areas of the welfare state, the burdens are equally shared between employees and employers. Moreover, the federal executive cofinances several social security schemes with general tax revenues. In the past, the legitimacy of this financial contribution by the state to the social security system was intensely debated (Bleses and Seeleib-Kaiser 2004; Jochem 2007).

Following the 1990 German Reunification, the institutional design of West Germany's welfare state was successfully expanded to the former East Germany. Despite challenges posed by the East, such as its severe economic crisis and high unemployment, massive financial transfers within social security schemes took place. Since 1990, considerable amounts of money have been transferred from West German to East German social security schemes, thus amounting to another layer of transfers in addition to the official transfer system that redistributes tax revenues between the national government and the now 16 states or "Länder" ("Länderfinanzausgleich"). In 2003, for example, €5.7 billion were transferred from West German to East German public pension funds alone. Between 1992 and 2003, these transfers in public pension funds amounted to approximately €55 billion in total (Jochem 2007).

German Reunification meant both an expansion of the state and a reduction of the role of the public sector in social policies. This seemingly contradictory reflection rests on the observation that, after German Reunification, the federal government had to inject more tax revenues into social-policy schemes, thereby gradually eroding the traditional emphasis on social insurance. However,, and especially visible in health policies, the "pure" public system of East Germany was terminated and the West German mix of public social insurance and private actors was transferred into the "neue Länder." From 1992–93, when this territorial transformation of the German welfare system was by and large completed, welfare reforms have attempted to alter the public-private mix. These reforms and their impacts on the public-private mix are discussed in detail in the following two sections.

Health care

Health insurance systems are often fragmented, yet to varying degrees governments intervene into their different components (Immergut 1992). Many analyses focus on the mode of financing or spending (for example, Castles 2004). The state may also serve as a provider of health services or as a more or less active regulator of private health services or private health markets. In this respect, the German social insurance system represents a peculiar mixture of public and private insurance schemes, of public and private services and, finally, of public governance and private self-regulation. Thus, as far as the public-private dichotomy is concerned, the German health care system was and remains a public-private hybrid.

Germany pioneered public and mandatory social security schemes. Already in 1883, the government of the German "Reich" under Chancellor Bismarck introduced a national statutory health insurance system. From the beginning, corporatist and federal elements in health policies dominated (Wehler 1995). The incorporation of organized labor and business interests as social partners into the administrative boards of the regionally differentiated statutory health insurance funds ("Krankenkassen") was meant to pacify the labor movement while enabling these social partners to regulate health issues in collaboration with the national government.

In the following decades, a trend not unique to Germany was the stepwise inclusion of many other collective actors into the health policy network, such as professional organizations representing pharmacists or statutory health insurance physicians. The governance of the German health care system has also been shaped by a national decision-making system where the central government not only has to negotiate reforms with organized interests but in many cases with the "Länder," which are represented through the "Bundesrat" (that is, the upper house of the German parliament). Both corporatism and federalism have survived dramatic regime changes in German history and they still determine the institutional configuration of this policy area (Schmidt 2005).

At the heart of the German health care system is statutory health insurance ("Gesetzliche Krankenversicherung" or GKV). This public insurance is de facto compulsory for all employees, but there are major exceptions. For example, under specific circumstances, self-employed individuals and civil servants ("Beamte") may opt out. The GKV coverage increased steadily after World War II, as particular public health insurance schemes for students, artists, and farmers were founded and integrated into the public system. However, this trend was reversed in the mid-1970s. Since then, the proportion of the population that opts out of the GKV has increased steadily. In 1975, 4.2 million people were insured under a private health insurance scheme; this figure increased to 5.2 million people in 1985 and reached 6.6 million in 1990. Since German Reunification, the number of privately insured people has increased even further. Today, approximately 8 million people participate in private health insurance schemes (approximately 10 percent of the German population). Political decisions taken during the 1980s opened several pathways for the insured to leave the GKV. This is especially true for civil servants ("Beamte") and high-wage employees, who have been granted more and more freedom to choose between public and private health insurances. In addition, since the early 1980s, private supplementary health insurance schemes, which deal with costs not covered by the GKV, have also proliferated. Today approximately 9 percent of the German population participates in these supplementary schemes (Rothgang et al. 2006: 324–25).

In the 1980s, to contain health spending, the center-right governments implemented various reforms. As early as 1983 and 1984, the first reforms were aimed at increasing private health co-payments. This trend was further strengthened by the major health care reform in that decade, the 1988 "Gesetz zur Strukturreform im Gesundheitswesen." Because the interests of the providers of heath care services were effectively protected by the smallest party in the coalition government (the liberal Free Democratic Party, FDP), most cost-containment measures favored the expansion of private co-payments in the German heath care market. This was especially the case for cost-intensive dental treatment. Despite the government's ambition to make efficient reforms to the institutional structure of the German health care system, this "Strukturreform" could not shake up the institutional status quo. Organized interests from the supply side of the health care market, such as pharmacists and physicians, as well as the FDP in government, blocked any attempts to promote greater competition between health service providers. Due to the pivotal position of the FDP, ambitions to restructure the public-private mix in health care were politically limited and the status quo remained mainly unchanged.

From 1990 to 1992, as the West German health care system was extended to former East Germany, further attempts to change health care institutions were launched. In general, the Social Democratic Party (SPD) in the East defended some public institutions of the former East Germany's health care system like outpatient centers. However, due to the time pressure of Reunification and the lack of political support for these interests within the West German SPD and other parties, these attempts failed (Ritter 2006). Thus, the health care system in reunified Germany is to a very great extent the system as it had developed in West Germany, with its peculiarly fuzzy public-private mix.

Political frustration over the 1988 reform and further increased health spending (as well as rising health contribution rates of the GKV) led the center-right government to activate new reform negotiations in 1992–93. In contrast to what occurred before the 1988 reform, organized interests were excluded from official negotiations. In contrast to the situation prevailing in the 1980s, the largest opposition party, the SPD, was included in the reform talks, which were held behind closed doors in Lahnstein, a small city near Koblenz. The government hoped the new reform would introduce more competition between health care service providers. At the same time, every employee was granted the freedom to decide which health insurance fund he or she would join. With this political "compromise from Lahnstein," a financial coupling of the different health funds was implemented and the unrestricted freedom for private physicians to enter the health care market was limited. Further, the financing of public hospitals was altered. The goal was to contain costs through switching the financing mechanism from overall transfers to specified individual transfers.

Politically, however, the "compromise from Lahnstein" became a "traumatic experience" for the FDP (Lehmbruch 1998: 172, translated by the author). Consequently, from its enactment to the end of the "Kohl Era" in 1998, the FDP blocked all further attempts to negotiate social-policy reforms again with the SPD (with the exception of the 1994 long-term care scheme, which falls beyond the scope of this chapter). A second consequence of the above-mentioned compromise was that the FDP strengthened its liberal profile, thus trying to further protect private suppliers in the health market. Under the circumstances of divided government after German Reunification, this strategy undermined the political foundation of further successful reforms and, hence, this political compromise on health care reform came at a high political price for the centre-right government.

The political stalemate became obvious during the 1996 and 1997 reform negotiations. This time, although organized interests again returned to the reform process, opposition parties were excluded from it. In addition to institutional rearrangements in the hospital sector and the greater freedom for the insured to switch to other health insurance funds (if the insurance funds increase their contribution rates), most measures resulted in a further expansion of private co-payments. After 1998, the newly elected red-green government immediately lowered co-payment rates. As a consequence, the total amount of the co-payments dropped significantly. Although the amount of the private co-payments increased from €0.6 billion in 1991 to €2.7 billion in 1998, it decreased to €2 billion in 1999 and remained stable at €1.8 billion until 2002 (Busse and Riesberg 2004: 74).

After intense political debates and a compromise between the red-green government and the largest opposition party (the Christian Democratic Union, CDU/CSU), the Health Care Modernization Act ("Gesundheitsmodernisierungsgesetz" or GMG) reversed the declining trend of private co-payments after 2004. This reform mainly switched the burden of containing public health care spending toward increased private co-payments. General exemptions due to poverty or other reasons were abolished and regulations for partial exemptions were tightened. It should be noted that this increased "risk privatization" (Hacker 2004, 2006) goes hand in hand with a decline in public funding. For example, the share of tax revenues used to finance the health care system declined from 13 percent in 1992 to 7.8 percent in 2002 (Busse and Riesberg 2004: 58). It should be further added that the overwhelming part of the costs is financed through the public health insurance funds. Official data classify these financial sources as public, which is problematic at best. As this money is injected through the employee and employer contributions, the label of "public" funding partially veils the private component of the German health care system and, consequently, overestimates the direct role of the state.

As elsewhere in the OECD, the health care business in Germany is a growth industry. Health spending relative to the national income in Germany has risen from 6.2 percent in 1970 to 10.3 percent in 1995 and, finally, to 10.9 percent in 2004. This increase is in line with the OECD trend (Rothgang et al. 2006). Within the OECD, only the United States (15.3 percent) and Switzerland (11.6 percent) devote a greater portion of their national income to health care. As for the public share of health care spending in Germany, it was 78.2 percent in 2004 (OECD 2006). Thus, among OECD countries, Germany ranks near the middle in terms of public health care spending, significantly below Luxembourg (90.4 percent public) and far above the United States (44.7 percent). It should be noted that since 1995, the relative financial weight of the public sector decreased by approximately 2 percentage points in Germany (OECD 2006).

But the public-private mix in Germany is more complex than these data imply *prima facie*. In fact, private households are responsible for the lion's share of financing. Analyzing cash-flows in the German health care system, it can be shown that, in 2004, private households spent €147.5 billion to finance the system. The employers' contribution amounted to €112.8 billion whereas the state only contributed €52.8 billion (SBA 2006: 22). These cash-flow data show that private households are the main revenue source for the German health care system. The SBA ("Statistisches Bundesamt") report further shows that the state's relative financial contribution to the German health care system has declined steadily. Although representing about 19 percent of health care spending in the mid-1990s, the state's share declined to 16.9 percent in 2004. Although there are no up-to-date spending data available, we can assume that, as a consequence of the 2004 reform, the share of private financing has continued to increase.

As suggested above, corporatism and federalism structure the organizational landscape of the German health insurance system. Policy competencies are delegated to membership-based, self-regulated organizations representing both the supply side (for example, physicians and regional sickness funds) and the demand side (for example, those who "consume" health services and which are mainly represented by the unions). These organizations are formally integrated into statutory insurance schemes. In the statutory health insurance system (GKV), regional sickness funds, their associations, and the associations of GKV-affiliated physicians have assumed the status of quasi-public corporations. Through joint committees, organizations from both the supply and the demand sides are entitled to define health care benefits, prices, and standards. These committees may even sanction their members, if they do not follow the defined rules of health services. Hence, the German health insurance system is a combination of horizontal corporatist negotiation and vertical negotiation within a federal state. Today, there are 320 different quasi-public sickness funds with slightly different contribution rates. On average, the contribution rate is today 13.8 percent in former West Germany and 13.5 percent in former East Germany (SVR 2006).

Due to the specific public-private mix in the provision of services, the German health care system has had a pronounced private, that is, market-based, profile. This market emphasis characterizes private pharmacies and office-based ambulatory care and dentistry. However, the role of the private sector is increasing even in traditionally state-dominated areas. Although there is no strong push toward "pure" privatization, a trend toward the multiplication of private, for-profit hospitals is observable. Between 1990 and 2002, for example, the share of public hospital beds declined from 62.8 to 53.9 percent of the total number of beds. During the same period, the share of private yet *nonprofit* beds increased slightly from 33.5 to 37.7 percent. Meanwhile, the share of private, *for-profit* hospital beds increased from 3.7 to 8.3 percent (Busse and Riesberg 2004: 56). This trend continues today.

Privatization and the strengthening of market rules have occurred in other aspects of the German health care system. During the 1990s, the federal government expanded choice in sickness funds. In a comparative perspective, choice is as "liberal" as in Switzerland, for example. Although comparing differences in health care regulations across countries is difficult, Greß (2006) shows that, on average, German citizens switch from one health insurance plan to another more often than Swiss or Dutch citizens. In a sense, this dimension of the German health care system has been liberalized with great success, as the population actively takes advantage of opportunities to switch from one insurer to another.

A disadvantage to this "liberalization," however, is that an increasing portion of the population has been excluded from the private and statutory components of the German health insurance system. Due to economic problems such as unemployment and national initiatives aimed at restricting access to statutory or private health insurance in order to fight adverse selection, the number of people without private or public health insurance increased during the 1990s. Relying on estimations based on "Mikrozensus" data, Greß and others (2005) suggest that between 1995 and 2003, the number of uninsured nearly doubled from 105,000 to 188,000. These uninsured individuals are mainly people who are excluded from the labor market. However, in recent years, even the share of self-employed living without private or statutory health insurance has increased. In 2007, the government reacted to this trend by introducing mandatory health insurance. Since April 2007, every citizen has the right to contract a basic private or statutory health insurance. Those who have lost their insurance coverage for one reason or another have now the right to gain health coverage from their last insurance fund.

Universal health insurance is only one aspect of what is known as the 2007 Statutory Health insurance Competition Strengthening Act ("Gesetz zur Stärkung des Wettbewerbs in der gesetzlichen Krankenversicherung"). This key legislation was intended to be the core reform project of the Grand Coalition (SPD and CDU/CSU) formed in the aftermath of the 2005 elections. Immediately after these elections, that coalition pushed negotiations for a "fundamental" health care reform. However, the results were meager. Already during the 2005 campaign, the two main political parties promoted different reform strategies. In the past and into the present, the CDU/CSU has wanted to reform the German statutory health insurance system in line with the Swiss model (cf. Bertozzi and Gilardi, this volume). The SPD, in contrast, has recommended and continues to recommend a citizens' health insurance scheme ("Bürgerversicherung") that would bring all blue- and white-collar workers as well as civil servants (up to a specified income ceiling) into public statutory health insurance, leaving only few opportunities to opt out of the public system. Hence, two contradictory policy alternatives clash: one favoring the expansion of market-based protection, the other favoring the strengthening of the public GKV.

Overall, the 2007 reform implemented a number of new health care regulations. First, as already mentioned, the reform transformed health coverage into a citizenship right according to which public and private insurers alike must offer basic benefit packages to all citizens. This innovation is based on a broad policy consensus between the Christian Democrats and the Social Democratic Party. Second, the reform implemented several measures that should increase the level of competition within the health care market. Health insurers may offer their clients differentiated tariffs and sickness funds may now negotiate more flexible arrangements with health care providers about the price and the quality of services. Third, the structure of financing of the GKV will soon be reformed. This will lead to the implementation of a unitary contribution rate across Germany as well as the expansion of the federal government's tax contribution to GKV financing. According to this new system, contributions and tax revenues will flow into one nationwide health care fund. Statutory health insurance funds will receive a flat amount for each insured person. Well-managed funds will then be able to refund a portion of each insured's contribution, whereas funds which will not able to cover costs will have to charge an additional premium to its insured. In the public debate, the introduction of the above-mentioned nationwide health fund was highly contested and, for that reason, postponed until 2009. It is doubtful that this united fund will in fact be implemented at that time, as the next federal elections take place in the same year (if the Grand Coalition holds together until then).

The results of the next national elections (expected in 2009) will be decisive for the future of the German public-private health care mix. The SPD proposes strengthening of the public GKV and a partial integration of private health insurance funds into the public system. In contrast, the CDU/CSU proposes strengthening the private insurance funds, and to differentiate between basic (public) and supplementary (private) health insurance. It is too early to tell which conception will triumph. It is clear, however, that the outcomes of the next federal elections will decide which political camp will win the majority and which reform will take place.

Pensions

The Disability and Old Age Insurance Act of 1889 ("Invaliditäts- und Altersversicherungsgesetz") marks the beginning of a public, compulsory pension insurance system in Germany (Frerich and Frey 1993: 95–101). This reform introduced mandatory insurance for blue-collar workers. Insured workers were entitled to benefits at the age of 70 with a minimum of 30 years of contributions, and they were entitled to invalidity benefits. Many workers could not benefit from this scheme because life expectancy at this time was in most cases lower than 70 years. Contribution rates depended on wage groups, but on average were 1.7 percent. In the early decades of the twentieth century, a white-collar scheme was introduced separately.

After World War II, the administrative separation between blue- and white-collar employees, which had been discarded by the Nazi dictatorship, was reestablished. As the calculation of pension benefits did not take into account inflation or wage increase, the level of benefits became inadequate by the early 1950s. During that decade, deliberations on a comprehensive pension reform resulted in the 1957 legislation. In 1956, both the government coalition (the Christian Democratic Party and two small liberal parties) and the SPD opposition submitted pension reform bills that envisioned gross wage indexation, a reform rejected both by the liberal FDP and the employers' association. Despite some resistance within the CDU/CSU, federal Chancellor Konrad Adenauer (CDU) pushed the innovation known as "dynamic pension" ("dynamische Rente") through the Bundestag on January 21, 1957. Since then, pension benefits have been coupled toward growth in gross wages. The immediate effect of this reform was an average 65 percent increase in old-age pensions.

In the field of occupational pensions, the 1974 Occupational Old-Age Protection Act ("Gesetz zur Verbesserung der betrieblichen Altersersorgung") emerged as the most crucial postwar legislation, setting the legal context for second pillar pensions. The Act regulated the vesting of pension entitlements for employees who move from one employer to another and safeguarded pension benefits against the risk of inflation and an employer's insolvency (Schmähl and Böhm 1996: 8). It is worth noting that, since the 1970s and following a "functional conversion" logic according to which the defining objectives of an institution are altered (Thelen 2004), the existing early retirement schemes have been increasingly used by labor and capital as an exit pathway for older workers. As a consequence, social partners shifted labor market problems, especially unemployment among older workers, to the pension system. This logic is not unique to Germany, and it has been used extensively in countries such as Belgium and France, among others (Immergut et al. 2007; Kohli et al. 1991).

Since the 1980s, several minor reforms were implemented by the federal coalition (FDP and CDU/CSU). However, most of these reforms aimed at cost containment and, by and large, did not shift the public-private mix in pension policies. The most important of these reforms, the 1989 Pension Reform Act, enacted the very same day as the Berlin Wall broke down but implemented in 1992, even strengthened the existing institutional design of the pension system. The change from gross- to net-wage indexation was the most influential change enacted through the 1989 reform. And, from a political perspective, this reform was the last one until 2007 that was backed by all major parties in parliament (Hinrichs 1998; Schulze and Jochem 2007). In 2001, the red-green government brought about a genuine "paradigm shift" (Hall 1993) in German pension policies by introducing a more or less "private" insurance pillar, the so-called "Riester-Rente." With this reform and two others in 2004, the red-green government reshaped the traditional goals and institutions of the German pension system and strongly altered the public-private mix (Rüb and Lamping 2005; Schulze and Jochem 2007).

Figure 8.1 presents the complexity of the highly fragmented German pension system. Representing the "sector" of a specific pension scheme, the first pillar stands for the public sector, the second for the occupational sector, and the third pillar for the private sector. This perspective makes use of the analytical distinction between the state and the market sectors. Furthermore, the term "tier" points to the distinction between various types of pension benefits. This distinction is important because it matters a great deal whether benefits are targeted, minimum, flat-rate, earnings-related, or defined-contribution. Moreover, the distinction between mandatory and voluntary pension schemes is essential for obvious reasons.

Disentangling this complex system further, it is also possible to differentiate between the schemes covering different occupational groups. Following

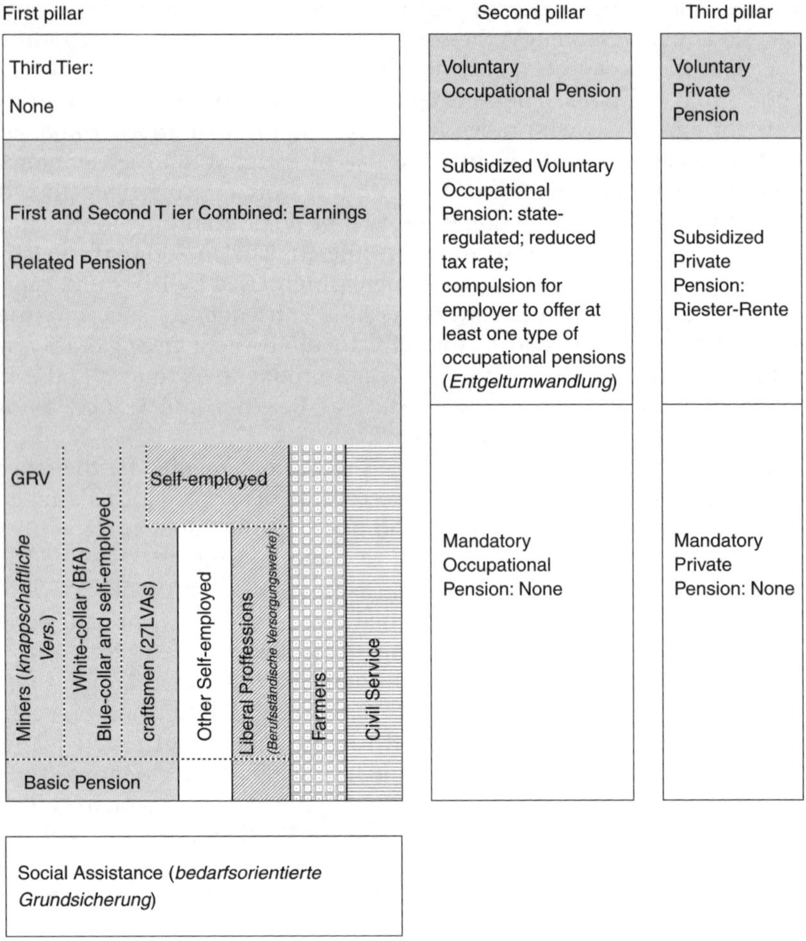

Figure 8.1   The German pension system today
Source: Schulze and Jochem (2007: 674).

a logic of occupational fragmentation that emerged under Bismarck, the contemporary German pension system is divided into the compulsory statutory pension insurance for blue- and white-collar employees, the pension scheme for the agricultural sector, coverage of civil servants ("Beamtenversorgung"), and several other occupational schemes. The statutory pension insurance ("Gesetzliche Rentenversicherung," GRV) covers approximately 82 percent of the workforce. Although Germany has no compulsory insurance system for all types of self-employed, they can voluntarily join the state pension system. As occupational and private pensions are not mandatory, the roles of the second- and third-pension pillars remain limited in scope. Since the introduction of the "Riester-Rente" (see below), however, their importance has increased steadily due to tax subsidies from the state. Although the major source of old-age income remains the first pillar pension scheme for current pensions, impacts of this first pillar will be reduced significantly in the near future (DIA 2007).

The 23 regional pension insurance funds are united in the Federation of German Pension Insurance Institutes (*Verband Deutscher Rentenversicherungsträger*, VDR). The VDR is an autonomous administrative institution with a board of directors composed of an equal number of business and labor representatives. One of the main tasks of the VDR is consultation and the preparation of expert reports aimed at informing the legislative process. Hence, in Germany, data collection on pension policy is more or less in the hands of the VDR, and the government relies to a great extent on its database (Nullmeier and Rüb 1993). Organizational reforms enacted in late 2004 fused the VDR and BfA (the white-collar umbrella pension fund) into a new "Deutsche Rentenversicherung Bund" (German National Pension Insurance). These reforms also reduced the number of regional pension funds through regional fusions.

The public pension system is financed on the pay-as-you-go principle. Contribution rates are shared equally between the employee and the employer. The employer pays the entire contribution for employees in apprenticeship and those earning less than €400 per month. Low-income earners with monthly wage between €400 and €800 wages must pay reduced but progressively increasing contributions. The German public pension system is partly tax-financed, as the government subsidizes pension insurance with a grant. Since April 1, 1998, there has been a supplementary federal subsidy to cover noncontribution benefits. This lump-sum payment is financed by having increased VAT by one percentage point and, since 2000, by the revenues from an "ecology" tax on energy. This reform increased the financial contribution of the state to the public pension funds. To guarantee that pension carriers always have balanced budgets, the contribution rate must increase as expenses grow.

Pensions are paid if the insured person reaches the standard retirement age of 65, meets the requirements for long service pensions, is incapacitated for work (disability), or dies leaving his or her spouse eligible for a survivor's pension. The value of pension benefits depends mainly on the contributions paid throughout the working career and, therefore, on the level of income from employment. Contributions paid are converted into personal earning points ("Entgeltpunkte"). "Entgeltpunkte" can also be earned through child-raising periods, military service or, until 2004, higher education.

Pensions are adjusted yearly by government decree. So far, the new pension value ("Rentenwert") has been calculated by multiplying the current pension value with the changes in the average gross wage (of the real contribution base since 2005) between the previous year and the year before that, and with the changes in pension contribution rates, including a private pension contribution rate of 4 percent in 2009. Since January, 2005, the indexation formula further includes a demographic factor known as the "Nachhaltigkeitsfaktor" (sustainability factor) that reflects the ratio of pensioners relative to contributors.

The most important shift in the public-private pension mix was made by the so-called Riester Reform. After some fumbling by the red-green government, in 2001 this pension reform changed the contours of the German pension scheme (Trampusch 2005). As Winfried Schmähl puts it, the 2001 reform marked a "paradigm shift" in German pension policies (Schmähl 2003; see also Hering 2002; Hinrichs 2004; Rüb and Lamping 2005). The replacement rate of the first pillar was significantly reduced. The joint (employer and employee) contribution rate was capped at 20 percent of gross wages. In order to compensate for the traditional principle that the first pillar should maintain the pensioner's standard of living ("Lebensstandardsicherung"), the government subsidized private pensions ("Riester-Rente"), especially targeting lower-income workers. After political negotiations and the intervention of trade unions, occupational pensions ("Entgeltumwandlung") were included in the system of tax incentives, thereby giving the labor market parties new opportunities to negotiate labor market pension schemes (Schmähl 2003). The reform was layered on top of the old pension system, which will alter the public-private income mix of future generations of pensioners. The 2001 reform also paved the way for new actors, mainly private insurance companies, to enter the inner circle of German pension policymaking. Because of the far-reaching tax incentives it created, this reform also gave the Ministry of Finance important veto power over this policy area, something it did not have in the past (Rüb and Lamping 2005).

As mentioned above, in 2004, this "direction setting law" (Rüb and Lamping 2005: 2) was complemented by two reforms that openly rejected the idea that pensions provided by the first pillar could maintain the pensioner's standard of living, which had been the norm since 1957. Under the heading of a "sustainability factor," the replacement rate of the first pillar was further reduced. Taken together, the gross replacement rate of the first (public) pillar was reduced by the reforms in 2001 and 2004 from 48.7 to 39.9 percent (DIA 2007, OECD 2007). Its construction enables the government to adjust pension increases in an ad hoc fashion if the combined contribution rate of employers and employees threatens to rise above the fixed limit of 20 percent. Additionally, following a verdict of the German Constitutional Court, the second reform will make future pension benefits taxable, which implies a further reduction in the net replacement rate.

Undoubtedly, many elements of the old system remain and, for most retired Germans, the first pillar is still the main source of pension income. In fact, the reduction of benefit levels will only become noticeable to those who retire after 2010 at the earliest. Nevertheless, the logic and the public-private mix of the German pension system have fundamentally changed. The role of the first pillar has been reduced and will further decline in the future. Until today, the incentives of the "Riester-Rente" have only been used sparingly, especially targeting lower-income workers. However, in 2005, under the Grand Coalition, the government announced that mandatory private and occupational pension schemes were not necessary because coverage rates for both private and occupational voluntary schemes had significantly increased (Rentenbericht 2005). Hence, a reform of these schemes is currently not on the political agenda. To further dampen future expenditure growth for the first pillar, the Grand Coalition decided to increase the current retirement age from 65 to 67. This change will be gradually implemented between 2007 and 2029.

Due to the above-mentioned reforms, the public-private mix and the logic of the whole German pension system have notably changed through incremental processes. The future replacement rate of the first pillar will be significantly lower than it is today, and the consensus among political leaders is that the growing importance of occupational and private supplementary pensions is unavoidable. The prototypical Bismarckian German pension system has thus started to change its path largely through the institutional layering (Béland 2007) of supplementary and voluntary pension schemes on the top of decreasingly generous public pension schemes.

Conclusion

Since the 1980s, the German public-private mix for health care and pension policies has changed significantly. For example, most post-1982 governments increased private co-payments in health care and, since 2001, the red-green governments have strengthened the market for private and occupational pensions. These market-building efforts involved the implementation of new state regulations aimed at regulating increasingly large social-policy markets. As a consequence, the relationship between the state and the market has become even more complex than before, never approaching a clear-cut division between the two sectors. The contours of the private and the public in German social policies are becoming increasingly blurred. The push toward "risk shifting" (Hacker 2004, 2006) has gone hand in hand with further increases in public market regulations. Hence, the state now faces the challenge of regulating dynamic markets in order to fulfill long-standing but less solidaristic social security goals in these new circumstances.

This greater policy complexity is most clearly observable in pension policies. On the one hand, the red-green governments built up the market for private and occupational pensions. On the other hand, intense regulations for these private pension products were introduced. For example, far-reaching tax subsidies that mainly targeted lower-income workers were implemented. In light of these changes, the OECD rightly concludes that the "recent pension reforms in Germany are among the most substantial and comprehensive among OECD countries" (OECD 2007). These changes do not imply a full retreat of the state. In contrast, recent pension reforms further blurred the boundaries between the public and the private sectors, and introduced tax policies into the pension policy framework.

Like in other countries, the political logic behind these developments is mediated through specific decision-making institutions and the policy legacies of existing social security schemes. Yet, even in the field of pension policy, the *locus classicus* of path dependency arguments (Myles and Pierson 2001), the red-green governments favored an incremental shift toward a new institutional path that combines private markets and comprehensive public regulation (Jochem 2007). These remarks about pension reform in Germany suggest that institutional accounts focusing on path dependency often neglect the consequences of institutional layering (Béland 2007) as well as the fact that small policy changes may culminate over time to generate path-departing dynamics (Thelen 2004).

As far as the German public-private mix is concerned, future developments are difficult to predict. Under the current Grand Coalition, further pension reforms have already been implemented (for example, the stepwise increase of retirement age). Today, most policy experts, even including the OECD (2007), argue that, in this policy area, structural reforms have been successfully accomplished. As for health care, the programmatic differences between the CDU/CSU and the SPD seem insurmountable. Considering this barrier, the outcome of the next national elections, which may take place in 2009, will probably shape the future of the public-private mix in health care. As mentioned above, although the CDU/CSU favors promarket liberalizations, the SPD, in contrast, supports solutions that strengthen the existing public statutory health insurance. Because health care issues remain very high on the political agenda, the next electoral campaign (expected in 2009) probably will focus on these issues, which are at the heart of the changing relationship between public and private social policy in Germany. However, it seems possible to predict that whatever reforms we will experience in the future, they will presumably further increase the complexity of the public-private mix in Germany and, as a consequence, blur the boundaries between "public" and "private" in German social policies even more.

References

Béland, Daniel. 2007. "Ideas and Institutional Change in Social Security: Conversion, Layering, and Policy Drift." *Social Science Quarterly* 88: 20–38.
Bleses, Peter and Martin Seeleib-Kaiser. 2004. *The Dual Transformation of the German Welfare State.* New York: Palgrave/Macmillan.
Busse, Reinhard and Annette Riesberg. 2004. *Health Care Systems in Transitions: Germany.* Copenhagen: WHO Regional Office for Europe on behalf of the European Observatory on Health Systems and Policies.

Castles, Francis G. 2004. *The Future of the Welfare State: Crisis Myths and Crisis Realities.* Oxford: Oxford University Press.

DIA (Deutsches Institut für Altervorsorge). 2007. Nachhaltigkeit verbessert—Gefahr der Altersarmut gestiegen: Das deutsche Rentensystem nach den Reformen. Pressemitteilung Retrieved on January 15, 2008 from www.dia-vorsorge.de

Frerich, Johannes and Martin Frey. 1993. *Handbuch der Geschichte der Sozialpolitik in Deutschland: Von der vorindustriellen Zeit bis zum Ende des Dritten Reiches.* München: Oldenbourg.

Greß, Stefan. 2006. "Regulated Competition in Social Health Insurance: A Three-Country Comparison." *International Social Security Review* 59: 27–47.

Greß, Stefan, Anke Walendzik, and Jürgen Wasem. 2005. *Nichtversicherte Personen im Krankenversicherungssystem der Bundesrepublik Deutschland—Bestandaufnahme und Lösungsmöglichkeiten. Expertise für die Hans-Böckler-Stiftung.* Essen: Hans-Böckler-Stiftung.

Hacker, Jacob S. 2004. "Privatizing Risk without Privatizing the Welfare State: The Hidden Politics of Social Policy Retrenchment in the United States." *American Political Science Review* 98: 243–60.

Hacker, Jacob S. 2006. *The Great Risk Shift: The New Economic Insecurity—And What Can Be Done About It.* New York: Oxford University Press.

Hall, Peter A. 1993. "Policy Paradigms, Social Learning, and the State: The Case of Economic Policymaking in Britain." *Comparative Politics* 25: 275–96.

Hering, Martin. 2002. "The Politics of Privatizing Public Pensions: Lessons from a Frozen Welfare State." Presentation prepared for American Political Science Association 98th Annual Meeting. Boston, August 29–September 1, 2002.

Hinrichs, Karl. 1998. "Reforming the Public Pension Scheme in Germany: The End of the Traditional Consensus?" ZeS-Arbeitspapier 11/98. Bremen: Centre for Social Policy Research.

Hinrichs, Karl. 2004. "Alterssicherungspolitik in Deutschland: Zwischen Kontinuität und Paradigmenwechsel." In Petra Stykow and Jürgen Beyer (eds), *Gesellschaft mit beschränkter Hoffnung: Reformfähigkeit und die Möglichkeit rationaler Politik*: 266–86. Wiesbaden: VSVerlag.

Immergut, Ellen M. 1992. *Health Politics: Interests and Institutions in Western Europe.* Cambridge: Cambridge University Press.

Immergut, Ellen M., Karen Anderson, and Isabelle Schulze. (eds). 2007. *The Handbook of West European Pension Politics: Political Institutions and Policy Outcomes in Comparative Perspective.* Oxford: Oxford University Press.

Jochem, Sven. 2007. *Reformpolitik im Wohlfahrtsstaat. Deutschland im internationalen Vergleich.* Habilitationsschrift Humboldt-Universität zu Berlin.

Kohli, Martin, Martin Rein, Anne-Marie Guillemard, and Hermann van Gunsteren. (eds). 1991. *Time for Retirement: Comparative Studies of Early Exit from the Labor Force.* New York: Cambridge University Press.

Lehmbruch, Gerhard. 1998. Parteienwettbewerb im Bundesstaat. Regelsysteme und Spannungslagen im Institutionengefüge der Bundesrepublik Deutschland 2, erweiterte Auflage. Opladen: Leske+Budrich.

Myles, John and Paul Pierson. 2001. "The Comparative Political Economy of Pension Reform. " In Paul Pierson (ed.), *The New Politics of the Welfare State*: 305–33. Oxford: Oxford University Press.

Nullmeier, Frank and Friedbert W. Rüb. 1993. *Die Transformation der Sozialpolitik: Vom Sozialstaat zum Sicherungsstaat* Frankfurt am Main: Campus.

OECD. 2006. OECD in Figures 2006–2007. Paris: OECD.

OECD. 2007. Pensions at a Glance. Paris: OECD.

Rein, Martin and Lee Rainwater. 1986. "Introduction." In Martin Rein and Lee Rainwater (eds), *Public/Private Interplay in Social Protection*: vii–vii. Armonk, NY: M. E. Sharpe, Inc.

Rentenbericht. 2005. Deutscher Bundestag. Drucksache 16/905.

Ritter, Gerhard A. 2006. "Der Preis der deutschen Einheit. Die Wiedervereinigung und die Krise des Sozialstaats." München: Beck.

Rothgang, Heinz, Mirella Cacace, Simone Grimmeisen, Uwe Helmert, and Claus Wendt. 2006. "Wandel von Staatlichkeit in den Gesundheitssystemen von OECD Ländern." In Leibfried and Zürn (eds), *Transformation des Staates*: 309–54. Frankfurt am Main: Suhrkamp.

Rüb, Friedbert W. and Wolfram Lamping. 2005. "The Politics of Reforming a 'Holy Grail.' Paradigm Shifts, Experimental Law-Making, and the Politics of German Pension Reform." Paper presented at the ESPAnet Conference, September 22–24, 2005, Fribourg.

SBA (Statistisches Bundesamt). 2006. *Gesundheit. Ausgaben, Krankheitskosten und Personal 2004*. Wiesbaden: Statistisches Bundesamt.

Scharpf, Fritz W. 1988. "The Joint Decision Trap. Lessons from German Federalism and European Integration." *Public Administration* 66: 239–78.

Scharpf, Fritz W. 2006. "The Joint-Decision Trap Revisited." *Journal of Common Market Studies* 44: 845–64.

Schmähl, Winfried. 2003. "Dismantling the Earnings-Related Social Pension Scheme: Germany Beyond a Crossroad." ZeS-Arbeitspapier 9/03. Bremen: Zentrum für Sozialpolitik, Universität Bremen.

Schmähl, Winfried and Stefan Böhm. 1996. "Supplementary Pensions in the Federal Republic of Germany." In Emmanuel Reynaud, Lucy Aproberts, and Bryn Davies (eds), *International Perspectives on Supplementary Pensions: Actors and Issues*: 7–15. Westport: Quorum Books.

Schmidt, Manfred G. 2005. "Sozialpolitik in Deutschland." Historische Entwicklung und internationaler Vergleich. 3, völlständig überarbeitete und erweiterte Auflage. Wiesbaden: VS Verlag.

Schulze, Isabelle and Sven Jochem. 2007. "Germany: Beyond Policy Gridlock." In Ellen M. Immergut, Karen Anderson, and Isabelle Schulze (eds), *The Handbook of West European Pension Politics: Political Institutions and Policy Outcomes in Comparative Perspective*: 660–710. Oxford: Oxford University Press.

SVR (Sachverständigenrat zur Begutachtung der gesamtwirtschaftlichen Entwicklung). 2006. Jahresgutachten 2006/2007. Wiesbaden: SVR.

Thelen, Kathleen. 2004. *How Institutions Evolve: The Political Economy of Skills in Germany, Britain, the United States and Japan*. New York: Cambridge University Press.

Trampusch, Christine. 2005. "Sozialpolitik in Post-Hartz Germany." *WeltTrends* 47: 77–90.

Wehler, Hans-Ulrich. 1995. *Deutsche Gesellschaftsgeschichte, Dritter Band: Von der Deutschen Doppelrevolution' bis zum Beginn des Ersten Weltkrieges 1849–1914*. München: Beck.

9

The Swiss Welfare State: A Changing Public-Private Mix?

Fabio Bertozzi and Fabrizio Gilardi

Introduction

Analyzing the changing boundaries between the public and the private spheres in the welfare state is particularly interesting in the Swiss case. In fact, the role of the private sector has always been important in social policymaking in this country, many decades before the contemporary pushes for privatization and market-based social protection in most industrialized countries (Cattacin 2006).

It is thus not surprising that in international comparison the Swiss welfare state has been often classified as a liberal welfare regime (Esping-Andersen 1990), despite the geographical location encircled by typical continental conservative regimes (Austria, France, Germany, and Italy). The major reasons for this situation can mainly be found in two institutional characteristics—direct democracy and federalism—which proved to be strong barriers to the expansion of the Swiss welfare state and have oriented the path of welfare state evolution in a rather liberal direction (Obinger 1998). The historical weakness of prowelfare parties also contributed to this situation (Armingeon 2001).

Nevertheless, a number of relevant reforms since the mid-1970s have partly modified the overall shape of the welfare state in Switzerland and also somewhat adjusted the balance between the public and the private spheres in the system. Four major welfare schemes that previously worked on a voluntary basis became compulsory at the federal level during these years: the unemployment insurance scheme (in 1977–84), the occupational pension schemes (in 1985), the health insurance scheme (in 1996), and the maternity insurance scheme (in 2005).[1] At the same time, to a certain extent because of these reforms, public social expenditure dramatically increased from approximately 15 percent of the GDP at the beginning of the 1980s to almost 30 percent at the end of the 1990s (OECD).

Switzerland can nowadays be considered as a continental European welfare state with a liberal face (Armingeon 2001; Bonoli and Mach 2000).

In fact, despite these transformations, some inherited liberal characteristics still strongly shape the Swiss system. This is for instance very well illustrated by the two social policy areas, health and pensions. In these two cases, as we will show in this chapter, private insurers still play a major role, both in managing some parts of the compulsory schemes and in providing complementary voluntary private social protection. The extension of the public compulsory schemes has regulated the activity of private actors but has ultimately not significantly reduced the role they play in the overall system.

In the following sections of this chapter we will focus on the health care system and the pension system in Switzerland focusing on historical developments, detailed description of the systems and looming issues on the horizon in these policy areas. We will then compare the two policy areas and discuss the different public-private mixes that can be identified. In the end, we will try to assess to what extent the traditional role of private actors in Swiss social policy is changing in an era of growing retrenchment pressures.

Health care

Introduction

Health care systems are usually divided into three categories: national health services, social insurance systems, and liberal systems (Freeman 2000; Palier 2004; but see Moran 1999; Moran 2000). With respect to this typology, the Swiss system is a hybrid because it is mainly liberal, but with several features typical of social insurance systems. Its current shape is defined by the 1994 law on health insurance, which preserved the fundamentally liberal nature of the system, but injected several important social elements that moved Switzerland closer to a social insurance model. Basic health insurance is compulsory for all residents, and is provided by more than 90 private health care funds. Although the market for the basic package is highly regulated and insurers cannot profit from it, the market for complementary coverage is quite free: insurers are for instance allowed to select people on the basis of their health status. In other words, this means that they can refuse to insure a person if coverage would not be profitable. Insurance premiums are independent of revenue, both for basic and complementary coverage: within the same fund, every person pays the same amount for the insurance, regardless of income. However, a public system of subsidies aims to reduce the burden for the less well-off. The implementation of this policy is, however, left to the cantons: as a result, the generosity of the system varies greatly across subnational units. Finally, doctors are professionals who, within the tight limits of a complex regulatory framework, can set their rates and are paid on the basis of the number and type of medical acts performed. With respect to inpatient care, both private and public hospitals need to be approved by cantonal authorities in order for patients to be reimbursed by their insurance schemes.

In this section we will first outline the broad historical development of the Swiss system, which confirms the relevance of path dependence and veto points in the preservation of a liberal model (Hacker 1998; Immergut 1992a). We will then describe the system in detail, notably with respect to its organization, financing and expenditures, eligibility and coverage, and its general public-private mix. Finally, we will discuss looming issues on the horizon, which include ongoing legislative reform.

Historical development

In Switzerland the first law on health insurance was passed in 1911. This law did not significantly change the existing system, but rather preserved both medical practice as a liberal profession and the multiplicity of private health funds. The outcome was a very liberal system: health insurance was not compulsory (although shortly before the 1994 reform more than 95 percent of the population was insured), and insurers could legally select customers on the basis of both age and health status, and also vary premiums as a function of these factors. Therefore, the risk structure of the various funds varied greatly, with an effect on premiums. In addition, there was no common basic insurance package, because insurers were free to define it.

Despite its many problems, this system survived until 1994. Ellen Immergut (1992a; 1992b) has provided one of the most authoritative accounts of the failure to introduce a national health insurance in Switzerland. Her well-known argument is that the Swiss institutional structure, which is characterized by many veto points, has given supporters of the status quo many opportunities to block reforms. The 1994 reform does not put her findings into question, since the new law largely preserved the main elements of the previous system. In addition to veto points, or rather, as a precondition for their activation, a second element that can explain the liberal nature of the Swiss system are the effects of the 1911 law, which allowed powerful interests to develop, namely liberal medicine and private insurers, not unlike in the United States (Hacker 1998). These groups have been able to consolidate their position at the core of the system, and to prevent a greater public role in health care through the activation of the various veto points of the Swiss system, including the referendum threat. The effects of the 1911 law extend until today: this is a clear example of path-dependence.

The 1994 law on health insurance constitutes the most important reform to date, which determines the current shape of the system. The reform was not path-breaking: the main elements of the liberal system were maintained. However, significant changes were introduced. In particular, basic insurance was made compulsory for all residents and social instruments were introduced, notably subsidies to reduce premiums for low-income groups, the obligation for insurers to accept all patients for the basic package, and a risk-adjustment scheme to reduce premium variations across insurers. A major objective was cost containment, and the main instrument was the market, or more precisely competition among insurers. We discuss these aspects of the Swiss system and their outcomes in the next sections.

Organization of the system

The main characteristic of the organization of the Swiss system is that public authorities, especially at the federal level, have little control over most aspects of health care.

On the supply side, doctors have complete professional freedom, and any therapies or acts they perform or prescribe are then reimbursed by the patient's insurance, as long as they are included in the basic or complementary package. Doctors' fees depend on three factors: the number and type of medical acts performed, the number of "points" associated with each medical act, and the monetary value of each point. The "points" and their corresponding value are negotiated between doctors' and insurers' associations in two steps: at the national level, peak associations establish the link between acts and points, whereas at the cantonal level subnational associations set the monetary value of points. The basic tool for these negotiations is a comprehensive list of medical acts called TARMED, which has been used since January, 2004. The list includes more than 4,500 acts and about 10,000 "coordination rules," which describe all possible combinations of acts. The result is highly complex. For instance, more than 50 entries are needed to describe certain hernia interventions. Public authorities are largely absent from the negotiations and intervene only if doctors and insurers are unable to find an agreement.

On the demand side, patients also enjoy extensive liberty. There is no form of gatekeeping, and people can freely consult both generalists and specialists. As long as the treatment is covered by either basic or complementary insurance, health funds have to reimburse the costs. To encourage moderation in health care consumption, insurers can propose discounts on premiums in exchange of higher deductibles,[2] which currently vary between SFr300 (about US $250) and SFr2,500 (about US $2,100), or of participation in managed care plans. Both insurers and public authorities have thus only very modest means to steer the behavior of patients: these are limited to persuasion and to the economic incentive structure, which have proved unable to move significant shares of the population into managed care plans, which are known to be less costly than traditional insurance models. In Switzerland, patients seem to value very highly their freedom, and seem willing to pay more in order to keep it.

Finally, insurers are the cornerstone of the system. More than 90 private insurance companies exist, which compete to attract patients. Indeed, competition between insurers is the main governance mechanism in the Swiss system, albeit a weak one. Premiums vary across funds, notably as a function of risk structures, despite the existence of risk-adjustment mechanisms intended to compensate for these differences. The basic insurance package is the same in all funds and no profit can be made from it. For both basic and complementary insurance, premiums are set by the insurers but are subject to the approval of federal authorities. However, for complementary insurance there is a real market in which funds can set premiums and also select people, including on the basis of their health status. Insurers have quite limited possibilities to influence health care demand, supply, and therefore expenditures: they cannot significantly influence the behavior of patients or doctors, and have to reimburse all the fees that are covered by the insurance scheme. However, they are the most visible part of the rise of health care costs, since these are almost automatically translated into higher premiums, and are the object of widespread popular discontent.

To sum up, nobody really governs the Swiss heath care system: its functioning and outcomes depend on the uncoordinated interaction of patients, insurers, and providers, within the loose framework set by public authorities. Competition between insurers has been the main governance mechanism, but largely an ineffective one in terms of expenditures growth.

Financing and expenditures

Figure 9.1 compares Switzerland and the other OECD countries with respect to the sources of financing. The Swiss health care system is financed primarily through health insurance premiums (41.4 percent), whereas out-of-pocket expenditures (31.9 percent) are the second source. If we add private insurance (8.7 percent) (in the Swiss context, this means complementary insurance), we see that more than 80 percent of the expenditures are financed through mechanisms that do not redistribute wealth across income categories. In effect, unlike in social insurance systems such as Germany or France, health insurance premiums do not depend on income and therefore constitute a much heavier burden for lower-income groups. In contrast, typically other OECD countries finance the health care system principally with taxation, a redistributive mechanism, and second with social insurance contributions, which usually are more redistributive than in Switzerland because they are linked to salaries and cofinanced by employers (in Switzerland social insurance is paid entirely by patients).

Figure 9.2 shows the evolution of total health care expenditures as a share of GDP in Switzerland, in comparison with the other OECD countries. In Switzerland not only has expenditure on health grown much faster than GDP, but also faster than in most other OECD countries, and about twice as much as the OECD average. Since the health care system is financed predominantly by nonredistributive mechanisms, this increase has affected disproportionately the less well-off. In this sense, this evolution constitutes

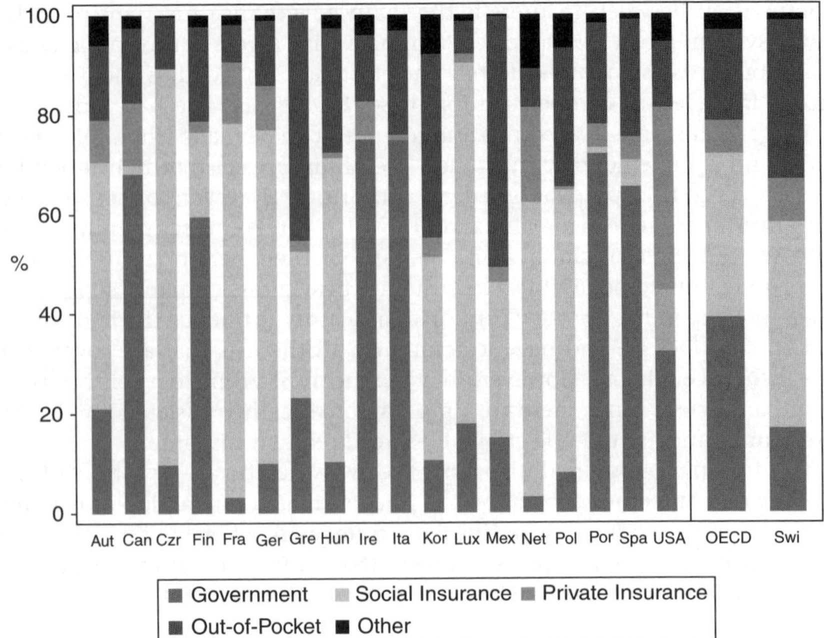

Figure 9.1   Financing sources
Source: OECD (2006).

an example of "policy drift" and "risk privatization without welfare state privatization" (Hacker 2004). After 1994 the policy framework has been essentially stable, but the system has nevertheless become less social. Today lower-income groups are in a worse situation than ten years ago. Unsurprisingly, the constant growth of costs, which is smoothly translated into higher insurance premiums, has been one of the main preoccupations of Swiss citizens.

Although the Swiss system is essentially a liberal one, there is one important social component. The 1994 law required all cantons to set up a subsidies scheme in order to lower health insurance premiums for people in need, the target (which is not part of the law) being that in no case should premiums exceed 8 percent of revenue. This target, however, is not only legally unenforceable, but also very difficult to observe. Although it seems that in many cases this threshold is exceeded, no broad comparative figures exist (Balthasar 2001). Subsidies are financed through matching funds. Cantons choose how much they want to spend within the limits set by the federal government, which then matches the funds. Subsidies have a double social component: they are financed through taxation, which is a redistributive instrument, and they are targeted to poorer people. With respect

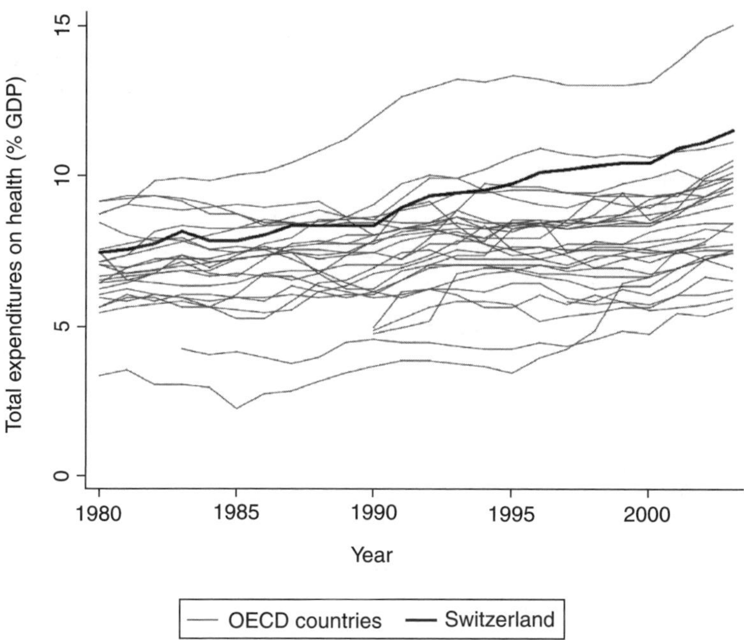

Figure 9.2 Total expenditures on health
Source: OECD (2006).

to the policy design, cantons are almost entirely free. For instance, they can choose eligibility criteria, generosity, and payment modalities. Given that the federal framework is very loose, it comes as no surprise that cantonal policies vary greatly, both in their set-up and in their outcomes.

Rising costs have a direct impact on cantonal policies: higher costs mean higher insurance premiums, which in principle require more money for subsidies. To cope with this pressure, cantons have followed two different strategies: either give more to fewer people, or give less to more people. Figure 9.3 shows that on average, generosity (defined as the share of premiums that, on average, is covered by the subsidy for each beneficiary) has tended to decline, whereas the share of beneficiaries has tended to increase slightly. On the other hand, insurance premiums have increased very rapidly. This is another example of 'policy drift' and 'risk privatization' (Hacker 2004): policies have been insufficiently adapted to the new context (that is, higher premiums), and as a result people are less protected now than ten years ago.

To sum up, although an important subsidy policy exists, the Swiss health care system is financed predominantly through nonredistributive mecha-nisms. Since costs have steadily increased during the past quarter of century

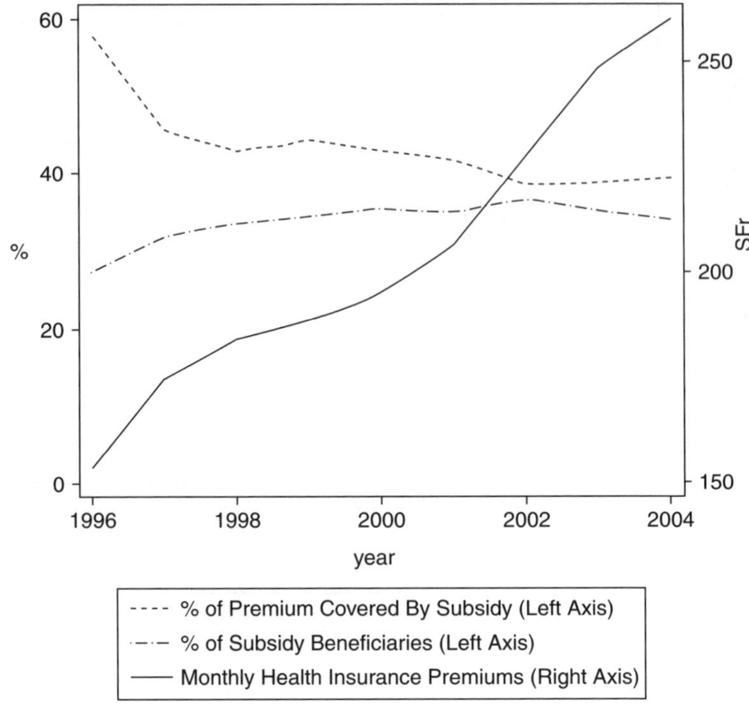

Figure 9.3   Subsidies

and subsidies have been inadequately adapted after their introduction in 1994, the result is an increased privatization of the risks associated to poor health.

Eligibility and coverage

Virtually 100 percent of legal residents are covered by the basic insurance scheme, which is compulsory. The basic package is relatively comprehensive: it includes inpatient and most outpatient care, as well as medicines and other forms of treatment such as physiotherapy, provided that they are prescribed by a doctor. Some types of natural medicine, however, have recently been left out of the basic package; other forms of care, such as dental care, have never been included. Complementary insurance is voluntary and a wide offering exists, which covers everything that is not included in the basic insurance, at a price, of course.

An important issue that undermines both eligibility and coverage is "cream-skimming," namely the fact that some insurers attempt to select people on the basis of their health status, obviously trying to attract healthy customers ("good risks") and get rid of sick ones ("bad risks"). Although for the basic package this kind of selection is illegal, insurers can legally make their plans more attractive for "good risks" (for example, bigger discounts for higher deductibles). In addition, a variety of semilegal practices push "bad risks" onto other insurers, such as delaying reimbursements or in general offering poor service. In principle, the risk-adjustment scheme set up by the 1994 law should prevent these abuses: insurers with "better" risk structures subsidize those with "worse" structures, which should eliminate all economic incentives to hunt "good risks," since if the risk structure improves, the insurance has to put more money into the risk-adjustment scheme. However, the calculations are made only on the basis of two criteria, namely sex and age. Although on average older people spend more on health care than younger ones, and women more than men, these two factors actually explain only a very small percentage of expenditures. Risk-adjustment calculations therefore do not accurately reflect the real risk structure, which leaves economic incentives for cream-skimming almost intact.

Summary: public-private mix

The Swiss health care system has a very interesting public-private mix. With the partial exception of hospitals, most care is provided by private actors. Insurance is compulsory but is also private, both because the insurers are private companies and because premiums are independent from revenue and, unlike in other social insurance systems, are not cofinanced by employers. Patients enjoy extensive freedom and indeed are expected to act as customers in a market. Public authorities have therefore delegated most functions to the private sector, and their role, with the exception of subsidies to reduce insurance premiums, is largely regulative. Basically, government simply defines the rules of the game and supervises their implementation. The result is that the health care system is not governed, and public authorities can merely try to influence the various actors by fine-tuning the incentive structure. This has not worked well: attempts to rein in the explosion of expenditures have so far proved vain. Of course, wide-ranging reforms are in principle possible. However, the historical development of the Swiss system has shown that these are unlikely.

Looming issues on the horizon

Two major issues will influence the evolution of the Swiss health care system during the next years, possibly with durable effects.

First, the 1994 law is currently being revised in a piecemeal fashion after an attempt at comprehensive reform failed in 2003. Most aspects of the system are being changed. One of the most controversial points is the proposal to allow insurers to reimburse only the fees of the providers they have selected. This would drastically change the power balance between insurers and providers, and give the former real means to influence the behavior of the latter. However, if the law will be passed a referendum is almost certain. Another controversial proposal is to increase coinsurance levels: once the deductible level is reached, patients currently pay 10 percent of the costs, and the government would like to raise this share to 20 percent. Other less controversial proposals aim to make managed care plans more attractive and to introduce patient classification systems as a hospital financing instrument. A change that has already been voted into law is an adjustment of subsidy policy, which however is very limited and leaves the policy virtually untouched. Although some of the proposals are quite path-changing, the final result will probably be incremental. These reforms are therefore unlikely to have big effects on the evolution of expenditures.

Second, in a referendum held on March 11, 2007, following a successful popular initiative, Swiss citizens rejected (with a majority of more than 70 percent) a proposal to establish a single health insurance fund at the national level, governed by representatives of patients, providers, and public authorities. If it had been accepted, this proposal would have constituted a major departure from the current path. Existing health insurers would have no longer been allowed to offer the basic package, and their role would have been limited to complementary insurance. In addition, premiums would have been linked to revenue, although the initiative did not specify how. A similar proposal to make premiums vary with revenue was rejected by 72 percent of voters in a referendum in 2003. The failure of these two initiatives shows clearly that, although direct democratic instruments can in principle short-circuit the normal veto-ridden policy process, path dependence remains a strong determinant of the evolution of the Swiss system.

The Swiss pension system

Introduction

In international comparison, the Swiss pension system is classified as a multipillar system (Bonoli 2000, 2005; Palier 2003). In fact, the system consists of a public basic pension (AVS-AHV)[3] which also includes means-tested complementary old-age benefits (PC-EL),[4] an additional professional pillar (LPP-BVG)[5] and voluntary private savings encouraged by tax concessions. The system thus comprises three distinct pillars organized along different logics.

Each tier of the Swiss pension system has distinctive features in terms of objectives, coverage, benefits, and financing mechanism (see Table 9.1). Whereas the first pillar aims essentially at guaranteeing a poverty-free retirement, the second pillar has an income maintenance objective, to allow pensioners to maintain the standard of living to which they are accustomed. Ultimately, the third pillar encourages people to establish voluntary private pension savings through tax concessions and is meant to meet further personal needs.

Table 9.1   The three pillars of the Swiss pension system

	1st Pillar		2nd Pillar	3rd Pillar
	Old-age insurance (AVS-AHV)	**Complementary benefits (PC-EL)**	**Occupational pension schemes (LPP-BVG)**	**Individual provision**
Principle	Universal	Need	Occupational	Personal
Coverage	Compulsory for all residents	Compulsory for all residents	Compulsory for employees*	Voluntary
Financing mechanism	Pay-as-you-go	General taxation	Funding	Funding
Contributions	Employment-related	—	Employment-related	
Benefits	Almost flat-rate	Means-tested	Contributions-related	
Objective	Poverty prevention	Basic needs	Income maintenance	Complementary individual needs

Note: *Coverage is compulsory for all employees earning more than SFr19,890 (about US $17,000) a year (2007).

Source: Bertozzi and Bonoli (2007).

Since the strength of the legal regulatory framework significantly decreases going from the first to the third pillar of the system, the role of private and public actors in the management of the scheme changes significantly along the selected pillar (Bertozzi and Bonoli 2007).

In this section we present the features of each pillar of the Swiss pension system. We first focus on the historical development of the system since its implementation. Second, we precisely describe the organization of the three tiers of the system, with particular attention to the financing mechanisms, the benefits levels, and the coverage. The role of public and private actors in each tier of the system is carefully analyzed. In the end, we will concentrate on the looming issues for the Swiss pension policy and politics, for example contemporary and future reform projects and future scenarios on the development of the system.

Historical development

In a typical Swiss way of social policymaking, which is strongly influenced by federalism and direct democracy, the historical development of the three pillars system has been slow and has followed a step-by-step trajectory. In fact, these features introduce many veto points in the Swiss decision-making procedure (Bonoli 2000: 87–95). Compared to other Western countries, Switzerland can be considered as a latecomer concerning the introduction of the core elements of the public retirement scheme (Armingeon 2001; Obinger 1998).

The first voluntary and compulsory pension schemes in the country were implemented at the level of the cantons.[6] The initial step toward the introduction of a federal compulsory retirement scheme was in 1925, when Swiss citizens adopted by referendum a new article in the federal constitution allowing the federal government to implement a federal compulsory old-age and survivors' insurance. Nevertheless, the first old-age and survivors' insurance law, which was put to popular vote in 1931, was refused (referendum).

It was only after World War II that the bases of the current system were finally laid down. In fact, in 1947 a second draft of the compulsory old-age and survivors' insurance law (AVS-AHV) was accepted by an overwhelming majority of the population (more than 80 percent). This law, the first pillar of the Swiss pension system, was enacted in 1948. In the beginning, the AVS-AHV granted only flat-rate benefits for the entire population, but the scope and the level of the benefits were expanded since then through frequent revisions of this law.

The first pillar was completed in 1966 when complementary benefits (PC-EL) were introduced. These means-tested benefits were first implemented as a transitional measure in order to span the period until AVS-AHV benefits would be high enough to guarantee a poverty-free retirement for the entire population. However, since the minimum AVS-AHV benefits have never been raised over the old-age social assistance threshold, complementary benefits became a permanent measure.

Whereas the principle of a three-pillars pension system has been included in the federal constitution already in 1972, the second occupational tier of the system became compulsory only in 1985 (federal law on occupational pension schemes, LPP-BVG). It must be underlined that the first professional pension funds were created on a voluntary basis in some branches over one century ago. Since 1916, tax concessions were granted for occupational pensions. The compulsory occupational pension scheme implemented in 1985 was thus largely inspired by the structure of the already existing pension funds, but it has introduced the principle of minimum provision guaranteed by the law, the so-called *Obligatorium*.

At the same time that professional pension schemes became compulsory, tax concessions for private voluntary pension savings—the third pillar of the system—were introduced in 1985.[7] Since the implementation of the first federal compulsory schemes, many reforms have been adopted in Switzerland in the area of pension policy. Up to now, the first pillar AVS-AHV law has been reformed ten times and the second pillar LPP-BVG only once. The result of this development and the shape of today's pension system are described in the following sections.[8]

The first pillar: state provision

The first pillar (AHV-AVS) provides universal coverage and is a fairly redistributive scheme, due to a compressed benefit structure: the highest pension is worth only twice as much as the lowest one. In 2007, the lowest and the highest pension are set at SFr1,105 (about US $945) and SFr2,210 (about US $1,890) per month, respectively. Within these limits, the amount of the benefit is related to the contributions paid while in work. The strong vertical redistribution is due to the fact that contributions are proportional to earnings without a ceiling. Even though its benefits are moderately related to earnings, the Swiss basic pension is a scheme of Beveridgean inspiration, geared toward poverty prevention rather than income maintenance. As a matter of fact, in international comparisons this pillar is often considered as a flat-rate pension scheme (Hinrichs 2000; Weaver 2003).

As far as financing is concerned, the AVS-AHV works on a pay-as-you-go basis. It is mainly financed through the contributions paid by those insured and their employers, but also receives a state subsidy financed by general taxation equal to 20 percent of total expenditures.[9] Coverage is universal: those who are not working after age 21, for instance students, are required to pay an annual flat-rate contribution or, if providing informal care, are entitled to contribution credits. Benefits are adjusted every two years according to the so-called *mixed index*, which corresponds to the arithmetic average between salary and price index.

Since 1997, as a result of the tenth AVS-AHV reform, contribution credits are provided for those with children younger than 16, and a contribution-sharing system between married people called *splitting* makes sure that nonworking spouses are credited with half of the contributions paid by their partner.

First pillar benefits in Switzerland do not guarantee pension benefits over the old-age social assistance level. The Swiss basic pension is thus not fully poverty preventing like in other Beveridgean countries (Hinrichs 2000). Persons that get pensions below the old-age social assistance threshold can apply for means-tested supplementary benefits (PC-EL). These benefits are financed out of tax revenue by the federal state, the cantons and partly by the municipalities. In 2005, up to 12 percent of first pillar beneficiaries (149,600 persons) also received complementary benefits (OFAS 2006). Complementary benefits recipients are particularly concentrated in some categories of the retired population—unmarried persons, divorced persons—and in some poorer cantons.

Concerning the administrative organization of the scheme, the Swiss government and in particular the Federal Social Insurance Office (OFAS-BSV) supervise the old-age insurance system. The scheme is administered by compensation offices, which collect contributions and pay benefits. There are about 100 offices, which operate under the auspices of various professional associations, of the cantons, and of the federal administration. Employers are bound by law to do their part in the operation of the system by deducting the employees' contributions from all salaries or salary-like benefits, and paying these, along with the contributions they as employers pay, to the compensation office to which they are affiliated.

The second pillar: privately administered compulsory occupational schemes

When the second pillar of the Swiss pension system, occupational pensions, was implemented in 1985, it became compulsory for all employees earning at least twice the amount of the minimum AVS-AHV pension. The first revision of the LPP-BVG law (2003), has lowered this threshold to 1.5 times the minimum AVS-AHV benefit, that is SFr19,890 (about US $17,000) a year (in 2007).

In the 1990s coverage was virtually universal among male employees but reached only approximately 80 percent among employed women (OFAS 1995: 10), mainly because part-time employment and wages below the threshold are more common in female employment. A full occupational pension is granted to employees with a contribution record of 39 years for women and 40 for men (possibly to be equalized over the next few years). When the affiliation to an occupational pension became compulsory in the mid-1980s, legislation needed to take into account the existence of an already relatively developed system of occupational pension provision. As a result, a compulsory minimum level of provision, known as the *Obligatorium*, was introduced, which is calculated on the basis of notional contributions. The Obligatorium leaves relatively wide room for existing pension funds to maneuver in how they deliver and finance that minimum level of provision. Many pension funds, especially in the public sector or those sponsored by large employers, still offer better conditions than the *Obligatorium* (Bonoli and Gay-des-Combes 2003; Vontobel 2000).

Minimum compulsory benefits are calculated on the basis of notional contributions. Depending on the employee's age, individual accounts must be credited with a percentage of insured earnings, ranging from 7 to 18 percent (rates are higher for older people). Pension funds are free to finance the set amount as they wish, unless the contribution of the employers are at least equal to the contributions paid by the employees.

Besides notional contributions, the occupational pension law prescribes also a government-set minimum nominal interest rate, which must be credited to second pillar pension funds. At the time of the introduction of the new law, this rate was set at 4 percent and remained at this level until 2003 when, as a result of the crisis in the stock market, it was reduced to 3.25 percent. In 2004 the rate was further reduced to 2.25 percent, and since 2005 it has been set at 2.5 percent. The Swiss government has recently decided to set the rate at 2.75 percent from January 2008, on.

When a worker reaches retirement age, or decides to take early retirement (possible from the age of 58, but with an actuarially determined benefit reduction), the retirement credit resulting from the notional contributions and the applicable minimum interest is converted into an annual pension, on the basis of a conversion rate set by the government. The conversion rate was originally set at 7.2 percent in the law of 1985 but was recently lowered to 6.8 percent with a transition period of ten years (until 2014). The Swiss government is currently planning to further lower this rate to 6.4 percent with a shorter transition period (until 2011).

The employer bears ultimate responsibility for subscribing to a second pillar scheme for employees and can choose the pension fund. In 2004, more than 2,800 different pension funds were available (for 3.21 million insured persons). The LPP-BVG lets pension funds freely choose the form of organization they prefer. The institutions that implement occupational pension schemes can be public or private, but must be registered and are subject to joint management by employers and employees.

The third pillar: privately administered, noncompulsory personal savings

The third pillar of the pension system, voluntary private provision, consists of tax concessions for payments made to personal pension schemes. Employees who are already covered by a second pillar occupational pension can deduct from their taxable income contributions paid into a third pillar pension up to SFr6,365 (about US $5,440) per year (in 2007). Tax concessions are more substantial for people who are not covered by an occupational pension such as the self-employed who can deduct up to SFr31,824 (about US $27,220). Personal pensions play a relatively small but fast growing role in the Swiss pension system. The number of personal pensions went from 560,000 in 1990 to just over 2 million accounts in 2003[10], but the assets held by third pillar pension providers (banks and insurance companies) amounted to "only" about US $26 billion in 1999, or 13 times less than those held by second pillar funds (OFAS 2004).

The function of the third pillar is to allow individuals to adjust their pension coverage on the basis of their individual preferences, which may differ and cannot as a result be satisfied by the one-size-fit-all solutions represented by the first and the second pillar. As such, third pillar pensions are widely considered as a somewhat marginal element in the system.

The public-private mix in the three pillars of the pension system

As the previous sections clearly illustrate, the public-private mix is very different in the three pillars of the Swiss pension system. The first pillar is strictly regulated by the state, and the central fund is managed by the federal administration. However, social partners do take part in the management of the scheme by running some branch funds. For second pillar occupational schemes, state regulation mainly concerns the guarantee of the minimum requirements (*Obligatorium*) and other technical details such as portability. The law also prescribes the obligation to involve employees' representatives in the joint steering bodies of the funds. Nevertheless, scheme managers have a large degree of freedom in deciding how to attain the objectives of the minimum requirements and in providing supplementary provisions. The legal regulations for third pillar private pension savings are even less binding, and are rather similar to the directives concerning any private insurance contract.

Looming issues on the horizon

Toward decreasing first and second pillar benefits?

The official target of the Swiss pension system is to ensure a combined—first pillar with second pillar's *Obligatorium*—replacement rate of approximately 60 percent of the last salary. This should allow pensioners to maintain their former standard of living. However, current and future reforms of the first two pillars might seriously challenge this objective (Bertozzi and Bonoli 2007).

Despite growing demographic pressures, up to now direct democracy and the high popular support of AVS-AHV have prevented major retrenchment in the first pillar of the system (Bonoli 2005). But the same cannot be said for occupational pensions. In fact, the benefits guaranteed by the *Obligatorium* are decreasing. The two government-set technical variables having an essential impact on final benefits—the minimum nominal interest rate and the conversion rate—have been reduced in recent years, and plans for further reductions are under discussion. As already mentioned, the Swiss government has recently published a proposal going in this direction. Even if the reduction of the minimum interest rate might be only a short-term decision depending on the performance of pension funds, it looks unlikely that this rate will be increased again at the level that was guaranteed in the 1980s and 1990s. The reduction of the conversion rate is linked to population aging and is thus a long-term change. To sum up, second pillar benefits have already decreased and are very likely to decrease even more in coming years.

Toward an increasing role for private pension provision?

The result of the previously mentioned reduction of second pillar benefits might be that these benefits will not guarantee preservation of living standards anymore. Second pillar benefits are likely to become a limited supplement to the basic pension benefit. The second pillar benefit will only enable individuals to avoid the risk of old-age poverty. Low- and middle-wage employees will likely face this scenario. In fact, recent economic and demographic developments suggest that in an increasing number of cases, the pensions provided by the first and the second pillar may not be sufficient to cover even basic needs. More atypical career profiles, lower returns on second pillar pension fund assets and higher life expectancy for retirees suggest that the target combined replacement rate of 60 percent of earnings may be far away for many current workers (Bertozzi and Bonoli 2007).

In this case, third pillar voluntary savings might become necessary for everyone to guarantee income maintenance. From the point of view of the public-private mix in the Swiss pension system, this would mean a decreasing role for public pension provision and a growing importance of private pension actors, such as private insurance companies.

Discussion: comparing the public-private mix for health care and pensions

Table 9.2 compares the Swiss public-private mix for health care and pensions. We can see that very little is purely public in Switzerland. For health care, only the means-tested system of subsidies to reduce insurance premiums can be considered to be essentially public, although responsibility for subsidies is at the cantonal level, which leads to considerable variations in generosity. For pensions, only the basic pension scheme, the first pillar, is mainly public. It is strongly redistributive, but does not fully prevent poverty, and is funded through about 100 compensation offices managed by both public and private actors. At the other extreme, two components are essentially private. For health care, complementary insurance is not only voluntary and provided by private companies, but is also quite weakly regulated. The same holds for the third pillar for pensions, which can also be seen as a form of complementary insurance.

A significant part of the Swiss public-private mix is in between these two poles. For health care, the basic health insurance package is both compulsory and tightly regulated, but premiums are disconnected from revenue and financed entirely by patients, although subsidies aim at reducing the burden for the less well-off. In addition, basic insurance is provided by private companies that can set their premiums, which vary considerably both across cantons and across insurers. The second pillar of the pensions system is also compulsory and tightly regulated, but provided

Table 9.2 The Swiss public-private mix

	Mainly public	Private actors, strong public regulation	Mainly private
Health care insurance	Subsidies for the reduction premiums	Basic health insurance	Complementary health insurance
Pensions	First pillar (AVS-AHV & PC-EL)	Second pillar (LPP-BVG)	Third pillar
Likely evolution	Relative erosion	Relative erosion	Relative increase

by private actors. This pillar is jointly financed by workers and employers and is very lowly redistributive. The federal government has a certain control over benefits, which are however strongly influenced by the evolution of financial markets.

For both pensions and health care, the likely evolution in the medium term is toward increased "risk privatization" (Hacker 2004). For health care, subsidy policies have been insufficiently adapted to the rise of insurance premiums, and increased co-payments are likely to be introduced. As a result, the risks associated with poor health will probably become more individualized. For pensions, replacement rates are likely to decline. The government has already reduced the minimum nominal interest rate and the conversion rate for the second pillar, and further cuts seem probable. As a result, a well developed third pillar may become necessary in order to maintain income after retirement. There seems thus to be a shift toward a greater role for private insurance in the Swiss pensions system, which also goes in the direction of increased "risk privatization" (Hacker 2004).

Conclusion

Despite a late expansion of the Swiss welfare state in the 1980s and 1990s, which enabled the Swiss welfare state to catch up to the average level of social protection offered by continental European states (Bertozzi et al. 2005), current economic and demographic pressures are likely to modify the shape of the social security system rapidly once again. This remodeling will probably highlight the historical characteristics of the Swiss model of social-policy making.

In fact, due to the importance of federalism and direct democracy, the evolution of the Swiss system has been highly path dependent and the establishment of social insurance schemes for pensions and health care has preserved its liberal characteristics. In these two domains, politics set the rules of the game, but the implementation is delegated to private actors. Moreover, political authority is fragmented at different levels.

The evolution of the system is likely to be characterized by "risk privatization" (Hacker 2004): the risks associated with ill health and with retirement will be increasingly borne by individuals rather than collectively. This will be particularly problematic for some groups of the population, in particular low-income workers and women. If private insurances—third pillar pensions or complementary health insurances—will become indispensable to compensate for the reduction of protection guaranteed by compulsory state insurances, not everybody will be able to afford such supplementary individual costs.

This problem will be faced by all the workers with low wages and in particular by women. In fact, part-time employment is very widespread among women working in Switzerland, and this has a major impact on the wages and social security rights earned through employment-related contributions (in particular first and second pillar pensions). In the health domain, lower-income categories are also the most exposed to the increased privatization of risks, since they are the most dependent on the public subsidies that, as we have seen, have not been sufficiently adapted to the increase of insurance premiums.

To conclude, the Swiss public-private mix is characterized by slow and incremental reforms, compounded by weak public control over social policies. In front of a changing social and economic context, policy stability does not mean that social protection is also stable, but rather that it increasingly fails to cover the people who most need it.

Notes

1. The maternity insurance scheme is financed through the already existing fund for loss of earned income(APG-EO). This fund, introduced during the World War II, provides compensation to cover the loss of earnings during the period in which the person is serving in the army, or carrying out civilian service and protection service.
2. A deductible is an all-inclusive amount paid by the patient before the insurance cover begins.
3. Old-age and survivors' insurance (Assurance Vieillesse et Survivants—Alters- und Hinterlassenenversicherung).
4. Supplementary benefits (Préstations complémentaires—Ergänzungsleistungen).
5. Occupational pension (Prévoyance professionnelle—Berufliche Vorsorge).
6. For instance, the cantons of Neuchâtel in 1898 and Vaud in 1907 have introduced voluntary pension schemes at the cantonal level. The first compulsory old-age scheme has been implemented in the canton of Glarus in 1916.
7. The regulatory framework for third pillar schemes is weak and mainly relies on article 82 of the LPP-BVG and on the OPP 3-BVV 3 (*Ordonnance sur les déductions admises fiscalement pour les cotisations versées à des formes reconnues de prévoyance—Verordnung über die steuerliche Abzugsberechtigung für Beiträge an anerkannten Vorsorgeformen*) implemented in 1985.
8. Some parts in the following sections build on Bertozzi and Bonoli (2007).
9. The Confederation contributes 16.4 percent of outgoings and cantons contribute 3.6 percent. Since 2000, the AVS-AVS also receives one percentage point of value added tax (VAT).
10. In 2006, the total population of Switzerland was 7.5 million and the working-age population (20–64) was approximately 4.5 million.

References

Armingeon, Klaus. 2001. "Institutionalising the Swiss Welfare State." *West European Politics* 24(2): 145–68.

Balthasar, Andreas. 2001. "*Efficacité sociopolitique de la réduction des primes dans les cantons.*" Rapport de recherche no. 02/01. OFAS: Berne.

Bertozzi, Fabio and Giuliano Bonoli. 2007. "The Swiss Pension Regime and Social Inclusion." In Traute Meyer, Paul Bridgen, and Barbara Riedmüller (eds), *Private*

Pensions Versus Social Inclusion? Non-State Arrangements for Citizens at Risk in Europe: 107–35. Cheltenham: Edward Elgar.

Bertozzi, Fabio, Giuliano Bonoli, and Benoît Gay-des-Combes. 2005. *La réforme de l'Etat social en Suisse. Vieillissement, emploi, conflit travail-emploi*. Le Savoir suisse, Lausanne: Presses polytechniques et universitaires romandes (PPUR).

Bonoli, Giuliano. 2000. The Politics of Pension Reform. Institutions and Policy Change in Western Europe. Cambridge: Cambridge University Press.

Bonoli, Giuliano. 2005. "Switzerland: Adapting Pensions within Tight Institutional Constraints." In Giuliano Bonoli and Toshimitsu Shinkawa (eds), *Ageing and Pension Reform Around the World*: 137–56. Cheltenham: Edward Elgar.

Bonoli, Giuliano and André Mach. 2000. "Switzerland: Adjustment Politics within Institutional Constraints." In Fritz W. Scharpf and Vivien A. Schmidt (eds), *Welfare and Work in the Open Economy*: 131–74. Oxford: Oxford University Press.

Bonoli, Giuliano and Benoît Gay-des-Combes. 2003. *L'évolution des prestations vieillesse dans le long terme: une simulation prospective de la couverture retraite à l'horizon 2040, Aspects de la sécurité sociale* (Rapport de recherche no. 3/03). Bern.

Cattacin, Sandro. 2006. "Retard, rattrapage, normalisation. L'Etat social suisse face aux défis de transformation de la sécurité sociale." *Studien und Quellen—Etudes et Sources* 31: 49–78.

Esping-Andersen, Gøsta. 1990. *The Three Worlds of Welfare Capitalism*. Cambridge: Polity Press.

Freeman, Richard. 2000. *The Politics of Health in Europe*. Manchester: Manchester University Press.

Hacker, Jacob S. 1998. "The Historical Logic of National Health Insurance: Structure and Sequence in the Development of British, Canadian, and U.S. Medical Policy." *Studies in American Political Development* 12: 57–130.

Hacker, Jacob S. 2004. "Privatizing Risk without Privatizing the Welfare State: The Hidden Politics of Social Policy Retrenchment in the United States." *American Political Science Review* 98(2): 243–60.

Hinrichs, Karl. 2000. "Elephants on the Move. Patterns of Public Pension Reform in OECD Countries." *European Review* 8(3): 353–78.

Immergut, Ellen M. 1992a. *Health Politics. Interests and Institutions in Western Europe*. Cambridge: Cambridge University Press.

Immergut, Ellen M. 1992b. "The Rules of the Game: The Logic of Health Policy-Making in France, Switzerland, and Sweden." In Sven Steinmo, Kathleen Thelen, and Frank Longstreth (eds), *Structuring Politics. Historical Institutionalism in Comparative Analysis*: 57–89. Cambridge: Cambridge University Press.

Moran, Michael. 1999. Governing the Health Care State. A Comparative Study of the United Kingdom, the United States and Germany. Manchester: Manchester University Press.

Moran, Michael. 2000. "Understanding the Welfare State: The Case of Health Care." *British Journal of Politics and International Relations* 2(2): 135–60.

Obinger, Herbert. 1998. "Federalism, Direct Democracy, and Welfare State Development in Switzerland." *Journal of Public Policy* 18(3): 241–63.

OECD. 2006. *OECD Health Data 2006*. Paris: OECD

OFAS [Office Fédéral des Assurances Sociales]. 1995. *La prévoyance professionnelle en Suisse*. Bern: OFAS.

OFAS [Office Fédéral des Assurances Sociales]. 2004. *Statistique des assurances socials*. Bern: OFAS.

OFAS [Office Fédéral des Assurances Sociales]. 2006. *Statistique des prestations complémentaires à l'AVS et à l'AI 2005*. Bern: OFAS.

Palier, Bruno. 2003. *La réforme des retraites*, Que sais-je? Paris: Presses Universitaires de France.
Palier, Bruno. 2004. *La réforme des systèmes de santé*, Que sais-je? Paris: Presses Universitaires de France.
Vontobel, Werner. 2000. "Die Säulen-Scheinheiligen—Pech hat wer in einem Kleinbetrieb arbeitet: Die Versicherung behält die Zinsen Zurück." *CASH*, December 1: 44.
Weaver, Kent. 2003. "The Politics of Public Pension Reform." *Center for Retirement Research Working Paper*, 2003–6.

10
The Japanese Familial Welfare Mix at a Crossroads

Toshimitsu Shinkawa

Japan as a familial welfare mix

Japan is sometimes referred to as a hybrid of the conservative and liberal welfare regimes (Esping-Andersen 1997). A major feature of social security in Japan is its occupationally fragmented, social insurance schemes modeled after the Bismarckian model, which is typical of a conservative welfare state (Bonoli and Shinkawa 2005). Japan, however, is deviant from the conservative model in some important respects, such as low generosity of social protection and extended roles of firm-specific welfare, which make Japan closer to the liberal welfare regime. Taking Japan as a hybrid, however, raises a theoretical difficulty. Once we accept the idea of a hybrid, all welfare states can likely claim to be hybrids. After all, no country can perfectly fit a single model, yet our typologies of welfare states are weakened by accepting the idea of hybrids.

Introducing the idea of a pan-Asian welfare type like the so-called East-Asian model is not a promising endeavor, either (Jones 1993). If Korea, Taiwan, Singapore, and Japan share certain collectivist features, their social policy developments vary according to different economic and political circumstances, and cannot be traced back to a common culture or tradition such as Confucianism. Some argue that East-Asian welfare states share the logic of the developmental state or productivism, according to which social policy is employed as an instrument of nation-building and economic development (Goodman and Peng 1996; Goodman et al. 1998; Gough 2000; Holliday 2000; Jones 1993; White and Goodman 1998). Such a phenomenon is not specific to East-Asia, but commonly witnessed elsewhere around the world. In the end, the East-Asian welfare state is a theoretically unclassified, residual category (Bonoli and Shinkawa 2005). Before asserting the existence of another welfare model, more comparative research about East-Asian welfare states is necessary (Hiroi and Komamura 2003; Lin 2005; Shiratori et al. 2006; Uemura and Suhehiro 2003; Wong 2004).

To avoid these pitfalls, I propose the addition of a fourth type to Esping-Andersen's typology of welfare capitalism by using his two indices of decommodification and social stratification (Esping-Andersen 1990). The fourth type is characterized by low decommodification and high levels of stratification, in which Japan is included, together with Southern European countries (Ferrera 1996). Japan shares with these countries a relatively small state, occupationally fragmented social protection, and respect for collectivist and, more specifically, traditional family values. Therefore, this new type can be called the "familial type." Instead of calling it the "familial welfare state," however, I would like to call it as the "familial welfare mix" since private welfare provision goes hand in hand with public welfare provision in this type of welfare capitalism.

Familial principles are prominent in Japan. The male breadwinner family is still a basic unit of welfare provision. Levels and standards of social protection for families reflect the positions of male breadwinners in the labor market. Company-based welfare, which is usually developed in the liberal welfare regime, is provided in a familial fashion in Japan. The company as a quasi-family delivers welfare to its employees as family members. Meritocracy is taken into account, but the bottom-line is firm loyalty. Employees are expected to grow their identification with their companies stronger, as they are employed longer. Corporate welfare provision is intricately linked with lifelong employment and seniority-based wages. Pension schemes and public health care allow large firms to have their own schemes, through which the employer provides more generous benefits and services. In the Japanese welfare mix, public and private welfare are combined to work complementarily while promoting efficient labor management.[1]

The Japanese familial welfare mix has a dualist structure. A majority of marginal workers are excluded from such familial industrial relations, whereas the family is assumed to provide care to children and older adults. Accordingly, facilities and services related to these kinds of care provision are not adequately provided so that housewives are overly burdened with family responsibilities, which discourages labor force participation of married women. When they return to the labor market at the later stage of their life, they are usually hired as inexpensive, low-skilled workers. In spite of the development of gender bias-free labor legislation since the late 1980s, female workers have difficulties in continuing to work after marriage and especially after childbearing due to tacit social pressures and unwritten labor practices.

The Japanese familial welfare mix stands at a crossroads, as do other welfare regimes. Two streams are discernible in the wave of social policy reforms that started in the 1980s. The first is the push to increase the fiscal sustainability of social programs by fixing institutional defects to deal with population aging. This type of reform can be called "reform for sustainability." Increased social expenditures become a more pressing problem to tackle in the second stream with accelerated population aging. Pressured by economic globalization, making the market more efficient and competitive by liberalizing the business sector and downsizing the state is the top priority in the second stream. This type of reform has been witnessed since the 1980s, but became predominant in the late 1990s, when the Japanese economy suffered a prolonged recession. Such a reform type can be called "neoliberal reform." These two reform types are interwoven in the actual political process, but they are conceptually distinct and have different impacts on the Japanese welfare mix. The first stream of reform does not necessarily weaken the familial feature of the Japanese welfare regime; rather, in some cases, reforms reinforce this familial feature. In contrast, the second stream clearly undermines it.

Welfare retrenchment is a very important part, but certainly not the only aspect of social policy reform in Japan. The most urgent pressure on finance comes from population aging, which provides a strong rationale for the retrenchment in health care and pensions. Yet, population aging can also justify welfare expansion. To make up for a shortage in the male labor force, the government introduced various measures by which to encourage female labor force participation, including long-term care for the aged and parental leave programs as well as the expansion and improvement of care services for the elderly. Welfare retrenchment and expansion go hand in hand to modify the familial bias of the Japanese welfare mix and move it toward a market-oriented welfare regime.

The next two sections clarify the structure and transformation of the Japanese welfare mix by focusing mainly on health care and pension policies.

Health

Structure

Under the Health Insurance Law (HIL) enacted in 1947 and substantially revised in 1952, Japanese employees are covered by two different types of public health insurance schemes. One is managed by health insurance associations (HIA) and the other by the state. A firm, or a group of firms in the same business, holding 700 employees, is qualified to establish a health insurance association. A group of firms in the same local area but in different industries can have their own association, if the number of their employees totals 3,000. As of March 2005, there were 1,584 heath insurance associations holding approximately 14.7 million members. Including their dependents, roughly 30 million people are covered by this scheme.

The state-managed health insurance (HI) holds 18.9 million members and, including their dependents, a total of 35.6 million people are insured. Individual insurance fees in each scheme vary according to their incomes.

The average monthly income of the state-managed health insurant is ¥283,624[2] as of March 2005 and the average contribution rate is 8.2 percent of the "monthly salary," whereas that of the HIA insurant is ¥371,200 and the average contribution rate is about 7.5 percent.[3] Contribution is split between the employer and the employee with ratios of 0.55 and 0.45, respectively.

Public employees have their own mutual-aid schemes. Mutual-aid associations (MAA) are classified into three categories. First, the State Employee Mutual-Aid Association is established by each State Ministry. There are currently 21 of such MAAs[4], which hold 1.1 million members and 1.4 million dependents as of 2005. The contribution rate varies from 4.52 to 7.46 percent, which is split equally between the employer and the employee. The second category is the MAA for public employees in local governments, public schools, and local police. Local mutual-aid health insurance schemes hold 2.87 million members and cover 6.34 million people in total. Contribution rates split equally between the employer and the employee vary from 5.5 to 7.4 percent. The third category is the MAA for private school teachers and clerks, holding roughly 468,000 members and 371,000 dependents. The contribution rate is 6.72 percent, split evenly between the employer and the employee.[5]

The National Health Insurance (NHI) is provided for those not covered by the aforementioned schemes, including the unemployed, the self-employed, retirees, students and, finally, workers employed in small establishments that have fewer than five employees. In principle, municipalities are the insurers. As of 2004, there are 3,144 municipal NHI schemes and 166 NHI associations. Together, they cover 51 million people in total. Contribution fees are fixed by municipalities based on their financial conditions. In rural areas whose populations have a high proportion of older residents, inhabitants usually have to pay more than those in urban areas, in spite of financial transfers from urban to rural areas. Since the NHI covers economically vulnerable social categories, such as the unemployed and the retired, the system allows those under a certain level of income to pay only half of contribution fees, or nothing at all. To make up for the balance, the state pours substantial subsidies from general revenues into the NHI (almost half of NHI expenditures are financed out of these revenues).

Reform towards financial rationality

Until the 1984 reform, employees' medical costs were 100 percent insured (their dependents must pay 30 percent of medical costs). In the NHI, a 30 percent co-payment was universal, except for those aged 70 and over who enjoyed free medical care. Free Medical Care for the Aged (FMCA) was initially introduced in a small village (Sawauchi) of the Iwate Prefecture in 1960 and became prominent after Tokyo's adoption of it in 1969. Tokyo's initiative was so popular that most of the local governments followed Tokyo, regardless of political partisanship. Witnessing the popularity of FMCA and pressured by the local governments, the central government eventually introduced a nationwide scheme of FMCA in 1972.

As politically comprehensible and reasonable as it was, the FMCA scheme was not financially sound (see Calder 1988; Campbell 1992). Free medical care was introduced without substantial increases in people's contribution burden. Therefore, financial as well as welfare bureaucrats were skeptical about its sustainability. Skyrocketing increases in medical expenditures and accumulating fiscal deficits in the late 1970s reinforced the push for the review of FMCA. Political leaders hesitated to act for a while because of the anticipated negative reaction from the population, but in 1982, they finally introduced the Elderly Health Act (EHA), which requested co-payment from elderly persons. Charges were initially nominal; the charge for outpatient service was fixed at ¥400 and ¥300 for hospitalization per day.

Equally noteworthy in the 1982 EHA is the creation of the Elderly Health System (EHS) to finance medical spending for the aged. The fragmented health insurance system had no devices by which to balance financial burdens among different schemes. Therefore, the NHI, which has more elderly members due to its aforementioned residual structures, is financially more vulnerable to population aging. The EHS introduced a device for transfers across the different health insurance schemes to finance health care for the elderly, thereby alleviating the NHI's heavy fiscal burdens.

Last but no less important in regards to the EHA is the course of policy development it suggested. It proposed a tightened linkage between acute and extended care as well as between institutional and home care. Unfortunately, due to scarce financial resources, no major steps in such a direction took place in the 1980s, when fiscal restructuring topped the political agenda. As population aging accelerated in the 1990s, however, elderly care became a pressing issue. Scarce facilities and public services for extended care resulted in a phenomenon called "social hospitalization," when frail elderly people who do not need acute treatment are hospitalized. Social hospitalization was considered to push medical expenditures substantially upward. As a result, in order to control medical costs, the government started increasing the number of long-term care facilities and staff in the mid-1990s.

When a co-payment was introduced in 1982, charges on the patient were nominal, as mentioned above, but periodically increased afterwards. Co-payment for outpatient services finally shifted from fixed-amount to fixed-rate payment as a consequence of the 2002 reform. Those aged 70 and over now have to pay 10 percent of medical costs and those whose annual income is over ¥6.2 million are obliged to pay 20 percent of these costs. The 2006 reform further increased financial burdens on older individuals who enjoy high incomes by raising the rate of their co-payment to 30 percent of medical costs. In addition, the number of those within the top category was increased by the measure of lowering the upper limit to ¥5.2 million.[6] The rate of co-payments for those below the upper limit was also scheduled to increase to 20 percent in April 2008, but the measure is currently (as of August 2008) suspended.[7]

In the face of endlessly increasing financial burdens due to the absence of upper limits on spending within the EHS system, health insurance associations called for a new independent insurance scheme for the elderly. The 2006 reform set the schedule to replace the EHS with a new independent health insurance for those aged 75 and over in April 2008. The new insurance is to be financed out of contributions, national subsidies, and transfers from the established health insurance schemes that are limited to 40 percent of total expenditures. In addition to alleviated financial burdens of the established health insurance schemes, the new insurance scheme deprives those between the ages of 70 and 74 of entitlements to privileged elderly medical care. Additionally, the new scheme urges those who are currently covered by their children's insurance schemes to join and contribute to the new scheme. In total, 2.4 million people, who currently are their children's dependents, will be affected by the measure.

One of the most noteworthy moves in the recent medical reform is the separation between acute and extended care for the aged, as witnessed in the introduction of the long-term care insurance in April 2000. Long-term care for the aged was brought onto the political agenda in the mid-1990s. Social policy experts across political persuasions acknowledged the necessity of introducing this measure to reduce the financial squeeze of health insurance and to alleviate burdens on those families looking after the frail elderly. Such an all-party consensus overcame the opposition of municipalities due to the concern of financial burdens that would be placed on them.

Neoliberal reform

The aforementioned changes that have been taking place since the 1980s are a mixture of welfare expansion and retrenchment, but can also be regarded as a wave of social policy reforms aimed at attaining fiscal balance by fixing institutional defects, separating acute and extended care, and expanding care facilities and services. These reforms do not introduce market mechanisms as means to restrain public medical expenditures or to improve medical efficiency. At the start of the twenty-first century, however, neoliberalism emerged as a promoter of private activity in medicine, as the Koizumi Cabinet (2001–2006) steered the course of policy development toward market-oriented principles under the flag of "structural reform." Koizumi's idea of structural reform with the slogan "let the private sector do what it can do" permeated across policy areas. The Koizumi government fought battles for liberalizing the financial markets, deregulating the labor market, and curbing public works as well as welfare expenditures.

Most enthusiastically pushed forward by neoliberals is the so-called "mixed medicine." The current principle of health insurance prohibits doctors from combining insured and uninsured medical treatment except for certain experimental cases in a limited number of authorized hospitals and selective services, including special bedrooms, reservations, and treatments performed during extra-working hours. After the Koizumi cabinet was formed in 2001, the governmental advisory committees, especially the one on deregulation and privatization, increasingly called for a change in the rules governing mixed medicine. They insisted that a broader coverage of mixed medicine would help restrain medical expenditures, and that mixed medicine would expand the health care market and employment in medicine, thereby providing profit-making opportunities for private insurance companies.[8] Financial bureaucrats and experts joined the neoliberal camp on this issue.

Mixed medicine, however, generates its own set of problems. First, it does not necessarily control total medical spending since uninsured medical services are more expensive on average and push total medical costs upward. Second, it is likely to produce a dual system that would favor the rich at the expense of the poor. The rich would purchase the best and most advanced medical care treatment, whereas the poor would have no choice but to receive insured service, regardless of its quality. Third, the Ministry of Health, Labor, and Welfare (MHLW) and the Japan Medical Association (JMA) doubt whether free competition can guarantee safe medical practices. Finally, related to the third point, free competition in medicine does not necessarily improve the quality of medicine since medical treatment is so highly specialized and technical that the patient cannot evaluate the appropriateness and validity of the delivered services and treatments (Asahi Newspaper March 14, 2003).

In spite of these criticisms, however, staunch neoliberal reformers continuously pressured the MHLW to introduce mixed medicine and finally extracted some concessions from policymakers. The MHLW modified the rules in July 2005 to broaden the range of uninsured medical treatments on the condition that a committee of specialists should check its validity. Since mixed medicine remains the exception and must go through peer-examination, it has not yet spread as broadly as expected by neoliberals. So far, few private firms find profit-making opportunities in mixed medicine (Nihon Keizai Newspaper August 11, 2006).

The liberalization of hospital management is another major goal of neoliberal reformers. The committee on the future of health care management proposed allowing nondoctors to be chief directors of the executive committees that govern hospitals, but the idea failed to gain support. The conventional view that medicine should be a nonprofit activity remains predominant in Japan. The MHLW rebuked the idea of liberalizing hospital management by contending that the for-profit logic dominant in the business sector contradicts the basic idea of medicine (Nihon Keizai Newspaper October 30, 2001).

The last major issue that merits discussion here is the control of total medical spending. The idea came in May 2005 from the Ministry of Finance (MOF) and the Advisory Committee on the Economy and Finance. They insisted that increases in medical spending be indexed to the nominal growth of GDP. The MHLW and the JMA again opposed the idea on the grounds that controlling medical expenditures by economic indices is impossible, considering the fact that they increased annually by about 3 percent even in the decade of economic stagnation starting in 1993. This argument points out the difficulty in controlling expenditures, but does not deny the necessity of total expenditure control. The MHLW conceded when it announced in June 2005 that it would set a goal for the appropriate size of medical care spending and take necessary measures to achieve that goal. The MHLW's plan that was finally released in October 2005, however, was far from a direct and efficient device for expenditure control. The MHLW only proposed the promotion of healthy life habits, the shortening of hospital stays, and the control of individual medical expenditures at the prefecture level. A compromise was hammered out that set the medium-term (approximately five-year) goal of controlling medical spending growth, considering both the appropriateness of individual item spending and economic growth (*Nihon Keizai Newspaper* September 15, 2005, October 8, 2005; Shakai Hosho Nenkan 2006).

Substantial changes in health insurance took place between 2002 and 2006 during the Koizumi era. The 2002 reform shifted co-payment of the elderly for outpatient service from fixed-amount to fixed-rate. Employees' co-payment was also raised from 20 to 30 percent. The 2006 reform increased the elderly co-payment from 10 to 20 percent and set the schedule to introduce an independent health insurance for those aged 75 and over. Substantial and more than incremental as they were, these reforms remained within the conventional reform pattern that has prevailed since 1982. In addition to these reforms, the Koizumi Cabinet attempted to introduce market mechanisms to medicine, but only partially succeeded. The limited effect of the neoliberal approach is due to the predominance in Japan of the idea that medicine should be separate from business or profit-making.

Pensions

Basic pension structure

The Basic Pension (BP) covers all Japanese citizens aged 20 and over. It was created in 1985 by integrating the first tier of employees' pension schemes (the Employees' Pension Insurance and Mutual-Aid Pension Insurance) with the flat-rate National Pension Insurance (NPI), which was provided for those not covered by the other schemes, including the self employed and farmers. The Basic Pension is pay-as-you-go in principle, but heavily subsidized by general tax revenues. All of its administrative costs and a third of the benefits are paid out of general tax revenues. Its insurants are separated into three categories. The first category is composed of the NPI insurants. About 22 million people are under this category as of March 2005 (Ministry of Health, Labor, and Welfare www.mhlw.go.jp/topics/nenkin/zaisei/01/index.html). Those under the first category pay flat-rate contributions. The current monthly payment for these insurants is approximately ¥14,140. A minimum contribution record of 25 years is necessary to receive a BP benefit. The 40-year record guarantees a full benefit of ¥792,100 per year.

The second-category insurants are employees in both the public and the private sectors. As of March 2005, 37,130,000 employees fall under this category (Ministry of Health, Labor, and Welfare www.mhlw.go.jp/topics/nenkin/zaisei/01/index.html). A percentage of their salaries is deducted automatically from their pay checks as pension contributions, which cover both the BP and second-tier fees. The current contribution rate is approximately 15 percent (half of which is paid by the employer). The BP entitlement age was set at the age of 65 by the 1985 legislation, but the second-type insurants were given special benefits at the age of 60 to protect their entitlements before the 1985 integration. The privilege is to be cancelled after the phase-in period between 2001 and 2013.

The membership of housekeepers in the NPI was voluntary before 1985. The 1985 revision gave housekeepers pension entitlements independent of their working spouses under the third category. When their yearly earnings are below a certain limit (currently ¥1.3 million), they are exempted from contribution payments. The number of the third-category insurants has risen to 10,990,000 as of March 2005 (Ministry of Health, Labor, and Welfare http://www.mhlw.go.jp/topics/nenkin/zaisei/01/index.html). Their benefits are financed out of the contributions of all employees.

Employees' pension structure

The second-tier provides employees earnings-related pensions. It is composed of the Employees' Pension Insurance (EPI), which is provided to private-sector employees, and Mutual-Aid Pension Insurance (MAPI), which is provided to public employees. Teachers and clerks working in private schools also have their own MAPI schemes. The second-tier schemes are almost fully financed by a pay-as-you-go method, except for their administrative costs which are financed from general tax revenues. Since the number of MAPI members is much smaller than the EPI (the number the MAPI holds is 4.6 million, whereas that of the EPI is 32.5 million) and the structures of MAPI are largely identical with those of the EPI[9], the EPI can be reasonably selected as representative of the second-tier.

In 1999 and 2004, two reforms reshaped the second-tier of the Japanese Pension system. The 1999 reform changed the age of entitlement under the second-tier pension, so that it will gradually increase from 60 to 65 between 2013 and 2025. The 2004 reform will also increase the contribution rate up to 18.30 percent by 2017.[10]

The second-tier is largely earnings-related: individual monthly earnings are classified into 30 classes, ranging from ¥98,000 to ¥620,000 and the amount of individual contributions is calculated based on each worker's earnings class. Earnings surpassing the amount of ¥620,000 per month are not pensionable. The average replacement rate before the 2004 reform was 59.2 percent, which would go down to approximately 50 percent by 2017, according to the schedule set by the 2004 reform.

Private pension structure

The third-tier of the Japanese pension system is composed of private pension schemes, most of which are employer-sponsored corporate pension plans. Before the 2001 grand-scale reform, corporate pensions were divided into two major types: the Employees' Pension Fund (EPF) and the Tax-Qualified Pension (TQP). The EPF is composed of a substitute part for the EPI and an additional part of firm-specific pension. Therefore, the EPF actually includes the function of the second-tier pension. A firm, or a group of firms, is allowed to opt out of the EPI if it satisfies certain requirements. A company with more than 500 employees can establish an EPF with the consent of more than half of the employees (and unions representing at least a third of the employees, if any). A business-affiliated group of companies can establish a fund with more than 800 employees. A group of companies with no specific ties is required to have at least 3,000 employees in total to institute a fund. An EPF benefit must be at least 10 percent higher than that one expects to receive from the EPI.

Employee Pension Funds are strictly regulated and supervised by the state.[11] They are not allowed to dissolve except for special cases such as the bankruptcy of sponsor companies. If investment returns are lower than the officially required interest rate, sponsor companies must make up the difference. When the economy was in good shape, most funds easily gained more than the official rate and enjoyed surpluses. As the Japanese economy suffered a prolonged recession in the 1990s, however, many EPFs had difficulties in keeping up with the official rate and suffered increased fiscal burdens.

In contrast, the TQP is a pure corporate pension scheme and it is rather loosely regulated. A company with 15 or more employees can establish a TQP scheme by contracting with a life insurance company or a trust bank. Naturally smaller firms adopted TQP schemes. Before the significant 2001 reform, 736,000 TQP schemes existed with 1.7 million members, whereas 1,737 EPFs covered 10.87 million employees.

Both the EPF and the TQP enjoy preferential tax treatment. Contributions paid by employers are deductible as social security expenses in the case of the EPF and as business expenses in the case of the TQP. In both cases, no income tax is levied on employees, until they retire and receive payments. A special corporate tax of one percent is levied on a tax-qualified pension fund's accumulated assets each year as interest for arrears. The same measure is applied to an EPF, only on the portion exceeding 2.7 times the funding required to meet the benefits of the substitute component.

In 1991, a new pension scheme was introduced on top of the NPI: the National Pension Fund (NPF). The NPF has the purpose of providing insurants of the National Pension additional pension entitlements. The basic annuity guarantees ¥30,000 per month. Contribution depends on the age of an insurant. NPFs are managed by local governments or occupational organizations. Joining an NPF is voluntary and only a small portion of NPI members join NPFs (approximately 750,000 people).

Reform towards sustainability

The decisive factor behind pension reform since 1985 has been financial concerns over the sustainability of the Japanese pension system. The NPI faced difficulties in collecting contributions and its finances further deteriorated due to the decreasing number of working-age members caused mainly by the shrinking size of the agricultural population. The 1985 reform not only introduced financial transfers across the different public pension schemes but also tightened the relationship between contributions and benefits (restraining benefits and increasing contributions). This "tightening up" policy was repeated in 1989, 1994, and 1999. Such incremental changes are a universally witnessed political strategy of reducing the visibility of an unpopular policy and avoiding blame for it (Weaver 1986). Incremental as it was, each round of pension reform in Japan was substantial enough to attract public attention. Seemingly endless changes brought about increased anxiety over the sustainability of public pensions and undermined public confidence in them. Against this backdrop, the government launched the 2004 reform by expressing its determination to make it the last one.

The 2004 reform set a cap on contribution increases. In the case of the NPI, a monthly payment of ¥13,300 in FY 2004 is scheduled to increase by ¥280 every year from FY 2005 to FY 2017, when it will reach ¥16,900. After 2017, the monthly contribution payment will not increase any further. As for the contribution rate of EPI, it will gradually increase from 13.85 percent of the yearly earnings (half paid by the employer) in 2004 to 18.3 percent of yearly earnings (half paid by employers) by 2017; after 2017, the rate is expected to remain the same. Meanwhile, the replacement rate of the EPI will decline from 59.2 to 50 percent. From 2017 onwards, benefits are expected to vary according to such variables as economic growth, interest rates, fertility, life expectancy, and other factors. The government calls it the "Macro Economic Indexation" (MEI) method. In short, Japan's public pension will shift toward the logic of notional defined-contribution (NDC).

Curiously, such a drastic change in the operating logic of the public pension system did not attract public attention during the reform process. The public's exclusive concern was whether the replacement rate in the future would not fall below the 50 percent level. In order to reassure the public, Prime Minister Koizumi repeatedly stated his commitment to the maintenance of the 50 percent replacement rate. If these words implied pouring subsidies into the system, Koizumi indicated his intention of violating the MEI rule, which was what his government was trying to push through the Diet. Otherwise, he simply did not understand the MEI method. The 50 percent replacement rate the MHLW suggested was based on assumptions regarding the demographic and economic variables indicated above. The MHLW admitted later that, even if the initial replacement rate could be 50 percent, the replacement rate would deteriorate afterwards (*Nihon Keizai Newspapers*, May, 13 2004; Shinkawa 2005b).

An important assumption of the MEI method has already changed since 2004. The population projection used in the 2004 reform was replaced with a more pessimistic, gloomy projection released in December 2006. The 2002 medium-variant population projection assumes that the ratio of the aged 65 and over to the whole population (the aging rate) would increase from 19.9 percent to 35.7 percent between 2005 and 2050, and, given the 1.39 long-term fertility rate, slowly decrease afterwards. The 2006 projection assumes that, based on the 1.26 long-term fertility rate, the aging rate would increase from 20.2 in 2005 (actual figure) through 39.6 percent in 2050 to the peak of 40.5 percent in 2055 (Shajinken 2006).

In addition to cutbacks in benefits, the rearrangement of the occupationally fragmented system into a unified system is necessary to stabilize pension financing. As a matter of fact, as early as 1984, the government had set a goal of integrating different schemes into a single scheme by 1995. The unification process went too slowly to achieve this goal on schedule, but some noteworthy milestones were achieved. In the 1990s, the mutual-aid pension schemes of the public corporations were absorbed into the EPI after their privatization, and due to the financial instability the cooperatives in agriculture, forestry, and fishery relinquished their own mutual-aid plans and joined the EPI by 2001. Strong resistance against unifying the EPI and MAPI within each ministry had slowed down the process of integration, but the government recently publicized its commitment to their integration in the next round of pension reform (the necessity of another reform was broadly perceived in the middle of the 2004 reform process). When it is accomplished, the most prominent feature of the traditional Japanese welfare state (that is, its occupational fragmentation) will become a thing of the past (*Nihon Keizai Newspapers* June 15, 2007).

The recession of the 1990s provided a critical momentum for a review of not only public pension schemes but also corporate pensions. Many firms have reduced corporate welfare to cut costs and insure the survival of their businesses. After reaching the peak of 92,500 in 1993, the number of TQP plans declined to 73,600 in March 2002. The strictly regulated EPF was unable to respond as promptly as the TQP, but after reaching a peak in 1996, its number started to decline. The number decreased by more than 150 to 1,737 in 2002. Consequently, the total number of employees covered by corporate pension schemes (including both TQP plans and EPFs) fell from 22.89 million in 1996 to 20.04 million in March 2002.

To rescue EPFs in trouble, the government lowered the officially required rate of return on invested funds from 5.5 to 4.5 percent, reduced the amount of fund reserves that an EPF was required to hold, and allowed the employer to transfer stocks and other securities to the EPF to make up shortfalls. However, employers calling for large-scale deregulation were not satisfied with these measures. The government was urged to take more radical action. The recession facilitated a review of the TQP as well, but in quite a different fashion. The sharply falling number of TQP schemes made urgent the need to reinforce the legal protection of its entitlement rights. Under the TQP law, the employer can fail to maintain the minimum level of funding with no legal sanctions.

The 2001 reform changed the world of the Japanese corporate pensions. The dissolution of the EPF scheme is no longer an exception but an institutionalized option available to the employer. The establishment of new TQP schemes is prohibited altogether and previously established TQPs are to be abolished by 2012. After the dissolution of an EPF or TQP, the employer has several options. The first is providing a fund-type corporate pension, which is assumed to take over the firm-specific pension of a dissolved EPF. To establish a fund-type corporate pension, the employer is required to hold 300 employees or more. Second, the employer can introduce a scheme of the defined-benefit corporate pension (DBCP). The DBCP is expected to replace the TQP so that its overall structure is similar to the TQPs. The important difference between the two is that the DBCP will make explicit the employer's obligation to protect pension assets. Moreover, portability between different DBCP schemes is guaranteed. No minimum number of employees is required for an employer to introduce a DBCP scheme.

Offered as the third option is the defined-contribution pension (DCP) known as the "Japanese version of 401(k)."[12] Although it still only covers a relatively small number of workers, the DCP symbolizes a change in the function and role of corporate pensions. In Japan as elsewhere, a defined-contribution plan provides security "through the market," whereas a defined-benefit plan provides security "against the market." In a defined-contribution plan, employers no longer have an obligation to pay a predetermined level of benefits to their workers. Instead, employees are responsible for the management of their pension assets. As with any other defined-contribution plan, the Japanese DCP thus transfers financial risks and the responsibility for pension management from the employer to the employee. It also provides full portability of pension assets, which makes it easier for the employee to move from one firm to another.

Fourth, a de facto option, which is not officially recommended, is for employers to abolish their corporate pension schemes without offering alternatives to their employees. The new legislation promoted the dissolution of corporate pension schemes. The number of the EPFs covered fell sharply from 11.4 million in 2001 to 6.15 million in 2005. As many as 137 EPFs relinquished the substitute part of the EPP within the first six months after the 2001 legislation came into effect. Coverage by the TQP declined from 9.7 million in 2001 to 6.55 million in 2005. This new type of pension schemes now enrolls 5.13 million in total.[13] Therefore, those covered by corporate pension schemes decreased in number by approximately 3.4 million during the period. Considering the absence of a matching decline in the labor force, this decline indicates a shrinking coverage of corporate pensions. A substantial number of employers simply abolished established firm-specific schemes and provided no alternative forms of protection to their workers.[14]

Neoliberal reform

Whereas it has never been predominant in health insurance reforms, the neoliberal orientation was explicit from the outset in the field of pension reform. The major concern and goal of pension reform was financial sustainability, which was frequently couched in the rhetoric of "small government." The fact that pension retrenchment went hand in hand with the privatization of public corporations in the mid-1980s indicates that pension reform took place in a neoliberal context. At that time, however, the neoliberal strategy was not to attack or damage the Japanese familial welfare mix; rather its compatibility with neoliberalism would reinforce it. Corporate pensions as a main pillar of the familial regime were expected to complement the lowered level of security granted by public pensions. In other words, familial corporate welfare was assumed to expand its function and role as public protection declined. Thus, paternalism inherent in the familial welfare mix would stand against the seemingly cruel market logic.

The promarket attack against such paternalism was witnessed for the first time in the 1994 reform. The most significant aspect of the reform was the increase in pension entitlement age, which was linked to labor market innovations. The Ministry of Labor had promoted the extension of the retirement age from 55 to 60 since the 1960s by providing employers with financial incentives. The retirement at age 60 finally became mandatory in 1994. The 1994 reform also eliminated the "double benefit" from pensions and unemployment insurance. Before 1994, unemployed individuals over age 60 were entitled to receive both a pension and unemployment benefits.

The practice was not only financially extravagant but also undermined work incentives. Since 1994, those who qualified for both benefits must choose between them. Thus, the 1994 reform favored a reduction in pension expenditures through the labor market activation of the aged. The substantial lowering of public pension standards in the 2004 reform makes the average replacement rate in Japan closer to its counterparts in liberal, market-oriented countries such as the United States and Canada (Béland and Shinkawa 2007).[15] Given the notional defined-contribution element embedded in the MEI method, uncertainties about future benefit levels are likely to be high.

The most noteworthy development related to neoliberalism is the 2001 corporate pension reform. Corporate pensions conventionally worked to complement the relatively thin protection offered by public pensions. When public pensions were temporarily frozen after World War II, employers started lump-sum payments and rearranged them into firm-specific pension schemes. Once the government embarked on pension retrenchment, corporate pensions were expected to compensate for lower state protection. The 2001 revision, however, unfettered corporate pensions from such a complementary role. The weakened complementary function of private pensions would lead to the undermining of the familial feature of the Japanese welfare mix. The 2001 revision aimed at reshaping corporate pensions in favor of flexibility in employment and management, thus making Japan more like the liberal welfare regime.

In 1995, the Japan Employers' Association (JEA) released a watershed report in which they presented a new employment strategy to cope with international competition intensified by globalization. The report classified three types of employment. The first type is the same as conventional lifetime employment based on seniority, but this type is limited to those who are potential future executives. The second type, including high-skilled labor and professionals, works on an annual contract basis. The wages of these workers are annually negotiated or depend on their performance. They will receive neither premiums nor retirement allowances. Rank and file employees, including general clerks, are classified as the third type and also hired on a contract basis, but their position is much more vulnerable due to low skills and expertise levels than the ones of the second-type employees. Their recruitment and dismissal are highly subject to market fluctuations. A majority of current employees will fall under this category (Shinkawa 1999).

To support such an employment strategy, the government deregulated the labor market in the late 1990s through a series of law revisions. Articles about "female protection" in the Labor Law were abolished to achieve equal treatment of men and women. Labor dispatching businesses, which were allowed only in limited types of occupation, such as research and development, are now allowed to operate freely. Flexi-time work is also available more broadly and freely than before (Shinkawa 1999). The neo-liberal trend since the late 1990s has enhanced flexibility in employment and has cancelled or at least undermined conventional practices, such as lifelong employment and seniority-based wages. The 2001 revision reflected such a new trend. The established corporate pension schemes became outdated, since they assumed lifelong employment and provided little portability across the different schemes. The new types of corporate pension, the schemes of DCP in particular, are designed to address flexible employment or increased turnover (Shinkawa 2005a,b).

In spite of all the changes, Japan's pension system still faces serious problems. In addition to the challenge of integrating the EPI and MAPI, at least two more problems are found in the NPI. Mandatory as it is, the NPI holds over three million of first-type insurants in arrears, who fail to pay their contributions. This happens because no serious sanctions have been exerted upon those in arrears. Unless the government takes serious actions against them, this would cause social tensions and further undermine the already shaken social solidarity necessary for a sustainable pension system.

Another looming issue also deals with fairness and social solidarity. As the number of working married women increases, third-type insurants are increasingly criticized as free riders. Ironically, feminists and neoliberals are on the same page on the issue. The elimination of the third-type category would help promote female labor force participation. However, considering the very low fertility rate (below 1.0) among working women in Japan, this issue should be carefully treated. Promotion of female labor force participation must be carried out with the provision of female-friendly policies such as the expansion of child care facilities, without which the already low fertility rate may further decline.

Conclusion

In Japan, the public-private welfare mix is closely linked with the occupational fragmentation witnessed in health care and pension schemes, which intersects with firm size. Large companies have their own health care associations, which provide additional health services and sometimes promise lower rates of co-payment. Large companies also opt out of the EPI and deliver more generous pension benefits than their counterparts of the EPI. Thus, not only corporate welfare but also public social provisions are mobilized to promote firm loyalty. The welfare mix in Japan worked effectively to maintain quasi-familial industrial relations during the period of rapid economic growth between the mid-1950s and the early 1970s. The familial welfare mix was, however, not a deliberately or intentionally created architecture. Rather, it arose from a number of various factors, including historical contingencies, institutional legacies, class politics, and political partisanship (Shinkawa 2005a,b; Shinkawa and Pempel 1996).

When rapid economic growth ended, the familial welfare mix was "discovered" as an effective way of avoiding the alleged pitfalls of the massive welfare state developed in a number of European countries. Popularized in the late 1970s, the argument of "Japanese-Style Welfare Society" (JSWS) consisted of a rediscovery of the Japanese familial welfare mix. The so-called "Western welfare state" is criticized as a cause of the "advanced-country disease," or the "British disease." Expanded public services, it argues, encourage people to depend upon the state, erode work ethics, and weaken incentives to invest and improve productivity. Consequently, according to this discourse, people would demand more state welfare. To avoid this vicious cycle, the idea of JSWS stresses the importance of private welfare provision. According to the JSWS thesis, self-help and mutual aids in families, local communities, and firms should play an essential role in restraining public welfare expansion and improving the nation's overall welfare (Shinkawa and Pempel 1996).

The government employed the expression "welfare society with vitality," instead of JSWS, when it embarked on welfare retrenchment in the 1980s, but no substantial differences can be found between these two approaches. The JSWS assumed that private welfare, including corporate and family welfare, would take over functions given up by the welfare state. Employers positively responded to the ideological notion of JSWS by making programs of the so-called "lifetime comprehensive welfare (LCW)." LCW was regarded as a new developmental form of corporate welfare from the late 1970s to the early 1980s. Various LCW plans were released by companies in such industries as distribution, food, textiles, electric machinery, and metal refining. They commonly stressed the idea that the company should provide regular employees with comprehensive physical and psychological security not only during their productive years but also after their retirement. If it materializes, LCW would integrate occupational welfare with personnel management in such a way as to involve every aspect of individual employee's life (Shinkawa and Pempel 1996). The LCW would have created an "ideal" familial welfare mix in a "perfect" corporate society.

The heightened importance of corporate welfare reflected the rearrangement of Japanese-style labor management taking place in the 1980s. The experience of the two oil crises in the 1970s forced Japanese firms to pursue more efficient labor management. Redundant employees were redeployed, dispatched, or transferred to subsidiaries, but rarely dismissed. By holding redundant employees within a group of subsidiaries or affiliated businesses (the so-called intermediate labor market), Japanese firms maintained the conventional practice of lifetime employment. In return for employment security, labor unions collaborated with management to reduce the number of regular employment. Consequently, the Japanese-style of labor management was rearranged peacefully in such a way as to shrink the core of employment with thick protection and enlarge the periphery composed of employees in smaller businesses, temporary workers, and part-time workers with thin protection, thereby exacerbating dualism in the labor market (Shinkawa 2005b). This mature form of the familial welfare mix was short-lived due to the prolonged recession that began in 1993. The aforementioned JEA's 1995 report explicitly promoted a departure from the conventional Japanese-style labor management. In addition to population aging, increased global competition inspired the government and employers to seek greater flexibility and abandon traditional forms of paternalism, including life-long employment.

Retrospectively, we can identify two different aspects of Japan's social policy reform. The first aspect was an attempt to upgrade the familial welfare mix in Japan by shifting its balance toward private welfare through the pro-motion of corporate welfare provisions. The conventional industrial rela-tions were maintained within the limited number of regular workers, thus reinforcing labor market dualism. Another aspect of the welfare reform was an attempt to introduce market mechanisms in welfare provisions and shift financial risks from employers to workers. In such a vein, corporate welfare is no longer complementary to public welfare, and welfare provision as a whole declines. This second aspect becomes more predominant in the most recent reforms. In short, the Japanese welfare mix is moving toward a liberal model. As a result, economic security of workers and their families is severely reduced.

It should be noted, however, that free competition in the global market creates fewer winners than losers, who would call for stronger social pro-tection. Eventually, economic globalization may facilitate the expansion of social protection (Garrett 1998; Weiss 2003). Granted that globalization brings about ambivalent pressures both for the curtailment and the empowerment of the state, how they are balanced depends upon domestic politics in individual countries. Considering the current political config-uration in Japan, the neoliberal strategy is likely to remain predominant at least for the time-being. Given the acceleration of population aging, however, it is also unlikely that Japan can rely simply upon the neoliberal, market-oriented approach. While encouraging women and the elderly to be more active in the labor market, the government must deal with the increasing number of frail elderly. In other words, after dismantling the familial welfare mix, Japan needs to find a way to rebalance private and public social policies in order to promote genuine economic security (Rein and Schmaehl 2004). What is to be done is clear, but how to accomplish it is yet to be found.

Notes

1. Japan's familial welfare mix is an ideal case of "welfare through work" (Goodin 2001).
2. A US dollar is roughly between ¥110 and ¥115 as of October 2007.
3. The "monthly salary" does not mean an individual's actual salary. It is divided into 39 classes from ¥98,000 to ¥980,000. These classified amounts are used as denominators in calculations.
4. In principle, each ministry has its own association. Some ministries have two or more associations along different functionary lines.
5. Seamen also have their scheme, but the number of the covered participants is very small (60,000 members).
6. Those who suddenly enter the high-income class by the revision are allowed to follow the old rule until 2008.
7. Soon after his Cabinet was formed in September 2007, Prime Minister Yasuo Fukuda decided to freeze the implementation of the 2006 reform from 6 to 12 months.
8. Retrenchment in public health insurance has already expanded room for private insurance businesses as people tend to protect themselves by purchasing private insurance goods. For example, the number of new life insurance contracts more than doubled between 1999 and 2003, reaching the figure of 2.8 million (*Nihon Keizai* Newspaper July 14, 2004).
9. MAPI schemes provide more generous benefits than the EPI in spite of the fact that their contribution rates are not much higher than that of the EPI. Those who benefit from MAPI schemes legitimize this advantage by claiming that it is a substitute for third-tier (firm specific) pensions.
10. Before April 2003, employees contributed 17.35 percent of their monthly salaries (half paid by their employers) and 1 percent of their bonuses (usually equivalent to 4–5 monthly salaries). The new method is designed to keep the total amount of payments identical, except for those whose incomes are based heavily on bonuses.
11. Described are conditions before the 2001 reform.
12. The DCP has a corporate type and an individual type. The former is much larger in number.
13. Fund-type corporate pension is so unpopular due to its strict regulation that it fails to take over the corporate specific part of the EPF.
14. Except for the dissolution of the sponsor firm itself, it is difficult for an EPF to abolish its firm specific part when it returns the substitute part to the EPI. The fourth case is more likely to take place when TQP schemes are abolished.
15. As far as the fund management is concerned, Japan is more liberalized than the United States. All pension reserves have been invested in the financial market since 2001 in Japan (partial investment was allowed from the late 1980s). The Canada Pension Plan started investment in the financial market only in the late 1990s, whereas the US Social Security is still not allowed to invest in the financial market (Béland 2006; Shinkawa 2005c).

References

Béland, Daniel. 2006. "The Politics of Social Learning: Finance, Institutions, and Pension Reform in the United States and Canada." *Governance* 19(4): 559–83.

Béland, Daniel and Toshimitsu Shinkawa. 2007. "Public and Private Policy Change: Pension Reform in Four Countries." *Policy Studies Journal* 35(3): 349–71.

Bonoli, G. and Toshimitsu. Shinkawa. 2005. "Population Ageing and the Logics of Pension Reform in Western Europe, East Asia and North America." In G. Bonoli and T. Shinkawa (eds), *Ageing and Pension Reform around the World: Evidence from Eleven Countries*: 1–23. Cheltenham: Edward Elgar.

Calder, E. Kent. 1988. *Crisis and Compensation*. Princeton, NJ: Princeton University Press.

Campbell, John C. 1992. *How Policies Change: The Japanese Government and the Aging Society*. Princeton, NJ: Princeton University Press.

Esping-Andersen, G. 1990. *The Three Worlds of Welfare Capitalism*. Princeton, NJ: Princeton University Press.

Esping-Andersen, G. 1997. "Hybrid or Unique? The Distinctiveness of the Japanese Welfare State." *Journal of European Social Policy* 7(3): 179–89.

Ferrera, Maurizio. 1996. "The Southern Model of Welfare in Social Europe." *Journal of European Social Policy* 6: 17–37.

Garrett, Geoffrey. 1998. *Partisan Politics in the Global Economy*. Cambridge: Cambridge University Press.

Goodin, Robert E. 2001. "Work and Welfare: Towards a Post-Productivist Welfare Regime." *British Journal of Political Science* 31: 13–39.

Goodman, Roger and Ito Peng. 1996. "The East Asian Welfare States." In G. Esping-Andersen (ed.), *Welfare States in Transition*: 192–224. London: Sage.

Goodman, Roger, R. G. White, and H. Kwon. (eds). 1998. *The East Asian Welfare Model*. London: Routledge.

Gough, Ian. 2000. "Welfare Regimes in East Asia and Europe: Comparisons and Lessons." Presented at Towards the New Social Policy Agenda in East Asia, Parallel Session to the Annual World Bank Conference on Development Economics Europe 2000. Paris. June 27, 2000.

Hiroi, Yoshinori and Kohei Komamura. (eds). 2003. *Ajia no Shakai Hosho (Social Security in Asia)*. Tokyo: University of Tokyo Press.

Holliday, Ian. 2000. "Productivist Welfare Capitalism: Social Policy in East Asia." *Political Studies* 48(4): 706–23.

Hughes, G. and J. Stewart. (eds). 2004. *Reforming Pensions in Europe*. Cheltenham: Edward Elgar.

Jones, Catherine. 1993. "The Pacific Challenge: Confucian Welfare States." In C. Jones (ed.), *New Perspectives on the Welfare State in Europe*: 198–217. London: Routledge.

Lin, Chen-Wei. 2005. "Pension Reform in Taiwan: The Old and New Politics of Welfare." In G. Bonoli and T. Shinkawa (eds), *Ageing and Pension Reform around the World*: 182–207. Cheltenham: Edward Elgar.

Nishizawa, Kazuhiko. 2003. *Nenkin Daikaikaku (Great Pension Reform)*. Tokyo: Nihon Keizai Shinbunsha.

Rein, M. and W. Schmaehl. (eds). 2004. *Rethinking the Welfare State*. Cheltenham: Edward Elgar.

Shajinken (Kokuritu Shakai Hosho/Jinko Mondai Kenkyjo, National Institute of Population and Social Security Research). 2006. Nihon no Shorai Suikei Jinko (The Future Projection of Population in Japan). Retrieved on February 13, 2008 from http://www.ipss.go.jp/index.html

Shibata, Yoshihiko. 1998. *Nihon no Shakaihosho (Social Security of Japan)*. Tokyo: Shin-nippon Shuppansha.

Shinkawa, Toshimitsu. 1999. *Sengo Nihon Seiji to Shakai Minshu-shugi (Social Democracy in Postwar Japan)*. Kyoto: Horitsu Bunka-sha.

Shinkawa, Toshimitsu. 2005a. "The Politics of Pension Reform in Japan: Institutional Legacies, Credit-Claiming, and Blame Avoidance." In G. Bonoli and T. Shinkawa (eds), *Ageing and Pension Reform around the World: Evidence from Eleven Countries*: 157–81. London: Edward Elgar.

Shinkawa, Toshimitsu. 2005b. *Nihongata Fukushi Rejimu no Hatten to Henyo (The Development and Transformation of the Japanese-Style Welfare Regime)*. Kyoto: Minerva.

Shinkawa, Toshimitsu. 2005c. "Fukushi Kokka no Sotaika (Putting the Welfare State in Perspective)." *Kikan Shakai Hosho Kenkyu (The Quarterly of Social Security Research)* 41(3): 186–99.

Shinkawa, Toshimitsu and T. J. Pempel. 1996. "Occupational Welfare and the Japanese Experience." In Michael Shalev (ed.), *The Privatization of Social Policy?*: 280–326. London: Macmillan.

Shiratori, R., D. Sungkawan, and S. E. Olson-Hort. (eds). 2006. *Ajia no Fukushi Kokka Seisaku (Welfare State Policies in Asia)*. Tokyo: Ashi Shobo.

Uemura, Y. and A. Suehiro. (eds). 2003. *Higashi Ajia no Fukushi Shisutemu Kochiku (Building the Welfare System in East Asia)*. Tokyo: Tokyo Daigaku Shakai Kagaku Kenkyujo.

Weaver, R. Kent. 1986. "The Politics of Blame Avoidance." *Journal of Public Policy* 6(4): 371–98.

Weiss, Linda. 2003. "Introduction: Bringing Domestic Institutions Back In." In L. Weiss (ed.), *States in the Global Economy*: 1–33. Cambridge: Cambridge University Press.

White, G. and R. Goodman. 1998. "Welfare Orientalism and the Search for an East Asian Welfare Model." In R. Goodman, G. White, and H. Kwon (eds), *The East Asian Welfare Model: Welfare Orientalism and the State*: 3–24. London: Routledge.

Wong, Joseph. 2004. *Healthy Democracies*. Ithaca, NY: Cornell University Press.

11
New Political Legacies and the Politics of Health and Pension Re-reforms in Chile

Christina Ewig and Stephen J. Kay[1]

Introduction

Chile was a pioneer in introducing market competition into its largely public-dominated health and pension systems. Numerous countries followed Chile's lead in privatizing pension provision; US President George W. Bush looked to Chile's pension reform as a model for the United States to follow. Chile's health reforms were also pioneering in that it was the first Latin American country to introduce private health providers and insurers into a largely public health care system, inspiring similar market-based reforms across the Latin American region. Yet, despite international and regional leadership in health and pension reforms, Chileans themselves have been less than satisfied with the new market-based systems. This discontent has manifested in recent "re-reforms" of both health and pension policies in Chile during the 2000s. The democratically elected center-left governments of Ricardo Lagos and Michele Bachelet attempted to pass reforms in which the state would increase its oversight over these social policy areas and would compensate to a greater degree for market failures.

These re-reforms are striking from a policy point of view given Chile's status as an international model. They point to the failure of market-based health and pension reforms to provide both sufficient social equity and efficiency. The re-reforms are also fascinating from a political perspective, in that a comparison of the two waves of reform allows one to see precisely how "policy makes politics" (see Pierson 1994). The early reforms created new political interests—policy legacies in the form of private-sector interests—which have had significant impacts on the re-reform process. Chile provides a very interesting case for this volume on the public-private divide in social policy because it allows one to see, over the course of less than 30 years, how the introduction of private actors into welfare provision during the first wave of reforms not only created a "hidden welfare state," but also spawned new political interests which significantly influenced the national politics of social policy formation in the second wave of reform.

We begin this chapter by briefly reviewing the political context that surrounded the initial reform of Chilean health and pension policies. We then focus on the two waves of Chilean reform of the early 1980s and 2000s, first outlining the health reforms and then the pension reforms and their changing character from largely public to significantly private. In health and then pension policy, we consider the implications of this shift toward private provision of benefits for the politics of the health and pension reforms in the 2000s under the Lagos and Bachelet governments. Our comparison of the two waves of reforms in both policy areas shows that the early reforms had significant ramifications for the politics of re-reform in the 2000s, specifically by institutionalizing private-sector forms of service delivery and creating a new set of vested private-sector interests.

Chilean political context

Prior to the 1973 military coup, the Chilean state had progressively expanded state financing and provision of social welfare policies to new segments of the population. Chile's social programs covered nearly all of the population; however, benefits tended to be skewed toward well-organized middle-class constituencies. Increases in social spending were accompanied by growing fiscal deficits that had reached 30 percent of GDP by 1973. At that time the country was politically polarized, and the elected administration of Salvador Allende was overthrown and replaced by a military dictatorship led by General Augusto Pinochet.

The military government brought an end to the existing universal redistributive welfare model. The new policy regime emphasized reduced public spending, privatization of social services, demand-driven subsidies, and decentralization. Economic growth was viewed as the best form of social policy, and social spending itself was considered an obstacle to growth. Social spending was targeted toward basic services such as primary education, health care, and maternal and infant nutrition, while expenditures on advanced services such as hospitals and universities were cut. Private, individually capitalized pension accounts were introduced to replace the state-run pay-as-you-go system, and private health insurance was expanded to complement the state-run health care system. Demand-driven subsidies were provided for housing, education, and health care in an effort to stimulate competition and improve the efficiency of service providers and many of the administrative responsibilities of the health and education ministries were decentralized to municipal governments (Raczynski 2000).

Unlike other Latin American countries, which were often pressured by international financial institutions or by pressing macroeconomic crises to introduce market-based reforms, Chile's reforms were due largely to the ideational influence of a group called "The Chicago Boys"—a group of University of Chicago-trained Chilean economists who worked at Catholic University in Santiago, Chile. The influence of these economists within the military regime, and the neoliberal approach of the regime itself, were strongest precisely at the time of the major health and pension reforms (Borzutsky 2002; Kurtz 1999). The dramatic reform of both the pension and health sectors was politically possible, despite Chile's history of a strong democratic Left, because of the centralized power of General Pinochet's dictatorship.

In 1990, Chile ended the longest dictatorship in Latin America when General Pinochet ceded to a democratic transition. Since the transition, Chile has been ruled in its first four governments by the center-left coalition, the Coalition of Parties for Democracy (*Concertación de Partidos por la Democracia*), composed of the center Christian Democratic Party (PDC), the Socialists (PS), the left-leaning Party for Democracy (PPD), the Radical Social Democrats (PRSD), and a handful of independents. Despite center-left governments, change from the neoliberal economic and social policy model has been slow and measured. This was due in large part to a controlled transition to democracy, in which the Right was designated nine seats in the Senate and the open-list electoral system was replaced with a binomial system in which the winning slate has to win two-thirds of the vote; otherwise the second seat goes to the second largest vote-getter—a system that has favored Right party candidates. The military was also given budgetary and political autonomy. Recently the designated seats were eliminated, and reform of the binomial system is now a point of debate. Slowly, and contrary to the expectations of many early analysts, the Chilean political system has moved from a restricted democracy to one of the most democratic of the region.

One cost of this slow change has been a preponderance of Right political power in the first ten years of democracy and its ability to defend the free-market reforms of Pinochet. But the institutional rules that favored the Right were not the only factor protecting the market reforms; the rise of new political interests vested in the neoliberal economic and social policy model also served to prevent major changes. These played a prominent role in the politics of re-reforms of the health and pension systems in the 2000s, in which the state sought to garner greater oversight over the private sector and to induce greater solidarity. By "solidarity" we mean sharing of the costs of social benefits across socioeconomic groups, as well as equalization of the type and quality of benefits received by different groups.

Health reform: restructuring and private sector incentives under dictatorship

The first wave of Chile's health sector reforms entailed combining existing state health systems, the separation of the financing and provision aspects of health care, and a new role for private health insurance and provision. The 1979 reforms created a number of problems with regard to equity and efficiency; issues that the second major wave of reforms sought to address beginning in 2002. The second wave of reform sought to reverse the trend of low levels of state investment in health care, long waiting periods, and low quality of care in the public sector that had existed since 1979. It also sought to pool costs between the public and private sectors, and to make private sector insurers more accountable to their clients. The establishment of private sector health insurers and providers during the first wave of reform would significantly impact the politics of the second wave, allowing only some of these reform proposals to succeed.

In the 1970s, prior to its major reform by the Pinochet dictatorship, Chile's state health system was considered the most comprehensive of Latin America. Although not universal by European standards, by Latin American standards its coverage was relatively comprehensive in that more than 85 percent of the population had a right to state-provided health services. Similar to the Conservative welfare state arrangements of Germany and Belgium, where different state health systems are segmented by beneficiary populations, the Chilean public health sector prior to the reform of 1979 was divided into two main insurance institutions: the Employee Medical Service (Servicio Médico Nacional para Empleados, SERMENA), which insured white-collar workers and civil servants; and the National Health Service (Servicio Nacional de Salud, SNS), modeled on the British National Health Service, which served blue-collar workers and the poor. These were financed with employee, employer, and state contributions with the exception of coverage for the poor, which was subsidized entirely by the state. In the 1970s, SERMENA covered 25 percent of the population, SNS covered 60 percent, private providers exclusively served 10 percent, and the remaining 5 percent were covered by separate health insurance programs for the military and police (Cartin 1998; Viveros-Long 1986). The blue-collar SNS system was reliant on government contributions for 60 percent of its operating costs, with the rest of its budget coming from blue-collar social security transfers (20 percent) and fees and income from health establishments (20 percent) (Viveros-Long 1986). It also absorbed 70 percent of public health expenditures.

The government's neoliberal approach, which sought to reduce dramatically the role of the state combined with perceived inefficiencies of the large, bureaucratic, and centralized SNS system, were motivating factors behind the health sector reform. In 1979 the government separated the health policy, insurance, and provision functions of both the white- and blue-collar systems. Health policy and oversight remained in the hands of the Ministry of Health. To take over the financing and insurance functions of the new system, reformers created a new entity, the National Health Fund (Fondo Nacional de Salud, FONASA). Financing of the public system was achieved via employee contributions and state subsidies. Employer contributions were eliminated. All insured employees initially were required to contribute 1.7 percent of their monthly earnings to the fund, a rate that was successively raised to 7 percent by 1986, which remains the current contribution level (Castiglioni 2001). In addition to the obligatory salary deduction, a scale of fees was determined based on beneficiaries' income levels.

The health provision infrastructure of the white- and blue-collar systems were combined and renamed the National Health Services System (Sistema Nacional de Servicios de Salud, SNSS). Beginning in 1981, provision of primary care (health posts and general consultations) was devolved to municipalities, and the secondary and tertiary care facilities to 27 autonomous regional health departments. These local governments were charged with the management of local health infrastructure, equipment and supplies, and personnel. Separate from secondary and tertiary care, financing of primary care was achieved primarily through fees for services and a common municipal fund.

The separation of the financing and provision aspects of health coverage made possible increased participation of the private sector in health care provision. The state allowed for the top income earners in the state health system to choose the private providers who would receive state contracts (Barrientos 2000). This change, in turn, led to the growth of the private health sector and the 1981 legalization of for-profit, private health insurers who also had the option of providing health care directly, which are called Health Provider Institutions, or ISAPREs (Instituciones de Salud Previsional). Once the ISAPREs were established, individual workers could choose health care coverage from the state or they could buy this care through an ISAPRE at a cost determined by the market.

The Pinochet reforms of the health care system resulted in a major shift from a largely public system of insurance and provision, to one in which the private sector played an important new role. The number of ISAPRE beneficiaries as a proportion of total health beneficiaries has varied over time. These reached a high of 24.6 percent in 1996, a proportion that has been declining since then, to 16.3 percent in 2003 (MIDEPLAN 2003). In terms of public-private expenditures, under the Pinochet regime the reform resulted in a dramatic decline in public health expenditures and a rise in private expenditures due to both private sector involvement and a radical decline in state public health care spending (Viveros-Long 1986).

The entry of the private sector into health insurance and health care provision had important consequences in terms of equity, efficiency, and politics. The shift of a major portion of health financing from the public sector to the private had a significant impact on equity. After their introduction, 11 percent of state health care beneficiaries moved to the ISAPREs. As these tended to be the best paid employees who have lowest health risks, they also took with them from the public to the private sector 48 percent of overall health insurance contributions (Titelman 2000). This flight of high-income beneficiaries provoked a financial crisis in the public health system. In 2005, the private sector collected 65 percent of revenues from health salary deductions to serve 23 percent of the population, whereas the public sector received 35 percent of these revenues to serve 62 percent of the population (MINSAL 2005).

Beyond the disproportion in income-to-beneficiary ratios between the two systems, populations with greater health risks were concentrated in the public system. For example, Chileans with high-cost chronic health needs were disproportionately affiliated with the public health care system, in part due to the rejection of high-risk beneficiaries by private insurance. In 2001, 82 percent of patients with HIV or AIDS, 90 percent of those with uterine cancer, 83 percent of those with kidney failure, and 80 percent of those with leukemia were affiliated with the public system (Blackburn et al. 2004). ISAPREs were allowed to deny coverage for any reason, though they could not terminate coverage of a beneficiary under contract. However, ISAPREs could adjust the price or benefits of beneficiaries under contract at any time, which often times forced high-risk patients out of the ISAPRE to the public system that was required to accept all applicants. Moreover, because the law allowed beneficiaries to move between the public and private systems, as an individual's earnings dropped and the cost of private health insurance increased (due to increased risk, such as old age) Chileans tended to return to the public system. As a result, the public system received disproportionately low contributions in relationship to the health risks of its beneficiaries, leading to its further impoverishment.

Related to this drop in risk pooling, the introduction of the private ISAPREs also led to greater class stratification. The introduction of the ISAPREs led to a new private class of health facilities of better quality that served to further distance the wealthy from the working class and the poor, as the wealthy could afford the higher rates of private insurance. In 1990, the spending per beneficiary in the private system was close to four times higher than the spending per beneficiary in the public system (Oyarzo 1994). Although the subsequent democratic governments significantly increased investment in the public health sector, by 1999 spending per beneficiary in the private sector was still twice that of the public sector (MINSAL 2005).

In addition, the new system exacerbated a male breadwinner bias. Because of the higher costs of private insurance for women, labor market inequalities and women's greater responsibilities for sociál reproduction, women were less likely than men to be enrolled in an ISAPRE and were concentrated in the public system. In 2003, 74.5 percent of women were in the public system compared to 69.5 percent of men (MIDEPLAN 2003). Because only 34 percent of Chilean women are in the paid workforce, and even fewer are in the upper earning quintiles, ISAPREs are not an option for the majority of women. In 2001 women represented just 34.4 percent of ISAPRE beneficiaries (Ramírez Caballero 2001). Women's participation in ISAPREs decreases faster than men's later in life, signifying their inability to maintain the cost of the ISAPREs into old age (Pollack 2002). Moreover, women's lower earnings (on average 40 percent of male earnings) results in an inability to pay for the best quality ISAPRE care (Ramírez Caballero 2001).

Compounding the male breadwinner bias, the Chilean system allowed for overt discrimination based upon gender and age, as a means of protecting private sector profitability. Law 19.381 of May 1995, at the behest of insurers, allowed private insurers to calculate health premiums based upon two risk factors: gender and age. Women's reproductive health care needs, coupled with greater longevity, makes them a greater "risk" for needing health care, especially in their reproductive and older years. Increasing age also increases risk of sickness. As a result, ISAPREs charged women more for insurance—premiums for women in the early 2000s were 3.2 times more expensive than men's for the same health care coverage (Pollack 2002). Even the premiums for coverage of women as dependents on a spouse's policy can be prohibitively expensive. In terms of age, the ISAPREs charged much more to the elderly, resulting in their return to FONASA, at precisely the time that their earnings disappeared or decreased due to retirement. Consequently, the overwhelming majority of older Chileans were affiliated with the public system in the early 2000s: 83.6 percent of men and 84.7 percent of women aged 70 and older (MIDEPLAN 2003). One study reported an ISAPRE charging 20 times more for health insurance for a male over age 69 than for a male between the ages of 2 and 18; when the risk factor of illness for the older male is only 14 times as great (Blackburn et al. 2004). Similar findings were found by researchers looking into sex-based differential fees, in which fees were much higher than actual increased risk based on sex (Pollack 2002).

The Pinochet reforms also generated new inefficiencies, including a duplication of technologies and equipment with the advent of parallel private and public systems, and an increase in overall health costs (Oyarzo 1994). The higher costs were due in part to private sector administrative costs. The ISAPREs administrative costs represented 20 percent of their expenditures compared to just 4 to 5 percent in the public sector (MINSAL 2005).

Politically, the introduction of the ISAPREs into the Chilean health system led to the creation of a powerful new set of political actors with a vested interest in maintaining the new health care system. Whereas prior to the reforms the major players in health policy were labor unions, medical doctors, and the state, the ISAPREs offer a new wrinkle in Chilean health care politics that will have a lasting effect—the introduction of private sector, profit-oriented business interests. The impact of this new political legacy of the Pinochet reform period is observable in the "re-reforms" carried out by the government of Ricardo Lagos (2000–2006) and his successor, Michelle Bachelet (2006–2012).

The "re-reform" of the health sector under democracy

The health sector was a priority of the first democratic governments, which quickly moved to increase public health expenditures. In the 1990s, the first two democratic presidential administrations spent six times more on public health care than the government had in the 1980s (Sandoval 2004). Although these administrations talked of reform and carried out some minor modifications, their contribution was mainly increased health spending, not policy change. It was not until the government of Ricardo Lagos (2000–2006) that a major health sector reform effort was initiated.

The Lagos government began discussion of re-reform of the health sector in its first year in office, and in 2002 sent a full reform package to the Congress composed of a series of bills. One of the central objectives of the reform was to reduce health inequalities, including gender and age discrimination (Bibilioteca Nacional del Congreso 1992 Anexo 2). Another was to address Chile's changing epidemiological profile. Chile's population has become older and thus chronic diseases such as cancer, diabetes, and HIV/AIDS play a much more important role, as opposed to childhood diseases and infant mortality, which had been the focus of the health system since the 1930s. By 2050, one in every four Chileans is expected to be over age 60 (Ministerio de Trabajo 2003). Changing demographics meant that the public system was facing even greater pressures serving the aged and chronically ill, who, as explained above, were served disproportionately by the public health system as a result of adverse selection.

Five major reforms constituted the proposed overhaul of the health sector. One of these reforms was a plan to create a universal package of health services that every health insurer and provider would be obligated to provide to each client. This was termed the "Plan de Acceso Universal con Garantías Explícitas" (Plan for Universal Access with Explicit Guarantees), or the "Plan AUGE". The Plan AUGE would provide care for a list of specific medical interventions which were to be selected based upon their cost-effectiveness in preventing death and disability in the population as a whole. The plan was envisioned as standard in its components, universal in its coverage of all Chileans regardless of insurance type, integral in that it would apply to any stage of the disease in question, and would encompass both curative and preventative care. Finally, it would be incrementally implemented with elements added only when it was fiscally possible to pay for coverage of additional pathologies (Biblioteca del Congreso Nacional 2002).

The universality of the AUGE was an important element in that even the ISAPREs would have to provide all of the medical services in the AUGE list—thus stopping the common practice of ISAPREs providing plans that did not include key services, such as reproductive health care for women. In an attempt to rectify the long waits for care in the public system—where, according to one Congressional report waitlists to see a specialist were sometimes 200,000 long—the Plan AUGE also outlined explicit timelines in which care would be guaranteed, dependent on the infirmity (Comisión de Salud 2002). Finally, the Plan sought to guarantee a standard level of quality of care as well. It was to be financed in part through an increase in the import tax and a tax on tobacco products.

Another crucial proposed reform, article 22 of the proposed AUGE law, was to create a "Fondo de Compensación Solidario" or a compensatory, universal health fund which was intended to make financing of the health system more solidaristic. Initially, President Lagos advocated that 3 percent of the standard 7 percent salary deduction go to a Solidarity Fund (Mensaje Presidencial 2001). In the bill that ultimately was sent to the Congress, the amount contributed to the fund, instead of the 3 percent, was to be the average cost of health care per person (to be determined every three years by the state), multiplied by the number of beneficiaries the insurer had under contract, and paid by insurers. The fund, in turn, would pay back the insurers based on the risk profiles of their beneficiaries. For those too poor to pay for health insurance, the state would pay insurers the average contribution per beneficiary. In this way, the fund would serve as a cross-subsidy between the healthy and the sick, the high and the low risk, and between the private and public sectors. In particular, the proposed fund sought to address one of the main discriminatory effects of the health system: the higher prices for insurance charged to women and to the elderly (Biblioteca del Congreso Nacional 2003).

In addition to the AUGE bill, three additional bills were introduced: two of which would provide more regulation over the ISAPREs and a third, the Sanitation Authority Law (Ley de Autoridad Sanitaria), which would give hospitals greater autonomy. The ISAPREs laws were aimed at making them more accountable—regulating the number of plans that an ISAPRE could offer (which had multiplied into the thousands), their ability to increase plan prices for beneficiaries under contract, or to deny coverage. The Sanitation Authority Law essentially gave public hospitals greater administrative autonomy within a network of geographically proximate hospitals under the assumption that greater autonomy and resource pooling would lead to more efficient operations.

All of these proposed reforms, with the exception of the Solidarity Compensation Fund, were passed by the Congress into law with few major changes. The Solidarity Compensation Fund, however, was modified in important ways by the Congress as a result of lobbying against the measure by the ISAPREs. In the end, the fund was reduced to only a compensatory fund among the ISAPREs rather than a fund that would bridge risk between the public and private sectors. By not encompassing public and private, the law that did pass failed to meet the reform objective of eliminating inequalities between the public and private sectors by creating financial and risk solidarity. Moreover, the more sweeping fund proposal failed despite overwhelming public support for the reform and Left control of the Presidency and Congress.

To pursue the health sector reform, President Lagos had set up a technical commission to generate reform proposals. Parallel to this reform, then Minister of Health Michelle Bachelet initiated a set of public forums to generate a set of national health objectives. The technical commission led the reform process by developing a range of potential reform proposals that were subsequently vetted by the inter-ministerial commission and formulated into bills to be presented to the Congress. The inter-ministerial commission was particularly important due to the presence of the Ministry of Finance (Ministerio de Hacienda) which evaluates and approves the financial viability of any major policy decision.

Reform of the sector was broadly popular. According to government polls, 90 percent of the population in 2002 was in favor of reforming the health system (Gálvez 2002). The preferred approach to reform differed, however, dependent on the interest group or party in question. Left parties generally preferred greater state oversight and class solidarity whereas Right parties preferred more consumer "choice," market freedoms, and decentralization.

In civil society, the Chilean Medical Association (Colegio Médico) and professional health care unions such as the National Confederation of Healthcare Workers (Confederación Nacional de Trabajadores de Salud, CONFENATS) loudly criticized the reforms from the Left, urging more sweeping reforms that would promote greater financial solidarity among Chileans and access to a broader range of health services from the state (Durán 2001). On the other side of the debate were the ISAPREs. Whereas the Colegio Medico and other health care unions appeared in the press regularly and threatened to demonstrate in the streets against the reforms, the ISAPREs lobbied largely behind the scenes. According to the head of the Association of the ISAPREs at the time of the reform, René Merino, the ISAPREs developed a very positive, close relationship with the government and political party members in the chamber of deputies and Senate— especially those on the health commissions. They opposed the creation of the solidarity fund most vehemently, and were ultimately successful in reducing this proposal to the inter-ISAPRE fund. According to Merino, their success was due to their close tracking of the legislation process, the presentation of their own research reports, and because, as he put it, "we had senators who understood very well what we were saying" (Merino 2005). In fact, it was representatives from the center-left government coalition on the health commission in the chamber of deputies that ultimately proposed the change from a public-private Solidarity Fund to a solely private inter-ISAPRE fund (Comisión de Salud 2002). By watering down the solidarity fund proposal, the ISAPREs essentially averted a reform that would have struck a major blow to ISAPRE profits.

Viewing the reforms in the Chilean health sector as two waves beginning in 1979 allows one to see how health care insurance and delivery has shifted from largely public to significantly private insurance and provision. This transformation has been accompanied by major changes in political dynamics. Although reforms efforts in the 2000s emphasized greater control over the market and broader guarantees for health care, political legacies from the first wave of reform prevented the pendulum from swinging back to a more solidaristic system. Despite the fact that the government coalition had a majority of seats in both houses of Congress as well as control of the executive branch, the private sector ISAPREs were able to use their influence to significantly modify the health sector reform package, and protect their profitability.

Pension reform: the public-private remix

With respect to pensions, Chile's first wave of reforms redefined boundaries between public and private. Although the state maintained a regulatory role, provided welfare pensions, and remained (whether *de facto* or *de jure*) the ultimate guarantor of pensions, the administration and investment of pension funds became increasingly the purview of the private sector. Recent reforms call for a more active role for the public sector, including a commitment to universal coverage, signifying that the boundaries between public and private are shifting once again. The fact that the paradigmatic case of privatization pursued a thorough reform of its pension system suggests that other countries that have followed Chile's example will likely follow suit.

The military dictatorship first eliminated special programs for high-ranking senior servants and standardized some entitlement conditions before introducing the individual savings scheme that began operation in 1981. Labor Minister José Piñera noted that there was widespread opposition to the pension reform from both the left and right, as well as from elements of the military government. Nevertheless, with General Pinochet's backing, the pension reform was approved (Piñera 1991).

Under the new pension system, which was compulsory for new workers and optional for those already in the workforce, workers paid 10 percent of their monthly salary to a private pension-fund administrator where the funds were invested in both domestic and international capital markets. An additional 2.3 percent of salary went toward a commission fee and disability and survivors insurance (FIAP 2007). Those already in the workforce had a powerful incentive to join the new private system because they received an 11 percent net salary bonus for switching as well as a recognition bond representing accrued rights under the old system. Upon retirement, workers could use their accumulated funds to purchase an annuity or schedule programmed withdrawals (or a combination thereof). Workers who contributed for at least 20 years and had not accumulated enough capital to purchase an annuity equivalent to a minimum pension were entitled to a government subsidy. The armed forces and police retained their state-sponsored programs.

As the Chilean pension system reached its twenty-fifth anniversary, several important policy challenges remained. Commission charges had dropped from earlier levels, but still remained high, at approximately 10 percent of total contributions. Expenses also remained high, in part due to the fact that competition was limited with three pension funds dominating the market. Contribution density levels were also far below expectations—the original reform forecasted that 85 percent of affiliated workers would contribute regularly, compared to an actual total of 52 percent (Consejo 2006). Low density of contributions and a large informal sector meant that nearly half of the workforce would not earn enough to receive a minimum pension, with projected levels being lower for women than for men (Berstein et al. 2006; see Table 11.1). This situation meant that replacement rates were forecast at 44 percent, compared to original projections of 70 to 80 percent (Consejo 2006). Furthermore, only about 5 percent of self-employed workers, who were not required to join the system, were enrolled in a pension fund.

Although the old pay-as-you-go systems did not differentiate benefits based upon gender, the strict actuarial logic of the new private system meant that women would receive lower benefit levels than men because of their lower earnings, they accumulate less capital, and live longer on average, leaving them with a lower monthly benefit after purchasing an annuity (Arenas de Mesa et al. 1999; Bertranou 2001). Finally, polls showed that the pension system had an image problem as surveys revealed that half of workers belonging to pension funds stated that the system was "bad" or "very bad" (Consejo 2006), whereas a majority of workers were unfamiliar with basic facets of how the system functioned (Arenas de Mesa et al. 2008).[2]

Table 11.1   Projected pensions 2020–2025 (prior to the 2008 reform)

	All (%)	**Men (%)**	**Women (%)**
Above the Minimum Pension	52	67	37
At Minimum Pension Level	2	1	2
Below the Minimum Pension	46	32	61
Total	100	100	100

Source: Berstein et al. (2006) (cited in Consejo 2006).

Strengthening individual savings accounts and universalizing coverage

Public dissatisfaction with the pension system made pension reform a topic of debate in the 2006 presidential election campaign as both candidates, Michelle Bachelet of the left-center *Concertacíon* coalition and conservative Sebastian Piñera of the *Renovación Nacional* party (brother of former labor minister José Piñera who introduced the 1981 reform), agreed that the system needed reform. Piñera pledged to provide pensions to housewives, to make government contributions to pension-fund accounts of low-income workers, and to increase competition. Meanwhile, Michelle Bachelet pledged a major reform, which her advisor (and later Finance Minister) Andres Velasco described as "a Chile II model" (Rohter 2006). Within six months of taking office, Bachelet's advisory committee (known as the "Marcel Commission" after its chair Mario Marcel), which had held numerous public hearings and consulted with interest groups and international experts, issued a series of recommendations which led to reform measures that were approved by the legislature in January 2008.

The commission directly addressed the flaws described above, noting that "the system has low coverage, low density of contributions, it leaves almost 95 percent of the independent workers outside the system, it shows very little competition and high commission charges, it does not take into account the complexities of modern workplace, high turnover, high level of informality...and discriminates against women...among other shortcomings" (Consejo 2006: 5–6). The stated goal of the legislation that President Bachelet sent to Congress was thus to "perfect" the system of individual accounts and to "complement it with a system of solidarity pensions for those who, for a variety of reasons, fail to accumulate sufficient funds to finance a dignified pension" (Mensaje 2006: 1). In pursuing its aim to "transform social security into an economic and social right" (Consejo 2006: 29) by guaranteeing universal coverage, and improving benefit adequacy and equity, the government will assume a more central role in the financing and provision of pensions.

In other words, the reform did not focus exclusively on improving the system of individual accounts with respect to lowering fees and administrative costs, or improving gender equity and competition. Rather, the reform also sought to create an adequate universal coverage system for workers who fall outside the system. In particular, the reform directly addressed Chile's challenges with respect to the sizable informal sector (a common feature in Latin American labor markets), arguing that rather than waiting for labor markets to adapt to the pension system, the pension system should be flexible enough to serve all workers, both informal and formal (Consejo 2006).

The reform thus had two basic components. It sought to correct inefficiencies and inequities in a system of individual accounts, and in that sense

Finance Minister Andres Velasco commented that the system had to be created "from scratch" (Rohter 2006). The initiative to include the sizable percentage of the labor force that would otherwise receive inadequate benefits through the Basic Solidarity Pension and the efforts to address gender inequity are indeed unprecedented in the region. The other element of the reform sought to strengthen the system of individual accounts, or as the legislation put it, to "perfect" it (Mensaje 2006: 1), maintaining the basic model of private individual accounts as the central locus of the pension system. In this sense, although the reform introduces important modifications, it reflects continuity rather than reinvention.

The reform is consistent with the "policies create politics" argument discussed elsewhere in this volume, in that no system of individual accounts in the region has been overhauled or retrenched since being adopted. This is not to say that such an event could not take place. Uruguay elected a president whose party had previously opposed that country's 1994 pension reform, yet his administration did not endorse a roll back (Matijascic and Kay 2006). The most significant effort to retrench a system of individual savings accounts occurred in Argentina, where in January 2007 President Kirchner reversed 14 years of policy by encouraging workers to join the public rather than the private system. In Chile, despite polls showing that the system was unpopular (Consejo 2006), altering the basic model was never on the agenda.

The reform's measures to lower costs, universalize coverage, restructure regulatory institutions, and improve gender equity are being closely studied in neighboring countries. With respect to the pension funds themselves, the reform sought to expand participation by requiring independent workers to contribute to a fund and provided subsidies to induce younger workers to join the system. It aimed to increase competition by allowing new entrants into the market, allowing the contracting out of some functions, and assigning those workers who have declined to pick a pension fund to the lowest cost operator (a proposal opposed by the pension-fund industry). Other measures included new investment rules (including ending limits on foreign investment), and allowing loyalty discounts for workers who stay with one pension fund. The reform also sought to consolidate supervision and regulation of the solidarity, savings, and voluntary pillars under one agency, and to improve transparency and accountability by creating an advisory council of workers, employers, pension-fund administrators, and pensioners charged with making recommendations to the government. Finally, given the system's image problem and workers' lack of familiarity with it described above, the law authorized a special education fund designed to improve pension-fund literacy (Mensaje 2006).

Perhaps the most significant feature of the new reform is the introduction of the *pension basica solidaria*, or Basic Solidarity Pension, intended to integrate into the pension system all Chileans, including nonwage earners. The basic pension will have a maximum value of approximately \$160/month, with the government subsidy gradually decreasing as workers self-financed pension levels increase (the gradual drop-off of the subsidy provides workers with an incentive to continue to contribute in order to maximize their pension benefits). Although the government previously provided a pension for the indigent, and a minimum pension guarantee that topped up pensions for workers who had contributed for 20 years but had not accumulated sufficient funds for a minimum pension, the new Basic Solidarity Pension is far more comprehensive, with the lower 60 percent of households on the income scale ultimately receiving a subsidy. Furthermore, to encourage workers age 35 and younger to participate, the government will subsidize half of their contributions if they earn the minimum wage.

Another significant milestone is the fact that, for the first time, gender equity is directly addressed in the pension reform legislation. President Bachelet remarked that the pension system discriminates against women, and the Marcel commission noted that women receive annuity benefits equivalent to just 42 percent of what men receive because of lower income, the division of household and reproductive work, demographics, the earlier retirement age (60 compared to 65 for men), as well as the fact that insurance companies use differential mortality tables which leads to lower wages due to greater female longevity (Consejo 2006).

The new law aims to ameliorate these conditions. Although it has been discussed by the Marcel commission, women who choose to work until 65 will be able to continue to contribute to their accounts. The government will also pay women retiring at age 65 a bonus for each child. In case of divorce or annulment, the assets in an individual retirement account will be divided between the spouses (no such provisions existed previously). With respect to survivors and disability insurance, women had been paying the same rates as men even though costs were lower given their greater longevity. With the reform, the difference in cost is to be refunded into her retirement account (Mensaje 2006).

With majorities in both houses of the legislature, the Bachelet administration's political strategy had been to present the reform as a package in order to avoid political conflict over specific measures (although ultimately amendments were introduced), whereas in countries where the president did not enjoy disciplined legislative majorities, such as Brazil, pension reform could take many years to make its way through the legislature (see Kay 1999). Some elements of the Marcel commission's report, such as raising the female retirement age to 65, were left out of the final law because they would likely cause too much controversy (although the legislation had a number of incentives to keep women in the labor force until age 65).

The pension-fund industry welcomed measures to reduce investment restrictions, such as lifting the 30 percent ceiling on foreign investment and government contributions into pension funds of younger low-income workers. It also did not oppose the Basic Solidarity Pension. However, it objected to the provision whereby cohorts of new workers would be assigned to the pension fund with the lowest commission cost. The pension funds objected that such a measure would restrict freedom of choice, legally guaranteed market share, and emphasize consumer costs over profitability, which it deemed more relevant (Diario Financiero 2006). Furthermore, it argued that lowering costs could lead to lower profitability if firms hired lower quality investment managers, a claim that Mario Marcel refuted (Diario Financiero 2007). In short, the pension-fund industry supported measures that improved overall contributions and reduced restrictions on investment, but objected to those actions that set new regulatory precedents or could potentially affect profitability.

Members of President Bachelet's coalition also sought to make changes in the law. Some *Concertación* legislators introduced an amendment that would allow a state-owned bank to operate a pension fund (already in place in both Argentina and Uruguay). This measure was never part of the Marcel Commission report and was opposed by the pension-fund industry, which opposed a public sector-owned entity entering the market.

Collectively these measures represent a more active role for the state in that it would now explicitly seek to eliminate pensioners' income insecurity by raising replacement rates, improving gender equity, and preventing poverty among the elderly. In making this commitment to provide universal benefits, the government would not alter the basic model of individual accounts, but would rather enact a series of redistributive measures to cover those who would otherwise not receive adequate pensions. In other words, even with more government intervention, the core public-private mix remained the same.

Conclusion

Chile has been a global model for introducing market-based health care and pension reforms, making its recent "re-reforms" all the more striking in that they reflect a more assertive role for the public sector. To be clear, these new reforms are not an effort to scale back market-based measures, but rather an attempt to incorporate citizens who have previously received inadequate coverage in the health care and pension systems and to make the private sector more accountable. A more assertive public role that expands and complements private provision was uncontested by the private sector. However, as we have described above, ISAPREs and private pension-funds did object to government proposals that would affect overall profitability.

These recent developments underscore the fact that policies create politics as institutions, once established, create new political actors. Neither the ISAPREs nor the private pension-fund industry objected to efforts to expand coverage—such as government funding required to support the AUGE in the public health system, or the proposed 2008 reform that included government contributions to the pension-fund accounts of younger low-income workers. However, those proposals that presented the greatest threats to private sector profitability were strongly opposed, and in the case of health, defeated. For example, although the AUGE attempted to improve health care in the public sector and make the private sector more accountable, the failed solidarity compensation fund would have forced some private and public sector risk pooling. Such a fund is not unheard of elsewhere in the region (Chile's proposal was drawn in part on lessons from the Colombian health system), but in Chile, where the private sector ISAPREs have gained significant political influence and institutional standing, the fund proposal which directly challenged profitability was defeated. In the pension sector, the mandatory allocation of new workers into the lowest cost pension-fund and the proposal to allow a state-owned bank to enter the market was opposed by the private funds. The latter would have signified a new level of government intervention.

Even more telling is what has not made it onto the reform agenda in Chile. Neither the health nor pensions reform proposals contested the private sector's role in social policy delivery, nor proposed any shrinking of that role. For example, with respect to pensions, it was never on the policy agenda to shrink or dismantle the private sector role, unlike Chile's neighbor Argentina, where a 2007 initiative by President Kirchner sought to expand the public pension system at the expense of the private system. This agenda-shaping power indicates the degree to which, in less than 30 years, private sector delivery has become an uncontested part of the Chilean social policy landscape.

What lessons does the Chilean case offer to our understandings of the politics of social policy? This case demonstrates that once the private sector is given a significant role in social insurance coverage or service provision, it is very difficult to roll back. Governments can attempt to increase regulation over the private sector, or compensate for the inequalities generated by that sector through increased public sector spending. However, the political power and social institutionalization of these actors into the social policy realm makes radical shifts quite difficult. As a result, the overall stratification created by the public-private split in coverage, between the better-off members of society with private services and the working class and poor majority of the population covered by the public sector, will likely persist.

Notes

1. The views expressed here are those of the authors and not those of the Federal Reserve Bank of Atlanta or the Federal Reserve System. The authors thank Daniel Béland and Brian Gran for their helpful comments on this chapter. Christina Ewig thanks the Fulbright New Century Scholars program for their generous

financial support of this research and the University of Wisconsin-Milwaukee which granted her leave from her regular teaching duties to direct their study abroad program in Santiago during the Spring of 2005. She also extends thanks to the many informants in Chile for their generosity of time and insights during the course of this research.

2. For example, according to the Social Protection Survey, 11.1 percent of workers knew how benefits were calculated, 21.4 percent knew the requirements for a minimum pension, and 36 percent knew how much money was in their private accounts (Arenas de Mesa et al. 2008).

References

Arenas de Mesa, Alberto, David Bravo, Jere R. Behrman, Olivia S. Mitchell, and Petra E. Todd. 2008. "The Chilean Pension Reform Turns 25: Lessons from the Social Protection Survey." In Stephen J. Kay and Tapen Sinha (eds), *Lessons from Pension Reform in the Americas*: 23–58. Oxford: Oxford University Press.

Arenas de Mesa, Alberto and Veronica Montecinos. 1999. "The Privatization of Social Security and Women's Welfare: Gender Effects of the Chilean Reform." *Latin American Research Review* 34(3): 7–37.

Barrientos, Armando. 2000. "Getting Better after Neoliberalism: Shifts and Challenges of Health Policy in Chile." In Peter Lloyd-Sherlock (ed.), *Healthcare Reform and Poverty in Latin America*: 94–111. London: Institute of Latin American Studies.

Berstein, Solange, Guillermo Larraín, and Francisco Pino. 2006. "Chilean Pension Reform: Coverage Facts and Policy Alternatives." *Economía* 6(2): 227–79.

Bertranou, Fabio M. 2001. "Pension Reform and Gender Gaps in Latin America: What are the Policy Options?" *World Development* 29(5): 911–23.

Biblioteca del Congreso Nacional de Chile. 2002. *Conceptualización del Plan de Acceso Universal con Garantías Explícitas (AUGE), Eje de la Actual Reforma de Salud*, Serie de Estudios de Anticipación /CEA/BCN Year 1 No. 1 April. Valparaíso: Biblioteca del Congreso Nacional de Chile.

Biblioteca del Congreso Nacional de Chile. 2003. *Reforma de Salud Fondo de Compensación Solidaria*, Serie UAPROL/BCN/ Year 3 No. 057 March. Valparaíso: Biblioteca del Congreso Nacional de Chile.

Blackburn, Stephen, Consuelo Espinosa, and Marcelo Tokman. 2004. *Alternativas para Reducir la Discriminación y Segmentación por Riesgo en el Sistema de Salud Chileno.* No. 152 Serie Financiamiento del Desarrollo. Santiago: Comisión Económica Para América Latina y el Caribe, Unidad de Financiamiento para el Desarrollo.

Borzutsky, Silvia. 2002. *Vital Connections: Politics, Social Security and Inequality in Chile.* Notre Dame: University of Notre Dame Press.

Cartin, Brian. 1998. "Chile: The Effectiveness of Reform." In María Amparo Cruz-Saco and Carmelo Mesa-Lago (eds), *Do Options Exist? The Reform of Pension and Health Care Systems in Latin America*: 205–24. Pittsburgh, PA: University of Pittsburgh Press.

Castiglioni, Rossana. 2001. "The Politics of Retrenchment: The Quandaries of Social Protection Under Military Rule in Chile, 1973–1990." *Latin American Politics and Society* 43(4): 37–66.

Comisión de Salud de la Camera de Diputados. 2002. "Informe de la Comisión de Salud Sobre el Proyecto de Ley Que Establece un Régimen de Garantías en Salud." Boletín No. 2947–11. Santiago: Biblioteca del Congreso Nacional.

Consejo Asesor Presidencial para la Reforma Previsional. 2006. *El Derecho a una Vida Digna en la Vejez: Hacia un Contrato Social con la Previsión en Chile*. Santiago: Presidencia de la República de Chile.

Diario Financiero. 2006. "AFP se preparan para una dura batalla por el proyecto de Reforma provisional." December 22, 2006.

Diario Financiero. 2007. "Mario Marcel: Preveo un cambio en el modelo de negocios de las AFP." January 12, 2007.

Durán, Victor Hugo. 2001. "Propuesta Gremio para reformar el sector." *La Tercera*. April 27, 2001,13.

Federación Internacional de Administradoras de Fondos de Pensiones (FIAP). 2007. "Estructura de Comisiones." Retrieved on January 12, 2007 from www.fiap.cl

Gálvez, Mario. 2002. "El Gobierno Retoma el Rumbo de las Reformas." *El Mercurio*. July 16, 2002,C3.

Kay, Stephen J. 1999. "Unexpected Privatizations: Politics and Social Security Reform in the Southern Cone." *Comparative Politics* 31(4): 403–22.

Kurtz, Marcus J. 1999. "Chile's Neo-Liberal Revolution: Incremental Decisions and Structural Transformation, 1973–1989." *Journal of Latin American Studies* 31: 399–427.

"Lagos Interpeló a Críticos de la Reforma de la Salud." 2002. *La Nación*. July 2, 2002.

Matijascic, Milko and Stephen J. Kay. 2006. "Social Security at the Crossroads: Toward Effective Pension Reform in Latin America." *International Social Security Review* 59(1): 3–26.

Mensaje Presidencial. 2001. "Discurso de S.E. El Presidente de la Republica. D. Ricardo Lagos Escobar." Inicio de la Legislatura Ordinaria en el Congreso Nacional. May 21, 2001. Valparaíso: Chile.

Mensaje de S. E. La Presidenta de la Republica. 2006. *Mensaje N° 558–354*. December 15, 2006. Santiago.

Merino, Dr. René. 2005. Ex-president of the Association of ISAPREs of Chile. Interview by Christina Ewig, July 7, 2005. Santiago.

MIDEPLAN (Ministerio de Cooperación y Planificación). 2003. *Encuesta de Caracterización Socioeconómica Nacional (CASEN): Principales Resultados de Salud*. Santiago: Ministerio de Cooperación y Planificación.

Ministerio del Trabajo y Previsión Social. 2003. *El Trabajo y la Protección Social en Chile 2000–2002*. Santiago: Ministerio del Trabajo y Protección Social.

MINSAL (Ministerio de Salud). 2005. Presentation by Dra. Nelly Alvarado Aguilar. División de Rectoría y Regulación Sanitaria, Ministerio de Salud.

Oyarzo, César. 1994. *Salud: La Mezcla Publico-Privada Una Reforma Pendiente*. Documento de Trabajo 216. Santiago: Centro de Estudios Públicos.

Pierson, Paul. 1994. *Dismantling the Welfare State? Reagan, Thatcher, and the Politics of Retrenchment*. New York: Cambridge.

Piñera, Jose. 1991. *El Cascabel al Gato: La Batalla por la Reforma Previsional*. Santiago: Editora Zig-Zag.

Pollack, Molly E. 2002. *Equidad de Género en el Sistema de Salud Chileno*, No. 123 Serie Financiamiento del Desarrollo, Santiago: Comisión Económica Para América Latina y el Caribe, Unidad de Financiamiento para el Desarrollo.

Raczynski, Dagmar. 2000. "Overcoming Poverty in Chile." In Joseph S. Tulchin and Allison Garland. (eds), *Social Development in Latin America*: 119–48. Boulder, CO: Lynne Reinner Publishers.

Ramírez Caballero, Apolonia. 2001. *Género y Sistema Isapre*. Santiago: Ministerio de Salud, Servicio Nacional de la Mujer.

Rohter, Larry. 2006. "Chile's Candidates Agree to Agree on Pension Woes." *The New York Times*. 18. January 10, 2006.

Sandoval, Hernán. 2004. "El Proceso de reforma de la salud en Chile." In Clarisa Hardy (ed.), *Equidad y Protección Social: Desafíos de políticas Sociales en América Latina*: 179–98. Santiago: Lom Ediciones.

Titelman, Daniel. 2000. *Reformas al Sistema de Salud en Chile: Desafíos Pendientes*, No. 104 Serie Financiamiento del Desarrollo. Santiago: Comisión Económica Para América Latina y el Caribe, Unidad de Financiamiento para el Desarrollo.

Viveros-Long, Anamaria. 1986. "Changes in Health Financing: The Chilean Experience." *Social Science Medicine* 22(3): 379–8.

Conclusion: Revisiting the Public-Private Dichotomy

Brian Gran and Daniel Béland

The public-private dichotomy is a controversial analytical device used by experts and policymakers to designate responsibilities for social policy. It is prominently referred to in debates over the futures of both health care and pension policies. This volume shows that lines separating public from private social provisions can be hard to draw, not only in the United States but in other countries as well. The volume calls into question the utility of a strict analytical separation between public and private policies while suggesting that its application to health and pension policies is problematic. This is true largely because, due to major institutional and political variations, the public-private dichotomy takes a different meaning from one country to another—or even from one policy area to another within the same country. Adopting a simplistic understanding of the public-private dichotomy is inappropriate because it may thwart democratic efforts to reform and improve existing social policy systems by obscuring their inherent complexity.

This brief chapter considers what this volume's contributors have shown about the nature and the consequences of the public-private dichotomy for social policy. After examining the often fuzzy boundaries separating public and private social policies, we review patterns that emerge in public and private health care and pensions. This chapter then considers factors that lead to public-private configurations in social policy, as well as how public and private social policies are institutions with which sociopolitical actors must contend when introducing and reforming health care and pension programs. We conclude by weighing the advantages and disadvantages of public-private health care and pension policies, then raise questions and concerns for future research on the public-private dichotomy for social policy.

Nature and forms of the public-private dichotomy

Fuzzy policy boundaries

The public-private dichotomy is complex and often fuzzy, suggesting that separating public from private efforts is seldom an easy task. Beyond this claim, contributions to this volume demonstrate that the meaning of the public-private dichotomy varies depending on the political and institutional context. On the one hand, pure public provision is made for health care and pensions, but this public provision can be undertaken in a variety of ways, as Debra Street shows in her chapter on health care provision. On the other hand, pure private provision, without any direct or indirect state intervention, is rare. Yet, even compared to state-regulated private schemes, public approaches to health care and retirement income tend to be oriented toward wider coverage and more modest benefits, typically providing a measure of socioeconomic security to an entire population.

States take different roles when it comes to private provision; four of which are to regulate, promote, finance, and mandate (Gran 2003). Across all of the examined countries, states *regulate* private old-age pensions and health care. For private pensions, states can regulate their coverage, contribution levels, benefit amounts, and vesting rights, among other aspects. As Sven Jochem demonstrates, Germany's federal state, for instance, restricts employers' abilities to set conditions an employee must meet before becoming entitled to a work-related, old-age pension. To *promote* private provision, some states offer *financial* incentives, but they reward these incentives only if the individual meets specified requirements. As for the Canadian Registered Retirement Savings Plans (RRSPs), Gerard Boychuk and Keith Banting indicate that these plans place limits on how funds can be withdrawn from these tax-preferred savings plans. Still, regulation is a matter of degree. Fabio Bertozzi and Fabrizio Gilardi find that only to a limited extent does the state regulate the health care market in Switzerland, leaving patients, insurers, and providers to negotiate many health care arrangements.

Although state regulation of voluntary private provisions is common, some states *mandate* private provision. A well-known instance is Chile's pension system. As Christina Ewig and Stephen Kay show, in 1981, participation in the new Chilean system was optional for workers already in the workforce; new workers had no choice but to join the privately administered system. From this perspective, the idea that Chile "privatized" public pensions is potentially misleading. The state still plays a major role in regulating privately administered personal savings accounts. The state's roles of regulating, promoting, financing, and mandating private provision highlight difficulties in drawing clear boundaries between public and private social policy efforts.

Beyond this example, the idea of privatization remains a potential source of misunderstandings. In the United States, President George W. Bush's proposal to "privatize" Social Security, "Strengthening Social Security in the 21st Century," paradoxically involved the maintenance of the federal state's key role in pension policy (White House 2005). As Christopher Howard and Edward Berkowitz put it, "Social Security privatization" would result in an *increase* in "federal regulation with no end to ultimate federal responsibility for the pension system." Both the Chilean and the US cases suggest that the term "privatization" is problematic and should be used with caution.

This discussion once again points to the potentially fuzzy nature of the public-private dichotomy for social policy. The German approach to health care provision particularly challenges the concept of a strict public-private dichotomy. In his chapter, Jochem demonstrates that the German public approach primarily relies on direct private financing, which generally takes the form of social insurance contributions paid by both employers and workers. By law, employers (paying 36 percent in 2004) and private households (paying 47 percent in 2004) are required to contribute to the German health care system with the state paying only a fraction (17 percent in 2004). Yet, a role many states play in *private* social policies is financial. A common financial approach states take to sponsor private provision is tax expenditures. As indirect state spending, tax expenditures are used to encourage individuals and organizations to establish health care and retirement savings plans. Susan St John and Toni Ashton show that in New Zealand, tax expenditures were avoided for a long time because of concerns over their inefficiency and their signaling of wrong incentives. New Zealand's reluctance to use tax expenditures, however, is unusual compared to their importance as social policy tools in many other countries. The Swedish welfare regime is characterized as state dominated (Esping-Andersen 1999), yet as Karen Anderson, Paula Blomqvist, and Ellen Immergut find, private pensions are important aspects of retirement-income security, and tax expenditures supplement these private pensions. Through tax expenditure policies, individuals and organizations receive state benefits, paid for by taxpayers, to pursue what can often be seen as private objectives. Tax expenditure policies are especially prominent in the United States, where their broad scope, considerable costs, and typically unequal distribution have raised critical questions that challenge tax expenditures and other stealthy measures used to subsidize wealthier citizens and businesses with public funds (but see Myles and Pierson 1997).

Overall, the willingness of states to regulate, promote, finance, and mandate private provision of health care and old-age pensions illuminates the often blurred nature of public-private boundaries for social policy. These four types of state involvement challenge the utility of a clear-cut vision of the public-private dichotomy.

Patterns in public-private policies

Even if boundaries separating public from private efforts tend to be fuzzy, important patterns emerge across public-private interactions in health care and pension policies. Contributions to this volume indicate that public-private provision of health care can be characterized as work-related, hybrid, or public. Public-private retirement pensions, on the other hand, are often described as pillars.

As Street shows, one approach to health care provision is work related, whether public or private. Individuals obtain health insurance either through their employment or because of their relationship to the employee, such as being their spouse or child. It is difficult to characterize this work-related approach as public or private. In Germany, as Jochem demonstrates, many individuals and their dependents enroll in employment-related sickness funds. These funds have public qualities in that they are regulated and ensure nearly universal coverage, but they are financed by employers, employees, and the state. In Japan, as Toshimitsu Shinkawa discusses, a firm, or a group of firms, can establish a health insurance association that insures employees and their dependents. Like the German sickness funds, these associations are regulated and insure many Japanese. Approximately 30 million people in Japan enjoy health insurance coverage through such associations.

Yet, the Japanese and German work-related plans are but one element of a hybrid approach to providing health care. For example, it is clear that the Japanese health care system is a hybrid: nearly the same number of Japanese is entitled to state-provided health insurance as is covered by the health insurance associations. Japan's public insurance plan provides health insurance coverage to individuals not covered by these health insurance associations. The German health insurance system is parallel, consisting of a range of public-private plans. Street comments that all health care systems of the examined countries are public-private hybrids of some kind, ranging from a strong public emphasis to a strong private emphasis. The US health care system may be characterized as an overly complex hybrid, consisting of a hodge-podge of private, employment-related plans, national insurance for retirees and the disabled, and a federal-state system for low-income individuals, which, all taken together, still fails to insure many Americans.

Public health insurance, through which nearly all residents are covered by state plans, is the third dominant approach to health care. The British National Health Service is internationally famous and considered a uniform model of public finance and public provision. Peter Taylor-Gooby and Lavinia Mitton show that as demographic and economic concerns have influenced this public model, sociopolitical actors have left room for private provision, with the central state increasingly taking on a regulatory role.

In contrast, the British retirement-income system has long been very complex. It is a tiered approach, with a flat pension at its base, an earnings-related pension as the second-tier, and tax-advantaged private occupational and personal pensions on top. This notion of pillars, which does not necessarily correspond to the model once advocated by the World Bank (1994), characterizes retirement systems found in other countries, for example, Canada, Switzerland, and the United States. Patrik Marier and Suzanne Skinner find that across all of the examined countries, states have established a basic pension as the first pillar. This basic pension may either provide social assistance or a flat-rate pension, but it is designed largely to prevent older residents from experiencing poverty. Consistently across these countries, this basic pension is public. Private provision is not involved in the first pillar, but can play a major role in the second pillar and, especially, the third pillar. Countries such as Canada and the United States feature private pensions prominently as their third pillars.

Rather than strict reliance on one approach, evidence presented in this volume indicates contemporary national health care and pension systems tend to combine different aspects of Titmuss' (1974) residualist, industrial-achievement, and universalist models. In Sweden, for instance, an individual may qualify for a public income-tested pension, whereas another may benefit from a state work-related pension along with a private, tax-advantaged work-related pension. Empirical material analyzed by this volume's authors demonstrates that health care does not readily fit Esping-Andersen's (1990) welfare regime typology. Whether their welfare regime is characterized as liberal, conservative, or social democratic, contributors show that health care systems consist of public, hybrid, and work-related approaches. Japan's system of health insurance associations covers some Japanese whereas state health insurance plans insure others. The public-private mix of health care and pensions is ever-present across all of Esping-Andersen's (1990) three worlds of welfare capitalism.

Why do states employ public-private collaborations?

Pursuit of public-private policies

Why do sociopolitical actors pursue public-private arrangements? A variety of factors lead to the establishment of public-private configurations in health care and pension policies.

Sociopolitical actors with neoliberal orientations advocate for private policies across all of the examined countries. These actors stress demographic, economic, and political factors to foster greater reliance on private schemes. For example, when demographic and economic concerns arise over the sustainability of public programs (true for nearly all of the examined countries), these sociopolitical actors argue that private alternatives are best. Taylor-Gooby and Mitton demonstrate that under the leadership of Margaret Thatcher, British Prime Minister from 1979 to 1990, the United Kingdom responded to population aging and economic difficulties by shifting public welfare provision to markets. Thatcher's marketization efforts encouraged individuals to save for retirement and state agencies to contract out their services. Even in the absence of strong neoliberal parties, market alternatives have been pursued in the face of demographic and economic pressures. In the case of Sweden, Anderson, Blomqvist, and Immergut show that private organizations compete with public authorities to provide health care, but this competition is played out in the relations between central and local powers.

Political institutions shape playing fields on which these political actors compete to realize their social policy ambitions. Bertozzi and Gilardi suggest that the development of modern Swiss social policy has been structured by federalism and direct democracy. Swiss federalism has limited the ability of the central state to pursue public social policies; public benefits can significantly vary across cantons. The Swiss referendum is another important institutional factor in social policy development. When a national pension policy was proposed, it was defeated by a referendum. As for the United States, multiple veto points associated with "checks and balances" can empower business interests and limit the extent to which the federal state can implement comprehensive reforms that challenge existing vested interests in both the public and the private sectors (on this issue see Steinmo and Watts 1995). As Howard and Berkowitz suggest in their chapter on the United States, the mobilization of such interests largely explain why President Bill Clinton's Health Security initiative failed.

Considering these two cases, it becomes clear that the *absence* of some political institutions can facilitate political attempts at making sweeping changes to public policies quickly. Without major forms of institutional fragmentation like federalism and "checks and balances" standing in the way, in the late 1980s, neoliberal political actors in New Zealand succeeded in eliminating all tax incentives for private savings. As St John and Ashton demonstrate in their chapter, New Zealand's centralized political system and the "first-past-the-post" electoral model used at the time meant that the national state faced comparatively few barriers to pursuing such a drastic reform. The radical reform enacted in New Zealand in the late 1980s would be hard to imagine in the US context, for example. Even in New Zealand, the electoral reform that became effective in 1996 should make this type of radical change harder to implement in the future.

Public-private policies as institutions

Political centralization does not necessarily mean that states do what they want to reshape existing public social programs. The New Zealand case reveals how public social programs can act as enduring policy legacies that create constraints for elected officials. The radical 1991 proposal to dismantle the universal flat pension did not succeed largely due to this pension's long-term popularity and the gray lobby's opposition to the reform. Even when formal political institutions do not stand in the way of a neoliberal government, private options are not necessarily pursued when popular public programs have created powerful constituencies capable of defending the program against direct political attacks (Pierson 1994).

In some countries, private welfare approaches have a comparatively long history, which have favored the emergence of strong vested interests in the private sector that frequently struggle against transformations of existing public-private arrangements. Private policies create legacies over time and interest groups often emerge to support their maintenance (Hacker 2002; Klein 2003). In the United States, as Howard and Berkowitz show, the absence of national health insurance gave ample room for the development of private health insurance, which expanded during the post-World War II era. As a consequence, today, political actors must keep health insurance companies in mind when reforms are pursued.

It would be misleading, however, to argue that vested interests in the private sector necessarily prevent departures from existing policy configurations. Boychuk and Banting show that private insurers in Canada were unable to thwart the creation of a universal health insurance system in the mid-1960s. The same conclusion applies to vested interests stemming from well-established public social programs, which may not always resist coordinated political efforts to transform or even abolish them. In the field of old-age pensions, the Swedish and the Japanese cases provide two examples of path-departing reforms amidst powerful vested interests in existing public social programs. In both countries, undeniable demographic challenges coupled with institutional vulnerabilities of existing public pension changes helped political actors secure consensus for the enactment of radical reforms that profoundly altered their national pension systems while increasing the role of private savings.

Shinkawa shows that employer-sponsored pension plans in Japan have been traditionally considered benefits that not only attracted employees and maintained their loyalty to the firm; they also represented key components of the Japanese-style familial welfare regime. Beyond providing essential retirement income, these employer-sponsored plans appeared as critical labor market mechanisms used to signify status and an employee's commitment to the firm. Yet, their key roles and the vested interests surrounding them have not prevented employers from restructuring existing pension schemes in ways that are often detrimental to workers and retirees.

As the Japanese case shows, the paths taken by public-private arrangements do change over time. In both the public and the private sectors, the existence of well-entrenched policy legacies does not mean that path-departing reforms cannot reshape public and private social programs. More generally, significant policy change affecting the relationship between public and private benefits is present across all the cases discussed throughout this volume. In other words: the public-private social policy landscape is everything but static. This claim is consistent with the growing literature on institutional change, which stresses the limitations of the concept of path dependence (Thelen 2004; Streeck and Thelen 2005).

Substitution or exclusion?

As public-private relationships change, do public or private benefits come to substitute for or even exclude one another? Clearly, in advanced industrial countries, cutting or at least limiting the expansion of public benefits is seen as a means to maintaining or even favoring the expansion of private benefits. In the post-World War II era, for example, policymakers in liberal countries such as Britain, Canada, and the United States explicitly advocated a limited expansion of public pensions so that these would not endanger existing private, albeit tax subsidized, schemes. In such countries, the apparent complementarity between—and even the integration of—public and private pension benefits emerged as both a common wisdom and an enduring institutional feature of modern liberal pension systems. In recent decades, these liberal countries have witnessed attempts to increase further the role of private savings and pensions through the curtailment of existing public pension benefits. The 1986 Social Security Act in Britain and, to a lesser extent, the 1983 amendments to the Social Security Act in the United States provide support to this claim. In both cases, cuts in public benefits favored the expansion of private provisions. In Canada, the attempt to eliminate or, at least, enact major cuts in Old Age Security failed. As Boychuk and Banting suggest, however, the already low replacement rates existing under the current public pension system leave plenty of room for private savings and occupational pensions in the Canadian retirement-income system.

Perhaps more interesting is the attempt to increase the role of private provisions in countries where public schemes have long been dominant. In Sweden, as Anderson, Blomqvist, and Immergut show, the mid-1990s pension reform increased the role of private savings partly by curtailing future public pension benefits. In the case of Japan, Shinkawa demonstrates that massive retrenchment in public pensions occurred simultaneously with the creation of a "Japanese 401(k)" aimed at increasing personal pension savings. These two examples are consistent with the existing literature on pension privatization, which emphasizes the close relationship between cutbacks in public programs and attempts to increase the role of private benefits (for example, Hacker 2004; Palier and Bonoli 2000).

Nevertheless, this discussion about the push for a greater reliance on private schemes should not hide the fact that private benefits, just like public benefits, are vulnerable to demographic, economic, and political pressures. Where private plans are emphasized, concerns have arisen over their stability. Concerning Chile, whose largely private pension system has been widely portrayed by neoliberals as a model of success, Ewig and Kay reveal that such private alternatives do not necessarily reach their objectives. After the shine wore off of the Chilean pension system created in the early 1980s, questions arose over administrative costs and information availability for investing, and whether middle-class and blue-collar workers were contributing enough to their personal pensions to guarantee their retirement security. Regarding the Chilean case, Ewig and Kay demonstrate that "privatization" does not eliminate concerns about the future and sustainability of social policy. These concerns can feed powerful political debates as they have in Chile.

An important instance in which political debates confronted problems arising from greater reliance on private benefits is the 1990s "misselling scandal" in Britain. Ironically, as Mitton and Taylor-Gooby show, pension privatization stemming from the 1986 reform of SERPS had unintended consequences that created strong political support for more stringent regulations of the British financial sector, among other changes (see also Jacobs and Teles 2007). The British case suggests that attempts to increase the role of the private sector may paradoxically result in new and growing state interventions and regulations. The extreme complexity of the US health care system is another instance of massive and ever-expanding state regulations stemming from the development of private benefits and the predictable political calls to protect workers and citizens against seemingly greedy employers and insurance providers.

Does reliance on private benefits promote social inequality?

Contributors to this volume have considered the impacts of public-private social policies on inequality. Although the cases of Japan and the United States suggest that private benefits increase income inequality, one must remain cautious when the time comes to discuss this issue. As mentioned above, the state can play a major role in regulating private provisions, and such a regulatory role may mitigate the ways in which the reliance on private schemes potentially increase social inequality. As Howard and Berkowitz's discussion of US health care shows, however, the presence of complex regulatory schemes does not necessarily prevent the emergence and the reproduction of widespread social inequality. Howard and Berkowitz remind us that approximately 47 million Americans, or one out of every six, lack health insurance. In other countries such as Switzerland, however, extensive state regulations guarantee universal or quasi-universal coverage. Yet, as Bertozzi and Gilardi show, it is important to keep in mind that even in the Swiss health care system, 80 percent of the expenditures are financed through mechanisms that do not redistribute wealth across income categories. In other words, the Swiss health care system is primarily financed through nonredistributive mechanisms. Furthermore, in recent years, costs have increased but subsidies have not, resulting in a privatization of risk. This risk privatization means that individuals, not collectivities, will bear responsibility, potentially undermining concrete social and economic solidarities.

Debra Street demonstrates that health care can redistribute resources in significant ways. Public provision of health care can redistribute resources from healthy to ill, from well-off to low- and middle-income residents.

Private provision can also be redistributive, but typically in a different direction. When a public health care system exists, but individuals pay for private health care, they are effectively paying twice for health care: via taxes, they pay for public health care, then pay for private health care out of their own pocket. Street points out that this approach maximizes redistribution to lower paid and less healthy citizens. According to Street, such a public-private division of labor within the same health care system may result in a two-tiered system. As a consequence, if the number of people who choose the private approach becomes large, political support for the public approach may weaken.

This type of dualism can also characterize old-age pension systems when public-private systems are in place. Marier and Skinner point out that across the examined countries, men and women may come to rely mainly on two separate sources of retirement income: private for men, public for women. They show that men more than women benefit from private sources of income during retirement. Yet, women do not necessarily experience lower levels of retirement income. Instead, women rely on public income sources. As public pensions are under attack in many countries, Marier and Skinner warn that women's retirement-income security may weaken.

Overall, because it is often hard to draw clear lines between public and private efforts in providing health care and pensions, it is problematic to attribute promotion of inequality to only one sector over the other. Instead, socioeconomic equality arises from state commitments that are revealed through policy designs that impact both public and private benefits. This is true because the state influences private benefits, especially through its regulatory powers. Using these regulations, the state can weaken inequality effects that may derive from relying on private benefits. Ultimately, the state's commitment to equality and economic security are often more important than the balance between public and private policies, which are directly affected by state regulations.

Agenda for future research

This book has stressed the complexity and the multifaceted nature of the public-private dichotomy for social policy while exploring the institutional logics that shape the changing relationship between public and private social programs. More specifically, drawing on both quantitative and qualitative analyses, our volume has examined the public-private dichotomy for health care and pensions in a number of advanced industrialized countries with a primary focus on countries that rely extensively on private schemes.

Returning to the US literature on private social policy discussed in the first chapter (for example, Hacker 2002; Howard 1997), this volume provides comparative support for the idea that private benefits can create powerful institutional legacies that affect the development of both public and private policies. Although it is clear that existing policy legacies and formal political institutions mediate the impact of private benefits on social policy development, several of the case study chapters send a clear warning against mechanistic institutionalist explanations that would depict path dependence as a universal rule. Although entrenched policy legacies can matter a great deal, changing economic and demographic factors, as well as the mobilization of powerful actors promoting new ideas about the public-private dichotomy, can reshape existing public and private policy legacies.

Drawing on the growing literature on institutional change in social policy (for example, Béland 2007; Hacker 2004; Streeck and Thelen 2005; Thelen 2004), future scholarship should further explore the economic, political, and ideological conditions under which path-departing changes to the public-private dichotomy for social policy are not only possible but likely. This type of analysis could take the form of small-N, qualitative comparisons between countries. Yet, our two quantitative chapters also stress the need for further quantitative research, which would greatly benefit from the creation of more complex databases that offer additional details about various public-private arrangements.

In their contributions, Street, as well as Marier and Skinner, highlight important concerns for available quantitative evidence of public and private qualities of health care and pensions. As states increasingly turn to private sources, they must demand that private providers maintain open and clear records of their work. In turn, public-private links must be made available. Contemporary data are often sketchy, presenting challenges to determining how well public-private efforts at health care and retirement income are performing, as well as who is benefiting and whether some are losing from existing policy designs. Further work is needed to generate more reliable data about the public-private dichotomy, which would in turn facilitate the development of more rigorous and systematic quantitative analyses.

Beyond this issue, it is clear that, because the public-private dichotomy is not only used in the fields of health care and pensions, scholars can use this volume as a starting point to tackle the development of this complex dichotomy in other policy areas such as housing, long-term care, and even social assistance and employment policy. It would be very useful to examine whether this volume's findings apply to these other policy areas.

Another issue that requires more systematic attention is the role of "social partners" (that is employers and labor unions) and collective agreements in the development of public and private social policies. In countries such as France and Germany, "social partners" play a major role in the development and management of these policies. Understanding the interaction between the state, "social partners," and public-private social programs is a major task that compels specialists of social policy to draw on the industrial relations literature. As the work of Christine Trampusch (2007; 2008) shows, drawing on this literature is an interesting way to improve our understanding of the role of social partners and collective agreements in the development and restructuring of public-private social policies.

This volume has primarily focused on wealthy, OECD democracies that have experience using public-private social policies on a larger scale. In addition to exploring developments of policy areas other than health care and pensions, future research should systematically analyze the transformation of the public-private dichotomy in less wealthy, non-OECD countries. Although excellent scholarship is available about social policy privatization in Eastern Europe, Latin America, and other regions of the world (for example, Brooks 2002; Roberts 2005; Weyland 2007), more systematic, comparative work on the public-private dichotomy in non-OECD countries could contribute to major contemporary debates about the value of the policy models the World Bank and other international organizations have put forward to reform existing social programs in these countries.

As we can see, much work lies ahead for students of social policy interested in the fate of the public-private dichotomy. It is hoped that the scholarship presented in this volume will contribute to such future research while helping to reframe contemporary debates over the relationship between public and private social policies. As suggested above, if not properly managed by the state, the expansion of private benefits can have truly negative consequences for economic insecurity and social inequality. This fact alone should encourage citizens, scholars, and policymakers alike to study and debate the complex nature and uncertain future of the public-private dichotomy for social policy.

References

Béland, Daniel. 2007. "Ideas and Institutional Change in Social Security: Conversion, Layering, and Policy Drift." *Social Science Quarterly* 88(1): 20–38.

Brooks, Sarah M. 2002. "Social Protection and Economic Integration: The Politics of Pension Reform in an Era of Capital Mobility." *Comparative Political Studies* 35(5): 491–525.

Esping-Andersen, Gøsta. 1990. *The Three Worlds of Welfare Capitalism*. Cambridge: Polity.

Esping-Andersen, Gøsta. 1999. *Social Foundations of Post-Industrial Economies*. Oxford: Oxford University Press.

Gran, Brian. 2003. "A Second Opinion." *International Journal of Health Services* 33(2): 283–313.

Hacker, Jacob S. 2002. *The Divided Welfare State: The Battle over Public and Private Social Benefits in the United States*. Cambridge: Cambridge University Press.

Hacker, Jacob S. 2004. "Privatizing Risk without Privatizing the Welfare State: The Hidden Politics of Social Policy Retrenchment in the United States." *American Political Science Review* 98(2): 243–60.

Howard, Christopher. 1997. *The Hidden Welfare State*. Princeton, NJ: Princeton University Press.

Jacobs, Alan M. and Steven M. Teles. 2007. "The Perils of Market Making: The Case of British Pension Reform." In Marc Landy, Martin Levin, and Martin Shapiro (eds), *Creating Competitive Markets*: 157–83. Washington, DC: Brookings Institution Press.

Klein, Jennifer. 2003. *For All These Rights: Business, Labor, and the Shaping of America's Public-Private Welfare State*. Princeton, NJ: Princeton University Press.

Myles, John and Paul Pierson. 1997. "Friedman's Revenge." *Politics and Society* 25(4): 443–72.

Palier, Bruno and Giuliano Bonoli. 2000. "La montée en puissance des fonds de pension." *L'Année de la régulation* 4: 71–112.

Pierson, Paul. 1994. *Dismantling the Welfare State? Reagan, Thatcher, and the Politics of Retrenchment*. New York: Cambridge University Press.

Roberts, Andrew. 2005. "Pension Privatization in Eastern Europe and Beyond." Paper Presented at the Annual Meeting of Research Committee 19 of the International Sociological Association. –September 8–10, 2005 (Chicago).

Steinmo, Sven and Jon Watts. 1995. "It's the Institutions, Stupid! Why Comprehensive National Insurance Always Fails in America." *Journal of Health Politics, Policy and Law* 20(2): 329–72.

Streeck, Wolfgang and Kathleen Thelen. (eds). 2005. *Beyond Continuity: Institutional Change in Advanced Political Economies*. Oxford: Oxford University Press.

Thelen, Kathleen. 2004. *How Institutions Evolve: The Political Economy of Skills in Germany, Britain, the United States, and Japan*. Cambridge: Cambridge University Press.

Titmuss, Richard M. 1974. *Social Policy: An Introduction*. London: George Allen and Unwin.

Trampusch, Christine. 2007. "Industrial Relations as a Source of Social Policy: A Typology of the Institutional Conditions for Industrial Agreements on Social Benefits." *Social Policy & Administration* 41(3): 251–70.

Trampusch, Christine. 2008. *The Privatization of Welfare States: Industrial Relations as a Source of Social Benefits* (Project Description). Berne: University of Berne. Retrieved on August 2, 2008 from http://www.ipw.unibe.ch/content/forschungsgruppen/prof_trampusch/index_eng.html

Weyland, Kurt. 2007. *Bounded Rationality and Policy Diffusion: Social Sector Reform in Latin America*. Princeton, NJ: Princeton University Press.

White House. 2005. "Strengthening Social Security for the 21st Century." February 2005.

World Bank. 1994. Averting the Old Age Crisis: Policies to Protect the Old and Promote Growth. Washington, DC: The World Bank.